Windows Small Business Server 2003

A Clear and Concise Administrator's Reference and How-To

Quickly find the information you need to install, configure, and maintain all the features of SBS 2003 and get the job done

Stephanie Knecht-Thurmann

BIRMINGHAM - MUMBAI

Windows Small Business Server 2003: A Clear and Concise Administrator's Reference and How-To

First published: August 2005.

Published by Packt Publishing Ltd.
32 Lincoln Road
Olton
Birmingham, B27 6PA, UK.

ISBN 1-904811-49-3

www.packtpub.com

Cover Design by www.visionwt.com

Translation from the German language edition of:
Small Business Server 2003 – Das Integrationshandbuch
für kleine und mittlere Unternehmen
published by Addison Wesley, an imprint of Pearson Education Deutschland GmbH, München.

Credits

Author
Stephanie Knecht-Thurmann

Translator
Sujeet Bhatt

Technical Editors
Niranjan Jahagirdar
Ashutosh Pande

Proofreader
Chris Smith

Layout
Niranjan Jahagirdar
Ashutosh Pande

Cover Designer
Helen Wood

Illustrator
Dinesh Kandalgaonkar

About the Author

Stephanie Knecht-Thurmann was born in 1975 in Itzehoe. She graduated in 1994, and went on to study classical philology (Latin and Ancient Greek) and German at the Christian Albrechts University in Kiel.

In 2001 she started working for a systems house in Hanover, where she was responsible for the technical documentation of complex IT systems for systems management in heterogeneous architectures. She earned various certifications, such as for Novadigm—RADIA. She also gained experience in the Microsoft Windows environment, especially Windows 2000 Server, Small Business Server, and their successors.

Stephanie Knecht-Thurmann started on her own with Knecht Consult in 2002 in Barsinghausen. Since then she has been advising companies on deployment of Microsoft products in mission-critical areas (consultation for a newspaper publisher in Vancouver, Canada, and Internet-based projects for several companies in Tashkent, Uzbekistan). Apart from this, she has also been active in the publishing field with books in German on these subjects. In 2003 her book *Active Directory* was published by *Addison-Wesley* with great success; in 2004 the book *Small Business Server 2003* appeared under the same label. Other publications are already in progress.

Table of Contents

Introduction

A fully functional and an easy-to-administer IT base is gaining importance even for small to medium-sized companies aiming for expansion. The Small Business Server 2003 operating system platform addresses this need. The Small Business Server 2003 unites the essentially important applications—the Windows Server 2003 operating system, the current version of the Exchange mail server, the Share Point Services for synergy within a team and, where applicable, the Internet Security and Acceleration Server (ISA), and the high-capacity MS SQL Server 2000 database—into one package. This package offers a very attractive price-to-performance ratio. The restriction to only one location is not a disadvantage for small companies; in fact, it simplifies the administration process.

This book helps the reader to plan, install, configure and operate a Small Business Server with all its components. The different types of licensing and the update possibilities are also discussed in this book. As this book cannot be an introduction to the operation of an operating system, it is primarily aimed at readers who have a working knowledge of Windows NT, 2000, XP, or Windows Server 2003.

The field of information technology has seen an explosion in the number of new businesses and startups. It is, however, important to take a realistic look at the needs as well as constraints of such a setup before investing in a solution—to not get extravagant, and also to stay practical. This is the thought that is gone behind the development of the Small Business Server 2003—to provide a server with a range of functions specially optimized for efficiently running such businesses.

What This Book Covers

Chapter 1 introduces SBS and talks about the possible scenarios that would demand its usage, the way it has improved over its predecessor, and about its base technology, Active Directory.

Chapter 2 discusses installation and basic configuration of SBS 2003, and various network and administrative tasks such as adding users and printers, configuring remote access, etc.

After the fresh installation, we move on to discuss the process of upgrading to SBS 2003 from previous versions in *Chapter 3*. We also present a few migration scenarios, and illustrate the how a migration differs from an upgrade.

Chapter 4 introduces Exchange Server 2003 and the fax services of SBS. *Chapter 5* follows with a discussion on Windows Sharepoint Services, for HTML-based central administration and access to documents, calendars, etc.

Chapter 6 and *Chapter 7* introduce you to Internet Security and Acceleration Server 2000 (a successor to Microsoft Proxy Server 2.0) and SQL Server 2000 (which can be used as a database for your business applications); both these applications are available only on the Windows Small Business Server Premium Technologies CD.

Chapter 8 is where we dig deep into SBS administration. We've discussed a host of topics, such as users, security and distribution groups, policies, their application, backup, software management, monitoring and reporting in SBS 2003, as well as network administration.

Chapter 9 discusses update management in the SBS network. *Chapter 10* discusses the role of a terminal server and client applications in an SBS environment.

Chapter 11 discusses the Business Contact Manager, an efficient customer-management add-on for Outlook 2003. This is followed by *Chapter 12*, on strategies for protecting the SBS network, from securing the router to restricting user rights.

Chapter 13 suggests solutions to various areas that might require troubleshooting.

Appendices A and *B* discuss configuring SBS 2003 and a firewall without ISA Server, and configuring an existing DHCP server.

Conventions

In this book, you will find a number of styles of text that distinguish between different kinds of information. Here are some examples of these styles, and an explanation of their meaning.

There are three styles for code. Code words in text are shown as follows: "To see the difference, you can print_r() the results of both functions".

A block of code will be set as follows:

```
User-agent: *
Disallow:  /_vti_bin/
Disallow:  /clienthelp/
Disallow:  /exchweb/
```

When we wish to draw your attention to a particular part of a code block, the relevant lines or items will be made bold:

```
User-agent: *
Disallow:  /_vti_bin/
Disallow:  /clienthelp/
Disallow:  /exchweb/
```

Any command-line input and output is written as follows:

```
Runas /netonly /user:NameSourceDomain\Administrator
    "mmc\"%ProgramFiles%\Active Directory Migration Tool\Migrator.msc\""
```

New terms and **important words** are introduced in a bold-type font. Words that you see on the screen, in menus or dialog boxes for example, appear in our text like this: "clicking the Next button moves you to the next screen".

> Tips, suggestions, or important notes appear in a box like this.

Reader Feedback

Feedback from our readers is always welcome. Let us know what you think about this book, what you liked or may have disliked. Reader feedback is important for us to develop titles that you really get the most out of.

To send us general feedback, simply drop an e-mail to feedback@packtpub.com, making sure to mention the book title in the subject of your message.

If there is a book that you need and would like to see us publish, please send us a note in the SUGGEST A TITLE form on www.packtpub.com or e-mail suggest@packtpub.com.

If there is a topic that you have expertise in and you are interested in either writing or contributing to a book, see our author guide on www.packtpub.com/authors.

Customer Support

Now that you are the proud owner of a Packt book, we have a number of things to help you to get the most from your purchase.

Errata

Although we have taken every care to ensure the accuracy of our contents, mistakes do happen. If you find a mistake in one of our books—maybe a mistake in text or code—we would be grateful if you would report this to us. By doing this you can save other readers from frustration, and help to improve subsequent versions of this book. If you find any errata, report them by visiting http://www.packtpub.com/support, selecting your book, clicking on the Submit Errata link, and entering the details of your errata. Once your errata have been verified, your submission will be accepted and the errata added to the list of existing errata. The existing errata can be viewed by selecting your title from http://www.packtpub.com/support.

Questions

You can contact us at questions@packtpub.com if you are having a problem with some aspect of the book, and we will do our best to address it.

1

Introduction to Small Business Server 2003

Small Business Server (SBS) 2003 is the successor to SBS 2000 and features vast improvements over its predecessor. This chapter gives you a brief overview of the areas of application, features, versions, requirements, and licensing issues related to Small Business Server 2003. You will also learn some basics about fundamental technologies supported by SBS 2003.

Area of Application of the Small Business Server

As the name suggests, SBS is meant for small- and medium-sized companies, where the maximum number of network clients does not exceed 75. For these companies SBS offers a range of specially optimized functions for collective access to the Internet, e-mail, and fax services, as well as file and printer sharing. The complete server solution of SBS 2003 combines all these services. The premium version of SBS additionally offers firewall and database server functionalities.

SBS 2003 does an even better job of providing a complete integrated solution for the infrastructure management of small and medium-sized companies than its predecessor. It covers the central requirements of companies such as e-mail exchange, secure Internet access, document management, collective work on documents, and database preparation as well as offering the advantages of Windows Server 2003 as the underlying operating system. The advantage of combining all these components into a single system is that it is not necessary to purchase a tool for any of these areas from a separate vendor. This means lower licensing costs and smaller investment in training for administering the system within the company.

Small- and medium-sized companies often do not have an adequate number of people for network maintenance at their disposal, and the time that these people can spend on this task is limited by their involvement in their primary activity. SBS 2003 can't really be administered by some hobby administrator after work, but the large number of administration wizards that have been provided make the job much easier.

The Expanding Middle Class

The middle class has expanded enormously from the end of the '90s until today. There was great willingness to invest in IT. The desktop and server market grew by eight to ten percent in this period, and broadband connections rose by almost 20%. At the same time data volumes also increased exceptionally. Whereas in 1999 the volume of e-mail was still 4 billion terabytes, by 2003 the figure had already reached 18 billion terabytes. Also, most companies now store their data in digital format.

Implementation Planning

If you are involved with the implementation of SBS 2003, you should give a thought to the extent to which such an implementation could encounter internal obstacles. These obstacles need not necessarily relate to company policy—they could also be based on objective constraints.

Decision Support: SBS 2003 or Windows Server 2003

Both SBS 2003 and Windows Server 2003 offer features that can fulfill the IT requirements of small and medium-sized companies. To help you choose between them some scenarios are presented below in which the deployment of one of the two products is advised. Keep the following points in mind when installing SBS 2003:

- All SBS 2003 components are installed on a single server. This ensures that all components are integrated. The primary SBS can, however, be extended to other servers.

- SBS 2003 represents the highest level of a new Active Directory. Therefore, a fresh implementation doesn't pose any problems. However, the SBS Active Directory does not support trust relationships with multiple domains. So, SBS 2003 can be used to implement only a single domain model.

Companies with One Head Office and up to 75 Employees

For a maximum of 75 employees, the standard version of SBS offers an all-in-one solution for Internet, e-mail, and fax services and intranet solutions with many features for teamwork. The premium version extends these capabilities to include Internet proxy and firewall functions, a database server, and extended functions for website creation and maintenance. If your company has more than 75 employees, you can either exchange individual products contained in SBS via the Migration Pack or purchase Windows Server 2003, which has no restrictions regarding the number of users.

Connecting a Branch to a Head Office

SBS 2003 can be used in this model if there is no integration with the Active Directory of the head office. Such integration cannot be guaranteed via SBS 2003 because the SBS domain must constitute the master domain in the Active Directory. If integration with the central Active Directory is required, you must use Windows Server 2003.

However, you can implement an SBS domain over two locations. The prerequisite for this is that one of the locations must have a Windows Server 2003 installation that mirrors the SBS. This ensures that registration can take place over the quick LAN connection at the location in situations where WAN connections are slow.

Dismantling an Existing Active Directory Environment

SBS 2003 cannot be implemented as a domain controller in an existing Active Directory environment because it must form the master domain. It is also not possible for SBS 2003 to have trust relationships with other domains. Windows Server 2003 on the other hand offers the possibility of extending an existing tree or forest in a flexible manner, adding additional domain controllers, or forming trust relationships with other Active Directory or NT 4.0 domains.

Extending an Existing Environment with Additional Servers

SBS 2003 must be the domain controller of the master domain. No further SBS 2003 machines can be added to this domain. It is however possible to add more Windows Server 2003 machines as additional domain controllers or member servers. If you wish to have more flexibility or plan to use a complex domain structure later, you should use Windows Server 2003 from the outset.

Setting up a Web Server for the Intranet/Internet

SBS 2003 includes a web server. This is Internet Information Server (IIS) 6.0. It has been improved greatly over IIS 5.0 and supports both ASP.NET and XML. In addition to this web server that all server versions of Windows have, there is also the special Windows 2003 Server web edition. This server is appropriate if you want to add just one web server. This edition can also be used to run an entire server farm.

Using a Terminal Server

SBS 2003 cannot itself be set up as a terminal server. However, any Windows Server 2000 or 2003 can be added to the SBS domain as a terminal server. SBS 2003 does, however, support the remote administration mode of the terminal server of Windows Server 2003. So, remote administration is guaranteed by a maximum of two simultaneous connections.

Features of Small Business Server 2003

In the following sections, we introduce you to the main features of SBS 2003. The biggest strengths of SBS 2003 are network security and remote access to the company network. You will also find information about features that have been improved in comparison with its predecessor SBS 2000.

Network, Internet, and E-Mail

SBS 2003 has all the features that small and medium-sized companies require for creating their presence on and accessing the Internet. These include Exchange and Outlook technologies for e-mail exchange, for example Outlook Web Access and Remote Workspace, a web server for Internet presence, a firewall function, the possibility of shared Internet access via broadband and PPPoE, security mechanisms for the local network, and productivity tools for team work. Each time that Internet and e-mail are configured, a VBS script is generated (`config.vbs`). With the help of this script, these settings can be relayed back to the computer later. It can also be used to configure other SBS 2003 clients.

The included SharePoint Services offer an already preconfigured website for comprehensive teamwork.

Exchange Server has an anti-spam function. Additionally, Outlook 2003 has other functions for filtering and blocking spam. For example, Exchange Server includes Microsoft Connector for POP3 mailboxes. This makes it possible to migrate existing e-mail accounts to Exchange and to download the e-mails of these accounts and make them available to the user under Outlook. For file attachments, a filter function has been provided.

SBS comes with a fix for the blaster worm. This fix is installed automatically. Any anti-virus software that is compatible with Exchange and Windows Server 2000 can be installed. The anti-virus software should, as far as possible, support a server-client configuration and not just be a client or desktop solution.

SBS 2003 can be configured like Windows Server 2003 for network services like DNS, DHCP, and WINS. The combination of Outlook/Exchange 2003 and Windows Server 2003 now also allows RPC over HTTP. This makes it possible to establish secure connections via the Internet to RPC server applications.

Security

SBS 2003 has a number of wizards for configuring the necessary security settings. Security-wise, Windows Server 2003, on which SBS 2003 is based, is a vast improvement on Windows Server 2000. Attacks on the server could be reduced by

60%, while the availability of services has increased by 275%. The standard version already has a firewall; the premium version integrates Internet Security and Acceleration (ISA) Server 2000.

SBS also supports hardware firewalls. Almost all UPnP (Universal Plug and Play) devices are automatically recognized by the Internet Connection and e-mail Configuration wizards. If the firewall device is not UPnP-enabled, it will have to be configured manually. Even UpnP devices can be problematic if they are based on proprietary protocols.

The built-in function of the Volume Shadow Copy service makes it possible to have regular data backups. These are carried out quickly and securely.

Team Work

SBS 2003 offers a central repository for large volumes of data. This data can be easily processed, used collaboratively, and archived. SBS 2003 even offers secure storage for mission-critical data.

Based on Windows, SharePoint Services makes available a preconfigured website. Using this central website, employees can use documents, announcements, events, or links together. The Outlook 2003-Enhanced Outlook Web Access enables the joint use of data or calendar functions via the Internet.

Remote Access and Mobility

SBS 2003 data can be accessed remotely, irrespective of time, location, and device used. Access can be configured for private as well as public files. A user can have access to his or her desktop and e-mails. Access takes place via the new remote portal Remote Workspace. A data synchronization function is also included. The integration of mobile devices like Smartphones and PDAs is given great importance in SBS 2003. Mobile users can access e-mails, calendar, schedules, and tasks via Outlook Mobile Access (OMA).

For the administrator there is of course a Remote Administration module. In addition, functions for virtual private networks (VPNs) are also included.

Setup and Administration

The installation and configuration of SBS 2003 uses convenient wizards and needs little time investment. SBS 2003 is already pre-installed on many OEM platforms. The setup of SBS clients has also been simplified in comparison to SBS 2000 since activation is no longer done by diskette but conveniently over the Internet via Online License Activation. OEMs can pre-install the complete SBS with their own logos, service numbers, etc.

The network configuration of clients is now done conveniently via a website and not by diskette. Pre-configuration of client applications is also possible. In contrast to earlier versions, in which only one user could be registered at a time, you can now register several users in one step on the basis of user submissions.

Monitoring functions have been improved. Performance and usage reports can now be received and evaluated by e-mail. The quicker reaction time resulting from this minimizes SBS downtime.

Versions of Small Business Server

The Small Business Server 2003 is available in a standard version and a premium version. The following table lists the components contained in each of the two versions.

Component	Standard Version	Premium Version
Windows Server 2003 (5 CAL)	x	x
Outlook 2003 (5 CAL)	x	x
Windows SharePoint Services	x	x
Exchange Server 2003	x	x
Shared Fax Services	x	x
ISA Server 2000 SP1	–	x
SQL Server 2000 SP3	–	x
Office Front Page 2003	–	x

The following table gives you a brief overview of the functions of various components and can help in choosing the right version:

Component	Description
Windows Server 2003	The standard version of SBS is based on this operating system. This makes it possible to set up the Active Directory Service, for example. Limitations are described in the paragraph following this table.
Exchange Server 2003 and Outlook 2003	E-mail and messaging server solution with features such as web access for remote access to mails and a calendar function that can be used jointly by a team.
SharePoint Services	Environment for teamwork and communication.

Component	Description
Shared Fax Services	Fax function that does not require a large number of telephone connections. Faxes can be received via printer, e-mail or SharePoint. Faxes can be sent directly from user desktops and can be delayed.
ISA Server 2000	Firewall service, routing, and NAT (Network Address Translation), secure Internet access for several users simultaneously.
SQL Server 2000	Powerful relational database for creating and implementing business applications.
Front Page 2003	Development environment for websites and SharePoint Services solutions

The Windows Server 2003 that comes with SBS 2003 is limited in the following ways as compared to the normal version of Windows Server 2003:

- Within a domain there can be only one computer running Windows Server 2003 for Small Business Server.

- It is not possible to remove the five operations master roles (FSMO, Flexible Single-Master Operation) from the SBS 2003 in the domain. You can add further domain controllers to the domain, but the five operations masters must remain on SBS 2003. Only the global catalogue (covered later in this chapter) can be executed on another domain controller to reduce the load on SBS 2003.

- Within the Active Directory, SBS 2003 must constitute the root domain or the highest level of the Active Directory structure. It cannot have any subordinate domains. So, it is not possible to integrate SBS 2003 in a company network and run it within this network as a branch server.

- The domain of Windows Server 2003 for Small Business Server cannot build a trust relationship with any other domain. So, it is not possible to access resources beyond the server.

- Additional servers must have an access license (CAL, Client Access License) for Windows Small Business Server.

In every other respect, the server supplied with SBS 2003 is a standard Windows Server 2003.

All server components of SBS 2003 must be installed on one computer. It is not possible, for example, to install the SQL server of the premium version on another server. Only Front Page 2003 from the premium version can be installed on any client within the SBS network.

Apart from the version of Windows Server 2003 included in Small Business Server, there is also a "Windows Server 2003 for Small Business Server". This is the pure server solution as a trimmed down version of SBS 2003 and does not contain the functions of the SBS standard or premium version. This version is subject to the same limitations as the Windows Server 2003 of SBS.

Windows Server 2003 for Small Business Server is available for a price of about 550 USD. With this, you get five CALs for the server. Additionally up to ten more CALs can be purchased for about 90 USD each. If you need more than 15 CALs, you should fall back upon Windows Server 2003, because this model works out cheaper.

While the premium version has ISA Server 2000 SP1 as an integrated firewall solution, the standard version only includes Windows Server 2003's Internet-connection firewall. In addition, Microsoft SUS server (Software Update Services) can be integrated with Small Business Server. This component can be downloaded free of cost. The current version is SUS 1.0 with Service Pack 1. The integration of SUS in a Small Business Server network is explained in Chapter 9.

> In contrast to SBS 2000, Terminal Services cannot be run in Application Mode under SBS 2003. It was removed since Application Mode on a domain controller is risky for the network. If Terminal Services still need to run in Application Mode, you should add a 'proper' Windows Server 2003 to the domain.

Hardware Requirements

The standard and premium versions of SBS 2003 differ in some respects with respect to their hardware requirements.

Requirements for the Standard Version

Given below is a list of the hardware specifications recommended by Microsoft for running the standard version of SBS 2003. In light of the hardware available today these requirements look modest. But remember that any savings you make on hardware will always be at the cost of performance.

Component	Minimum	Recommended
Processor	300 MHz	550Mhz and above
RAM	256 MB	384 MB (Maximum 4 GB)
Disk capacity	4 GB	4 GB

Component	Minimum	Recommended
Drives	CD-ROM	CD-ROM or DVD
Graphics	VGA	SVGA (minimum 800 x 600 pixel)
Other components	Network card	Two network cards
For Internet access	Broadband or high-speed modem Internet connection. Additional connection costs may be incurred with the service provider.	Broadband or high-speed modem Internet connection. Additional connection costs may be incurred with the service provider.
For the network	Dedicated class-1 fax modem for the fax service	Dedicated class-1 fax modem for the fax service
		For Outlook Mobile Access (OMA) Pocket PC Phone Edition 2003 or Smartphone 2003
		Windows XP or Windows 2000 as the client operating system

Requirements for the Premium Version

Given below is a list of the hardware specifications recommended by Microsoft for running the premium version of SBS 2003.

Component	Minimum	Recommended
Processor	300 MHz	550 MHz and above
RAM	256 MB	512 MB (Maximum 4 GB)
Disk capacity	5 GB, 2 GB for an installation SBS 2000	5 GB, 2 GB for an installation SBS 2000
Drives	CD-ROM	CD-ROM or DVD
Graphics	VGA	SVGA (minimum 800 x 600 Pixel)
Other components	Network card	Two network cards
For Internet access	Broadband or high-speed modem Internet connection.	Broadband or high-speed modem Internet connection
	Additional connection costs may be incurred with the service provider.	Additional connection costs may be incurred with the service provider.
For the network	Dedicated class-1 fax modem for the fax service	Dedicated class-1 fax modem for the fax service

Component	Minimum	Recommended
For the network (continued)		For Outlook Mobile Access (OMA) Pocket PC Phone Edition 2003 or Smartphone 2003
		Windows XP or Windows 2000 as the client operating system

Both versions support a maximum of two real physical CPUS or four virtual CPUs.

License Information and Costs

For running SBS, both a Windows Small Business Server 2003 license as well as a Windows Small Business Server 2003 CAL (Client Access License) are required. The first license permits the installation and use of SBS 2003; the second allows access to the server software on a per-user or per-computer basis. The CALs do not refer to simultaneous connections. The CALs of the standard and premium versions do not differ in price. A maximum of 75 licenses may be used in a SBS 2003 domain. The SBS package comes with five CALs.

A user CAL allows a specific user to access SBS 2003. The computer from which the user makes the connection (desktop, mobile device, etc.) is unimportant. On the other hand, a computer CAL is valid for only one computer. Any user can log on from this computer. You are free to decide whether you want to use the five included licenses per user or per computer. Automatic license monitoring is not a feature of SBS 2003.

The CAL is valid not just for the SBS itself but also for other Windows-based servers within the SBS domain. However, this does not apply to other Exchange Servers, SQL Servers, etc.

If you have acquired Software Assurance for the Small Business Server 2000 CALs, you can convert all these CALs to CALs for SBS 2003 free of cost. If this is not the case, you have to purchase new CALs.

If you have acquired Software Assurance for SBS 2000 as well as SBS 2000 CALs, you have a claim to SBS 2003 Premium.

If you have acquired Software Assurance for SBS 2003-CALs, you can exchange user-based CALs for computer-based CALs and vice versa free of cost at the time of renewing the Assurance.

In contrast to SBS 2000, the activation of CALs is no longer done by diskette, but with a special activation key over the Internet. Alternatively, you can use the wizard to add new SBS licenses and activate them by phone (local call charges). SBS 2003 Standard Version costs about $599 and SBS 2003 Premium Version about $1499. Detailed pricing information can be found at `http://www.microsoft.com/windowsserver2003/sbs/howtobuy/pricing.mspx`.

Sometimes an existing SBS domain needs to be extended. For example, there may be more than 75 users in the domain or the server components of SBS may need to be distributed over several physical systems or higher functionality may be required, like that of an Exchange 2003 Enterprise Server. In such cases, the purchase of the Small Business Server 2003 Transition Pack is recommended. Further details about the contents and pricing of the Transition Pack can be found at the above link.

Active Directory as Base Technology for SBS 2003

The tips and instructions given here about Active Directory as the base technology of SBS 2003 are meant primarily for those users who have had little or no experience with Active Directory-based networks, e.g. users migrating from Windows NT 4.0 or Novell NetWare. A comprehensive treatment of this complex subject would be beyond the scope of this book.

Active Directory has been the integrated directory service solution for the central administration of network objects since Windows Server 2003. Under SBS 2003, you can administer all the network objects of the SBS 2003 network via the Active Directory.

Setting Up the Active Directory

The rest of this chapter introduces you to the Active Directory. To begin with, a brief description of Active Directory is given, and the mode of functioning of a directory service is explained in detail. The primary access protocol for Active Directory is LDAP (Lightweight Directory Access Protocol). At the end, a summary is presented of the core features of Active Directory that are new in relation to Windows NT.

With Active Directory in Windows 2000, Microsoft made its entry into the world of directory services. Novell Netware's Novell Directory Service (NDS) has been in the market longer. Active Directory is based on standard Internet technologies. It is fully integrated with the operating system of SBS 2003. With Active Directory, the domain model of Windows NT has been extended. The primary access protocol for Active Directory is LDAP (Lightweight Directory Access Protocol) Version 3.

How Does a Directory Service Work?

A directory service works in a manner analogous to a telephone directory. In a telephone directory, a telephone number is linked to each name entry. You can also find optional information such as the address of a subscriber there. In a directory service, network resource objects like users, printers, and databases are linked to items of information. This information includes the name of the object, the location, and many object-specific details. The more information you give about the characteristics of an object, the more quickly and precisely can it be found by network users later, even though entering details of objects in the database will naturally take time.

When the name of an object is known, all information pertaining to it can be directly obtained. This corresponds to looking up a known name in a standard telephone directory to find out the associated telephone number. This, however, does not exhaust the reference functions of the directory. Let us say you do not know the exact name of an object but have some information about it. Then you can search for all objects in the directory that meet these criteria. This process is analogous to looking up the Yellow Pages. In this case you then get a list of all the relevant names. The directory is, however, superior to the yellow pages to the extent that you can search the latter only based on predefined entries, whereas the directory allows you to define your own search criteria.

A directory service makes it possible to administer all network objects centrally. In Active Directory all information about users, servers, computers, printers, etc., can be maintained and administered at one place, and can be accessed by all users throughout the network. This greatly simplifies administering and finding network resources.

Objects in the Directory

The directory stores objects. An object is a stored piece of information linked to a network resource. The directory service makes these resources available to network users as well as applications. This network service is responsible for the identification of resources so that users can access them. Millions of objects can be stored in Active Directory. Each object has a unique identifier called the **GUID** (Globally Unique Identifier). The GUID is a value of length 128 bits. This value is assigned to each object when it is created.

There are two types of Active Directory objects: **containers** and **non-containers**. Non-containers are also called **end nodes** or **leaves**. A container holds further containers or end nodes; an end node cannot contain any further objects. An example of a container is an organizational unit. In this are computers, users, etc. Even computers are classified as end nodes, although theoretically they can also contain objects such as printers.

Directory and Directory Database

Even though the directory is often referred to as a database (or directory database), there are fundamental differences between these two terms. A directory offers functions that go way beyond what is offered by a traditional relational database.

A major difference consists in the fact that the information in a directory is more often *consulted* than *changed*. In a database, more and more updated data is written. In a directory, therefore the search and read functions are optimized rather than the write function. After all, read access is available to all users of the directory whereas write access is restricted to administrators. The data stored in the directory is relatively static because it is not subjected to frequent changes. Directory users can ask for the e-mail address of a specific user hundreds of times or even more often, while this address will, in all probability, not be changed by the administrator in the same period.

A second difference between directory and database lies in how the relevant component is accessed. A database is usually accessed by means of a standardized, complex SQL (Structured Query Language) query. With this, complex queries and updates of the database are possible, but this is unfortunately at the cost of the complexity and size of the application. Directories such as Active Directory use **LDAP** (Lightweight Directory Access Protocol) for access. This is a simple, optimized, and lean protocol. LDAP is described in detail later in the following section.

Client-Server Communication

The information in the directory is accessed via the client-server communication model. In this model, an application running on a client that needs information from the directory cannot directly access the directory on the server. An **API** (Application Programming Interface) is called, which in turn calls a new process, the Directory Client, which executes the request over the TCP/IP protocol. Direct access to the directory takes place using the Directory Server. The information is then sent back in reverse order via this mechanism.

A directory service is only one example of client-server communication. Other services are the printing service, the web service, etc. They can all coexist on one computer.

Security

It should be possible for all directory users to find public information such as the e-mail address of a colleague, and for members of the personnel department to read information such as the complete private address of an employee; but only administrators should be able to change these entries. Access to objects is controlled via Access Control Lists (ACL). For each object, a list containing the access rights of specific users for that object is automatically generated.

Lightweight Directory Access Protocol (LDAP)

For communication between Active Directory clients and servers for network registration or locating resources, **LDAP** (Lightweight Directory Access Protocol) Version 3.0 is used as the standard access protocol. This section first gives you an overview of the development of LDAP. This is followed by an overview of the defined LDAP standards.

LDAP is a communication protocol that defines the transport and message format used by clients to access a directory working on the X.500 standard. The entire LDAP communication takes place over port 389. The LDAP protocol specifies how the directory server may be accessed, which directory actions are permitted, which published data may be used, and how secure access is to be executed. Administration, querying, and listing of objects takes place via LDAP.

An application may never directly access directory data—the access is controlled by an API that is called via a message. This LDAP API is initiated by an LDAP message. The LDAP client can directly access the directory on the LDAP server via TCP/IP.

LDAP has developed into an open industry standard. Products from different manufacturers and operating systems can communicate with each other via this protocol and, in a manner analogous to the HTTP standard of the Internet, support a global directory structure with the help of it.

LDAP Architecture

This section introduces you to the logical model of LDAP. As already mentioned, LDAP is the access protocol for X.500-based directory services. LDAP with active directory offers the following improvements over DAP and OSI:

- LDAP uses TCP/IP and not the resource-intensive OSI protocol stack.
- The functional model is simplified and seldom-used functions have been removed.
- Normal character strings are used for representing data and not complicated syntaxes such as ASN.1 (Abstract Syntax Notation).

LDAP defines the message that is exchanged between an LDAP client an LDAP server. The client-side message describes the action to be carried out, such as searching or deleting, while the server-side message contains the resulting reply and the format of the data to be transported. Data transport always takes place over the TCP/IP protocol. For the design of Active Directory it is important to know how the directory is structured, which operations can be carried out, and which data is to be secured in transit.

All communication between an LDAP client and server has the same format. It can be divided into the following steps:

1. The LDAP client makes the connection with the server. To do this it gives the IP address or the hostname of the server along with the TCP port (389). Authentication can take place in three ways: anonymous authentication with standard access rights, username and password authentication, or the connection can be encrypted.

2. The client now accesses the directory data. This access can be either a write or read process. Search processes will be the most frequent. Users can employ Boolean operators to filter out the information they need.

3. The connection to the server is closed once the executed action is over.

Since LDAP is based on the X.500 model, the data is stored accordingly as entries in the directory. Each directory entry describes a single object that has an unambiguous **Distinguished Name** (DN), which in turn consists of a series of **Relative Distinguished Names** (RDN). This chain of names is comparable to a directory path in Windows Explorer. These objects are arranged in a hierarchical tree structure based on the DNs of the objects. This structure is also called the Directory Information Tree (DIT).

Each entry consists of one or more entries. Each attribute consists of a type and a value.

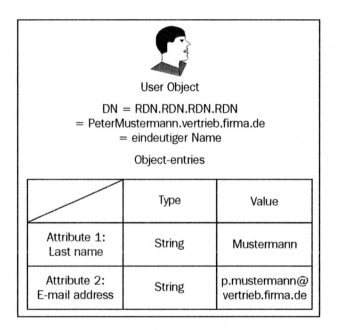

User Object

DN = RDN.RDN.RDN.RDN
= PeterMustermann.vertrieb.firma.de
= eindeutiger Name

Object-entries

	Type	Value
Attribute 1: Last name	String	Mustermann
Attribute 2: E-mail address	String	p.mustermann@ vertrieb.firma.de

In our example the attributes surname and e-mail address have been taken. The syntax of the attribute determines that the e-mail address is an alphanumeric string. An e-mail address can have letters, numbers or even special characters such as a hyphen (-).

Directory entries specify an object more precisely. At the same time, an object class describes an object. For example, the object class User is described by the attributes Surname and E-mail Address. Each object class has its own attributes and each attribute has its own value. For example, in a printer object you will not find the values Surname and E-mail Address. Instead it will have an attribute called Color Printer. All these object classes and their possible values are called the Active Directory Schema.

The actions that can be carried out on a directory entry are also determined over LDAP. These include adding, deleting, editing, and renaming entries, which require write access to the directory, as well as searching for and comparing an entry. These last two require only read access to the directory data.

Features of Active Directory

Active Directory offers the following solidly integrated yet flexibly configurable features that were not available in the Windows NT domain model:

- **Simplification of administration through centralization**: Each domain can have several domain controllers of equal rank. This ensures that changes you make on one domain controller are automatically replicated in the others. An administrator can log on from any computer on the network and administer resources on other computers in the domain from there.

- **Delegation of specific administration operations from the central administrator to sub-admins**: Permission is granted to a user from a higher level of authority to carry out a specific set of actions on a defined group of objects in an allocated section of the domain structure. This allows precise control over who can perform which action, without the need to assign higher privileges to the user.

- **Storage of objects in a structured hierarchy mirroring the organization of the company**: For example, domains can be set up according to geographical or functional aspects; in organizational units, the physical structure of the company, e.g. distribution over floors, can be represented.

- **High availability of the data as well as load distribution through multimaster replication of the directory on all domain controllers**: Through this, the directory is made available to a larger group of users. In the event of failure of a domain controller, a high degree of redundancy is available since the realization of Active Directory is no longer linked to one PDC but can take place on any Domain Controller.

- **Easier and quicker finding of resources in the network**: for example, a network printer can be found even if the complete address is not known. Specifying just parts of the qualities known to you in the search is enough, for example, duplex—yes or no, and color—yes or no.

- **High scalability**: The Active Directory database has a much higher capacity than the Windows NT user database. It is possible to first set up a small domain structure with maybe 200 objects, which can later be extended to millions of objects as the company grows.

- **Extensibility and individual adjustment of the Active Directory schema**: Each object can have its own attributes added, which can be highly company-specific, e.g. an attribute for signing authority, etc.

- **Support of standards such LDAP, NSPI (Name Service Provider Interface), HTTP, and DNS**: Active Directory supports Internet standards and builds on them. Support of the LDAP 3.0 and NSPI standards ensures collaboration with other directory services using these protocols. With DNS, the Internet naming concept has been integrated into Windows 2000. Windows 2000 even supports Dynamic DNS (DDNS). Using this, clients with IP addresses acquired over DHCP can register dynamically with the DNS server. In a pure Windows 2000 environment, the WINS name service can be replaced by DDNS if there are no legacy client-server applications that require the WINS service.

- **Improvement in security**: In Active Directory precise access control can be defined not just at the object level but also at the object properties level. Domain-wide security guidelines can be defined for the user accounts using group Policies.

Operation and Description of Active Directory

After giving you an insight into the operation of the directory service and the advantages of Active Directory over Windows NT, we introduce here the essential components and keywords of Active Directory such as domains, structures, and replication.

Domains and Domain Controllers

In contrast to a workgroup, all accounts and resources are administered centrally in a domain. This means that with a single login into the domain a user has automatic access to all resources of the entire domain for which he or she has the appropriate rights. The log in takes place exclusively on the domain controller of the domain. This is where the central database, which contains entries about user accounts, rights, resources, etc., is located. A domain controller does not have a local security database. Up to two million objects can be stored in a single domain. In an SBS 2003 network, SBS 2003 is the domain controller.

A Windows Server 2003 domain can have several domain controllers with equal rights. However, SBS 2003 is restricted to being the only domain controller in an SBS 2003 domain. Domain controllers in a non-SBS 2003 domain automatically synchronize their databases with each other ensuring that updated data is always available to the network. This process is known as replication. With the installation and configuration of SBS 2003, the domain itself is set up anew.

In contrast to Windows Server 2003, you do not have to run the installation wizard for Active Directory here. Since the SBS 2003 domain can consist of only one domain that has just one domain controller with no trust relationships to other domains, the configuration of Active Directory is considerably simpler and takes place automatically in the background. A domain controller is responsible for the registration and authentication of users in its environment as well as for object searches carried out on the directory. It stores all the Active Directory data.

A domain does not have to be identical with the physical boundaries of a company location. It is possible for a domain to have objects from several physically separated domains.

Under Windows NT if no domain controller was available for a client, it could not access any network resources. This problem was recognized and addressed from Windows 2000 onwards. Clients running Windows 2000 or later automatically use login caching.

In login caching, every successful login to the domain is cached on the client. By default, ten entries can be stored on the client. This value can be changed in the security guidelines. If this client wants to log in to the domain again later and cannot connect to the domain controller, it can still do so. The settings pertaining to rights, group memberships, etc. are taken over from the client's cache based on the last successful login to the domain. Even if these entries have been changed on the domain controller in the meantime, these settings in the client's local cache are still valid. The cache is updated at the next successful connection to the domain.

An SBS 2003 domain can have the following types of domains: a domain controller, client computers, and optionally member servers that can act as file and print servers.

Trees and Forests

Structures are a hierarchical arrangement of several Windows 2000/2003 domains. As you have already learned, no structures can be built with SBS 2003, which can only form a single domain. Nonetheless, this topic is discussed here briefly.

There are higher-level domains and subordinate domains. Structures are of two types—**trees** and **forests**. Trees are often referred to as just structures.

In a tree, all domains are in a continuous DNS namespace. The name structure is hierarchical. Each domain has a unique domain name.

Within a tree, all domains use the same Active Directory schema, the same replication information, and the same global catalogue.

In a structure, a subordinate domain inherits the name of the higher-level domains. The relative name of the subordinate domains is placed in front of these. For example the domain `vertrieb.firma.de` inherits the name of the higher-level domain `firma.de` and the relative name `vertrieb` is put in front of it (see the following figure). This is called a continuous or coherent namespace.

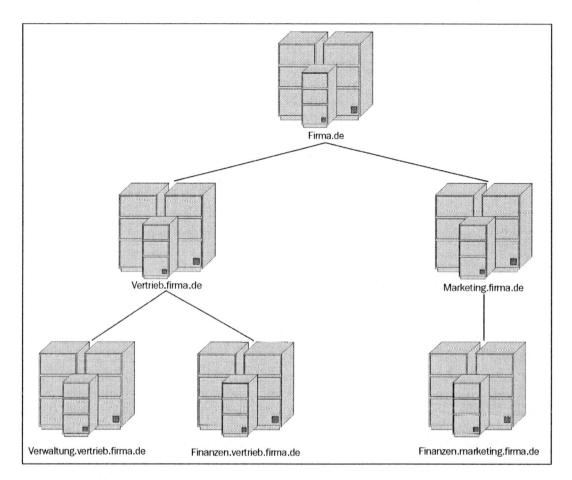

A tree is at the same time also a complete forest.

A **forest** is a hierarchical arrangement of either just one tree or several separate, independent trees. Even a single domain such as `firma.de` without any subordinate domains forms a self-contained forest.

In all the domains of a forest the same Active Directory Schema, the same replication information and the same global catalogue are used. The namespace is coherent only within the trees. In the figure, the two structures `firma.de` and `filial.de` constitute separate trees within the forest. Only within the two structures is the namespace continuous. The first domain in a forest is also called the master domain of the forest—here `firma.de`.

The installation wizard for Active Directory helps you determine at what level in the hierarchy the new domain should be placed. The following possibilities exist:

- First domain in a forest, for example `firma.de`
- First domain of a new tree, for example `filial.de`
- Subordinate domain in an existing tree, i.e. all other domains subordinate to the two domains

After setting up the first domain controller of one of the above-mentioned domain types, you can install additional domain controllers for this domain.

Trust relationships are created automatically between all Windows 2000 domains within the forest. This holds only for Windows 2000 domains. If you are still using Windows NT domains in the forest, trust relationships to these will have to be configured manually. The automatic set up refers to trust relationships between higher-level and subordinate domains as well as to those between the master domain of the forest and the first domains of new trees.

The Global Catalogue

The global catalogue is responsible for object searches in the directory. It is created automatically on the first domain controller of the master domain of the forest. This special domain controller is therefore also called the catalogue server. In the SBS 2003 environment, the SBS 2003 machine also acts as the catalogue server.

Two separate copies of the object attributes are maintained in the global catalogue. The catalogue server gets on the one hand a complete copy of all the object attributes in the entire directory and, on the other hand, a partial copy consisting of only the object attributes found in the directories of individual domains of the forest. Although the partial copy contains all the objects, the number of attributes is limited. Search requests for objects in the directory are dealt with via this partial copy. It contains only those object attributes that come up most frequently in search requests—e.g. user names—or are required to find the full copy of the object. To ensure secure access to the objects in the global catalogue, these objects inherit the access rights of their source domains.

The distinguished name of an object is enough to find the path to the complete copy of this object. In many cases, however, the user does not know the complete distinguished name. The global catalogue makes it possible for the user to find the desired object even from a few known attributes. It is therefore not necessary for the user to know the precise location of the object within the forest.

It is therefore also important to specify as many characteristics as possible at the time of creating an object so as to be able to use the efficacy of the global catalogue optimally.

The use of the global catalogue greatly reduces network traffic. Since the catalogue contains information about all objects in all domains of the forest, the search request can be processed within the domain to which the user making the search request is logged on. So, there is no search, and therefore no network traffic, across domain boundaries.

The catalogue server plays an important role when users log on to the domain. It makes user account information available to the domain controller. When a client logs on, a list containing all the groups of which this client is a member is generated. However, this feature is used only in multi-domain environments in which the client can be a member of several groups in several domains. The global catalogue servers contain membership lists of all universal security groups. These lists are used when clients or servers need to verify membership in the security groups.

The catalogue server has to play one more role if you deploy Microsoft Exchange Server 2000 or 2003 in your environment. The catalogue servers are responsible for looking up address book entries and resolving e-mail addresses for Outlook clients from Outlook 98 SP2 onwards. Older e-mail clients use the Exchange Server itself for this purpose, which again requires access to a catalogue server.

Locations

Locations structure networks as much as domains do. Domains reflect the logical structure of a company while locations reflect its physical structure. Organizational units also contribute to the logical structuring of the network.

A location corresponds to a group of computers that belong to a specific IP subnet. These computers are taken to be well connected with each other. The computers at a location can also belong to different subnets. In this case, however, there must be a fast connection between them. This fast connection is required because within a location the replication as well as resource requests from Active Directory consume a not insignificant part of the network bandwidth. For this reason, it is makes more sense to configure several locations for a WAN. For the relationship between locations and domains, the following points hold: a domain can contain several locations (see the following figure) and the other way round a location can contain several domains. From this, it follows that there does not have to be any correspondence between location boundaries and the namespace of the domains. So, in an SBS 2003 environment you can configure several locations for the SBS domain.

In this model, a domain has several locations. Each of the three locations has its own subnet range. The computers in locations 1 and 2 have slow connections to the domain (dial-up or WAN). That is why a separate location was created for each of them. The third location comprises computers with a fast LAN connection to the domain. The computers in all the locations are members of the domain firma.de.

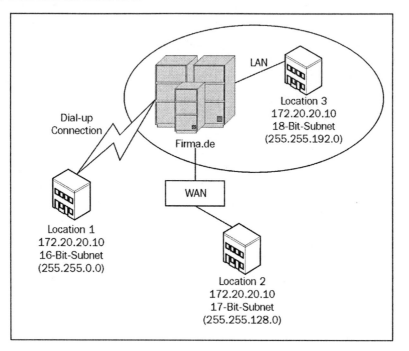

In this example, there is only one subnet with a coherent 16-bit subnet. Computers that by their logical structure belong to the domain firma.de, are part of this location. The location says nothing about the logical affiliation of the computers.

If you open the Microsoft Management Console (MMC) ACTIVE DIRECTORY LOCATIONS AND SERVICES, you will find that it does not list computers belonging to a particular location. Searching a domain returns computers only in their logical structure. You will find individual computers only under their domains and organizational units. Under ACTIVE DIRECTORY LOCATIONS you will only find elements that are responsible for configuring the replication between the locations.

Organizational Units

Apart from domains, organizational units are the second way of grouping network resources. The members of organizational units are all members of the domain that contains the organizational unit(s). In contrast to a location, an organizational unit does not have its own domain controllers. Organizational units are used instead of the resource domains in the Windows NT domain models. In an organizational unit, objects are divided into groups. These groups reflect the company structure. An organizational unit can contain objects such as computers, contacts, groups, other organizational units, printers, users, and released files. The fact that organizational units have fewer objects makes it easier to administer and display them.

Administrative tasks can be delegated to an organizational unit. The rights that a user needs for carrying out his or her administrative tasks can be assigned either to a separate organizational unit or to a higher-level organizational unit, which then passes on these rights to the subordinate units. This makes it possible to distribute the administration of the domain among several administrators. In this way, you can perform special administrative tasks for the organizational unit. By default, there are no pre-configured organizational units in the MMC ACTIVE DIRECTORY USERS AND COMPUTERS. This would not make sense because it is precisely the individual characteristics of the administration units that should structure your company network.

The following figure gives an overview of the organizational units within a domain as well as the different object that an organizational unit can contain.

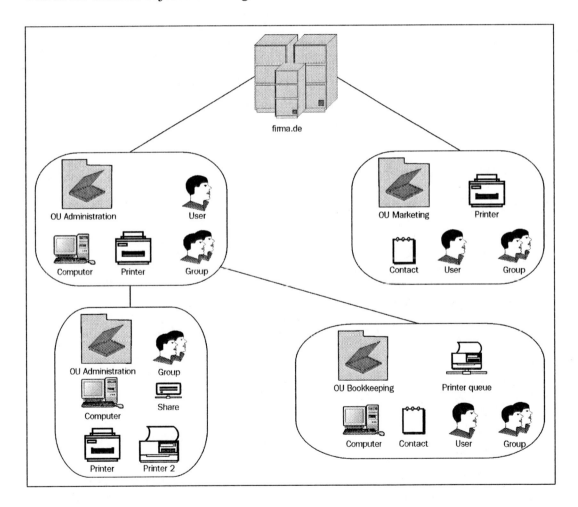

The figure shows a domain with four organizational units. The two organizational units Administration and Marketing are at a higher level; the organizational unit Administration contains the organizational units Personnel and Accounts as subordinate objects.

Each individual organizational unit has its own independent structure and resources. Objects that are present in an organizational unit do not have to occur in all organizational units of the domain, and conversely, all objects do not have to be bound to an organizational unit.

Active Directory Objects and Schema

All resources are stored as objects in Active Directory. Objects can be computers, accounts, printers, contacts, etc. Each object consists of a definite set of characteristics or attributes that are specific to this object. For example, a domain controller object has the following attributes under general characteristics: computer name, DNS name, function, and description. For Active Directory these characteristics serve as patterns for the objects. These patterns must be known to the directory service to store the objects.

The Active Directory Schema has a pre-given set of definitions for the objects and information in Active Directory. There are two types of definitions—attributes and classes. These are also known as schema objects or metadata. The Active Directory Schema is compulsorily the same for all domains within a forest. The information in the schema is replicated automatically.

Attributes

An attribute is defined only once in a schema and can be used by any classes. So, for example, you will find the Description attribute in various objects such as computers, accounts, etc. In each of these classes, the attribute fulfils the general purpose of explaining the corresponding object more precisely, but the description of the special object is different in each class.

Classes

Classes determine the types of objects that can be created in Active Directory— computers, accounts, etc. Each class has a specific set of all possible attributes. When you create a new object, the attributes get the values that describe the object concretely. Classes are also called object classes.

Under Windows Server 2000 and 2003, you have the option of customizing the schema according to your individual requirements.

The Active Directory Schema is object-oriented. A set of object instances is stored in the directory. This is how Active Directory is different from other directory services in which the schema is stored as a text file that is read when the directory service is started. From the objects stored in Active Directory applications we can, for example, find out what objects and characteristics are available. The Active Directory Schema can be dynamically updated. For example, an application can add new classes and attributes to the schema and immediately use this newly added metadata. Creating or modifying the metadata stored in the directory suffices to change the schema. Like all other objects in Active Directory, the metadata is also protected by Access Control Lists (ACLs). This ensures that only authorized users can change the schema.

Group Policies

Group Policies are the central component of Active Directory for the effective management of rights. Group Policies are an extension of the System Policies under Windows NT.

Group Policies can be applied at the level of locations, domains, and organizational units. A group policy object gives the user a collection of company rules in relation to available resources, access rights, and configuration of these resources. The desktop settings of a user are configured using a group policy. For example, you can assign software or determine which items the user is allowed to see in the start menu. Under Windows NT, you had the System Policy for this purpose, even though its scope was not as wide. Group Policies are a part of IntelliMirror. IntelliMirror is the generic term for regulating client desktops under Windows 2000/XP. You can determine policies for each client based on its function, location, and group membership. The user receives the settings defined for him or her in the Group Policy irrespective of the computer from which he or she logs on. IntelliMirror covers the administration of user data and settings as well as assignment, and the installation and configuration of software. The administration and configuration of group policies is discussed in detail in the Chapter 8.

Replication

Replication means the exchange of directory information between several domain controllers. All domain controllers in a domain must have access to current directory information at all times. If you make changes on any domain controller in the domain, these changes must be accessible to the other domain controllers as quickly as possible. In replication, the changed directory information is sent from the one domain controller to all the others.

Features of ADSI

This chapter briefly shows you the important features of **ADSI** (Active Directory Services Interface). ADSI offers you an interface for your own applications in a number of operating systems for accessing various directory services.

- ADSI gives you easy access to directory services via the Component Object Model (COM). The applications are not bound to any particular programming language and can be written in Visual Basic, C/C++, Java, etc.

- ADSI is independent of the directory service. You can develop applications without having to know the various vendor-specific directory APIs. Even administrative applications are not bound to any fixed directory service.

- You can use any automatable scripting language (VB Script, REXX, Perl, etc.) to develop applications for the directory service.

- ADSI can be extended by directory service providers, software developers and administrators by the addition of new objects and functions. This is important if your directory has to meet very special requirements.

- ADSI offers an OLE Database Interface so that even database programmers can quickly start working productively via this interface.

2

Installing SBS 2003

This chapter describes preparing for the installation of SBS 2003, the installation itself, and the subsequent base configuration. Here we start with a fresh installation. Migration from SBS 2000 or 4.5 and other update scenarios are described in Chapter 3.

Determining the Network Structure

Before you install SBS 2003 on a server or add a pre-installed OEM server to a network, you must first analyze the existing network structure to determine where SBS should be added.

The two most common network models are **peer-to-peer networks** and **server-based networks**. If you don't have a network, follow the steps described in the section *Fresh Installation of SBS 2003* to implement SBS 2003.

In a **peer-to-peer network** computers are connected to each other for data exchange and other communication. This connection can be via a switch or a hub but could also be implemented via a hardware firewall for Internet connectivity. An Internet connection on one computer can be used simultaneously by several computers.

In a **server-based network** on the other hand, there is at least one server. Clients are provided Internet connectivity via this server, which is most often a domain controller (the central database repository for the network) and also serves as a print server. A hardware or software firewall runs on the server to protect the Internet connection. In contrast to a peer-to-peer network, here the server (domain controller) is the central overriding authority for administering user accounts, client computers, and other network resources. To access network resources, clients have to log on to the server and be authenticated. The implementation steps for SBS 2003 vary depending on whether you are running a peer-to-peer or a server-based network.

Adding SBS to a Peer-to-Peer Network

This section describes the implementation of SBS in a peer-to-peer network. Such a network can be with or without a hardware firewall.

Peer-to-Peer Network with Hardware Firewall

When adding SBS to a network with a hardware firewall, ensure that the firewall remains on until you have completed the process.

The SBS is connected to the LAN as well as the Internet using a network card. To set up an Internet connection, consider the following example. A router is used as a standard gateway that obtains its IP address from the ISP (Internet Service Provider). This can either be a dynamic address assigned by the ISP's DHCP server or a static IP address. The username and password valid for this Internet connection for PPPoE (Point-to-Point Protocol over Ethernet) connections must also be entered in this device. This is true even if the device supports UPnP.

The gateway's internal interface must have an IP address that is in the same range as the network card of the SBS. If the gateway is simultaneously also configured as a DHCP server, an IP address from the range of the gateway's internal interface is suggested to you during SBS setup. The setup program also suggests an IP address if the gateway is not configured as a DHCP server.

The firewall function must compulsorily be implemented on this gateway or a hardware firewall must be available. In this scenario you *cannot* use the firewall function of SBS 2003 because the SBS is not acting as the gateway. To use this function, you will need to install a second network card in the SBS. If the hardware firewall deployed is UPnP (Universal Plug & Play)-enabled, it can be configured automatically during Internet configuration. For manual configuration of the firewall, please see Appendix A.

Peer-to-Peer Network without Hardware Firewall

In this setup you have to choose between a dialup connection (analog modem, ISDN) and a broadband connection (e.g. DSL) for Internet access.

Dialup Connection

If you use a dialup connection, you must connect the SBS to the LAN via a network card. On the other side the SBS is connected to the modem or the terminal adapter. In this setup the SBS becomes a standard gateway. SBS's integrated firewall is configured to protect the Internet connection.

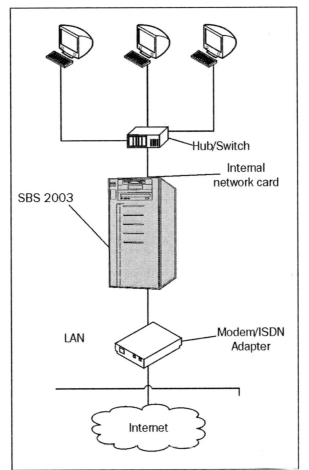

SBS without a hardware firewall and with a dialup connection

Broadband Connection

If you have a broadband connection such as DSL without a firewall in the LAN, you must equip SBS 2003 with two network cards. Its internal network adapter is connected to the switch or hub to which the LAN clients are connected. The second network adapter is connected to the DSL modem. In this model you will activate the firewall on SBS 2003 to protect the Internet connection. The SBS becomes the standard gateway in this set up. The user information for Internet access is asked for at the time of configuring the Internet connection.

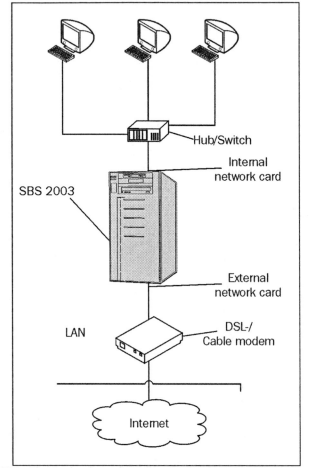

SBS without a hardware firewall and with a broadband connection

Adding SBS to a Server-Based Network

In this model there are various possibilities for the existing network set up:

- If the existing server runs Windows Server 2000, Windows Server 2003, or SBS 2000, you can update it so that all existing data and settings are preserved. The network configuration of the server is always available in this case and is taken over by SBS 2003.

- If the existing server runs Windows NT 4.0 Server or SBS 4.5, you will have to carry out a migration. In this case a fresh installation is done on a new system. The existing data and settings are then transferred from the old to the new system. Migration is also possible from an existing Windows Server 2000/2003 or SBS 2000.

- If there is already a server in the network that is neither set up as a domain controller nor meant to become one, you must do a fresh installation of SBS and configure it as a domain controller. The existing server can then be added to the SBS network as a member server.

Fresh Installation of SBS 2003

As already mentioned, SBS 2003 comes pre-installed on a wide range of OEM products. If this is the case, you can skip this section and go straight to *Task List for Concluding Configuration*.

To install the standard version of SBS 2003 three CDs are required. CD 1 contains Windows Server 2003 for Small Business, CD 2 has Exchange Server, and CD 3 SharePoint Services. To install the premium version you first run these three CDs and then the CD called "Small Business Server 2003 Premium Technologies". Both versions include the CD "Office Outlook 2003", and the premium version additionally has the CD "Office FrontPage 2003".

The complete installation and configuration process of SBS 2003 can be divided into three stages. They are:

1. Installation and configuration of Windows Small Business Server
2. Installation of other server components
3. Task list for final configuration

The next three sections are structured in accordance with these three sets of tasks.

Installation and Basic Configuration

Before installing SBS 2003 ensure that the hardware used is compatible with Windows Server 2003. To find this out, consult the Hardware Compatibility List (HCL).

Automatic hardware detection is carried out during the installation of Windows Server 2003. This can cause problems with a connected UPS. There is a danger of the UPS switching to battery mode and the setup failing. To prevent this problem, you should disconnect the UPS from the server before beginning installation and reconnect it only after installation is complete.

As soon as you insert the first installation CD of SBS 2003, the same setup that you are familiar with from Windows Server 2003 appears. This installation process takes about 40 minutes. Only when you log on to the system for the first time do you see the logo and the legend Windows Server 2003 for Small Business Server in the welcome window. After you have logged on to the system, some more installation components are copied and loaded. You will see the corresponding progress bars. When this process is over, you can start the basic configuration of SBS 2003. This configuration and installation process takes about 30 minutes.

If you want to continue the configuration process later, you can always do so by inserting the first installation CD and selecting the Install Small Business Server 2003 Now option.

Default values are offered at many points during the installation. These are usually adequate for small and medium-sized companies. If you want to change these values, click on the FURTHER Information button.

All the paths in the start menu of SBS 2003 assume that the classical start menu has been activated. If the modified start menu has been activated in your environment, the paths given may vary slightly in some cases.

1. To begin with you see a welcome message. You learn that the following steps will now be carried out one after the other:
   o Configuration of the operating system
   o Installation of other server applications such as Exchange 2003
   o Execution of a task list that completes the configuration of SBS 2003

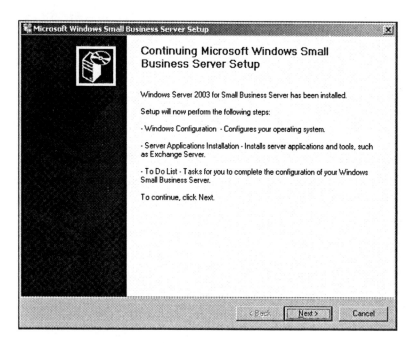

2. Click on Next.

3. The Setup Requirements dialog box appears. In the Requirements text field you see information about problems that could arise during installation.

The problems are divided into three categories. Double-click a listed requirement to get more information about the problem.

Category	Description
Information	The points listed under this category are things you should be aware of before beginning configuration. They do not necessarily lead to problems during installation.
Warning	Points in this category draw attention to possible problems during installation.
Obstruction	Points in this category indicate that installation cannot continue due to the problems mentioned. Problems listed here must therefore be removed before installation can be carried out.

This dialog box appears if there is any information in any of the three categories just mentioned. Then click on Next.

Enter the requested information in the Company information dialog box (telephone and fax numbers as well as address). SBS uses this information to configure its server components. Then click on Next.

4. The next step is the DNS configuration of the server in the Internal Domain information dialog box. Enter the DNS name of the domain, the NetBIOS name of the domain and the name of the server in the appropriate fields and click on Next.

The DNS domain name may consist of the following characters:

- The letters A–Z and a–z
- The numbers 0–9
- The hyphen character (-)

By default the NetBIOS domain name is the same as the DNS domain name. However, it is possible to have a NetBIOS domain name different from the DNS domain name. The computer name may consist of the following characters:

- The letters A–Z and a–z
- The numbers 0–9
- The hyphen character (-)

By default the use of .local as the TLD (Top Level Domain) is recommended to you. The use of this TLD has the advantage of clearly separating the internal domain from external Internet domains, which are not allowed to use .local as TLD.

You can also use another TLD such as .de or .com. Just ensure that it does not overlap with a previously registered domain on the Internet. The moment you select a TLD other than .local, a confirmation message appears.

Here the advantages of using .local as TLD are explained to you once again. If you do want to use this TLD, click Yes. If you want to retain the selected TLD, click No.

Once the installation of SBS 2003 is completed, you cannot change the DNS domain name, the NetBIOS domain name, or the computer name. So consider the name you want to use carefully! A change in name requires a reinstallation of SBS 2003.

5. If there is more than one network card in the SBS 2003 machine, select the card to be used for access to the local network in the Local Network Adapters Information dialog box. During setup all network cards on the SBS that have not been selected as the card for connecting to the local network will be

disabled. Any existing settings for the disabled cards will be saved and will not be lost.

To ensure that there are no mix-ups between the network cables connecting to the local network and to the Internet, you should label the cables accordingly.

6. The DNS configuration is followed by the DHCP (Dynamic Host Control Protocol) configuration. If there is another DHCP server in the same network, you get a confirmation message as shown in the following figure. Here you have the option of installing the DHCP server of the SBS (Yes button) or retaining the existing DHCP server (No button).

7. In the next step the selected network card of the SBS (which may be the only one in the server) is configured. If you have decided to retain the existing server in the previous step, the IP address, subnet mask, and standard gateway are provided by this DHCP server.

If the information is not provided by a DHCP server, a configuration is suggested to you. You should keep these settings. If no address has been specified for the network adapter so far, 192.168.2.1 is suggested (since routers often use the address 192.168.2.1, this should usually not result in an address conflict). If an address has already been given, this will be suggested.

8. In the Login information dialog box you specify whether you want to log in manually or automatically during the setup process (see following figure). Since further configuration will require a number of restarts, you should select the Automatic login option. Automatic login only works if a password is given for the administrator account. Click on Next when you are done.

> The password can consist of the characters A-Z, a-z, and 0-9 as well as special characters such as $, *, or !. To make the password secure you should use between eight and 127 characters and combine the various character types.

Automatic login of the administrator is limited to the setup period. As soon as this is over, the administrator will have to log in manually.

9. The Windows Configuration dialog box (shown in the following figure) displays information about the subsequent configuration. This configuration procedure will take about half an hour. During this period all windows and

applications (except, of course, those pertaining to the setup process) should be closed. To start the configuration, click Next.

If the configuration cannot be completed successfully, the message Continue Setup appears on the next restart. The new configuration begins again with step 1.

10. The components are installed after you click on Next. This installation process takes about 30 minutes. During this process you will see the Component status dialog box (see the following figure). This gives you information on the status of the installation and configuration. You also see this information at each restart. If you have selected automatic login, do not make any further adjustments until the configuration is completed.

The configuration of the server should in principle be carried out as soon as the operating system is installed. If you stop setup after installation, SBS will automatically shut down in seven days because the licensing requirements have not been met.

If setup has not been carried out after installation of the operating system, the message Continue Setup appears on the desktop. If you have closed this message dialog box or wish to carry out the setup later, you can run SETUPSBS.EXE from installation CD 1.

> If you start setup on a server that is already configured, you can add new components, remove old ones, and even repair or reinstall faulty ones.

What Happens during Basic Configuration?

During the basic configuration numerous changes are made on the server in the widest variety of applications, services, and components. This section gives you an overview of the changes made in the server configuration according to subject area.

Changing the Computer Name

In the Internal Domain information dialog box, if the computer name has been changed to something other than that given by the operating system, all the data on the server containing the computer name is modified.

Testing the Network Configuration

In this step the configuration of the network cards is first checked. Finally all the necessary network services and protocols are installed and configured.

Installation of Other Components

Internet Information Services (IIS 6.0) is installed during the basic configuration. IIS is required for the web-based portion of the SharePoint Services for the intranet website, Outlook Web Access (OWA), and Remote Workplace. Furthermore, the NNTP service (Network News Transfer Protocol), ASP.NET, RPC over http proxy, and the SMTP service (Simple Mail Transfer Protocol) are installed.

Installation and Configuration of Active Directory

Since the SBS 2003 domain can only be implemented as a root domain, the configuration of Active Directory is much simpler than for Windows Server 2003. The SBS domain is configured as an Active Directory domain in the standard operating mode of Windows 2000. This operating mode ensures support for the server tools. The password for restoring the directory service is synchronized with the administrator password specified during installation.

Installation of Microsoft Search

Microsoft Search is required for the support of indexes and for searches in Exchange Server 2003.

Installation of other Server Components

After the basic configuration is over, the server applications are installed along with their corresponding tools. The selection and installation of server components takes about 90 minutes in the standard version of SBS 2003.

1. In the Component Selection dialog box you will see the components that are typically selected in a standard installation.

If you want to modify this selection, click on the small arrow in the Action column. You have a choice between Install and No Action. In the second case the components will not be installed. The Server Tools and Client Deployment components both have a list of sub-features (indicated by the + symbol) that can be separately installed. Using the Change Path button you can specify a different installation path for the Server Tools and Exchange Server components. Clicking the Disk Information button will give you information about the free space available on your drives. Once you have made your choice, click Next.

2. In the Data Folders dialog box you can specify the installation path for the data folders (see the following figure).

If your system has a second NTFS-formatted hard drive, use this drive as a storage location for the data folders. To change the path click Change Folder. If you have selected the paths or accepted the standard settings, click Next.

What Are Data Folders?

Data folders are required during installation for applications such as Exchange Server or fax services. If a second drive is available on the system, you should install the data folders separately from the system drive. This improves system performance. This also facilitates backup and restoration of the data. The following default permissions have been specified for the data folder Users Shared Folders:

- Domain user: Read and write
- Administrators: Full access
- Folder Operators: Full access

The following additional standard permissions are also valid:

- Not inheritable by higher-level objects
- Administrators: Full access (inheritable)
- Folder Operators: Full access (inheritable)
- Domain user: Read and execute (not inheritable)

The following standard permissions for the folders of all users are also valid for the folder Users Shared Folders:

- Name of the user: Full access
- Administrators: Full access
- Folder Operators: Full access

You can change these default permissions. However, the moment you reinstall SBS 2003, the permissions for Users Shared Folders are reset to the default values mentioned above. The default values are also restored if you update SBS 2000 to SBS 2003.

3. The Component Summary dialog box appears next. Here you will see a summary of the installation options selected by you in step 1. If you still want to make changes, click the Back button until you reach the desired place. Otherwise click Next.

4. As in the basic configuration, you will again see the Component status dialog box, which will inform you about the progress of the installations and configuration. The installation takes about 60 minutes.

5. After all server applications and tools have been successfully installed, the dialog box Completing the Installation appears. Click on Complete and then on OK. This begins the final restart of the system.

Task List for Concluding Configuration

After the server components have been installed, SBS restarts and you see a list of tasks for the concluding configuration of server applications and tools. After you have worked through this final list, SBS 2003 is ready for use. To make changes or adjustments later, you will have to run the server administration program of SBS 2003. To begin, click the Start button. You will see the To Do List dialog box:

When working through the list you should maintain the given sequence of steps. The configuration will take about 30 minutes (not counting the setup time for individual clients).

The task list is divided into two categories: **network tasks** and **administration tasks**. The individual tasks in both categories are presented in detail in the following sections.

Network Task: Show Proven Security Methods

You will be taken to the SBS 2003 help screens. There you will get information about security recommendations in various security areas, for example, the configuration of password guidelines, remote access, implementation of an antivirus solution, implementation of security tools, or granting of access rights. Decide for yourself which of these recommendations are most meaningful for your network.

Network Task: Setting Up an Internet Connection

With the help of this wizard you will configure the network, the firewall, secure website publications, and e-mail settings for SBS 2003.

1. After a welcome message, first select the desired connection type.

Here you can choose between Broadband connection and Dial-Up. Choose Broadband connection if you have a high-speed connection such as DSL or faster.

The Do not change connection type option is available only if you have already run this wizard before and now want to make changes on some of the pages. The settings skipped using this option are not changed. You will find the Do not change option on a number of pages in all wizards of the task list.

If you use a dial-up connection, choose the Dial-up option. In this case make sure that the modem has been correctly recognized and installed. Otherwise it cannot be configured. Then click on Next.

2. If you have selected Broadband connection, you must now indicate how this connection is made. From the My server list box select one of the following entries: A local router with an IP address, A connection that requires a username and password (PPPoE), or A direct Broadband connection. Then click on Next.

Help about which method applies to your network is available via the More Information
button and the Display a network diagram link.

3. In the Router Connection dialog box enter the data required for the router to
    make the connection. In our example we assume that you have selected A
    local router with an IP address in step 2.

In the Preferred DNS server field enter the IP address of the DNS server. If you are using a second DNS server, you can enter its IP address beside Alternate DNS server. In the Local IP address of Router field enter the IP address of its internal interface. If you have only one network card, the checkbox My Server uses a single network connection for both Internet access and the local network is automatically selected. Then click on Next.

4. If only one network card is installed in the server, you will be shown the corresponding message dialog box, which informs you that the firewall contained in SBS 2003 cannot be installed. To protect the network with a firewall, you should either configure an external firewall or add a second network card. To continue anyway, click on No.

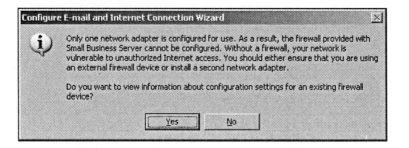

5. On the Web Services Configuration page you specify which web services of the server will be accessible from the Internet over the firewall. By default only the services Outlook Web Access and Remote Web Workplace are activated.

You can select the following services:

Outlook Web Access: This provides access to e-mails over the Internet or a web browser. For a secure connection between web servers, users must use https://.

Remote Web Workplace: This establishes a connection to the local network over a web browser. This enables Outlook Web Access, Remote Desktop connections to clients in the network, and access to server performance and usage reports and the SharePoint Services intranet site, apart from allowing you to download the connection manager. For a secure connection, users must enter https://. The Remote Workplace has the advantage that the user does not have to make a VPN connection for access to the local network.

Server performance and usage reports: These reports keep the administrator informed about the state of the server, its load, and any problems and bottlenecks that may have arisen on it. In the usage reports you also get statistical data about the load on the server.

Outlook Mobile Access: Users can access their e-mail over the Internet through mobile devices such as PDAs.

Outlook via the Internet: This provides access to Outlook 2003 e-mail without having to make a VPN connection. The Exchange Server is accessed via Remote Procedure Calls (RPCs) over HTTP.

Windows SharePoint Services intranet site: This gives access to the intranet site for SharePoint Services set up during installation.

Business Web site (wwwroot): This provides access to the intranet site of the company.

If you select the Allow access to the Entire Web site from the Internet option, all authenticated users can access all website directories over the Internet. Anonymous access is not possible. However, for security reasons, you should think carefully before selecting this option. If you select the option Do not allow access to the Web site from the Internet, none of the services just described will be available to users over the Internet. Then click on Next.

6. In the Web Server Certificate dialog box you will find the settings for certificates. A certificate is necessary for communication over SSL (Secure Sockets Layer) between the web server and browser for some web services. You can either have the wizard create a certificate for you or select a certificate file from a certification authority.

To create a new certificate, select the **Create a new Web server certificate** option. This creates a self-signed certificate, which is saved in the \Clientapps\SBScert folder and has a validity of five years. This certificate is made available to clients via the client setup wizard. In the Web server name field enter the name with which you want to access your server over the Internet.

Select the **Use a Web server certificate from a trustworthy authority** option if you have already received a certificate file. You can select this file using the **Browse** button. If you do not yet have a certificate file, you can request one using the Web Server Certificate Wizard in Internet Information Services (IIS). Since this a trustworthy certificate, it is not made available to clients like the self-signed certificate. If you have received a certificate, run the wizard once again for e-mail and Internet access. Then click on **Next**.

7. The configuration of Internet e-mail is next. The Exchange Server is configured here for sending and receiving Internet e-mail. For sending, the Small Business SMTP connector is created. For receiving e-mail the Microsoft POP3 connector is used.

To configure the Exchange Server, select the Enable Internet e-mail option. The Disable Internet e-mail option deletes the Small Business SMTP Connector and deactivates the Microsoft POP3 Connector. You will then not be able to send or receive Internet e-mails via Exchange Server. Only e-mails in the internal network can be sent and received. Then click on Next.

8. If you have activated Internet e-mail in the last step, you must first specify the e-mail transmission method.

Select the Use DNS to route e-mail option if DNS is to be used for sending e-mail. In this case the Exchange Server will send mail via the appropriate DNS resource entry for Mail Exchanger (MX).

If, however, your Internet Service Provider (ISP) requires that you send your e-mails to a dedicated mail server, choose the option Forward all e-mail to e-mail server at your ISP. Sending e-mail via the mail server of the Internet Service Provider is also known as **relaying**. The Exchange Server sends all mail to the SMTP Smarthost of the Internet Service Provider. Enter the name of the Internet Service Provider's mail server in the E-mail server field. If it has several names, enter all the names separated by semicolons. Then click on Next.

A Smarthost or relay host is a computer that processes outgoing messages from remote domains. It can also be configured as a mail gateway since it is connected to the Internet as well as the intranet.

9. In the E-mail Retrieval Method dialog box you specify the way in which e-mail is to be received from the Internet.

```
Configure E-mail and Internet Connection Wizard                              [X]

E-mail Retrieval Method
   You can specify how to receive e-mail from the Internet.

   [✓] Use the Microsoft Connector for POP3 Mailboxes

   [✓] Use Exchange

      (•) E-mail is delivered directly to my server

      ( ) E-mail is held at my ISP until my server sends a signal

            Specify the e-mail server to send the signal to:

            [                                                    ]

            Select the type of signal to send to your ISP:

            ( ) ETRN

            ( ) Turn after authentication

   [ More Information ]

                                    < Back    Next >    Cancel
```

Mark the checkbox Use the Microsoft Connector for POP3 Mailboxes, if you want to move the e-mails from the Internet Service Provider's POP3 account to an Exchange account. The advantage of this is that the user needs to check only the Exchange mailbox and not both. Moreover, mails sent to an Exchange mailbox can also be checked via Outlook-Web Access.

If you select the Use Exchange option, mails are received via SMTP from the Internet. For this you must ask your Internet Service Provider to make the necessary mail exchanger resource entries (MX).

The retrieval method E-mail is delivered directly to my server is used when incoming e-mails are directly sent to the Exchange Server and not collected at the ISP.

The E-mail is held at my ISP until my server sends a signal option requires the Exchange Server to send a signal to the mail server of the ISP when it has an Internet connection. Until the Exchange Server sends this signal, the e-mails are stored at the ISP. Enter the DNS name or the IP address of the ISP's mail server in the appropriate field. The Exchange Server sends its signal to this address. However, you must first specify the signal type.

ETRN: This is the standard method for the signal. It is often necessary for SBS 2003 to have a static IP address that is assigned by the ISP for a dial-up modem or a router when needed.

Turn after authentication: For this signal type the SBS can also have a dynamic IP address. If you choose this option you will see an additional dialog box in which you will enter the username and password for Exchange authentication with the ISP.

In either case you should check with your ISP which signal can be used. If you configure the wrong type, the forwarding of e-mails to the Exchange Server may fail.

Click on Next.

In the E-mail domain name dialog box, enter the registered Internet domain name. This name is used for the Internet reply address. When using Exchange you should make sure that the name entered is in conformity with the MX resource entry.

If you do not have a registered Internet domain name, keep the name field blank. This is also the case if you want to use the Exchange Server only for internal mail traffic. Then click on Next.

10. In the POP3 Mailbox Accounts dialog box you specify the POP3 accounts from which the POP3 Connector will retrieve the e-mails and forward them to the Exchange Server.

To set up a new account, click on Add. You will see the POP3 Mailbox dialog box.

In this dialog box you will add information about the POP3 mailbox. For E-mail server enter the full name of the mail server of your ISP, and for User name and Password add the authentication information. For Mailbox type you can select the type of mailbox you have. The following options exist:

- User Mailbox: A user mailbox contains e-mails that have been sent to a particular user. The moment these e-mails are retrieved by the POP3 Connector, the To line in the e-mail header changes to the specified Exchange recipient. In the Exchange User field enter the username or distribution group.

- Global Mailbox: In a global mailbox all e-mails addressed to you are collected at the ISP. As soon as Exchange fetches these mails, the recipient is determined on the basis of the To or Cc line and the e-mail is sent to his mailbox. In the E-mail Domain field enter the name of the mail domain to which all e-mails meant for your company are sent.

Then click on OK. You come back to the dialog box POP3 Mailbox Accounts. Here you can add more POP3 accounts, and update or delete existing ones. Then click on Next.

11. Under Mail Schedule, specify the intervals at which the Exchange Server and the POP3 Connector will retrieve e-mails from the mail server of the ISP.

From the Use the following schedule list box select the desired interval. The available intervals lie between every 15 minutes and every 24 hours. This schedule is only valid if you have selected Forward all e-mail to e-mail server at your ISP under the E-mail Delivery Method. If you have a broadband connection, e-mails are in principle sent immediately.

If you have selected the POP3 Connector under E-mail Retrieval Method, the specified schedule applies to receiving e-mail. If you have a broadband connection and have selected Exchange, the schedule has no effect on the receipt of e-mails.

If e-mails are sent by the ISP only after it gets a signal from the Exchange Server, the specified schedule comes into effect for the transmission.

If the schedule is to be defined under Exchange, run the Server Administration and select Properties from the context menu of Small Business SMTP Connector. Here select the relevant option so that the entered schedule remains unchanged.

Then click on Next.

12. In the Remove E-mail Attachments dialog box you can specify whether specific types of e-mail attachments should be removed from Exchange Server.

Mark the Enable Exchange Server to remove e-mail attachments that have the following extensions checkbox and select from the list all file types that that the Exchange Server should automatically delete. Using the appropriate buttons you can also add, delete, or edit entries. The deletion of these file types applies only to SMTP-based mails and POP3 mailboxes, not to internal e-mails that are sent from within the company network.

When an attachment is deleted, a notice is added to the e-mail informing the user that the attachment was deleted. The default text for this notice can be found in the file \Program Files\Microsoft Windows Small Business Server\Network\Attachment.txt.

If the removed attachments are not to be immediately deleted but saved in a folder, mark the Save removed e-mail attachments in a folder checkbox and give the path of the storage folder. Then click on Next.

13. Then the Finishing the Wizard dialog box appears. Here you see the configuration settings you have made and have the option of changing them if required. To accept the settings, click on Finish. After completing the configuration you will see the status window. Close this window.

```
Configure E-mail and Internet Connection Wizard

The wizard has completed successfully.

    ✔ Network Configuration
    ✔ Firewall Configuration
    ✔ Secure Web Site Configuration
    ✔ E-mail Configuration

                                              [  Close  ]
```

14. After you have closed the window, you will see a dialog box asking you to configure the password policies. Confirm with Yes. The Configure Password Policies dialog box appears.

For security reasons you should lay down requirements for the passwords by creating password policies. Mark the Password must meet minimum length requirements checkbox and select a length. Passwords shorter than the specified length will not be accepted. The minimum length is seven characters.

If the checkbox Password must meet complexity requirements is activated, the passwords must have characters from three of the following four categories:

- Upper case letters A–Z
- Lower case letters a–z
- Digits 0–9
- Special characters such as %, #, or $

Moreover, the password should not be the same as the user's account name (even in part).

If the Password must be changed regularly checkbox is activated, you can specify the number of days after which the password has to be changed. The longest validity period for a password is 42 days.

Finally, with the Configure password policies list box you specify when the new policy comes into effect. To begin with you should keep an interval so that you don't have to use any complex passwords when logging in to clients in the course of client configuration. After client configuration is done, you should set the value to Immediately.

To accept the settings, click OK.

15. When the configuration of the passwords is completed, the following dialog box appears, asking you to download the available updates and patches for the SBS 2003 operating system after establishing an Internet connection.

Configure E-mail and Internet Connection Wizard   [X]

⚠ Your server is now connected to the Internet. We highly recommend that you protect
your server by installing the latest critical and security updates. Click OK to connect to a
Microsoft Web site, which will scan your server to determine which updates and service
packs you should install.

[OK]

16. As soon as you click OK, you are connected to the Microsoft Update site on the Internet. All updates and patches available for SBS 2003 are listed and can then be installed. The server may have to be restarted during the course of installation.

Network Task: Configuring Remote Access

With the help of this wizard, SBS 2003 is configured for remote access by dial-in and VPN.

1. In the welcome dialog box click on Next. You will then see the Remote Access Method dialog box.

Remote Access Wizard   [X]

Remote Access Method
You can enable the server for remote access through either dial-in or VPN.

● Enable remote access

    ☑ VPN access

    ☐ Dial-in access (requires a modem)

○ Disable remote access

[More Information]

[< Back] [Next >] [Cancel]

If you want to permit remote access, select the Enable remote access option. The Disable remote access checkbox is only available if you have activated remote access services.

As the connection type you can select VPN access and Dial-in access. In the second case a modem must be installed on the server. Otherwise this option is not available.

VPN access: In a VPN connection the user first connects to his or her ISP. As soon as this connection is made, a connection to the server is established using tunneling protocols. This connection is called a secure connection.

If you have to use a local router for connecting to the Internet, make sure that the PPTP ports are not blocked by the firewall. You will find the appropriate configuration settings in your router's documentation. If on the other hand you are using the SBS 2003 firewall, the VPN filter is activated. This ensures that VPN traffic is not blocked by the firewall.

Dial-in access: In this mode of access the connection is made with the help of a telephone line and a modem on the server. For using dial-in access you should preferably use a modem other than the one used for fax services (see *Administrative Task: Configuring Fax*). Using a modem for several services can lead to complications.

If you have permitted remote access for at least one mode, the remote access Policies are automatically configured in such a way that all members of the security group Mobile Users have remote access.

Then click on Next.

2. The Client Addressing dialog box appears if the DHCP service is not implemented on SBS 2003. Here you must select an option for assigning IP addresses to remote clients.

If there is a device on your network that acts as a DHCP server, select the Use DHCP to assign IP addresses option. It makes no difference whether this device is another server or a router. Enter the IP address of the device in the appropriate field.

As soon as the routing and remote access service is active, the DHCP server automatically assigns ten addresses from its current address range for use by remote clients. If all ten IP addresses are used by remote clients, ten more addresses are made available.

If DHCP has not been configured in the network, select the option Use static IP addresses. Then specify the start value and end value of the IP address range to be assigned by SBS 2003.

Make sure that there are no conflicts with IP addresses already assigned in the network. Moreover, the address range selected for the remote clients must coincide with the address range of the network clients.

Then click on Next.

3. Finally, in the VPN Server Name dialog box specify the name or the IP address that will be used for access to the server from the Internet. When remote access services are configured, the server is also called a VPN server.

Enter the name of the server in the Server name field. This should be the complete host name of the server in the format servername.firma.de. This name must also be registered on the DNS server of the ISP. The name given here serves as the default name of the target server in the configuration file of the client connection manager. By default the local name of the server is entered in the field Server name. You could also enter the IP address of the server as an alternative to the full name.

Then click on Next. You get a summary of your entries and can allow the wizard to carry out the configuration by clicking Finish.

4.   If after completing the Internet Connection Wizard you have still not configured the password policy, you are asked one more time to complete this step. To do the configuration, carry out the processes described previously.

Network Task: Activating the Server

As with Windows XP, activation is required for Small Business Server 2003. Activation is done conveniently over the Internet. Here you have the choice of just activating the server or simultaneously both activating and registering it.

Until the server is activated, you cannot begin the next step (adding client licenses).

Network Task: Adding Client Licenses

The last of the network tasks is adding client licenses. SBS 2003 comes with only five Client Access Licenses (CALs). If there are only five clients in your network, you can skip this task.

1.   After the welcome message you see the License Agreement dialog box. Read the terms of the Microsoft Client Access License agreement and then select I agree. If you don't agree, you cannot continue with this task. Then click on Next.

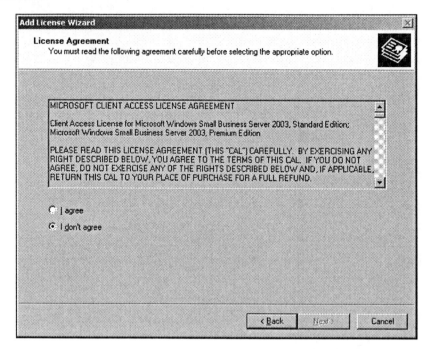

2. In the Contact Method dialog box specify whether you want to add client licenses over the Internet or by Telephone. Then click on Next.

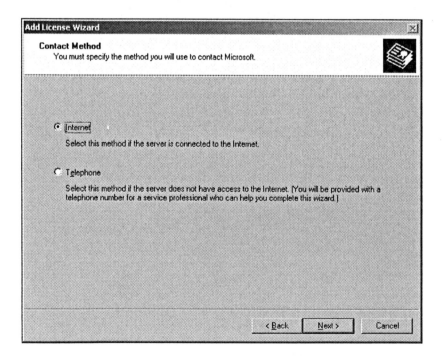

3. In the License Code Information dialog box you must now enter the 25-digit license code in the License Code field and click on Add. Here you can enter as many licence codes as you want one after the other. In the License codes to be added section you will see how many licenses each code represents. Check whether the license numbers have been added correctly. If you spot an error here, delete the number and re-enter it. Wrongly entered license codes delay the activation of the licenses. Then click on Next.

4. The license activation is now completed. Follow the instructions of the wizard to do this. If you want to add more CALs later, you will have to call up this point in the task list again.

Administrative Task: Adding Printers

After completing the network tasks, you must perform some administrative tasks. To start with, printers are added to the network.

> You don't need to run the Add Printer Wizard if you have a Plug & Play printer that connects to the server via USB, infrared, or IEEE 1394. In this case just plug in the printer and it is automatically installed.

1. After the welcome window you will see the Local or Network Printer page. Specify here whether the printer is connected locally to SBS or to another computer. If you are using a print server read the documentation of the device. Then click on Next.

2. In the Select Printer Port dialog box specify the port to which the printer is connected. This is usually LPT1. Then click on Next.

3. In the Install Printer Software dialog box you can select the printer from the manufacturer and printer list. If the printer is not in the list or if you have a

separate disk containing the driver, click on Have Disk and follow the subsequent instructions. Then click on Next.

4. The next step is to give the printer a name in the Name Printer dialog box. This name may have a maximum of 31 characters. Also specify whether this is the default printer. Then click on Next.

5. In the Printer Sharing dialog box you can indicate whether you want to share this printer with other users. If the printer is to be shared, enter a name for the printer in the Share name field. Then click on Next.

6. In the Location and Description dialog box you can then optionally add information about the location of the printer as well as a description of the printer in the appropriate text fields. Then click on Next.

7. Finally in the Print Test Page dialog box you are asked if you want to print a test page after the printer driver is installed. You should do this to convince yourself that the printer is correctly installed. Then click on Next.

8. At the end the wizard gives you a summary. Click on Finish to add the printer.

Administrative Tasks: Adding Users and Computers

This configuration step consists of a series of tasks. A user account, mailbox, and base folder are created for each user. Furthermore, membership of the user in the security and distribution groups is specified. SharePoint access and disk quotas are also configured. Finally a client computer is assigned to the user.

1. Before you create the user you must select a template in the dialog box Template Selection. The following four templates are available by default:

    o User Template: In this template, access to the Internet, e-mail, network printers, fax machines, and shared printers is permitted. This template should be used for normal user accounts.

    o Mobile User Template: This template has the all the rights of the User Template. Additionally, a connection can be made to SBS 2003 via VPN or dial-in.

    o Power User Template: This template has all the rights of the Mobile User Template. Additionally, users working on the basis of this template can administer users, groups, printers, faxes, and shared folders. They can even make a remote connection to the server. However, a local login on the server is not possible.

    o Administrator Template: This template provides unrestricted access for server and domain administration.

Apart from these pre-defined templates you can even create your own templates. You can also change the template for each user later. After you have selected the appropriate template, click on Next.

2. In the User Information dialog box you can create a new user for the selected template by clicking Add. If you have already created some users for this template, you will find them listed under Users.

3. After you have clicked on Add, fill in the appropriate fields in the dialog box Enter User Information. For the Logon name field you can pick one of the four available formats from the list. In our example you can choose between *Pmustermann*, *MustermannPeter*, *PMustermann* and *PeterM*. The value chosen here is also taken as the default for the field e-mail alias, although you are allowed to change it. If you are done with the entries, click OK.

4. In the Set Up Client Computers dialog box you can set up a client computer. If you choose the Set up computer now option, you can begin to configure it.

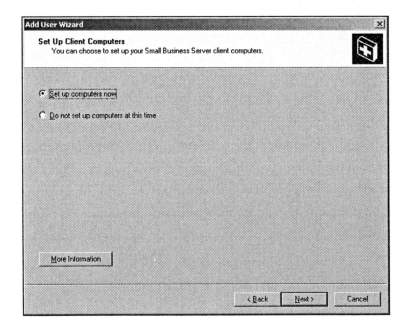

5. In the Client Computer Names dialog box enter the name of the computer and click on Add. Valid characters for the computer name are A–Z, a–z, 0–9, and - (hyphen). All information entered via the wizard applies to all the computers in the Accounts will be created for list. You can even remove computers from this list. The default name for the computer account is always *Username01*, in our example *PMustermann01*. However, this name can be deleted and replaced by another one. Click on Next.

6. Next the applications to be installed on the computer are selected in the dialog box Client Applications. By default the applications Client Operating System Service Packs, Internet Explorer 6.0, Outlook 2003, and the Fax Client are installed. You can, however, change and extend this choice.

Unchecking a checkbox for an installed application does *not* uninstall the application from the client computer.

If you have selected Outlook 2003 for installation and a previous Outlook version is already installed on the client, you must disable the COM Add-Ins on the client. To do this, take the following steps:

- Select Options from the Tools menu and click on the Next tab.
- Click on Advanced Options and then on COM Add-Ins.
- Uncheck the checkbox next to the Add-In.

7. In the Client Applications dialog box mark the During Client Setup, allow the selected applications to be modified checkbox if you want to allow the user to change the installation or not install an application during the setup process. You should mark the After Client Setup is finished, log off the client computer checkbox if the user is not able to wait till setup is completed and you don't want unauthorized access to the computer after the installation is over.

8. If you click on Edit Applications, you will see the Available applications dialog box. All applications available for installation are listed here. By clicking Add you can make more applications available for installation on the clients.

If you decide to add an application, you will see the Application Information dialog box.

Before you can add an application, you must copy its installation program in a share. It is best to put these applications in the default folder \ClientApps on SBS 2003. Domain users must have *Read* and *Execute* rights for the shared folder; otherwise they cannot carry out the installation.

9. Give a name for the application in the Application name text field and choose the path to the application by clicking Browse. A link to this application is created on the client's desktop. Then click on OK. You are brought back to

the Available Applications dialog box. Here you can modify the list of available applications at any time. The modification option is not available for the default applications. It is also possible to delete applications from the list. Click Next to complete the Add New Applications Wizard.

10. You then return to the page Client Applications. Clicking on Advanced brings up the Advanced Client Computer Settings dialog box.

For each of the points in the list you can accept the default settings by checking the appropriate checkbox.

The default settings for the various points are as follows:

- Internet Explorer Settings: The default home page is the company's internal website (http://Companyweb). The Favorites have links to various internal websites. If ISA Server has been installed, Internet Explorer is also configured to use the proxy server.

- Outlook Profile Settings: Outlook is configured for using the Exchange Server. Thus the account information and exchange server settings for new users are used in the profiles. If there are pre-existing profiles on the computer, the Exchange profile is added to them and set as the default profile. Furthermore, the fax mail transport is configured. This makes it possible to send faxes from Outlook and other e-mail applications. If Remote Access has been configured for the client computer, the manual synchronization of Outlook Folders is set up in Outlook.

- Desktop Settings: Links are created in the Network Neighborhood folder.

- Fax Printer: A fax printer is set up on the computer for connecting to the fax server.

- Printer: The printer published in the Active Directory of the SBS is added to the clients as the default printer. If, however, there are several printers in the Active Directory or a local printer is connected to the client, no default printer is specified.

- Fax Configuration Information: The fax information stored on the SBS is passed on to the clients. This includes, for example, the fax cover page with sender information so that users do not have to enter this information each time they send a fax.

- Remote Desktop: Remote Desktop and Remote Desktop Support are activated for clients. Using Remote Desktop users can, for example, start a session on their client computer from home or while on the road. Remote Desktop Support makes it possible for other users to connect to the client for troubleshooting.

If the checkbox is disabled, you can configure the settings on the client manually. Then click on OK.

11. You will next see the Mobile Client and Offline Use page.

Here you have the option of installing Connection Manager and ActiveSync 3.7.

- Connection Manager: With the help of the Connection Manager, users can make a Remote Connection with SBS 2003.

- ActiveSync 3.7: Using ActiveSync, users can synchronize mobile gadgets such as Microsoft Smartphone or Microsoft Pocket PC Phone Edition with the client computer and server.

Users can only use the Remote Connection after you have closed the Remote Access Connection wizard. Moreover the user should have been added to the user template Mobile Users (see step 1 in this section).

Finally, click on Next.

12. You will now see the Completing the Add User Wizard dialog box. If the settings are OK for you, click Finish. Click Back to make changes in the configuration.

13. While the user settings are being configured, you will see a dialog box. To complete the configuration of the client computer including its network configuration and application access, you must log on to the client and enter the address http://SBSServername/ConnectComputer in the browser. Click OK to confirm.

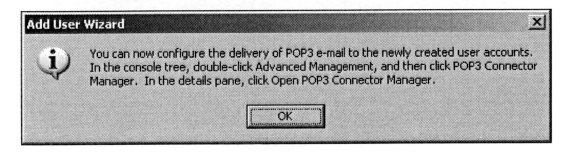

Finishing Your Installation... ✕

To finish setting up the client computer(s), including network configuration and application deployment and configuration, go to the client computer(s), start Internet Explorer, and type http://SBS2003/ConnectComputer in the Address bar.

☐ Don't show this dialog box again

OK

14. After the user account has been created, you are asked if you want to restart the wizard to create another user. If you select No here, another dialog box appears informing you that you can now configure the transmission of POP3 e-mail for the user accounts. Confirm this dialog with OK.

Add User Wizard ✕

ⓘ You can now configure the delivery of POP3 e-mail to the newly created user accounts. In the console tree, double-click Advanced Management, and then click POP3 Connector Manager. In the details pane, click Open POP3 Connector Manager.

OK

Administrative Task: Configuring Fax

This wizard helps to set up SBS 2003 for receiving, sending and forwarding faxes. You can only carry out this administrative task if at least one fax modem is installed on the server.

1. In the Provide Company Information dialog box you first enter the information that will be sent on the fax cover page.

Fill in the fields. The pre-filled values are based on your entries at the time of configuring the server. These entries can, however, be changed here. Then click on Next.

2. In the Outbound Fax Device dialog box you see a list of fax devices recognized by Windows.

Mark the checkboxes for the devices that you want to use. If several faxmodems are installed, you can change the usage sequence. If a fax device is in use, the next one in the list will be used automatically. Click on Next.

3. After this the devices for receiving faxes are specified.

Mark the checkboxes for the devices that you want to use for receiving faxes. If there are several devices, you can specify whether you want to use the same routing method for all devices (Set routing destinations for all devices option) or whether the devices are to be configured separately (Set specific routing destination for each device option). Then click on Next.

4. In the Inbound Fax Routing dialog box you specify the routing method for each fax device. Make sure you specify at least one routing method for each fax device.

Four routing methods are available:

- Route through e-mail: The faxes are forwarded to an e-mail address. This can either be an address inside or outside the SBS network.

- Store in a folder: Under this option the faxes are sent to a folder. This folder must be in a share.

- Store in a document library: The faxes are forwarded to the document library in the company's internal website. Under SBS 2003 the standard folder for incoming faxes is
`http://SBSServername/companyweb/incoming%20faxes`.

- Print: The faxes are sent directly to an installed printer and printed out.

When the wizard is run first, the link Configure appears as soon as a routing method is selected. If you run the wizard again later, select the method and click Edit to modify the entry. Then click on Next.

5. At the end you again get a summary of the settings. Confirm this with Finish.

Administrative Task: Configuring Monitoring

With the help of this wizard you can configure warning messages as well as server performance and usage reports. A schedule is set up here in accordance with which reports and messages are sent by e-mail. The reports can also be displayed via the server administration.

1. In the Reporting Options dialog box you specify how the individual reports are to be displayed and received.

After the wizard is completed the performance reports are displayed automatically in the server administration under monitoring and reporting. Performance data is collected hourly. Moreover you can also have the report sent to you by e-mail via the option Receive a daily performance report in e-mail.

The usage reports contain information about the Internet, e-mail, fax, and remote usage of the server. If the option View the usage report in Server Management is selected, you can simultaneously also specify the following: Receive a usage report in e-mail every other week. Then click on Next.

2. In the E-mail Options dialog box you can specify whether the reports are to be sent to one or more e-mail addresses. If you want to enter several e-mail addresses, separate them with a semicolon (;). The e-mail address selection is displayed only if you have activated the e-mail function in one or both reports in the previous step.

3. Under Business Owner Usage Report you can specify who is allowed to see the usage reports on a specific page of the intranet website. By default only members of the domain administrator group can see these reports.

To allow other users to view these reports, select the desired users from the All users list and click on Add. All selected persons receive an e-mail informing them about the function of the usage reports and the fact that they now have access to them. The usage report is available at http://SBSServername/monitoring. Then click on Next.

4. In the Alerts dialog box you can specify whether you want immediate notification by e-mail in the event of a performance warning.

To be notified immediately when a performance threshold is crossed, enter one or more e-mail addresses. Addresses are separated from each other by a semicolon (;). By default the address that you specified in step 2 is already entered in the field E-mail address.

The threshold values for the various performance areas can be specified in the server administration after completing the wizard under Monitoring and Reporting/Configuring Warning Messages. This procedure is described in greater detail in the *Monitoring and Reporting* section in Chapter 8. Then click on Next.

5. This completes the wizard. To end click on Finish.

Administrative Task: Configuring Backups

This wizard runs you through the planning and configuration of backups for SBS 2003.

1. After the welcome message you will see the Backup Location dialog box. Here you can decide whether the backup is to taken on a tape drive, hard

disk, or network share. The first option is available to you only if the backup wizard has found a tape drive. Otherwise you get an appropriate message at the bottom of the dialog box because a tape drive or other such removable medium is recommended.

2. If you want to back up to a hard drive, select the path to the backup folder using Browse. Then click on Next.

In the Backup Data Summary dialog box you will see the server data that is going to be backed up. By default all the data in all partitions is included in the backup. When backing up to a hard drive, only the folder that you selected in step 1 as the backup location is excluded.

If you want to exclude more folders from the backup, click on Exclude Folders. The window that opens has the same name and lists only the backup folder. If you want to exclude other folders, click on Add Folder and select the desired folders. Folders that have already been added can also be deleted. Then click on OK.

If in the Backup Data Summary dialog box there is a folder whose size is not shown in the Size column, you can have it calculated by clicking Calculate Folder Sizes. Depending on the size of the folder this process can take a few minutes.

3. The next dialog box is Define Backup Schedule. Select the days on which backups should be taken. By default the working days Monday to Friday are selected.

Specify the time under Start backup at. As a rule this will be in the evening or at night.

Ideally the backup should start before 02:00h to be sure that it is over before the server status report is sent. In this way you will know in time if any problems have occurred in the backup.

Under Store this number of backups specify the number of backups to be taken. If the backup is taken on a removable medium, one is usually enough. On a hard drive two backups should be taken.

Then click on Next.

4. You will next see the Storage Allocation for Deleted Files and E-mail dialog box.

Under Number of days specify how long e-mails deleted by users should be kept on the server. The default setting is 30 days. Within this period users can restore their e-mails in Outlook 2003. This function is only available in an Exchange environment. If you have unchecked the retain copies of permanently deleted e-mail messages checkbox, the deleted e-mails are not kept on the server.

The Enable periodic snapshots of users' shared folders checkbox allows you switch the new shadow copy functionality on and off. This enables the server to take a snapshot of all shared folders so that the user can restore a deleted file or a previous version of an existing file.

Snapshots are taken automatically at 07:00h and at 12:00h. When going back to a previous version, the file used is always the one that was created during the last snapshot. The default setting for the disk space allotted to snapshots is 1000 MB. Ideally you should specify a value that is ten percent of the disk capacity. For the shadow copy feature to be available, a minimum of 310 MB of disk space should be available. Then click on Next.

The shadow copy feature is not available if a shared folder has been renamed or deleted. If the entire Users Shared Folders folder has been deleted, you should rerun SBS and reinstall the components.

5. You can now either complete the wizard or click Back to make changes in the configuration. Then click on Finish.

Installed Hot Fixes

During the installation of SBS 2003 a number of patches and hot fixes are automatically installed. Here is a list of the individual hot fixes:

- QFE#47846 – KB822745
- QFE#47937 – KB822744
- QFE#47987 – KB822743
- QFE#47990 – KB822742
- QFE#48802 – KB824073
- QFE#47607 – KB822132
- QFE#50566 – KB824146
- QFE#49367 – KB824139
- QFE#48628 – KB823559
- QFE#48713 – KB823980
- QFE#46104 – KB819696
- QFE#50449 – KB826238
- QFE#50009 – KB826936
- QFE#50147 – KB825117
- QFE#48165 – KB822925
- QFE#48087 – KB824105

You can find further information about these hot fixes in the Microsoft Knowledge Base. The expression QFE#xxxxx refers to the patch and KBxxxxxx to the corresponding article in the Microsoft Knowledge Base, under which you will find the specific information.

3

Upgrade and Migration

This chapter deals with the migration from older versions of SBS to the current version, 2003. In general it is possible to *migrate* from the versions SBS 4.5 and SBS 2000 as also from Windows Server 2000, 2003, and NT 4.0.

An *upgrade* to SBS 2003 is possible from SBS 2000 as well as from Windows Server 2000 and 2003. In this chapter you will first find some tips that will help you decide whether an upgrade or a migration is more suitable for you.

Thereafter you will first be given detailed instructions on migrating an SBS 2000/Windows Server 2000 system and an SBS 4.5/Windows Server NT 4.0 system along with its clients to SBS 2003, followed by tips for upgrading an SBS 2000/ Windows Server 2000 installation to SBS 2003. It is not possible to upgrade systems older than this.

Considerations

Before you begin the switch to SBS 2003, you must decide whether you want to carry out an upgrade or a migration. If you are using SBS 4.5 or Windows NT 4.0 Server, the only option you have is migration—no upgrade is possible.

In a migration, SBS 2003 is installed on a new computer. Thereafter all the data and settings of the old system are migrated to the new one. In an upgrade, the new version is installed over the old one. If all goes well, all the data and settings are preserved in this process. An upgrade is not very different from the usual fresh installation and requires less planning and expenditure.

Upgrade Options for Existing Operating Systems

The following table gives you an overview of the options for upgrading existing operating systems to SBS 2003. For operating systems that do not support an upgrade, you can only carry out a migration.

Operating system	Upgrade possible to
Windows NT Server 3.51	No upgrade possible
Windows NT Server 3.51 Enterprise	No upgrade possible
Windows NT Server 3.51 with Citrix	No upgrade possible
Windows NT Server 4.0	Windows Server 2003 Standard and Enterprise
Windows NT Server 4.0 Enterprise	Windows Server 2003 Enterprise
Windows NT Server 4.0 Terminal Server Edition	Windows Server 2003 Enterprise
BackOffice SBS 4.0/4.5	No upgrade possible
Windows 2000 Server	Windows Server 2003 Standard and Enterprise, SBS 2003 Standard and Enterprise
Windows 2000 Advanced Server	Windows Server 2003 Enterprise
Windows 2000 Datacenter Server	Windows Server 2003 Datacenter
SBS 2000	SBS 2003 Standard and Premium
SBS 2003 Standard	SBS 2003 Premium
Windows Server 2003 Standard	Windows Server 2003 Enterprise, SBS 2003 Standard and Premium

Keywords

In this chapter you will encounter a number of keywords. For the sake of clarity these are explained briefly first.

Migration

In a **migration**, SBS 2003 is installed on a new computer. Thereafter the data and settings of the original system are migrated to the new one. A migration can also refer to migration of the data and settings of one existing SBS 2003 system to another.

Do not confuse the terms **migration** and **upgrade**!

Source Server

The **source server** is the one from which all existing data and settings are transferred to the new one. This can be an SBS 2000 or an SBS 4.5 server. Even a Windows Server

2000 or a Windows Server NT 4.0 can be the source server. You must make sure that the source server is online during the migration process.

Target Server

The **target server** is the one to which the data and settings of the source server are to be transferred. In our context the target server is an SBS 2003 system.

Active Directory Migration Tool (ADMT)

The **Active Directory Migration Tool** (ADMT) is a program that helps you move users, groups, and computers between Active Directory Domains or from a Windows 2000 domain to an Active Directory domain. This program is used in SBS migration.

The Steps in the Migration Process

SBS migration is a process that needs to be planned carefully and cannot be implemented hastily and without forethought in a production environment. Ideally you should have a test environment with identical source and target servers. The preparation for the migration can be summarized in seven steps. Detailed instructions for the individual steps can be found in the section *Migration from Small Business Server 2000 and Windows Server 2000* (for SBS 2000 and Windows Server 2000) and the section *Migration from Small Business Server 4.5 and Windows Server NT 4.0* (for SBS 4.5 and Windows Server NT 4.0).

1. **Preparing for the migration**: In this step all the information required for the subsequent procedure is collected. This includes information about the name, the domain name, the IP address, and all shares. On the old Exchange Server export the mail account of the administrator including all the rules created and save the public folders in a .pst file. You should also request all users to delete all mails and folders that they no longer need. Then take a backup of the source server and check whether all the current Service Packs and patches are installed on it. During the migration no user may be connected to the domain.

2. **Preparing the target server for the installation**: To prepare the target server for the installation of SBS 2003, you must first stop the DHCP service on the source server. The source and target servers are then connected to each other and SBS 2003 is installed on the target server. After you have completed the necessary network steps during the installation, disconnect the cable from the network card used for Internet access and install suitable anti-virus software. This ensures that this process does not interrupt the data transfer between the two servers.

3. **Preparing the clients for the migration:** The next step is to prepare the clients for the deployment of the SBS 2003. The preparation relates to all clients with the operating systems Windows NT 4.0, 2000 Professional, XP Professional, and Windows Server 2003. The same holds for member servers running Windows Server NT 4.0, 2000, and 2003. The migration of the computer accounts themselves is done with the help of the ADMT (see step 4), which only supports the above-mentioned operating systems. If you are running Windows 95, 98, or ME, you must either configure the computer accounts manually (see step 6) or first upgrade the client operating system.

4. **Carrying out the migration:** The migration is carried out with the help of ADMT. ADMT is installed on the target server and migrates existing user and group accounts. If DNS forwarders are installed on the source and target servers, ADMT can work with both servers. If Exchange 2000 is implemented on the source server, you may have to change existing mail quotas on the new server. The Exchange mailboxes are migrated thereafter. Furthermore, all shared folders, application data, and SQL databases must be migrated to the target server.

5. **Configuration of the target server:** After you have migrated the existing data to the target server, the server still needs to be configured. To do this, connect the user accounts with the account templates of SBS 2003 and distribute applications to the client computers. You must also work through the task list on the target server. All user-defined settings on the source server must also be transferred. You must also configure the mail distribution lists, mail receiving policies, and the Microsoft Connector for POP3 mailboxes.

6. **Configuration of the clients:** For Windows 2000 and XP clients the e-mail and proxy settings have to be configured next. For all operating systems older than Windows 2000 Professional, you will have to make these settings for the target server and the installation of the software manually. Even the public Exchange folders can now be imported so that the client can use the new Exchange Server. In each case you should check whether the client can access all the necessary data and resources.

7. **Completing the migration:** To complete the migration, uninstall ADMT from the target server. Then lay down a password policy that asks all users to change their password when they first log on. After you are sure that all the data and settings from the source server have been migrated, you can finally switch it off. Do not forget to remove all the permissions that were set during the migration process but could pose a security risk in an operational context.

Scheduling the Migration

The migration process is a relatively resource-intensive process that can take a few days to complete. Ideally you would first carry out a migration in a test environment. To do this, however, you need to make available separate hardware and install the source and target servers and various types of clients on it. Setting up a test environment may not be possible in small and medium-sized companies for cost and time reasons. This makes it even more important to plan individual steps carefully.

You should plan to spend the whole day for the first step, in which you collect information, ask users to delete unnecessary data, and apply current patches to the source server. The installation of SBS 2003 on a new computer can take place in parallel.

On the next day you should proceed to export the above-mentioned data from the Exchange Server. Finally, you will take a complete backup of the source server. Ideally this should be done after regular working hours so that you can be sure that the most current data is backed up. Since migrations are best carried out on a weekend, the backup can also be taken at this time.

For the subsequent tasks you can calculate one or two days depending on the size of the company. With the help of ADMT accounts are migrated and client computers manually configured if required.

After the migration to the new system is completed, the administrator must always be available to solve problems during actual operation and to answer user questions.

Problems during Migration

For the migration to proceed without problems, you should look into a number of things that are listed separately here once again. In the case of a misconfiguration they can quickly turn into pitfalls in the migration process.

Please also make sure that you carry out the individual migration steps in the above-mentioned order.

Names of the Two Servers

The source and target servers must have different names. This applies to both the DNS name for the internal domain and the NetBIOS domain name. Remember that the links with the old names have to be deleted and replaced with new ones pointing to the new SBS server on all clients for this reason.

Disabling the DHCP Service

The DHCP service must be disabled on the source server before it is connected to the target server so that it can be installed correctly on the latter. If the DHCP service is provided by a router on the network, you must ensure that it is connected with SBS 2003 during the course of the installation.

ADMT and Exchange Migration Wizard

You will use the ADMT program for migration of user and group accounts. Security Identifiers (SIDs) are maintained for this purpose. Detailed help on ADMT can be found in the installation folder in the DomainMig.chm file.

The Exchange Migration Wizard is responsible for the migration of the user mailboxes. However, it cannot export the mailbox of the administrator account, the rules for the public folders, or the rules for the mailboxes. You must execute these three steps manually by exporting them from the source server and importing them on the target server. More information about this can be found in Microsoft KB article 328871.

Transferring User-Defined Settings

At the end of the migration you must apply user-defined settings manually on the target server. This includes the following configurations: DHCP range options, DNS records, settings for routing and remote access services, group policy settings, the SMTP Connector of the Exchange Server, and settings of the ISA Server 2000. If you additionally have websites running over IIS, you must copy the files on to the new server and set up the websites afresh. Alternatively you can use the *IIS 6.0 migration tool*.

Desktop Profiles

Although desktop profiles under Windows 2000 and Windows XP are preserved during migration, all references in them to the source server are invalid and must be changed.

Premature Creation of Computer and User Accounts

Computer, user, and group accounts can only be created after you have completed the administrative tasks in step 5, *configuration of the target server*. If you try to create new accounts before this, the attempt will fail.

DNS-Forwarder

You must set up DNS forwarders on both the source and the target server. DNS forwarders are required because ADMT must work with both servers.

Migration from Small Business Server 2000 and Windows Server 2000

This section describes in detail the different work stages of the migration with an SBS 2000 or a Windows Server 2000 system as the source server.

Step 1—Preparing for the Migration

In the course of preparing for the migration you will first collect the following information from different areas:

Server-Related Information

- **Names of the source and target servers**: These two names must be different. You will find the computer name under the properties of the workstation on the Computer Name tab.

- **Complete DNS name in the internal domain and NetBIOS domain name**: These two names should also be different for the source and target servers. By default you can accept the values suggested during installation for the internal DNS domain. To find out the NetBIOS name enter dsa.msc under Run. In the MMC *Active Directory Users and Computers* select the Properties context menu for the domain. The NetBIOS domain name is the first part of the complete domain name. For a domain name firma.de the NetBIOS name is FIRMA.

- **IP address of the source server and target server**: To find out the IP address of the source server, enter cmd under Run, then issue the command ipconfig /all. The IP address of the target server must of course be a free IP address in the same range as the source server. If you are using a router as a DHCP server, the address must be in the range provided by the router. If the source server is functioning as the DHCP server, you will find valid addresses in its range options. In the DHCP console double-click the entry Range. Then click on Address Leases. Here you will find all the IP addresses currently in use.

- **Administrator account**: If you have renamed the administrator account on the source server, you must set it back to the original name 'administrator'. The account can be renamed once the migration to the target server is completed. You must ensure that the administrator password is identical on the source and target systems. One password must be used; otherwise the migration cannot be carried out.

Information about Shared Folders, Applications and Settings

- Users' shared folders: Note the name of the user folder. By default it is Users in SBS 2000 and SBS 2003.

- Client applications folder: If there are applications here that are going to be used even after the migration, copy the contents of this folder into the directory on the target server. The default name for the directory for client applications under SBS 2000 is ClientApps5, and under SBS 2003 ClientApps.

- The application *Modem Sharing Client* is, however, not available after migration because SBS 2003 does not support this function.

- Company shared folder: Under SBS 2000 the name of the folder is Company. Under SBS 2003 on the other hand a company website is created via SharePoint Services. The URL for this is http://companyweb.

- Other shared folders: The contents of the following shared folders cannot be migrated: Printers, Planned Tasks, and SYSVOL. Also, do not migrate the NETLOGON folder if you are not using any customized login scripts. These folders cannot be migrated from SBS 2000 or Windows Server 2000. In a migration from SBS 2000 the following folders may also not be migrated as SBS 2003 has updated versions: Mspclnt, MpClients, and Fax Clients.

- Even the TsClient folder cannot be migrated since terminal services are not available in application mode in SBS 2003. If you still want to use this functionality, you must set up a separate server.

- If there are other shared folders, check their contents and note the names of the shares so that these can be created afresh on the target system. To get an overview of all the shares on the source server enter the following under Run: \\Sourceservername.

- Next note the names and installation paths of all applications that you wish to use after the migration.

- If you have set up distribution groups under Exchange 2000, note their names. When transferring these groups to the target server you must put them in the Organizational Unit (OU) distribution groups. If the distribution groups contain pre-defined groups (such as administrators) as members, you must make a note of these memberships, as the memberships of pre-defined groups cannot be migrated. Write down user-defined rights to public folders and user-defined recipients so that you can configure them afresh once the migration is over.

- Then check if you have saved all the user-defined settings in the following areas: DNS entries, DHCP range options, routing and remote access, group policies, websites on the IIS, Exchange, and ISA Server 2000. These settings are configured afresh on the target server after the migration is completed. The public folders and the mailbox of the administrator account are exported to a .pst file. If specific rules have been laid down for the administrator mailbox, you must export these as well. It is not possible to migrate these settings with the Exchange Server Migration Wizard.

If you have not permitted any user-defined settings on the source system and have retained the default settings, you do not need to make a note of the configuration for these areas because the standard settings of SBS 2003 can be accepted.

Deleting Unnecessary Files and E-Mails

Before beginning the migration you must always delete all unnecessary files and e-mails. Ask all users to delete their Outlook mails from the Deleted Items and Sent Items folders. The same holds for unnecessary files in the individual user directories. Also search all shared directories for file fragments.

If a user's mailbox is greater than 200 MB even after deleting superfluous e-mails, you will definitely have to change the quota settings on the target server. The default threshold value for the mailbox size is 200 MB. If this size is exceeded, e-mails can no longer be sent or received. By default a warning is issued at a mailbox size of 175 MB.

There is also a limit for the user folder. The default limit value for the user folder is 1 GB. If a user's folder exceeds 1 GB, the quota settings for all users will have to be changed. More information about this can be found in the SBS 2003 help pages.

To determine the mailbox sizes of individual users, do the following in SBS 2000:

1. Open the administrations console. Double-click Exchange Organization and then Server.
2. Double-click First Storage Group and then Mailbox Store.
3. Click on Mailboxes. In the K column in the right pane you will find the mailbox size for the user.

If the user is using rules under Outlook, you must save these, because Outlook rules are excluded when mailboxes are migrated to the target server.

Hardware and Software Compatibility

If you intend to use hardware, for example an internal modem, or software from the source system on the target server, you must make sure that it is compatible with SBS 2003. Use the Windows Server catalog page at http://www.microsoft.com/windows/catalog/server/ to verify this.

Installing Current Service Packs

Ensure that the latest Service Pack is installed. For trouble-free migration at least the following Service Packs must be installed:

SBS 2000: Service Pack 1

To check if this Service Pack is installed, open the administration console. Click on Server Status. In the right window pane, click About. There you will find the version installed. For more information on installing Service Pack 1 for SBS 2000, see Microsoft KB article 326924.

Exchange Server 2000: Service Pack 2

To check if this Service Pack is installed, open Start/Programs/Microsoft Exchange/System Manager. Double-click on Server and then click on your Exchange Server. Under the Action menu, select Properties. The Service Pack version is displayed here. You can download the Service Pack from http://www.microsoft.com/Exchange/Downloads/2000/Sp3/default.asp.

SQL Server 2000: Service Pack 3

To check if this Service Pack is installed, open Start/All Programs /Microsoft SQL Server/Enterprise Manager. Double-click on SQL Server Group and select Properties from the context menu of the server name. The version number must be 8.00.760. This version number corresponds to an installation of Service Pack 3. You can download the Service Pack from http://www.microsoft.com/sql/downloads/2000/sp3.asp.

Windows Server 2000: Service Pack 4

To check if this Service Pack is installed, enter the command winver under Run. To install Service Pack 4, insert CD 3 of SBS 2003, change to the folder \SBS\Clientapps\Win2k_SP4\i386\ and run the file Update.exe.

Backing up the Source Server

The source server should be backed up after all users have completed their work. Ideally this should be done in the evening or at the weekend. Before starting the backup you should scan all drives for viruses.

Make sure you do not scan the Exchange drive M: when scanning for viruses. This can damage the Exchange database. By default the IFS (Installable File System) is mapped to the drive M: in Exchange 2000.

Then take a complete backup of the system data and Exchange.

Make sure you do not backup the Exchange drive M: when taking the Exchange backup. This can damage the Exchange database. By default the IFS (Installable File System) is mapped to the drive M: under Exchange 2000.

To make sure that the backup was done correctly, you should restore randomly selected files from the backup at another location and check whether the original file and the backup are identical.

Notifying Users about the Impending Migration

It is necessary to notify users about the impending migration only if some users are still logged on to the domain at that time. If you are carrying out the migration at a time when no users are working, this point is irrelevant. Otherwise you can reach users via the Net send command. The pre-requisite for this that the messaging system should be running on the server and on the clients. Here is an example of a command you can issue:

Net send * Please log off the domain in the next 5 minutes. No network and Internet connections will be available thereafter. (Enter)

The symbol * used here means that the message will be sent to all members of the domain.

Step 2—Preparing the Server for the Installation

This section describes all the steps you have to carry out on the source and target systems before installing SBS 2003. The installation of SBS 2003 has already been described in Chapter 2.

DHCP Configuration

Before beginning the installation of SBS 2003 you must stop the DHCP service on the source server if it is running there. As soon as source and target servers are connected, only the DHCP service configured on the target server should remain active. To end the service on the source server, enter the command Services.msc under Run. Double-click the entry DHCP-Server. In the Properties window that comes up click Stop. Then set the Startup Type to Disabled.

If you are using a router that acts as a DHCP server, you should not carry out the procedure just described. This router should be connected with the target server during the installation of SBS 2003 so that the DHCP settings can be configured correctly. You can choose between using the router or the SBS 2003 as the DHCP server.

Network and Internet Connection

Furthermore, it is recommended that you remove the cable from the network adapter responsible for connecting to the Internet. Whether this is a network card with broadband access or a modem with a dial-up connection is immaterial.

Next connect the network adapter of the target server that you want to use for accessing the internal network, with the network of the source server.

Faxmodem

If a faxmodem is to be removed from the source server and installed in the target server, this exchange should be made before beginning the installation.

Administrator Password

When performing a migration remember that the administrator password on the target server must be the same as the password on the source server and can only be changed after the migration is completed.

Network Information

When entering the internal domain information you should make sure that the NetBIOS domain name is not the same as the NetBIOS domain name of the server. Otherwise the migration will fail.

The IP addresses of the source and target servers must be in the same address range. If by oversight you have entered an incorrect IP address for the target server, you can only change this via the *Change Server Address* tool. To do this, open the Internet and E-Mail link in the Server Administration window and click Change Server IP Address. This is the only way to ensure that the IP address change is applied correctly to all the services on the target server. If you have the Premium Edition of SBS 2003, you can install the SQL Server and the ISA Server after working through the task list. However, do not yet distribute the firewall clients. This should only be done after the migration of the clients is complete as described in step 6.

Before the target server first connects to the Internet, you should install and configure antivirus software.

Performing Network Tasks

After you have completed the installation on the target server, you must carry out the network tasks on this server as described in Chapter 2. These include configuring the Internet connection, security settings, and remote access, activating the server, and adding additional client licenses. To do this, you must temporarily attach the network cable for the Internet connection. After completing these steps you should again disable the Internet connection to ensure undisturbed migration of data. Any real-time virus protection should be temporarily switched off for the same reason.

Step 3—Preparing the Clients

In the next step clients with the following operating systems must be prepared for migration to SBS 2003:

- Windows NT 4.0 Workstation
- Windows 2000 Professional
- Windows XP Professional
- Windows Server 2000
- Windows Server 2003
- Member server running Windows Server NT 4.0 or later

All these client computers are migrated with the help of ADMT. For Windows NT 4.0 clients (Workstation and Server), the installation of Service Pack 6a is mandatory. To check whether this is installed, enter the command winver under Run. The installed Service Pack is displayed in the About Windows NT dialog box. The Service Pack can be downloaded from http://www.microsoft.com/ntserver/nts/downloads/recommended/SP6/allSP6.asp.

If you have clients running Windows 95, 98, or ME, you will have to migrate them manually. This procedure is described in step 6. If Windows Server 2000 systems are to be migrated as additional domain controllers, you must first uninstall Active Directory from them. To do this, enter the command DCPROMO under Run. The computer account can then be migrated to the target domain and the computer added as a second server. Remember that you need an SBS 2003 CAL for every member server within the SBS 2003 domain.

The details of the tasks to be performed are as follows:

- If users have not exported their Outlook rules, you must do this now.
- Make sure that the domain administrators group on the source server belongs to the pre-defined administrators group. If you deleted the group on any client from the pre-defined group, you will have to add it again.
- If firewalls are running on the client computers, for example, the Internet Connection Firewall under Windows XP, these should now be disabled.
- When upgrading from SBS 2000 you must also uninstall the Microsoft Shared Modem Service Client. If you were using ISA Server under SBS

2000 and don't want it any more, you must also uninstall the Microsoft Firewall Client.

- To ensure the correct DHCP configuration, you must release and renew the IP address for each client. This ensures that all clients have acquired their IP address from the new DHCP server on the SBS 2003.

- Next delete the desktop links for the shared folder and the company folder. You must also delete or update all links that point to the source server. The same holds for entries in the folder Internet Favorites that point to the source server, for example, the Microsoft Small Business Server Web Site or the Small Business Server Administration.

- Even network printers or fax printers that point to the source server must be deleted. The printers are configured anew on the target server (see step 5) and will again be available to the clients.

- Finally you must carry out a virus scan on each computer and then disable the real-time virus protection. Then log off from each client.

Step 4—Carrying Out the Migration

ADMT is installed on the target server and existing computers, users, and group accounts are migrated. Since ADMT also works with the source server, you must set up DNS Forwarders on both servers. Based on the client information collected in steps 1 and 2, you must decide whether the quotas for Exchange need to be modified. Furthermore, all shared folders and application data must be moved to the target server. If you are using SQL Server, the SQL databases must also be transferred to the target server. Once again, you should take a backup of the source server if you have not done so already.

Installing ADMT

First install ADMT on the target server. You will find the program on CD 1 of SBS 2003 in the folder \i386\Admt\Admigration.msi. Follow the instructions of the installation wizard to install the program.

DNS Forwarding

For ADMT to function you must set up DNS forwarding on both servers. To do this, perform the following steps:

1. On the source server navigate to Start/All Programs/Administrative Tools/DNS.

2. From the context menu of the server select Properties. On the Forwarders tab enter the IP address of the target server and click Add.

3. Open the Forwarders tab on the target server. Click New.

4. In the New Forwarder window enter the complete domain name of the source domain, for example, sbs2000.local.

5. Then enter the IP address of the source server in the Selected domain's forwarder IP address list field and click Add.

ADMT Configuration on the Target Server

If you have clients in your domain running Windows NT 4.0 Workstation or member servers running Windows Server NT 4.0, you must first perform the following steps:

1. Enter the command cmd under Run. At the command line enter the following:

```
Net local group "Pre-Windows 2000 Compatible Access" everyone /add

Net local group "Pre-Windows 2000 Compatible Access" "anonymous logon" /add
```

Make sure you type the quotation marks in both the command lines.

2. Restart the target server.

Migration of User Accounts

1. Open a command line on the target server and enter the following command:

```
Runas /netonly /user:NameSourceDomain\Administrator
    "mmc\"%ProgramFiles%\Active Directory Migration Tool\Migrator.msc\""
```

Replace NameSourceDomain with the appropriate NetBIOS domain name.

If you close ADMT, you can only start it from the command line and not from the entry in the Start menu.

2. Enter the password for the administrator account when asked. The ADMT GUI appears.

3. In the Action menu, click on User Account Migration Wizard. Configure the Wizard with the following information:

User account names more than 20 characters long are automatically abbreviated to 20 characters after migration and may thus appear truncated on the target server.

ADMT Wizard page	Action to be taken
Test or Make changes	Click on Test the migration settings and migrate later?. The log files will help you identify and remove any errors. To start the final migration, click on Migrate now.

ADMT Wizard page	Action to be taken
Domain Selection	Enter the names of the source and target domains here. If after clicking Next you get the error message `Access denied` `(Error=5)`, close the ADMT Wizard and check whether the passwords for the administrator account are identical on the source and target servers and the password has been entered correctly when restarting ADMT from the command line.
User Selection	Click on Add and then Advanced. The Select this object type entry is automatically set to search for user accounts. Then click on Find Now. You will see a list of all user accounts. Select all the user accounts you want to migrate and then click OK. Remember that the following user accounts cannot be migrated: Administrator, Guest, IUSR_Servername, IWAM_Servername, Krbtg, and the TsInternetUser accounts.
	When migrating from SBS 2000 the following accounts may also not be migrated: Small Business Administrator, Small Business Power User and Small Business user accounts.
	When migrating from Exchange Server 2000 the SystemMailbox account and in SQL Server 2000 the SQLDebugger and SQLAgentCmdExec accounts may not be migrated.
	For other applications that require a separate user account, refer to their documentation to find out whether migration from Exchange Server 2000 is possible.
Organizational Unit Selection	For the target OU navigate to MyBusiness\Users\SBBUsers.

ADMT Wizard page	Action to be taken
Password Options	Click on Same as user name. This automatically sets the password to the first 14 characters of the username. By default these entries are saved in the following file: \Program Files\Active Directory Migration Tool\Logs\Passwords.txt. These temporary passwords can be changed after the migration is completed. If you want to migrate the original passwords, click on Migrate passwords. Instructions about the appropriate configuration for password migration can be found in article KB 325851 of the Microsoft Knowledge Base.
Account Transition Options	Click on Target same as source. Enable the checkbox Migrate user SIDs to target domain. Then click on Next and then Yes.
	You must then restart the source server and log in with the administrator account. Only then can you click OK on the target server to continue.
User Account	Under User Name enter the pre-defined administrator account and enter the password. Make sure that the name of the source domain is entered under Domain.
User Options	Activate the Translate roaming profiles and Update user rights checkboxes. Also make sure that the checkboxes Fix users' group memberships and Do not rename accounts are checked.
Object Property Exclusion	By default no particular properties of objects are excluded from the migration. To preserve this setting, click on Next.
Naming Conflicts	Here you should select Ignore conflicting accounts and don't migrate.
Completing the User Account Migration Wizards	As soon as you click Finish you will see a status window for the migration. The migration of user accounts is over if the status displayed is Completed. To check if there are any errors, click on View Log. The log file is available for the simulated migration as well as the real one.

Migration of Group Accounts

1. Open a command line on the target server and enter the following command, provided ADMT is not running:

```
Runas /netonly /user:NameSourceDomain\Administrator
    "mmc\"%ProgramFiles%\Active Directory Migration Tool\Migrator.msc\""
```

Replace NameSourceDomain with the appropriate NetBIOS domain name.

If you close ADMT, you can only restart it with the above command-line and not from the entry in the start menu.

2. Enter the administrator password when asked. The ADMT GUI appears.

3. In the Action menu, click on Group Account Migration Wizard. Configure the Wizard with the following information:

ADMT Wizard page	Action to be taken
Test or Make Changes	Click on Test the migration settings and migrate later?. The log files will help you identify and remove any errors. To start the final migration, click on Migrate now?.
Domain Selection	Under Source domain the name of the source domain must be entered, for example sbs2000.local, and under Target domain the name of the target domain, for example sbs2003.local.
Group Selection	Click on Add and then Advanced. The entry Select this object type is automatically set to search for group accounts. Then click on Object Types and disable the Built-in security principals checkbox. Then click on Find Now. You will see a list of all group accounts. Select all the group accounts you want to migrate and then click OK.
	The following user accounts cannot be migrated: Predefined security groups, Cert Publishers, DHCP Administrators, DHCP Users, DNS Admins, DnsUpdateProxy, domain administrators, domain computers, Domain Controllers, Domain Guests, domain users, Enterprise Admins, Group Policy Creator Owners, RAS and IAS Servers, Schema Admins and WINS Users

ADMT Wizard page	Action to be taken
Group Selection (contd.)	When migrating from SBS 2000 you may also not migrate the following groups: Back Office Fax Operators, Back Office Folder Operators, Back Office Internet Users, Back Office Mail Operators, Back Office Remote Operators, and Back Office Template Users.
	When migrating from Exchange 2000 Server you may not migrate the Exchange Domain Servers and Exchange Enterprise Servers groups, and in SQL Server 2000 the OLAP administrators and Domain Name$$$ groups.
Organizational Unit Selection	For all security groups navigate to MyBusiness\SecurityGroups, for distributor groups to MyBusiness\DistributionGroups as the target OU.
Group Options	Select the entries Update user rights, Fix membership of groups, Migrate group SIDs to target domain and Do not rename accounts.
Object Property Exclusion	By default no particular properties of objects are excluded from the migration. To preserve this setting, click on Next.
User Account	Under User Name enter the pre-defined administrator account and its password. Make sure that the name of the source domain is listed under Domain.
Naming Conflicts	The Ignore conflicting accounts and don't migrate option should be selected here.
Completing the Group Account Migration Wizard	As soon as you click Finish you will see a status window for the migration. The migration of group accounts is over if the status displayed is Completed. To check if there are any errors, click on View Log. The log file is available for the simulated migration as well as the real one.

Migration of Computer Accounts

Computer accounts can only be migrated for computers running Windows NT 4.0 Workstation and Server, Windows 2000 Professional and Server, Windows XP Professional, and Windows Server 2003.

If there are clients in your domain running Windows NT 4.0 Workstation or member servers running Windows Server NT 4.0, you must first:

1. Enter the command cmd under Run. At the command prompt type the following lines:

```
Net local group "Pre-Windows 2000 Compatible Access" everyone /add
```

```
Net local group "Pre-Windows 2000 Compatible Access" "anonymous logon" /add
```

Make sure you type the quotation marks in both command lines.

2. Then restart the target server.

After you have restarted the source server wait about 15 minutes so that the DNS entries on the source server can be refreshed. If you do not wait this long, the configuration of the clients for the target domain will not function. Furthermore, you should make sure that the domain administrators group on the source server is a member of the pre-defined administrator group. If this default setting is missing, you must add the group. Moreover, all real-time virus protection programs and software firewalls on the client computers should be disabled.

1. Open the command prompt on the target server and enter the following command, provided ADMT is not yet running:

```
Runas /netonly /user:NameSourceDomain\Administrator
"mmc\"%ProgramFiles%\Active Directory Migration Tool\Migrator.msc\""
```

2. Replace the NameSourceDomain with the appropriate NetBIOS domain name.

   If you close ADMT, you may start it only with the above command and not via the entry in the start menu.

3. Enter the administrator password when asked. The ADMT GUI appears.

4. In the Action menu, click on Computer Account Migration Wizard. Configure the Wizard with the following information:

ADMT Wizard Page	Action to be Taken
Test or Make Changes	Click on Test the migration settings and migrate later?. The log files will help you identify and remove any errors. To start the final migration, click on Migrate now?.

ADMT Wizard Page	Action to be Taken
Domain Selection	Under Source domain the domain name of the source domain must be entered, for example sbs2000.local, under Target domain the name of the target domain, for example sbs2003.local.
Computer Selection	Click on Add and then Advanced. The entry Select this object type is automatically set to search for computer accounts. Then click on Object Types and disable the Built-in security principals checkbox. Then click on Find Now. You will see a list of all computer accounts. Select all the group accounts you want to migrate and then click OK. Make sure you do not select the computer account of the source server or computer accounts on which the operating systems Windows 95, 98, or ME are running.
	Furthermore, you should ensure that all the computers to be migrated are switched on and connected to the network.
	For all server computer accounts (other than the source server, which is not migrated), rerun the Computer Migration Wizard and add the servers on the Organizational Unit Selection page of the OU SBS Servers.
Organizational Unit Selection	For all client computers navigate to MyBusiness\Computer\SBSComputer, and for servers to MyBusiness\Computer\SBSServer as the target OU.
Translate Objects	Make sure that all the checkboxes on this page are enabled.
Security Translation Object	The Replace option must be enabled here. Then click on Next. Click OK if the following message is displayed: User rights translation will be performed in 'Add' mode only. Any other objects will be translated in accordance with your mode selection.
Computer Options	Enable the option Do not rename Computers and set the number of minutes for a restart after completing the migration to 1.

ADMT Wizard Page	Action to be Taken
Object Property Exclusion	By default no particular properties of objects are excluded from the migration. To preserve this setting, click on Next.
Naming Conflicts	The Ignore conflicting accounts and don't migrate option should be selected here.
Completing the User Account Migration Wizard	As soon as you click Finish you will see a status window for the migration. The migration of group accounts is over if the status displayed is Completed. To check if there are any errors, click on View Log. The log file is available for the simulated migration as well as the real one. After you click on Close you will see a status dialog in the Migration Tool Agent Monitor window about the connection to client computers.

If the migration of a computer fails after the migration of the agent in the course of configuring the client, do the following to solve the problem:

1. Check all entries in the log files.
2. Make sure that the computer account has not been created in Active Directory. To do this, open the MMC Active Directory Users and Computers on the target server.
3. Run the Computer Migration Wizard and migrate the account again.

As long as you are migrating computer accounts only in test mode, you will get a message with the event ID 37075 in the event display. This is normal in test mode because the domain is not changed when accounts are migrated in this mode.

After you have migrated all clients successfully, you still cannot log on to them. Logging on is possible only after completing step 6—configuration of the client. Otherwise Outlook Profiles are not migrated.

Changing Exchange Quotas

When migrating from Exchange 2000, if the mail quota on the source server is set to 200 MB (200,000 KB) for sending and receiving e-mails and the warning threshold is set at 175 MB (175,000 KB), you must not change the settings on the target server. If, however, higher values have been set on the source system, you must change the quota values for the target system accordingly. To do this, perform the following steps:

1. On the source server open the Server Administration window from the Start menu and click on Advanced Administration.

2. Double-click on Organization Name (Exchange), Administrative Groups, First Administrative Group, then on Server and Your Server. Double-click on First Storage Group and select the Properties entry from the context menu Mailbox Store.

3. Open the Limit Values tab on the source server and make a note of the values for the maximum mailbox size and the warning threshold.

4. Then open the Limit Values tab on the target server as just described and enter the values from the source server in the appropriate fields.

Moving Exchange Mailboxes

The mailboxes of Exchange Server 2000 are migrated to the target server with the help of the *Exchange Server Migration Wizard*. At this point you cannot log on to any clients and open Outlook. Starting Outlook is only possible after completing step 6—configuring the client.

During the migration, all real-time virus protection programs and disk utilities on this server should be stopped. To migrate the mailboxes, perform the following steps:

1. On the target server open Start/Programs/Microsoft Exchange/Preparation/ Migration Wizard. Enter the following information while the Migration wizard is running:

Migration Wizard Page	Action to be taken
Migration	Select Migration of Microsoft Exchange.
Migration of Exchange Server	Click Next.
Migration target	Here you can only accept the default option Migration to a Computer running Exchange Server.
Source Exchange Server	Disable the checkbox Exchange 5.5 Server. Enter the computer name, the administrator account and the administrator password.
Migration information	Confirm the setting Creation of E-Mail Accounts.
Account migration	Select all the accounts that you want to migrate. The wizard cannot however be used for migrating the administrator's mailbox. To export this account, save the mails in a PST file from an Outlook client and then re-import them. The rules for the administrator account must also be exported. The migration of the mailboxes for the user accounts can only be carried out after the user accounts have been migrated to the target system with the help of ADMT.

Migration Wizard Page	Action to be taken
Container for New Windows Account	Navigate to Domain Name\MyBusiness\Users\SBSUsers.

2. Follow the instructions to close the Migration Wizard.

Moving the Shared User Folders

The easiest way to move the shared user folders is with the xcopy command on the command line. Alternatively you can also use the *Robo Copy* program. This program is a part of the Windows Server 2003 Resource Kit Tools and can be downloaded from http://go.microsoft.com/fwlink/?LinkId=20249.

Before starting the copying process, make sure that the user folders are not larger than 1 GB. By default the quota for the user folders is fixed at 1 GB under SBS 2003.

To move the user folders open a command line on the target server and enter the following command:

```
Xcopy \\Sourceserver\Users \\Targetserver\Users /e /o /d /h /v
                    /c>>c:\Kopier.txt
```

The meaning of the parameters in this command is as follows:

- /e: All sub-directories are copied, even if they are empty.
- /o: The information in the Discretionary Access Control List (DACL) and information about the ownership of the files is copied.
- /d: Only those files are copied whose source time is later than the target time. If only those files are to be copied that have been created after a specific time, use the option /d: m-d-y, where the date must be given in the format month-day-year.
- /h: Hidden and system files are also copied.
- /v: Each newly written file is verified.
- /c: All errors are ignored.
- >>C:\Kopier.txt: The results of the copying action are written to the file Kopier.txt on drive C. Check this file after completing the copying process to see if there are any errors. You can also compare the number and size of the files in the source and target servers.

User-Defined Login Scripts

If you have been using user-defined login scripts on the source system, copy these from the NETLOGON folder of the source server to the NETLOGON folder of the target server. If these scripts reference other files, these files should also be copied to the target server.

Moving other Shared Folders

For each folder to be moved create a share of the same name on the target server and assign the same rights to it as on the source server. Then move the contents of these folders as described in the previous section.

When creating the shares on the target server remember that the quota settings apply even to these folders if they have been created on the same partition as the user folders.

Moving the Company Folder to the Intranet Website

The Company folder used in SBS 2000 is not available in the same format under SBS 2003. The contents of this folder are moved to the internal website created by the SharePoint Services. To move the folder, perform the following steps:

1. Open Server Administration on the target server and click on Internal Web Site.

2. In the detail view click on Import Files. A wizard appears.

3. On the File and Document Library Path page enter under Copy Files From the path \\Sourceserver\Company. Under Copy Files To you can either accept the default setting http://companyweb/General Documents or specify/create another library via Browse.

4. By default all files larger than 50 MB are not copied. To change this setting, open a browser window and enter the address http://Targetserver:8081. Click on Configure Virtual Server Settings, then on Companyweb, and finally on General Settings. Here you can specify the maximum size.

5. Furthermore, all files with specific extensions (for example .exe or .vbs) are blocked by default. To change these settings, again enter the address http://Targetserver:8081 in a browser window. Then click on Manage Blocked File TYPES to modify the settings.

In general only files with data are copied.

Moving Other Data

If more data is to be moved that is not in any of the folders just described, it must likewise be copied. This also holds for application data. If rights are irrelevant for this data, it can simply be copied. On the other hand if the ownership of the files and the settings in the DACL are to be preserved, use the program *Xcopy* or *Robo Copy*. The exact procedure was described in the section *Moving the Shared User Folders*.

If you are using SQL databases that need to be migrated, perform the following steps:

1. Enter the following command at the command prompt on the target server:
   `\\Sourceserver\Driveletter$`
2. Navigate on this drive to the storage location of the desired files and copy these to the desired location on the target server. Repeat this process for the data folders of all applications.

If you have created your own websites on the source server under IIS (Internet Information Server), you must copy these files to the target server and then create the websites afresh under IIS 6.0. For this procedure you can also use the *IIS 6.0 Migration Tool*.

You can now install all the necessary applications on the target server.

Moving SQL Databases

If you are using the Premium Version of SBS 2003 and want to migrate existing SQL Server databases, perform the following steps:

If SQL Server 2000 is not yet installed on the target server, perform this installation now.

More information about moving SQL databases between SQL servers can be found in the Microsoft Knowledge Base Article 314546 and on the subject of restoring databases in Chapter 7.

Step 5—Configuring the Target Server

In this step you will connect the user accounts with an SBS 2003 user template and distribute applications to the clients so that they can access the SBS 2003 network the very first time they log in. Additionally, further configuration settings will have to be made on the target server, such as creation of distributor lists or configuration of Microsoft Connector for POP3 mailboxes. The detailed steps are as follows.

Rights for the Migrated Accounts

To ensure that users have the correct rights to access the resources on the SBS 2003 network, you must specify the user rights on the target server.

In the course of making these settings you will also, if required, specify rights for remote access. You can also distribute the Connection Manager Configuration Package, with which the required settings for the connection of mobile and remote clients are configured.

For specifying user rights perform the following steps:

1. Open the Server Administration link on the target server. Click on User and then on User Administration.

2. On the Template Selection page select an SBS 2003 account template for each migrated account. You should accept the default setting for preserving the user rights.

If a user account does not appear on the user selection page, make sure that this account is not disabled. To verify this, open Server Administration on the target server, click on Users, and select Enable from the context menu of the disabled account.

3. Then follow the instructions to complete the wizard.

If you were not using Exchange Server before the migration, a new mailbox is now created automatically for each user.

Distribution of Applications

Applications can only be distributed to clients using the operating systems Windows 2000 and XP Professional. For all other operating systems the installation must be done manually on the client. For member servers under Windows Server NT 4.0 you will find additional instructions in the Server Administration area under Server computers/More Information/Configuring additional Servers.

To configure more than five clients, you must first add additional licenses. SBS 2003 comes with only five CALs.

1. Open the Server Administration area on the target server and click on Client Computers.

2. In the right pane click on Assign Applications to Client Computers. Enter the following information in the wizard that appears:

Wizard page	Action to be taken
Client computers	Select all the clients here to which you want to distribute client applications.
Client applications	Confirm the default settings here. If you are using ISA Server 2000 on the target system, you must distribute the Firewall Client to all clients. To do this, click on Change Applications. On the Available Applications page click on Add. Then enter the application name Firewall Client or navigate via Browse to \\Targetserver\Mspclnt\Setup.exe

3. Follow the wizard's instructions to complete the process.

Completing the Task List of Administrative Tasks

If you have closed this list during the above activities, you can reopen it now by clicking Task List in Server Administration. Now perform the following administrative tasks:

- **Adding a new printer**: You can set up all the printers afresh here.
- **Adding users and computers**: This step is only required if you are adding new accounts to the migrated ones.
- **Fax configuration**: If you have a faxmodem, you can set it up now.
- **Configuring monitoring**: Here, you can configure server performance and load reports. Messages for alarm options are also specified here.
- **Backup configuration**: Here you can specify options for Windows Backup. If you are using a third-party backup program, you should not make any entries here.

These administrative tasks have already been described in detail in Chapter 2.

Transferring User-Defined Settings from the Source Server

In this step all user-defined configurations such as DHCP range options (scopes), settings for routing and remote access, group policies, or DNS settings are transferred to the target server. In short, all the relevant settings that cannot be migrated using a wizard are transferred manually to the target server in this step.

E-Mail Distribution Lists and Retrieval Policies

All user-defined retrieval policies must be recreated on the target server. The same holds for migrated distribution groups that contained pre-defined groups such as the administrator group as members. You must now again add the pre-defined groups of the target server to the distribution groups. To do this, perform the following steps:

1. Open Server Administration and click on Distribution Groups.
2. Click on the desired distribution group in the right pane. On the Members tab you can again add the desired pre-defined user accounts.

Microsoft Connector for POP3 Mailboxes

This configuration is required if you have POP3 mailboxes that you want to download to the Exchange Server. To do this, perform the following steps:

1. Open the entry Internet and E-Mail in Server Administration.
2. In the right pane click on Manage POP3 E-Mail. Then click on Open POP3 Connector Manager.

3. The remaining configuration of POP3 e-mail is as described in the context of the task list in Chapter 2.

Updating User-Defined Login Scripts

After you have copied the user-defined login scripts into the NETLOGON directory of the target server, they have to be made usable for the users. To do this, you must update each user account so that it references the login script on the target server. Also, in the login script you must change all references to the source server to point to the target server.

Step 6—Configuration of the Clients

In this step Windows 2000 and XP Professional clients automatically receive the settings for e-mail and proxy. On all other client operating systems you have to perform the configuration manually. Moreover, you can now also import the Exchange folders so that the clients are fully configured for connecting with the new Exchange Server. The detailed steps are as follows:

Configuration of Windows 2000 / Windows XP Clients

1. Log on to each client computer with the respective user account. You will be prompted to change the password for the account. Make a note of the password you enter in each case. Choose a secure password, because after the migration is completed the target server will be connected to the Internet. If you have not migrated the old user passwords, the default location for the passwords is the file \Program Files\Active Directory Migration Tool\Logs\Passwords.txt. As already mentioned, the default password consists of the first 14 characters of the username.

2. If you have selected the client under step 5 for the distribution of applications, the Client Installation Wizard appears; click on Start Now.

3. Open the Control Panel and double-click on Mail. Then update the e-mail properties in accordance with the target server.

If you are using ISA Server, you must configure the proxy settings of Internet Explorer.

1. To do this, open Internet Explorer. In the Tools menu click on Internet Options.

2. On the Connections tab click on LAN Settings.

3. Enable the checkbox Use a proxy server for your LAN and enter the name of the target server for Address and 8080 for Port.

4. If you have ISA Server only on the source server and not on the target server, make sure that the proxy checkbox in LAN Settings and the Automatically detect settings checkbox under Automatic Configuration are disabled.

After this you can again reactivate the real-time virus protection on the client.

Configuration of Older Windows Clients

Client computers with operating systems older than Windows 2000 must be configured manually for the target domain. The applications are then installed manually on them.

1. After you have made these two preparations, log on to each client computer with the respective user account. When you log on you will be prompted to change the password for the account.

Make a note of the password you enter in each case. Keep the security of the password in mind as after the migration is completed the target server will be connected to the Internet. If you have not migrated the old user passwords, the default location for the passwords is the file \Program Files\Active Directory Migration Tool\Logs\ Passwords.txt. As already mentioned, the default password consists of the first 14 characters of the username.

2. Next, open the Control Panel and double-click on Mail. Then update the e-mail properties in accordance with the target server.

3. Delete all Internet Explorer Favorites that reference the source server as these are no longer valid.

4. Delete or update all links to the shared user and company folders. This also holds for links to network folders and other links that refer to the source server.

5. If printers and fax devices that point to the source server have been configured here, delete them. Updated printers and fax devices have already been set up in *Step 5—Configuring the Target Server*.

6. If the Firewall Client of the ISA Server has already been installed, you must modify the name of the target server on the clients in accordance with that on the target server. To do this, double-click the Firewall Client icon in the System Tray. Enter the new name of the server in the options that appear.

If you are also using ISA Server, you must configure the proxy settings of Internet Explorer. To do this:

1. Open Internet Explorer. In the Tools menu click on Internet Options.

2. On the Connections tab click on LAN Settings.

3. Enable the checkbox Use Proxy Server for LAN and enter the name of the target server for Address and 8080 for Port.

4. If you have ISA Server only on the source server and not on the target server, make sure that the proxy checkbox in the LAN Settings and the Automatically detect settings checkbox under Automatic Configuration are disabled.

After this you can again reactivate the real-time virus protection on the client. Then proceed to the section *Setting up an Internet Connection.*

Testing the Network Connection

Finally you must check whether the migrated clients have functional network access. To test this, disconnect the source server from the network and send a test e-mail to the users. If the e-mail reaches the recipients, it indicates that the Internet settings have been configured correctly.

You must also test if shared folders, shared applications, and network printers are available and functional.

After completing the last step you can log on to a client as administrator and import the mailbox as well as the rules for the administrator account to the target server.

The earliest offline address books will become available will be one hour after the installation of SBS 2003. If you attempt to access them before this, you will not succeed as the offline address book has not been generated at this point in time.

Importing Public Folders

The next step is to import the public folders of the source server that have been exported to a .pst file. To do this, perform the following steps:

1. Log on to a client with the administrator account and start Outlook.
2. Double-click Public Folders and then All Public Folders.
3. Import the .pst file into the currently selected folder.

If special rights had been configured for the public folders, you must restore these.

1. To do this, open Server Administration on the target server. Double-click on Advanced Administration, Administrative Groups, First administrative Group, Server, Your Server, First Storage Group, Information Storage for Public Folders, and Public Folders.
2. In the right pane select Properties from the context menu of the desired folder.
3. On the Rights tab click on Client Rights. Update the Name, Role, and Rights fields with the desired values.

Step 7—Completing the Migration

After completing the migration you can stop the source server. It does make sense, however, to keep it in readiness for a period of time so as to be able to solve configuration problems on the new server to the extent that these relate to information that can be transferred manually from the old server. Only after this transition period should the old server be completely taken out of operation and formatted. You can set this machine up as a second server.

Furthermore, ADMT must again be uninstalled from the target server, and all pre-Windows 2000 rights, which could have been applied temporarily in the course of the migration, set back to the original values.

Deleting DNS Forwarders

To use ADMT you had to enter DNS forwarders to the source server on the target server. These entries are now superfluous and must be deleted.

1. To do this, open the *DNS* MMC on the target server. From the context menu of the target server select Properties.
2. On the Forwarders tab click the name of the source domain under DNS Domains and then click on Delete.

Resetting Rights

You need to carry out this step only if you have configured extended rights on the source server for pre-Windows 2000 compatible access in *Step 4—Carrying Out the Migration*. If you are using member servers running Windows Server NT 4.0, skip this step so that these servers can access the domain.

1. To reset the rights, open the command prompt on the target server and enter the following command:

    ```
    Net localgroup "pre-windows 2000 compatible access" everyone
            /delete
    ```

    ```
    Net localgroup "pre-windows 2000 compatible access" "anonymous
            logon" /delete
    ```

2. Restart the target server and log on using the administrator account.

Uninstalling ADMT

After all the accounts have been migrated you should uninstall ADMT from the target server. This can be done via Control Panel/Software/Add or Remove Programs.

Specifying Password Policies

If you have not migrated the old user passwords along with the accounts, you should now lay down a password policy that prompts users to change their passwords when they first log on.

1. To do this, open the Users entry in the Server Administration.
2. In the right-hand window, click on Specify Password Policies. If possible you should select all the three options offered.
3. Click on Configure Password Policies, and then click on Immediately.

If you are going to allow access to the server over the Internet, you should always activate password complexity. The complex password requirement comes into effect only after three days, so you have enough time to set up further user accounts in peace.

4. You should also delete the password file created during account migration. This is the file \Program Files\Active Directory Migration Tool\Logs\Passwords.txt.

Consider whether you want to give your users the option of changing their passwords. The advantage of permitting password changing is higher security; the disadvantage is that the administrator often has to reset passwords because users forget them. You will have to decide in each case (depending on your users) which option you want to exercise.

To enable or disable password changing open the Users entry in the Password Administration. Double-click on the desired account. On the Accounts tab you can enable or disable the checkbox that allows users to change their password.

Connecting the Target Server to the Internet

Finally, connect the target server's network adapter for Internet access to the appropriate cable. To test the Internet connection, open a website from any client. Also send a test e-mail to a mail account on the Internet. If you have configured the fax service, you should also send out a test fax.

Migration from Small Business Server 4.5 and Windows Server NT 4.0

As already mentioned, an upgrade to SBS 2003 from SBS 4.5 or Windows Server NT 4.0 is only possible via a migration. A direct upgrade to SBS 2003 is not available for these operating systems. Many of the steps involved in this migration are similar or identical to the steps in the migration from Windows Server 2000 or SBS 2000. So as not break the flow of this chapter, however, and to obviate the need to keep going back to the corresponding section of the SBS 2000 migration, we will now descrive the complete migration of a SBS 4.5 or Windows Server NT 4.0.

The steps described here are not applicable to SBS 4.0. If you are still using this version, you must do a fresh install of the server and perform a complete manual migration.

This section describes in detail the various steps in the migration with an SBS 4.5 Windows Server NT 4.0 server as the source server.

Step 1—Preparing for the Migration

In the course of preparing for the migration you will first collect the following information from different areas:

Server-Related Information

- Names of the source and target servers. These two names must be different. To find out the computer name, open the Control Panel and double-click on Network. You will find the computer name on the Identification tab.

- Complete DNS name in the internal domain and NetBIOS domain name. These two names should also be different for the source and target servers. By default you can accept the values suggested during installation for the internal DNS domain. To find out the NetBIOS name, open the Control Panel and double-click on Network. You will find the DNS and NetBIOS domain names on the Identification tab. The NetBIOS domain name is displayed under domains. A complete DNS domain name is not available under Windows NT.

- Find out the IP address of the source server and assign a free address to the target server. To find out the IP address of the source server, enter cmd under Run then issue the command ipconfig /all. The IP address of the target server must of course be in the same address range as the source server. If you are using a router as a DHCP server, the address must be in the range provided by the router. If the source server is functioning as the DHCP server, you will find valid addresses in its range options. To do this, open Start/Programs/Administration (General)/DHCP-Manager. Double-click on the local server and then Range. Here you will find all the currently used IP addresses.

- If you have renamed the administrator account on the source server, you must set it back to the original name "administrator". The account can be renamed once the migration to the target server is completed. Ensure that the administrator password is identical on the source and target systems. One password must be used, otherwise the migration cannot be carried out.

Information about Shared Folders, Applications, and Settings

- **Users' shared folders**: Note the name of the user folder. By default it is Users under SBS 4.5 and SBS 2003.

- **Client applications folder**: If there are applications here that are going to be used even after the migration, copy the contents of this folder into the directory on the target server. The default name for the directory for client applications under SBS 4.5 and under SBS 2003 is ClientApps.

The application *Modem Sharing Client* is not available after migration because SBS 2003 does not support this function.

- **Company shared folder**: Under SBS 4.5 the name of the folder is Company. Under SBS 2003 on the other hand a company web site is created via SharePoint Services. The URL for this is http://companyweb.

- **Other shared folders**: The contents of the following shared folders cannot be migrated: Printers and Planned Tasks. Also, do not migrate the folder NETLOGON if you are not using any customized login scripts. These folders may be migrated neither from SBS 4.5 nor from Windows Server NT 4.0. In a migration from SBS 4.5 the following folders may also not be migrated as SBS 2003 has updated versions: Mspclnt and the shared client folders. The individual user folders do not have to be migrated separately as their contents follow automatically during the migration of the shared user folders.

- If Exchange 5.5 is installed, you cannot migrate the following shared folders: Add-Ins, Address, Resources and Tracking.log.

- If there are other shared folders, check their contents and note the names of the shares so that these can be created afresh on the target system. To get an overview of all the shares on the source server enter the following under Run: **Sourceservername**.

- Next note the names and installation paths of all applications that you wish to use after the migration.

- If you have set up distribution groups under Exchange 5.5, note their names. When transferring these groups to the target server you must put them in the Organizational Unit (OU) distribution groups. If the distribution groups contain pre-defined groups (such as administrators) as members, you must likewise make a note of these memberships as the memberships of pre-defined groups cannot be migrated. Furthermore, you must write down user-defined rights to public folders and user-defined recipients under Exchange 5.5 so that you can configure them afresh once the migration is over.

- Check if you have saved all the user-defined settings in the following areas: DNS entries, DHCP range options, routing and remote access, group policies, websites on IIS 4.0, and Exchange 5.5. These settings are configured afresh on the target server after the migration is completed. The public folders and the mailbox of the administrator account are exported to a .pst file. If specific rules have been laid down for the administrator mailbox, you must export these, too. It is not possible to migrate these settings with the Exchange Server Migration Wizard.

If you have not permitted any user-defined settings on the source system and have retained the default settings, you do not need to make a note of the configuration for these areas because the standard settings of the SBS 2003 can be accepted.

Deleting Unnecessary Files and E-Mails

Before beginning the migration you should always delete all unnecessary files and e-mails. Ask all users to delete their Outlook mails from the folders Deleted Items and Sent Items. The same holds for unnecessary files in the individual user directories. Also search all shared directories for file fragments.

If a user's mailbox is greater than 200 MB even after deleting superfluous e-mails, you will definitely have to change the quota settings on the target server. The default threshold value for the mailbox size is 200 MB. If this size is exceeded, e-mails can no longer be sent or received. By default a warning is issued at a mailbox size of 175 MB.

There is also a limit for the user folder. The default limit value for the user folder is 1 GB. If a user's folder exceeds 1 GB, the quota settings for all users will have to be changed. More information about this can be found in the SBS 2003 help pages.

To determine the mailbox sizes of individual users, do the following in SBS 4.5:

1. Open Start/Programs/Microsoft Exchange/Microsoft Exchange Administrator.
2. Double-click on Exchange Location and then Servers on your Exchange Server. Here, double-click on Private Information Storage and then Mailbox Resources.
3. In the Total KB column you will find the mailbox size for each user.

If the user is using rules under Outlook, you must save these, because when mailboxes are migrated to the target server Outlook rules are not included in the migration.

Compatibility of Hardware and Software

If you intend to use hardware, for example an internal modem, or software from the source system on the target server, you must make sure that it is compatible with SBS

2003. Use the Windows Server catalog page at http://www.microsoft.com/windows/catalog/server/.

Installing Current Service Packs

Ensure that the latest Service Pack is installed. For trouble-free migration at least the following Service Packs must be installed:

Exchange Server 5.5: Service Pack 4

To check which Service Pack is installed, open Start Menu/Programs/Microsoft Exchange/Microsoft Exchange Administrator. In the Help menu click About Microsoft Exchange Server. The Service Pack version is displayed here. You can download the Service Pack from http://www.microsoft.com/exchange/downloads/55/sp4dl_de.asp.

If you have changed the Exchange SA password so that it is no longer the same as the password of the pre-defined administrator account, you will get an error message during the installation of the Service Pack saying that a connection could not be established between the account name and the Security ID (SID). In this case you must change the Exchange password back to its original value. Further instructions can be found in article 285297 in the Microsoft Knowledge Base.

SQL Server 7.0: Service Pack 4

To check which Service Pack is installed, open Start Menu/Programs/Microsoft SQL Server 7.0/Enterprise Manager. Double-click on SQL Server Group and select Properties from the context menu of the server name. The version number must be 7.00.1063. This version number corresponds to an installation of Service Pack 4. You can download the service pack from http://www.microsoft.com/sql/downloads/sp4GER.asp.

Windows Server NT 4.0: Service Pack 6a

To check which Service Pack is installed, enter the command winver under Run. You can download Service Pack 6a from http://www.microsoft.com/downloads/details.aspx?displaylang=de&FamilyID=e396d059-e402-46ef-b095-a74399e25737.

Windows Server NT 4.0: Internet Explorer High Encryption Pack

The High Encryption Pack must also be installed. To verify this, double-click the Internet Explorer icon on the desktop. In the Help menu click About Internet Explorer. Under Cipher Strength the value 128-bit should be displayed. If the key strength is not displayed there, navigate in Windows Explorer to the file \System32\Schannel.dll and open its Properties. On the Version tab you should see under Description the entry TLS/SSL Security Provider (US and Canada).

You can download the High Encryption Pack for Internet Explorer from
`http://www.microsoft.com/downloads/details.aspx?FamilyID=bbcaae86-f80d-4d0c-8fa2-78a8868652e0&displaylang=en`.

Backing up the Source Server

The source server should be backed up after all users have completed their work. Ideally this should be done in the evening or at the weekend.

1. Before starting the backup you should scan all drives for viruses. Also create an emergency diskette for the source server or update an existing one.
2. Then take a complete backup of the source server.
3. To make sure that the backup was done correctly, you should restore randomly selected files from the backup at another location and check whether the original file and the backup are identical.

Notifying Users about the Impending Migration

It is necessary to notify users about the impending migration only if some users are still logged on to the domain at that time. If you are carrying out the migration at a time when no users are working, this point is irrelevant. Otherwise you can reach users via the `Net send` command. The pre-requisite for this that the messaging system should be running on the server and the clients. Here is an example of a command you can issue:

`Net send * Please log off the domain in the next 5 minutes. No network and Internet connections will be available thereafter.`

The * symbol means that the message will be sent to all members of the domain.

Step 2—Preparing the Server for the Installation

This section describes all the steps you have to carry out on the source and target systems before installing SBS 2003.

DHCP Configuration

Before starting the installation of SBS 2003 you must stop the DHCP service on the source server if it is running there. The moment source and target servers are connected, only the DHCP service configured on the target server should remain active.

1. To stop the service on the source server, open Start Menu/Settings/Control Panel and double-click Services.
2. Mark the entry Microsoft DHCP Server and then click on Stop. Then set the Start Type to Disabled.

If you are using a router that acts as a DHCP server, you should not carry out the procedure just described. This router should be connected with the target server during the installation of SBS 2003 so that the DHCP settings can be configured correctly. You can choose between using the router or the SBS 2003 as the DHCP server.

Network and Internet Connection

It is recommended that you remove the cable from the network adapter responsible for connecting to the Internet. Whether this is a network card with broadband access or a modem with a dial-up connection is immaterial.

Next connect the network adapter of the target server that you want to use for accessing the internal network, with the network of the source server.

Faxmodem

If a faxmodem is to be removed from the source server and installed in the target server, this exchange should be made before beginning the installation. Also make sure that the hardware is compatible with SBS 2003.

File system

During the installation on the target server, you must specify the file system. Always choose NTFS here and not FAT or FAT32.

Administrator Password

When performing a migration remember that the administrator password on the target server must be the same as the password on the source server and can only be changed after the migration is completed.

Computer Name

The computer name to be selected for the target server should not already exist on the network. Valid characters for a computer name are A–Z, 0–9, and the hyphen (-). The name can have a maximum of 15 characters.

Network Information

When entering the internal domain information you should make sure that the NetBIOS domain name is not the same as the NetBIOS domain name of the server. Otherwise the migration will fail.

The IP addresses of the source and target servers must be in the same address range. If by oversight you have entered an incorrect IP address for the target server, you can only change this via the *Change Server Address* tool. To do this, open the Internet and E-Mail link in the Server Administration and click Change Server IP Address. This is the only way to ensure that the IP address change is applied correctly to all the services on the target server.

If you have the Premium Edition of SBS 2003, you can install the SQL Server and the ISA Server after working through the task list. However you should not yet distribute the firewall clients. This should only be done after the migration of the clients is complete as described in step 6.

Before the target server first connects to the Internet, you should install and configure antivirus software.

Performing Network Tasks

After you have completed the installation on the target server, carry out the network tasks on this server as described in Chapter 2. These include configuring the Internet connection, security settings, and remote access, activating the server, and adding additional client licenses. To do this, you must temporarily attach the network cable for the Internet connection. After completing these steps you should again disable the Internet connection to ensure undisturbed migration of data. Any real-time virus protection should also be temporarily switched off for the same reason.

Step 3—Preparing the Clients

In the next step clients running the following operating systems must be prepared for migrating to SBS 2003:

- Windows NT 4.0 Workstation
- Windows 2000 Professional
- Windows XP Professional
- Windows Server 2000
- Windows Server 2003
- Member servers running Windows Server NT 4.0 or later

All these client computers are migrated with the help of ADMT. For Windows NT 4.0 clients (Workstation and Server) installation of Service Pack 6a is mandatory. To check whether this is installed, enter the command winver under Run. The installed Service Pack is displayed in the About Windows NT dialog box. The Service Pack can be downloaded from http://www.microsoft.com/ntserver/nts/downloads/recommended/SP6/allSP6.asp.

If you have clients running Windows 95, 98, or ME, you will have to migrate them manually. This procedure is described in step 6. If Windows Server 2000 systems are to be migrated as additional domain controllers, you must first uninstall Active Directory from them. To do this, enter the command DCPROMO under Run. The computer account can then be migrated to the target domain and the computer added as a second server. Remember that you need an SBS 2003 CAL for every member server within the SBS 2003 domain.

The migration of a backup domain controller (BDC) under Windows Server NT 4.0 is not possible because SBS 2003 natively uses the Windows 2000 Active Directory function mode. This mode does not allow any NT-based BDCs. To continue using a BDC, you must reinstall it and then add it as a member server to the SBS 2003 domain.

The details of the tasks to be performed are as follows:

- If users have not exported their Outlook rules, you must do this now.

- Make sure that the domain administrators group on the source server belongs to the pre-defined administrators group. If you deleted the group on any client from the pre-defined group, you will have to add this again.

- If firewalls are running on the client computers, such as the Internet Connection Firewall under Windows XP, these should now be disabled.

- When upgrading from SBS 4.5 you must also remove the *Modem Sharing Client*, *Microsoft Fax Server Client*, and *WinSock Proxy Client* applications. The last is sometimes also called the *Microsoft Proxy Client*.

- To ensure the correct DHCP configuration, you must release and renew the IP address for each client. This ensures that all clients have acquired their IP address from the new DHCP server on SBS 2003.

- Make sure that Service Pack 6a is installed on all Windows NT 4.0 Workstations and member servers.

- Next delete the desktop links for the shared folder and the company folder. You must also delete or update all links that point to the source server. The same holds for entries in the Internet Favorites folder that point to the source server, for example, the Microsoft Small Business Server Web Site.

- Even network printers or fax printers that point to the source server must be deleted. The printers are configured anew on the target server (see step 5) and are then again available to the clients.

- Finally you must carry out a virus scan on each computer and then disable real-time virus protection. Then log off from each client.

Step 4—Carrying out the Migration

To carry out the migration, ADMT is installed on the target server and used to migrate existing computers, users, and group accounts. Based on the client information collected in steps 1 or 2, you must decide whether the quotas for Exchange need to be modified. Furthermore, all shared folders and application data must be moved to the target server. If you are using SQL Server, the SQL databases must also be transferred to the target server. This is your last chance to take a backup of the source server, if you have not done so already.

Installing ADMT

First install ADMT on the target server. You will find the program on CD 1 of SBS 2003 in the folder \i386\Admt\Admigration.msi. Follow the instructions in the installation wizard to install the program.

ADMT Configuration on the Target Server

If you have clients in your domain with the operating system Windows NT 4.0 Workstation or member servers running Windows Server NT 4.0, you must first perform the following steps:

1. Enter the command cmd under Run. At the command line enter the following lines:

```
Net local group "Pre-Windows 2000 Compatible Access" everyone /add
```

```
Net local group "Pre-Windows 2000 Compatible Access" "anonymous logon" /add
```

Make sure you type the quotation marks in both the command lines.

2. Restart the target server.

Migration of User Accounts

1. Open a command line on the target server and enter the following command:

```
Runas /netonly /user:NameSourceDomain\Administrator
"mmc\"%ProgramFiles%\Active Directory Migration Tool\Migrator.msc\""
```

Replace NameSourceDomain with the appropriate NetBIOS domain name.

If you close ADMT, you may only start it from the command line and not from the entry in the start menu.

2. Enter the password for the administrator account when asked. The ADMT GUI appears.

3. In the Action menu click on User Account Migration Wizard. Configure the Wizard with the following information:

User account names more than 20 characters long are automatically abbreviated to 20 characters after migration and may thus appear truncated on the target server.

ADMT Wizard page	Action to be taken
Test or Make Changes	Click on Test the migration settings and migrate later?. The log files will help you identify and remove any errors. To start the final migration, click on Migrate now?.
Domain Selection	Enter the names of the source and target domains here. If after clicking Next you get the error message Access denied (Error=5), close the ADMT Wizard and check whether the passwords for the administrator account are identical on the source and target servers and the password has been entered correctly when restarting ADMT from the command line.
User Selection	Click on Add and then Advanced. The entry Select this object type is automatically set to search for user accounts. Then click on Find Now. You will see a list of all user accounts. Select all the user accounts you want to migrate and then click OK.
	The following user accounts cannot be migrated: Administrator, Guest, IUSR_Servername, and IWAM_Servername.
	When migrating from SQL Server 7.0 the SQLAgentCmdExec account may not be migrated. For other applications that require a separate user account, refer to the application's documentation to find out whether a migration is possible.

ADMT Wizard page	Action to be taken
Organizational Unit Selection	For the target OU navigate to MyBusiness\Users\SBSUsers.
Password Options	Click on Same as user name. This automatically sets the password to the first 14 characters of the username. By default these entries are saved in the following file: \Program Files\Active Directory Migration Tool\Logs\Passwords.txt. These temporary passwords can be changed after the migration is completed. If you want to migrate the original passwords, click on Migrate passwords. Instructions about the appropriate configuration for password migration can be found in article KB 325851 of the Microsoft Knowledge Base.
Account Transition Options	Click on Target same as source. Enable the checkbox Migrate user SIDs to target domain. Then click on Next followed by Yes. You must then restart the source server and log in with the administrator account. Only then can you click OK on the target server to continue.
User Account	Under User Name enter the pre-defined administrator account and enter the password. Make sure that the name of the source domain is entered under Domain.
User Options	Activate the checkboxes Translate roaming profiles and Update user rights. Also make sure that the checkboxes Fix users' group memberships and Do not rename accounts are checked.
Naming Conflicts	Here you should select the option Ignore conflicting accounts and don't migrate.
Completing the User Account Migration Wizard	As soon as you click Finish you will see a status window for the migration. The migration of user accounts is over if the status displayed is Completed. To check if there are any errors, click on View Log. The log file is available for the simulated migration as well as the real one.

Migration of Group Accounts

1. Open a command line on the target server and enter the following command, provided ADMT is not running:

```
Runas /netonly /user:NameSourceDomain\Administrator
"mmc\"%ProgramFiles%\Active Directory Migration Tool\Migrator.msc\""
```

Replace NameSourceDomain with the appropriate NetBIOS domain name.

If you close ADMT, you can only restart it with the above command-line and not from the entry in the start menu.

2. Enter the administrator password when asked. The ADMT GUI appears.
3. In the Action menu click on Group Account Migration Wizard. Configure the Wizard with the following information:

ADMT Wizard page	Action to be taken
Test or Make Changes	Click on Test the migration settings and migrate later?. The log files will help you identify and remove any errors. To start the final migration, click on Migrate now?.
Domain Selection	Under Source domain the name of the source domain must be entered, for example sbs2000.local, and under Target domain the name of the target domain, for example sbs2003.local.
Group Selection	Click on Add and then Advanced. The entry Select this object type is automatically set to search for group accounts. Then click on Find Now. Then click on Find Now. You will see a list of all group accounts. Select all the group accounts you want to migrate and then click OK.

Remember that the following group accounts cannot be migrated: Administrators, Users, Domain Administrators, Domain Users, Domain Guests, Print Operators, Guests, Account Operators, Replicators, Server Operators, and Security Operators.

The groups Domain Name$$$ and MTS Impersonators may also not be migrated. |

ADMT Wizard page	Action to be taken
Organizational Unit Selection	For the groups select MyBusiness\SecurityGroups as the target OU.
Group Options	Select the entries Update user rights, Fix membership of groups, Migrate group SIDs to target domain, and Do not rename accounts.
User Account	Under User Name enter the predefined administrator account and its password. Make sure that the name of the source domain is displayed under Domain.
Naming Conflicts	Here, the Ignore conflicting accounts and don't migrate option should be selected.
Completing the Group Account Migration Wizard	As soon as you click Finish you will see a status window for the migration. The migration of group accounts is over if the status displayed is Completed. To check if there are any errors, click on View Log. The log file is available for the simulated migration as well as the real one.

Migration of Computer Accounts

Computer accounts can only be migrated for computers with the operating systems Windows NT 4.0 Workstation and Server, Windows 2000 Professional and Server, Windows XP Professional, and Windows Server 2003.

If there are clients in your domain with the operating systems Windows NT 4.0 Workstation or member servers running Windows Server NT 4.0, remember to first run the command described in the *ADMT Configuration on the Target Server* section before starting ADMT.

Also make sure that the domain administrators group on the source server is a member of the pre-defined administrator group. If this default setting has been changed, you must add the group again. Moreover real-time virus protection programs and hardware firewalls must be disabled on all client computers.

1. Open the command prompt on the target server and enter the following command, provided ADMT is not yet running:

```
Runas /netonly /user:NameSourceDomain\Administrator
    "mmc\"%ProgramFiles%\Active Directory Migration Tool\Migrator.msc\""
```

2. Replace the NameSourceDomain with the appropriate NetBIOS domain name.

If you close ADMT, you may start it only with the above command and not via the entry in the start menu.

3. Enter the administrator password when asked. The ADMT GUI appears.
4. In the Action menu click on Computer Account Migration Wizard. Configure the Wizard with the following information:

ADMT Wizard Page	Action to be taken
Test or Make Changes	Click on Test the migration settings and migrate later?. The log files will help you identify and remove any errors. To start the final migration, click on Migrate now?.
Domain Selection	Under Source domain the domain name of the source domain must be entered, for example sbs45, under Target domain the name of the target domain, for example sbs2003.local.
Computer Selection	Click on Add and then Advanced. The Select this object type entry is automatically set to search for computer accounts. Then click on Find Now. You will see a list of all computer accounts. Select all the computer accounts you want to migrate and then click OK. Make sure you do not select the computer account of the source server or computer accounts on which the operating systems Windows 95, 98, or ME are running.

Furthermore, you should ensure that all the computers to be migrated are switched on and connected to the network.

For all server computer accounts (other than the source server, which is not migrated), rerun the Computer Migration Wizard and add the servers on the Organizational Unit Selection page of the OU SBS Servers. |
| Organizational Unit Selection | For all client computers navigate to MyBusiness\Computer\SBSComputer, and for servers to MyBusiness\Computer\SBSServer as the target OU. |
| Translate Objects | Make sure that all the checkboxes on this page are enabled. |

ADMT Wizard Page	Action to be taken
Security Translation Object	The option Replace must be enabled here. Then click on Next. Click OK if the following message is displayed: Userrights translation will be performed in 'Add' mode only. Any other objects will be translated according to your mode selection.
Computer Options	Enable the Do not rename Computers option and set the number of minutes for a restart after completing the migration to 1.
Naming Conflicts	The Ignore conflicting accounts and don't migrate option should be selected here.
Completing the User Account Migration Wizard	As soon as you click Finish you will see a status window about the migration. The migration of computer accounts is over if the status displayed is Completed. To check if there are any errors, click on View Log. The log file is available for the simulated migration as well as the real one. After you click on Close you will see a status dialog in the window Migration Tool Agent Monitor about the connection to client computers.

If the migration of a computer fails after the migration of the agent in the course of configuring the client, try the following to solve the problem:

1. Check all entries in the log files.
2. Make sure that the computer account has not been created in Active Directory. To do this, open the MMC Active Directory Users and Computers on the target server.
3. Run the Computer Migration Wizard once more and migrate the account again.

As long as you are migrating computer accounts only in test mode, you will get a message with the event ID 37075 in the event display. This is normal in test mode because the domain is not changed when accounts are migrated in this mode.

After you have migrated all clients successfully, you may still not log on to them. Logging on is possible only after completing *Step 6—Configuration of the Clients*. Otherwise Outlook Profiles are not migrated.

Changing Exchange Quotas

When migrating from Exchange 5.5 if the mail quota on the source server is set to 200 MB (200,000 KB) for sending and receiving e-mails and the warning threshold is set at 175 MB (175,000 KB), you need not change the settings on the target server. If, however, higher values have been set on the source system, you must change the quota values for the target system accordingly. To do this, perform the following steps:

1. On the source server open Start Menu/Programs/Microsoft Exchange/Microsoft Exchange Administrator.

2. Double-click on Exchange Location, Configuration, then on Server and Your Server. Then double-click on Private Information Store.

3. From the File menu open Properties. Make a note of the values there.

4. On the target server open the Server Administration from the Start menu and click on Advanced Administration.

5. Double-click on Organization Name (Exchange), Administrative Groups, First Administrative Group, then on Server and Your Server. Then double-click on First Storage Group and select the entry Properties from the context menu of Mailbox Store.

6. Open the Limit Values tab and enter the values of the source server for the maximum mailbox size and the warning threshold in the appropriate fields.

Moving Exchange Mailboxes

The mailboxes of Exchange Server 5.5 are migrated to the target server with the help of the *Exchange Server Migration Wizard.*
At this point you may not log on to any clients and open Outlook. Starting Outlook is only possible after completing *Step 6—Configuring the Clients.*

During the migration of the Exchange Server, all real-time virus protection programs and disk utilities on this server should be stopped. To migrate the mailboxes, perform the following steps:

1. On the target server open Start/Programs/Microsoft Exchange/Preparation/Migration Wizard. Enter the following information while the Migration Wizard is running:

Migration Wizard Page	Action to be taken
Migration	Select Migration of Microsoft Exchange.
Migration of Exchange Server	You must now make sure that LDAP (Lightweight Directory Access Protocol) is enabled. To verify this, open Start Menu/Programs/Microsoft Exchange/Microsoft Exchange Administrator on the source server. Double-click Exchange Location, Configuration, Protocols and LDAP (Directory) Site Defaults. This protocol must be enabled.
Migration Target	Here you can only accept the default option Migration to a Computer running Exchange Server.
Source Exchange Server	Enter the name of the source server, the administrator account, and its password.
	If you have changed the Exchange SA password so that it is no longer the same as the password of the pre-defined administrator account, you must change the Exchange password back to its original value. Further instructions can be found in article 285297 in the Microsoft Knowledge Base.
Migration Information	Confirm the default setting Creation of E-Mail Accounts.
Account Migration	Select all the accounts that you want to migrate. The wizard cannot be used for migrating the administrator's mailbox. To export this account, save the mails in a PST file from an Outlook client and then re-import them. The rules for the administrator mailbox must also be exported.
	The migration of mailboxes for the user accounts can only be done after you have migrated the user accounts themselves to the target server with the help of ADMT.
Container for New Windows Account	Navigate to Domain Name\MyBusiness\Users\ SBSUsers.

2. Follow the instructions to close the Migration Wizard.

Moving the Shared User Folders

The easiest way to move the shared user folders is with the xcopy command on the command line. Alternatively, you can use the program Robo Copy. This program is a part

of the Windows Server 2003 Resource Kit Tools and can be downloaded from
`http://go.microsoft.com/fwlink/?LinkId=20249`.

Before starting the copying process, make sure that the user folders are not larger than 1 GB. By default the quota for the user folders is fixed at 1 GB under SBS 2003.

To move the user folders perform the following steps:

1. Open a command prompt on the target server and enter the following command:

```
Xcopy \\Sourceserver\Users \\Targetserver\Users_/e /o /d /h /v
                             /c>>c:\Kopier.txt
```

The meaning of the parameters in this command is as follows:

- /e: All sub-directories are copied, even if they are empty.
- /o: The information in the Discretionary Access Control List (DACL) and information about the ownership of the files is copied.
- /d: Only those files are copied whose source time is later than the target time. If only those files are to be copied that have been created after a specific time, use the option /d: m-d-y, where the date must be given in the format month-day-year.
- /h: Hidden and system files are also copied.
- /v: Each newly written file is verified.
- /c: All errors are ignored.
- >>C:\Kopier.txt: The results of the copying action are written to the file Kopier.txt on drive C. Check this file after completing the copying process to see if there are any errors. You can also compare the number and size of the files in the source and target servers.

Since the pre-defined groups of the source server have not been migrated, you must modify the rights for the user folder on the target server. To do this, perform the following steps:

1. Select Properties from the context menu of the user folder on the target server.
2. Select the Security tab. Remove all user names and group names listed here as unknown accounts. Then click on Advanced.
3. Disable the checkbox Subordinate objects to inherit the rights of higher-level objects, if applicable. Include those with the entries defined here. Then click on Add and add the user groups with the rights given in the following table:

User group	Rights
Domain administrators	Full access. Enable the checkbox Only transfer rights for objects and/or containers in this container.
Folder operators	Full access. Enable the checkbox Only transfer rights for objects and/or containers in this container.
SYSTEM	Full access. Enable the checkbox Only transfer rights for objects and/or containers in this container.
Domain users	Browse folders/run files, list folders/read files, read attributes, read advanced attributes, create folders, attach files and read rights. Disable the checkbox Only transfer rights for objects and/or containers in this container.

4. Take these steps for each user folder.

User-Defined Login Scripts

If you have been using user-defined login scripts on the source system, copy these from the NETLOGON folder of the source server to the NETLOGON folder of the target server. If these scripts reference other files, these should also be copied to the target server.

Moving other Shared Folders

For each folder to be moved create a share of the same name on the target server and assign the same rights to it as on the source server. Then move the contents of these folders as described in *Moving the Shared User Folders* above.

When creating the shares on the target server remember that the quota settings apply even to these folders if they have been created on the same partition as the user folders.

Moving the Company Folder to the Intranet Website

The Company folder used in SBS 4.5 is not available in the same format under SBS 2003. The contents of this folder are moved to the internal website created by the SharePoint Services. To move the folder, perform the following steps:

1. Open Server Administration on the target server and click on Internal Web Site.
2. In the detail view click on Import Files. A wizard appears.
3. On the page File and Document Library Path enter under Copy Files From the path \\Sourceserver\Company. Under Copy Files To you can either accept

the default setting http://companyweb/General Documents or specify or create another library via Browse.

4. By default all files larger than 50 MB are not copied. To change this setting, open a browser window and enter the address http://Targetserver:8081. Click on Configure the Virtual Server Settings, then on Companyweb, and finally on General Settings. Here you can specify the maximum size.

5. Furthermore, all files with certain extensions, for example .exe or .vbs, are blocked by default. To change these settings, again enter the address http://Targetserver:8081 in a browser window. Then click on Manage Blocked File Types to modify the settings.

In general only files with data are copied.

Moving Other Data

If more data is to be moved that is not in any of the folders just described, it must likewise be copied. This also holds for application data. If rights are irrelevant for this data, it can simply be copied. On the other hand, if the ownership of the files and the settings in the DACL are to be preserved, use the program *Xcopy* or *Robo Copy*. You will find the exact procedure described above.

If you are using SQL databases that are to be migrated, perform the following steps:

1. Enter the following command at the command prompt on the target server: \\Sourceserver\Driveletter$.

2. Navigate on this drive to the storage location of the desired files and copy these to the desired location on the target server. Repeat this process for the data folders of all applications.

If you have created your own websites on the source server under IIS 4.0 (Internet Information Server), you must copy these files to the target server and then create the websites afresh under IIS 6.0. For this procedure you can also use the *IIS 6.0 Migration Tool*.

Now you can install all the necessary applications on the target server.

Moving SQL Databases

If you are using the Premium Version of SBS 2003 and want to migrate existing databases of the SQL Server, perform the following steps:

If SQL Server 2000 is not yet installed on the target server, perform this installation now. More information about moving SQL databases between SQL servers can be found in the Microsoft Knowledge Base Article 314546 and on the subject of restoring databases in Chapter 7.

Step 5—Configuring the Target Server

In this step you will connect the user accounts with an SBS 2003 user template and distribute applications to the clients so that they can access the SBS 2003 network the very first time they log in. Additionally, further configuration settings will have to be made on the target server, for example the creation of distribution lists or the configuration of the Microsoft Connector for POP3 mailboxes. The detailed steps are as follows:

Rights for the Migrated Accounts

To ensure that users have the correct rights to access the resources on the SBS 2003 network, you must specify the user rights on the target server.

While making these settings you can also—if required—specify the rights for remote access. You can also distribute the Connection Manager Configuration Package. With this the required settings for the connection of mobile and remote clients are configured.

For specifying user rights perform the following steps:

1. Open Server Administration on the target server. Click on User and then on User Administration.
2. On the Template Selection page select an SBS 2003 account template for each migrated account. You should accept the default setting for preserving the user rights.

If a user account does not appear on the user selection page, make sure that this account is not disabled. To verify this, open the Server Administration on the target server, click on Users, and in the detail view select Enable from the context menu of the disabled account.

3. Then follow the instructions to complete the wizard.

If you were not using Exchange Server before the migration, a new mailbox is now created automatically for each user.

Distribution of Applications

Applications can only be distributed to clients with the operating systems Windows 2000 and XP Professional. For all other operating systems the installation must be done manually on the client. For member servers running Windows Server NT 4.0 you will find additional instructions in the Server Administration under Server computers/More Information/Configuring additional Servers.

To configure more than five clients, you must first add additional licenses. SBS 2003 comes with only five CALs.

1. Open Server Administration on the target server and click on Client Computers.

2. In the right pane click on Assign Applications to Client Computers. Enter the following information in the wizard that appears:

Wizard page	Action to be taken
Client computers	Select all the clients here to which you want to distribute client applications.
Client applications	Confirm the default settings here. If you are using ISA Server 2000 on the target system, you must distribute the Firewall Client to all clients. To do this, click on Change Applications. On the page Available Applications click on Add. Then enter the application name Firewall Client or navigate via Browse to \\Targetserver\Mspclnt\Setup.exe

3. Follow the wizard's instructions to complete the process.

Completing the Task List of Administrative Tasks

If you have closed the task list during the above activities, you can reopen it now by clicking Task List in Server Administration. You can now perform the following administrative tasks:

- **Adding a new printer**: you can set up all the printers afresh here.

- **Adding users and computers**: This step is only required if you are adding new accounts to the migrated ones.

- **Fax configuration**: If you have a faxmodem, you can set it up now.

- **Configuring monitoring**: Here, you can configure server performance and load reports. Messages for alarm options are also specified here.

- **Backup configuration**: Here you can specify options for Windows Backup. If you are using a third-party backup program, you should not make any entries here.

These administrative tasks have already been described in detail in Chapter 2.

Transferring User-Defined Settings from the Source Server

In this step all user-defined configurations such as DHCP range options (scopes), settings for routing and remote access, group policies, or DNS settings are transferred to the target server. In short, all the relevant settings that cannot be migrated using a wizard are transferred manually to the target server in this step.

E-mail Distribution Lists and Retrieval Policies

All user-defined retrieval policies must be recreated on the target server. The same holds for migrated distribution groups that contained pre-defined groups such as the administrator group as members. You must now again add the pre-defined groups of the target server to the distribution group. To do this, perform the following steps:

1. Open Server Administration and in it the entry Distribution Groups.
2. Click on the desired distribution group in the right pane. On the Members tab you can again add the desired pre-defined group accounts.

Microsoft Connector for POP3 Mailboxes

This configuration is required if you have POP3 mailboxes that you want to download to the Exchange Server. To do this, perform the following steps:

1. Open the entry Internet and E-Mail in Server Administration.
2. In the right pane click on Manage POP3 E-Mail. Then click on Open POP3 Connector Manager.
3. The remaining configuration of POP3 e-mail is as described in the context of the task list in Chapter 2.

Updating User-Defined Login Scripts

After you have copied the user-defined login scripts into the NETLOGON directory of the target server, they have to be made usable for the users. To do this, you must update each user account so that it references the login script on the target server. In the login script you must change all references to the source server to point to the target server.

Step 6—Configuring the Clients

In this step Windows 2000 and XP Professional clients automatically receive the settings for e-mail and proxy. On all other client operating systems you have to undertake the configuration manually. You can now also import the Exchange folders so that the clients are fully configured for connecting with the new Exchange Server. The detailed steps are as follows:

Configuration of Windows 2000 / Windows XP Clients

1. Log on to each client computer with the respective user account. You will be prompted to change the password for the account. Make a note of the password you enter in each case. Keep the security of the password in mind as after the migration is completed the target server will be connected to the Internet. If you have not migrated the old user passwords, the default location for the passwords is the file \Program Files\Active Directory Migration Tool\Logs\Passwords.txt. As already mentioned, the password consists of the first 14 characters of the username.

2. If you have selected the client under step 5 for the distribution of applications, the Client Installations Wizard appears when you start the computer. Here, click on Start Now.

3. Then open the Control Panel and double-click on Mail. Then update the e-mail properties in accordance with the target server.

If you are using ISA Server, you must configure the proxy settings of Internet Explorer.

1. To do this, open Internet Explorer. In the Tools menu click on Internet Options.

2. On the Connections tab click on LAN Settings.

3. Enable the checkbox Use a proxy server for your LAN and enter the name of the target server for Address and 8080 under Port.

4. If you have ISA Server only on the source server and not on the target server, ensure that the proxy checkbox in LAN Settings as well as the checkbox Automatically detect settings under Automatic Configuration are disabled.

After this you can again reactivate the real-time virus protection on the client.

Configuration of Older Windows Clients

Client computers with operating systems older than Windows 2000 must be configured manually for the target domain. The applications are then installed manually on them.

1. After you have made these two preparations, log on to each client computer with the respective user account. When you log on you will be prompted to change the password for the account.

Make a note of the password you enter in each case. Keep the security of the password in mind as after the migration is completed the target server will be connected to the Internet. If you have not migrated the old user passwords, the default location for the passwords is the file \Program Files\Active Directory Migration Tool\Logs\Passwords.txt. As already mentioned, the password consists of the first 14 characters of the username.

2.   Then open the Control Panel and double-click on Mail. Then update the e-mail properties in accordance with the target server.

3.   Delete all Internet Explorer Favorites that reference the source server as these are no longer valid.

4.   Delete or update all links to the shared user and company folders. This also holds for links to network folders and other links that refer to the source server.

5.   If printers and fax devices that point to the source server have been configured here, delete them. Updated printers and fax devices have already been set up in *Step 5—Configuring the Target Server*.

6.   If the Firewall Client of the ISA Server has already been installed, you must modify the name of the target server on the clients in accordance with that on the target server. To do this, double-click the Firewall Client icon in the System Tray. Enter the new name of the server in the options that appear.

If you are also using ISA Server, you must configure the proxy settings of Internet Explorer.

1.   To do this, open Internet Explorer. In the Tools menu click on Internet Options.

2.   On the Connections tab click on LAN Settings.

3.   Enable the Use a proxy server for your LAN checkbox and enter the name of the target server for Address and 8080 for Port.

4.   If you have ISA Server only on the source server and not on the target server, make sure that the proxy checkbox in the LAN Settings as well as the checkbox Automatically detect settings under Automatic Configuration are disabled.

After this you can again reactivate real-time virus protection on the client.

Testing the Network Connection

Finally you must check whether the migrated clients have functional network access. To test this, disconnect the source server from the network and send a test e-mail to the users. If the e-mail reaches the recipients, it indicates that Internet settings have been configured correctly.

You must also test if shared folders, shared applications, and network printers are available and functional.

After completing these steps you can log on to a client as administrator and import the mailbox as well as the rules for the administrator account to the target server.

The earliest offline address books will become available is one hour after the installation of SBS 2003. If you attempt to access them before this, you will not succeed as the offline address book has not been generated at this point in time.

Importing Public Folders

The next step is to import the public folders of the source server that have been exported to a .pst file. To do this, perform the following steps:

1. Log on to a client with the administrator account and start Outlook.
2. Double-click Public Folders and then All Public Folders.
3. Import the .pst file into the currently selected folder.

If special rights had been configured for the public folders, you must restore these.

1. To do this, open Server Administration on the target server. Double-click on Advanced Administration, Administrative Groups, First administrative Group, Server, Your Server, First Storage Group, Information Storage for Public Folders, and Public Folders.
2. In the right-hand pane select Properties from the context menu of the desired folder.
3. On the Rights tab click on Client Rights. Update the fields Name, Role, and Rights with the desired values.

Step 7—Completing the Migration

After completing the migration you can stop the source server. It does make sense, however, to keep it in readiness for a period of time so as to be able to solve configuration problems on the new server to the extent that these relate to information that can be transferred manually from the old server. Only after this transition period should the old server be completely taken out of operation and formatted. You can set this machine up as a second server, for example.

Furthermore, ADMT should again be uninstalled from the target server, and all pre-Windows 2000 rights, which could have been applied temporarily in the course of the migration, set back to the original values.

Resetting Rights

You need to carry out this step only if you have configured extended rights on the source server for pre-Windows 2000 compatible access in *Step 4—Carrying Out the Migration*. If you are using member servers running Windows Server NT 4.0, skip this step so that these servers can access the domain.

1. To reset the rights, open the command prompt on the target server and enter the following commands:

```
Net localgroup "pre-windows 2000 compatible access" everyone /delete
```

```
Net localgroup "pre-windows 2000 compatible access" "anonymous logon" /delete
```

2. Restart the target server and log on using the administrator account.

Uninstalling ADMT

After all the accounts have been migrated you should uninstall ADMT from the target server. This can be done via Control Panel/Software/Add or remove Programs.

Laying down Password Policies

If you have not migrated the old user passwords along with the accounts, you should now lay down a password policy that prompts users to change their passwords when they first log on.

1. To do this, open the Users entry in Server Administration.
2. In the right window pane click on Specify Password Policies. If possible, you should select all the three options offered.
3. Then click on Configure Password Policies, and then click on Immediately.

If you are going to allow access to the server over the Internet, you should always activate password complexity. The complex password requirement comes into effect only after three days, so you have enough time to set up further user accounts in peace.

4. Always delete the password file created during account migration. This is the file \Program Files\Active Directory Migration Tool\Logs\ Passwords.txt.

Consider whether you want to give your users the option of changing their passwords. The advantage of permitting password changing is higher security, the disadvantage is that the administrator often has to reset passwords because users forget them. You will have to decide in each case (depending on your users) which option you want to exercise.

To enable or disable password changing open the Users entry in the Server Administration. Double-click on the desired account. On the Accounts tab you can enable or disable the Users cannot change their password checkbox.

Connecting the Target Server to the Internet

Finally, connect the target server's network adapter for Internet access to the appropriate cable. To test the Internet connection, open a website from any client. Also send a test e-mail to a mail account on the Internet. If you have configured the fax service, you should also send out a test fax.

Upgrading Small Business Server 2000

In contrast to a migration, in an upgrade SBS 2003 is installed on the original system. An upgrade is only possible if SBS 2000 or Windows Server 2000 or 2003 is installed. It is not possible to upgrade from SBS 4.5 or Windows Server NT 4.0.

In the course of the upgrade, the following steps are executed on the system:

- Operating system upgrade
- Configuration of the operating system
- Updating pre-existing SBS tools and server applications
- Working through the task list after completing setup

To upgrade an SBS 2000 machine, the SBS 2000 Service Pack 1 must be installed on it. Moreover, you must verify that the hardware requirements for SBS 2003 are fulfilled on the server. You should also carry out disk clean-up and defragmentation on all drives. You can start disk clean-up by entering the command cleanmgr.exe under Run and defragmentation by the command dfrg.msc. At lest 2 GB of free disk space must be available. This disk space is temporarily used during the setup. The hardware and software used so far must also be compatible with SBS 2003. The latest drivers for all hardware components must be installed on the SBS 2000. Even the BIOS should have the latest version number. Immediately before the upgrade you should carry out a complete virus check of the system.

Make sure you do not scan the Exchange drive M: when scanning for viruses. This can damage the Exchange database. By default the IFS (Installable File System) is mapped to the drive M: under Exchange 2000.

1. Take a complete backup of the system so that you can restore it in the event that there are problems with the upgrade. Test the backup by restoring some data at another location and comparing with the original.

> Make sure you do not backup the Exchange drive M: when taking the Exchange backup. This can damage the Exchange database. By default the IFS (Installable File System) is mapped to the drive M: under Exchange 2000.

2. If users are still connected to the SBS network at this time, request them to log off the network. You can do this using the following net send command:

`Net send * Please log off the domain in the next 5 minutes. No network and Internet connections will be available thereafter.`

The symbol * means that the message will be sent to all members of the domain.

3. If no firewall has been implemented on the network adapter that connects to the Internet, you should disconnect it at this time. The connection to the local network remains.

4. On SBS 2000 you should now stop all applications that use the local system account. If these applications are active at the time of the upgrade, they could lock the operating system files thus preventing them from being updated. To find out which applications use the local system account, enter the command `services.msc` under Run. Check for which applications Local System is displayed in the column Log in as. Note the start type of each of these services and stop it.

5. Finally, stop all real-time virus protection programs and other hard drive tools such as backup software.

Step 1—Installation

With the installation of SBS 2003 the operating system of the existing SBS 2000 is upgraded. After the upgrade installation is complete, no settings may be changed on the server until the task list that appears after the installation has been worked through.

The upgrade installation takes about 45 minutes on a server meeting minimum hardware requirements.

Step 2—Configuration of Windows

The installation of the operating system is followed by the configuration of Windows by SBS 2003. To put it more precisely, you are presented with the task list described in detail in Chapter 2 even in an upgrade.

The tasks are described only briefly here. About half an hour is required to complete the task list. You must log on to the system using the administrator account. Clicking the appropriate desktop link will take you to the page Continue Microsoft Windows Small Business Server Setup. Here, click on Next.

Enter the following configuration information in sequence:

- **Company information**: Verify the existing information about your company here.

- **Login information**: Select the Automatic login option so you do not have to enter the username and password after each restart.

- **Windows configuration**: Here you will see the Windows components that must be installed first before you can proceed further. Click on Next.

You will then see the Component Status dialog box that informs you about the installation and configuration status. This installation and configuration phase takes about 20 minutes. If the Component Selection dialog box is displayed, the installation of the components is over and you can install the server applications of SBS 2003.

Step 3—Installation of Server Applications

Now the existing server applications, for example Exchange and the system tools, are upgraded. In a standard installation this step takes 1.5 hours.

Even if SQL Server 2000 is installed on SBS 2003, an instance of Microsoft Data Engine (MSDE) is installed during the installation of SharePoint Services. This, however, has no effect on SQL Server 2000.

In the Component Selection dialog box all the components required for the installation are listed.

In the Data Folder dialog box you can enter an alternative storage location for Internet files. Moreover, you must also specify a storage location here for applications that were not installed under SBS 2000.

You can view the settings just made in the Component Summary dialog box and make changes if required.

As before, the Component Status dialog box informs you about the status of the installation. If problems or errors occur during the installation, you will see the Component Message dialog. Any messages, including error messages, are displayed.

You will then see the Finishing the Installation dialog. Click on Finish and then on OK. The system is then restarted.

Step 4—The Task List

To complete the installation you must work through the final task list. It is recommended that you follow the sequence shown here. This step takes about half an hour.

To begin working, click on Start. As soon as you have completed a task on the list, you can check the corresponding checkbox to mark the task as completed.

The task list comprises two areas—network tasks and administrative tasks. You can get more information about each task by clicking More Information. The options for the various tasks have already been described in detail in Chapter 2.

Network Tasks

The following tasks need to be completed here:

- **Display proven security methods**: For the security of the network you should implement the methods and procedures suggested here.

- **Set up the Internet connection**: Before you begin with this, you must reconnect the server to the Internet. Start the e-mail and Internet connection wizard. You can configure the network settings, e-mail settings, firewall, and secure website of the server here. When configuring password policies you should always opt for complex passwords if the server is going to be accessed from the Internet.

- **Configure remote access**: This configuration is required if you want to allow clients to connect to the SBS 2003 network via VPN or a dial-up connection. The Remote Access Wizard is started for the configuration. All users who currently have permission to access the network from outside must be added to the Mobile Users group. This is done via the task Migrate Users in administrative tasks. SBS 2003 also offers the Connection Manager Configuration Package. The configuration settings for mobile and remote clients can be made with the help of this package. To do this, click on the Add users and computers task in the task list.

- **Activate the server**: Activation is required for SBS 2003. This is done most conveniently via the Internet. Follow the instructions of the Activation Wizard.

- **Add client licenses**: If you have more than five clients you must add more licenses to the five included CALs. To do this, the server must first be activated.

Administrative Tasks

The following tasks need to be completed here:

- **Migrate users**: In this step the SBS 2000 user templates are updated to SBS 2003. If you do not update them, the new features will not be available to the users.

- **Update client computers**: In this step the clients receive the settings for SBS 2003. If you do not update the client computers, new features will not be available.

- **Configure fax**: Here you can configure a faxmodem for sending and receiving faxes.

- **Configure monitoring**: Notifications about various alarms and reports about the performance and load of servers can be configured here.

- **Configure backup**: Configure the options for Windows backup.

After you have completed these tasks, the upgrade of SBS 2000 is over. For further administrative tasks you can use the Server Administration console.

Finally you must restart all the services that you stopped before beginning the upgrade and restore their start type to the original values.

Upgrade of Windows Server 2000/2003

The upgrade of Windows Server 2000 or 2003 proceeds in more or less the same way as the upgrade process for SBS 2000. To prepare for the installation execute all the steps described in the section *Upgrading Small Business Server 2000*.

However when upgrading a Windows 2000 or 2003 server you must keep in mind the role that this server is to play in the network as the SBS 2003 can only form one domain which must also be the root domain. If, for example, the server to be upgraded is the domain controller of a subordinate domain, you can definitely configure this for a new domain, but no trust relationships to other domains can be set up with the SBS domain.

Step 1—Installation

This step proceeds exactly as described the section *Upgrading Small Business Server 2000*.

Step 2—Configuration of Windows

In the second step, after the company information dialog you will see the Internal Domain Information dialog box. The DNS and NetBIOS names for the domain are specified here. If possible you should accept the recommended default values. Remember that, by default, you cannot change the computer name, DNS name, or NetBIOS name after installing SBS 2003. To change these you will have to fall back on the Active Directory support tool **Domainrename (RENDOM)**.

If the server has several network cards, you will also see the Information about local Network adapters dialog. Select the card for internal network access here. While this network card is being configured, the others are automatically disabled by the setup program. The settings of these cards remain intact.

You will see the Login Information dialog only if the server is not a domain controller. You have the option of logging on automatically until the installation is completed.

The Data folder dialog is displayed only if the storage location for the Active Directory is not valid. You must then select another directory.

This is followed by installation of the components. The installation status is displayed.

Step 3—Installation of the Server Applications

The installation proceeds exactly as in the upgrade from SBS 2000.

Step 4—The Task List

You are presented with a task list in the end even when upgrading from a Windows Server 2000/2003 system. The network and administrative tasks contained in it are as described in the section for upgrading SBS 2000.

4

Exchange Server 2003 and Fax Services

This chapter introduces you to Exchange Server 2003 and the fax services of SBS along with their administration and configuration. Both these components can be installed and run separately from each other. They are discussed together only because both the services belong to the area of communication.

The version of Exchange Server 2003 bundled with SBS 2003 does not differ functionally from the separately purchasable standard edition of Exchange Server 2003.

Structure of Exchange Server 2003

We begin with a brief description of the Exchange Server database.

The Exchange Server Database

As with Exchange 2000, Exchange 2003 uses an **ESE** (Extensible Storage Engine) database. This is a further development of the ESE97 database used by Exchange 5.5. In this database, the private mailboxes of users are located in the mailbox data store and the public folders are located in the public data store. When creating the database the administrator must decide which storage function to use. This cannot be changed later.

Each data store consists of a series of individual files. An **EDB file** (.edb) contains all the e-mails and appointments that the user has created under Outlook. This file is optimized for quick access to the information contained inside it. It is stored in the EDBF format internal to Exchange.

Apart from the EDB file the data store also contains an **STM file** (.stm). This is a stream file. It contains the information placed in the data store via the two supported internet protocols. To enable access to the information in the STM file, the corresponding message header is also stored in the EDB file.

Storing an E-Mail in the Database

When a user receives an e-mail via the Internet, the contents of the e-mail are first stored in the STM file. At the same time the mail header is stored in the EDB file. The moment the user accesses the e-mail from his or her copy of Outlook, it is converted on the fly while being transmitted to the user. In the STM file on the other hand, the e-mail remains preserved as original content. The moment the user stores the e-mail under Outlook or changes it in any way, the STM file is deleted and a copy is stored in EDBF format in the EDB file.

Administering Exchange Servers

This chapter gives you an overview of the fundamentals of administration as well as the administration programs of Exchange Server 2003.

Administration Aspects

The configuration settings of Exchange are made at two different places. Via the System Manager you can access all the components of Exchange Server. In this management console (see the following figure) all the Exchange organizations are shown hierarchically ordered and can be administered.

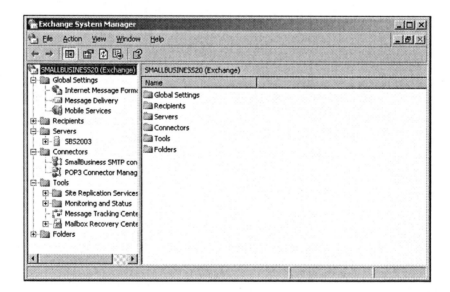

To start the System Manager, select the SMALLBUSINESS20 (Exchange) entry in the SBS administration console or click on System Manager under Start Menu/All Programs/ Microsoft Exchange/. This MMC is stored in the file Exchange System Manager.msc.

If, on the other hand, mailboxes are to be configured for the users, click on Active Directory Users and Computers for this purpose. This can also be opened via the appropriate option in the SBS administration.

After the installation of Exchange 2003, administrative groups and routing groups are disabled by default. In small and medium-sized companies, this offers the advantage of a simplified user interface as these groups are generally not required.

Administrative Groups

Administrative groups are created to give specific users administrative rights for certain tasks. In contrast to Exchange 2000, no administrative group is available by default under Exchange 2003 on SBS 2003. The reason for this is that administrative groups are generally used in larger environments. So, to avoid confusion, administrative groups are initially disabled.

To create an administrative group, perform the following steps:

1. Open the System Manager and from the context menu of Exchange Organization select Properties.
2. Mark the Display Administrative Groups checkbox. You must then restart the System Manager.
3. In the new container Administrative Groups you will find the First Administrative Group entry. To create a new group, click New in the context menu of the container.
4. Give the new group a name and click OK.
5. To assign rights to the group, click Assign Object Administration in the context menu of the new group. A wizard is started.
6. On the Users and Groups page select the persons to whom you wish to delegate parts of the administration. You can modify the rights of already existing users and groups through the Edit button. Users however may not carry the Inherited attribute for this. Properties for the administrative group are inherited if the user or group has already been given administrative rights for the higher-level Exchange Organization. You cannot add a user who is a member of one of the groups that carry the predicate Inherited.

    After you have selected a user via Add, you can assign him or her one of the three following rights:

    o   Exchange Full Administrator: Complete administration of the Exchange system information along with changing of rights is possible.

    o   Exchange Administrator: Complete administration of the Exchange system information is possible.

     o   Exchange View Only Administrator: Only the Exchange configuration information can be displayed.

7. Click on OK and Finish to close the wizard.

Security Implementation under Exchange

This section gives you basic instructions for the implementation and configuration of the settings relevant to security. You should carry out the procedures described in this section before you undertake further administrative tasks under Exchange.

Rights under Exchange

To set rights for the Exchange objects, you should use the wizard for assigning administrative rights. The rights for the following Exchange objects can be specified individually. You can assign default Active Directory rights such as read or write and also advanced rights such as Create Public Folders.

To use the wizard, take the following steps:

1. Open the System Manager and select Object Administration from the context menu of the organization or administrative group that is to be given an administrative right.

2. In the wizard first click on Next and then under Users and Groups click on Add. Use Browse to select the desired user or group.

3. In the Delegate Control window (see the following figure) select one of the following three options under Role:

     o   Exchange Full Administrator: Complete administration of the Exchange system information along with changing of rights is possible.

- o Exchange Administrator: Complete administration of the Exchange system information is possible.
- o Exchange View Only Administrator: Only the Exchange configuration information can be displayed.

4. If existing rights for a user or group are to be modified, click on Edit. You can delete users and groups from the list via Remove.

To configure rights for individual objects, do the following:

1. Open the System Manager and select Properties from the context menu of the object to be administered.

2. Open the Security tab and assign the appropriate rights to the user there. In the upper part of the tab you will find the default Active Directory rights and in the lower part the special Exchange rights. For each right select Allow or Deny if the setting can be changed. You can configure the special rights via Advanced.

Authentication on the Virtual Server

A virtual server under Exchange is a collection of services that are seen by a client as a virtual server. This is an instance of a specific protocol, such as SMTP or POP3, with a definite quantity of IP address/connection combinations and a set of configuration properties. The virtual server thus has all the resources such as network name, IP address, etc. that are required for running an application.

To determine whether the user is authorized to log in under Exchange 2003, the virtual server uses four different authentication methods. These are:

- **Anonymous access**: Any user can access the virtual SMTP and NNTP servers without giving a username and password.

- **Standard authentication**: The user must supply a Windows username and password. This information is sent unencrypted. For encryption on virtual NNTP, HTTP, IMAP4, and POP3 servers, you should use SSL (Secure Sockets Layer)/TSL (Transport Layer Security) with the standard authentication.

- **Integrated Windows authentication**: This authentication method is available for SMTP and NNTP. The user enters his or her Windows username. The information is passed on to the server so that the user does not have to enter a password and thus no unencrypted data is sent over the network.

- **Simple authentication and security**: The username and password are encrypted using the NTLM security package (NT LAN-Manager). However, the message data is not encrypted.

To configure the authentication, take the following steps:

1. Open the System Manager and navigate to Server/Server name/Protocols. Double-click the desired protocol and select Properties from the context menu of Virtual Default Server.

2. Open the Access tab and click on Authentication (see the following figure).

3. Select the available authentication methods for each virtual server. To make the standard authentication secure, you should select the Enable SSL Client Authentication checkbox. Then click on OK.

Authentication on the Virtual HTTP Server

Authentication on the HTTP server is not done via the System Manager—it is done through the Internet Information Services (IIS). The virtual HTTP server of Exchange displays the default website of IIS. To set up the authentication for this virtual server, take the following steps:

1. In the Administration open the Internet Information Services Manager. Navigate to Server name/Websites/default website.

2. Open Properties and switch to the Directory Security tab. Under Authentication and Access Control click on Edit (see the following figure).

3. Under Authenticated access mark the checkboxes for the desired authentication methods. Apart from the Integrated Windows Authentication and Basic authentication methods, you can also select the Digest Authentication for Windows domain servers and .NET Passport authentication options.

- **Digest Authentication for Windows domain servers**: This method is similar to the standard authentication except that a challenge-response mechanism is used for the user authentication on the server. The password is not sent to the server.

- **.NET Passport authentication**: This authentication is done with the help of a .NET passport account.

4. To allow anonymous access, select the Enable anonymous access checkbox and select a user account for the access.

Monitoring Connections with Virtual Servers

In addition to choosing the authentication method, to increase security you can also allow or deny access to specific computers, subnet ranges, or domains. By default, access is granted to all computers. To change this, take the following steps:

1. In System Manager open the desired virtual server. Open its Properties and switch to the Access tab.

2. In the Connection Control area click on Connection.

You can select the Only the list below option. To do this, you must select the desired computers via Add. Or you can select the All except the list below option. Here, too, you can use Add to make a choice. While adding you can either select Individual Computers and give their IP address, Group of Computers and enter their subnet, or Domain and enter its name. If you want to add a computer whose name you know but do not know its IP address, click on DNS Lookup. Then click on OK.

Monitoring Connections to the Virtual HTTP Server

As already described in the last section, the connection to the virtual HTTP server is also monitored via the IIS Manager console.

1. In the Administration open Internet Information Services Manager. Navigate to Server name/Websites/Default Website.

2. Open Properties and change to the Directory Security tab. Under Restrictions for IP Addresses and Domain Names click on Edit.

3. Select the Access allowed or Access denied option and enter individual computer names, a group of computers, or a domain name via Add. Then click on OK.

Enabling Logging for the SMTP, NNTP, and HTTP Protocols

For the Internet protocols SMTP, NNTP, and HTTP you can log all the commands that the respective virtual server receives. The following contents are logged: IP address and name of the client, date and time of the e-mail, and the number of bytes sent. You will find these entries in the event log after activating logging. You should activate logging for security reasons.

1. Open the System Manager and navigate to the SMTP or NNTP virtual server. Open Properties and then the General tab.

2. Select the Enable logging checkbox there. The default log format for SMTP is W3C extended, and for NNTP it is Microsoft IIS.

Click Advanced to select the log file and schedule. On the Advanced tab you can select the options to be logged, for example server IP address, protocol version, or cookies. Then click on OK.

The logging for the HTTP protocol is done using the IIS MMC.

1. As described above, open the Properties of the default website and change to the Website tab.

2. Select the Enable logging checkbox and select a log format. The log options are set for the SMTP and NNTP protocol.

Configuration of the Exchange Server

To configure the Exchange Server navigate in the System Manager to the Server container and open the server's Properties from its context menu.

On the General tab you will first see the version of the server (see the following figure). Version 6.5 stands for Exchange 2003. The build number gives the patch level—the installed Service Pack of the Server.

A brief word about the Service Pack for Exchange Server: Service Pack 1 has already been published for the *normal* Exchange Server. Theoretically, this can be installed for the SBS Exchange Server also. However, this can lead to problems later. Due to contradictory statements and reports about the mode of functioning of the Service Pack, we advise against its installation here.

Logging

The checkboxes Enable subject logging and display and Enable message tracking both stand for the Exchange Server's function of tracking the messages within the Exchange Organization (see the following figure). This option is particularly useful for locating problems in e-mail transmission.

First select the Enable message tracking checkbox to enable logging. If you want to collect more information, also enable the Enable subject logging and display checkbox. Remember, however, that enabling logging on the Exchange Server has an impact on its performance. Especially in the SBS 2003 environment, this can have a very negative effect since Exchange Server has to be installed on the same server as the operating system and the other SBS 2003 components. So, you should only activate logging if you want to analyze a specific problem.

Since the log can quickly grow to several megabytes, select the Remove log files checkbox and select a value for the number of days after which the log files should be deleted. Under Log file directory you can also specify the storage location for log files.

The This is a front-end server checkbox is only of interest in larger environments. A front-end server serves as a proxy server and forwards all e-mail requests to the back-end server. The front-end server itself does not provide any information, it only forwards the requests. For this scenario there should be at least two Exchange Servers available.

On the Diagnostics Logging tab you can specify the Exchange Services to be logged. To do this, select the desired services under Services. Under Category you can specify the degree of logging for each category of service: None, Minimum, Medium, or Maximum.

Language Settings

Language support for Outlook clients is set from the Country information tab. To ensure that a user of the Outlook client receives all information in accordance with his or her Outlook language setting, you must add the existing languages to the Exchange Server. By default the only country information available is English (US). After you have added new country information, the appropriate code pages for supporting country-specific formats must be installed manually on the server. The system must then be restarted.

Mailbox Administration

On the Mailbox Management tab you can specify when mailboxes should be searched for old data that is to be deleted.

Under Start mailbox management process you can either select the option Run at midnight on Friday (or Saturday or Sunday) or create a user-defined schedule. If you want details about the administration process, select the Send summary report to administrator or Send detailed report to administrator option. Under Administrator you can select the user who is to receive the report.

Full-Text Indexing

The Full-text indexing tab controls the capacity utilization of the Exchange Server for searching the information store and creating index files. This accelerates the search process. For the System capacity Utilization, you can set the level to Minimum, Low, Medium, or Maximum. When making the choice ensure that the indexing process does not load the server so much that it cannot perform its usual tasks.

Monitoring

Under Monitoring you can specify which services of the Exchange Server are to be monitored. By default Exchange Services are only added if you click on Microsoft Exchange Default Services under Name. You can enable monitoring for some hardware components and connectors as well. Click on Add to monitor the following components (these are shown in the screenshot that follows the list):

- Available virtual memory: The more memory there is, better the performance of the server.

- CPU Utilization: Less load on the CPU guarantees quick response time.

- Free disk space: There should be enough disk space available for an emergency evacuation.

- SMTP queue growth: The queue should not overflow due to network problems.

- Windows 2000 service: Select the services to be monitored here. Bear in mind that you should only select services that really require monitoring.

- X.400 queue growth: As with the SMTP queue, overflowing should be prevented here.

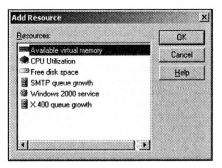

Setting Up New Monitoring Policies

To set up a new monitoring policy on the Exchange Server, click on Add in the Monitoring tab and select one of the six components just mentioned. You will get a separate window for each component with individual monitoring options. If, for example, you select CPU utilization (see the following figure), then under Duration you can specify the number of minutes for which the selected condition must be obtained. Under Warning state and Critical state you can specify the processor load percentage. Click on OK.

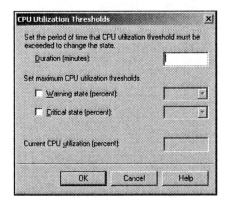

The configuration of values for other components is analogous and self-explanatory. To change the configured values later, select the components and click on Details. Monitored components can also be removed later using Remove.

If you click on Microsoft Exchange Default Services (see the following figure), you will see a list of Exchange Services (the moment one of these services stops, the status is set to Warning or Critical):

Receiving Monitoring Messages

You can set things up so that you are notified as soon as a warning threshold is crossed or a critical situation develops on the server. For example, you can be informed when a service repeatedly fails and could possibly damage the information store in the process. Otherwise there is the danger that the repeated failure goes unnoticed if the service again becomes available as soon as a user requests it.

To configure messaging, take the following steps:

1. In System Manager navigate to Extras/Monitoring and Status/Messages and select New/E-Mail Message from the context menu.

2. By default, the Monitoring server field (see the following figure) is set to the local mail server from which you are starting System Manager (you can select another server).

   Under Servers and connectors to monitor you can select the servers and/or connectors that are to be included in the notification. Next choose whether the notification should be sent when the monitored objects are in the Warning state or the Critical state. Finally enter the e-mail addresses of the persons who are to receive warning messages.

Properties [?] [x]

E-mail

Monitoring server:

[   ] [Select...]

Servers and connectors to monitor:

[This server   ▼] [Customize...]

Notify when monitored items are in:

[Critical state   ▼]

[To...] [   ]

[Cc...] [   ]

[E-mail server...] [   ]

Subject: [%TargetInstance.ServerStateString% on %TargetInstan]

%TargetInstance.Name% has reported a
%TargetInstance.ServerStateString%. Reported status is:
Queues - %TargetInstance.QueuesStateString%
Drives - %TargetInstance.DisksStateString%
Services - %TargetInstance.ServicesStateString%

[OK] [Cancel] [Apply] [Help]

In addition to e-mail notification, you can also set up script notification.

1. Open the path in System Manager as just described and select New/Script notification.

2. Carry out the configuration as just described.

3. Under Path to executable (see the following figure) give the location of the script to be run. Instead of a script you can also run a program.

Properties [?] [x]

Script

Monitoring server:

[   ] [Select...]

Servers and connectors to monitor:

[This server   ▼] [Customize...]

Notify when monitored items are in:

[Critical state   ▼]

Path to executable:

[   ]

Command line options:

[   ]

[OK] [Cancel] [Apply] [Help]

4. Optionally, you can specify parameters for starting the script or program under Command line options.

For example, you can have the failed service restarted via the script and simultaneously have a message sent to the administrator. A sample script can be as follows:

```
Net start pop3svc
If errorlevel 1
Net send Administrator There was an error in starting the POP3 Server
```

Server Policies under Exchange

The real purpose of configuring server policies is to simplify the administration of multiple Exchange Servers. Although it is true that, as a rule, only one Exchange Server is deployed in the SBS 2003 environment, the policies are briefly discussed here.

In contrast to the group policies of Active Directory, the application of an Exchange Server policy irrevocably overwrites an object's property. This means that the original value of the property cannot be restored even if the server policy is withdrawn. With an Active Directory group policy, on the other hand, the property is affected only so long as the policy is in force. As soon as the group policy is removed, the original value of the property is restored.

To configure an Exchange server policy, take the following steps:

1. In the System Manager navigate to Exchange Organization/Administrative Groups. From the context menu of the desired administrative group select New/System Policy Container.

The Administrative Groups container is not available by default. The creation of a new administrative group has already been described in the *Administrative Groups* section.

2. You cannot choose a name for the container as it is always set to System Policies. This folder cannot even be renamed later. There can be only one System Policies folder within an administrative group.

3. To set up a new server policy, select New/Server Policy from the System Policy container.

Other Settings

The Policies tab tells you what policies have been applied on the server. To edit these policies you have to modify them via the security policies and group policies in the Administration program group.

Via the Security tab you can view and change the rights configured for the individual Users and Groups.

E-Mail Administration

Below we give an overview of the fundamental administrative tasks pertaining to e-mail traffic. These include setting up distribution groups, a schedule for retrieval of e-mails, addition of connectors, and the synchronization of e-mails.

Setting Up Mailboxes

A mailbox is automatically set up for a user in Active Directory when you add a new user. By default all SBS users are in the Organizational Unit (OU) MyBusiness/Users/SBSUsers of the domain. To add a new user here or in another OU, select New/User from the context menu of the OU. To create a user:

1. First enter the full name and username of the user. Then click on Next. Then enter the password and password options for the user. Click on Next.

2. In the next dialog (see the following figure) make sure that the Create an Exchange Mailbox checkbox is checked.

The user's mail alias is entered under Alias. This is used for identifying the user on the Exchange Server. The Exchange Server on which the user's mailbox is stored is entered under Server. If several servers are available, you can pick one from the drop-down list. The Mailbox Store indicates the storage location on the Exchange Server.

3. Click on Next and Finish to create an Exchange mailbox for the new user.

Editing the Mailbox

After you have created a user you can edit the settings for the user. To do this, select Exchange Tasks from the user's context menu. A wizard is launched.

On the Available Tasks page (see the following figure) you can perform four different tasks on the mailbox. Select the desired task in each case and click on Next.

- Move Mailbox: The user's mailbox is moved to another Exchange Server. This will not normally be used in the SBS environment.
- Delete Mailbox: The user's mailbox is deleted.
- Configure Exchange Features
- Remove Exchange Attributes

Setting Up Distribution Groups

A distribution group is a group of users who are meant to receive specific e-mails not a group of users to whom specific rights can be assigned. No user or file rights can be given to a distribution group.

1. To set up a distribution group, open the server administration and select Add Distribution Group from the context menu of Distribution Groups.
2. Give the new distribution group a Name, a Description, and an E-Mail Alias. Then click on Next.

3. In the Group Membership window select the users and/or groups that are to be members of the new distribution group. Then click on Next.

4. In the Groups Manager window you can select a user or a group from the Leaders list. This user can later add users to the distribution group. He or she can do this later from Outlook 2003. The leader must be a person or group that is a member of the distribution list. If you do not select a group leader, only an administrator can edit group memberships. Click on Next.

5. In the Group Options window you can specify whether this distribution group may receive Internet e-mails and whether these should be archived. To permit the former, enable the Allow this Group to receive e-mail messages from outside the network checkbox. Disable the checkbox if this is an internal distribution group. This reduces the risk of e-mail viruses and spam. By marking the Create public folder for archiving e-mail messages sent to this group checkbox you specify that a Group name Archive folder be created for this group under the public folders. Copies of all e-mails sent to this group are stored in this folder. Then click on Next and close the wizard.

Setting Up Distribution Groups from Outlook 2003

If you have specified a leader of the distribution group in step 4 above this user can edit the membership list of the distribution group. This procedure is carried out from the leader's local copy of Outlook 2003, and not the server administration. An administrator can also create new distribution groups via Outlook 2003.

1. In Outlook 2003 click File/New/Distribution list. Enter the name of the group under Name.

2. Then click on Select members to add users from the address book. In the Display names from the following address books dialog you can choose from various address books. Via Add new you can also add members to the distribution who are not in an address book.

3. To create the group, click on Save and Close. The distribution group is saved in the Contacts folder under Outlook.

After creating the distribution group you can also assign a leader for the group who is allowed to administer it.

1. In the server administration open the Properties of the desired distribution group and switch to the Administered by tab.

2. Click on Change and enter the username. This user can now administer the distribution group.

Schedule for E-Mail Delivery

You can specify a schedule for Exchange Server in accordance with which e-mails are retrieved and received. This schedule is set up via the Set up Internet connection wizard in the task list of the server administration and is self-explanatory.

Editing Mailbox Size Restrictions

If a user repeatedly has problems in sending or receiving e-mails because he or she has exceeded the size limit for his or her mailbox, you can increase this limit for that user. To do this, take the following steps:

1. Open the Users entry in the Server Administration.

2. From the context menu of the relevant user account select Properties.

3. In the Properties window of the user switch to the Exchange—General tab and click on Storage limits. You will see the Storage limits dialog.

4. Disable the Use mailbox store defaults checkbox.
   Thereafter you can specify all values for Issue warning at (KB), Prohibit send at (KB), and Prohibit send and receive at (KB). Confirm with OK.

The POP3 Connector and the SMTP Connector

The POP3 and SMTP connectors are installed by default with SBS. A connector's task is to ensure the flow of messages between two e-mail systems. The POP3 connector is responsible for message exchange between POP3 e-mail systems and the SMTP connector for the exchange between Exchange systems. The SMTP connector plays a subordinate role in the SBS 2003 environment as several Exchange Servers have to be deployed within the Exchange Organization for it to be used.

Of much more interest is the POP3 connector. With the help of the POP3 connector you can retrieve messages from external POP3 mailboxes and distribute them to user mailboxes under Exchange. The connector downloads these e-mails from the POP3 mailbox and resends them to the Exchange mailbox. For this to function, the username of the POP3 mailbox must be assigned to an individual mailbox or a distribution group.

In addition to forwarding to a user mailbox, the POP3 connector can also manage forwarding to a global mailbox. A global mailbox is set up to receive all e-mails sent to the domain. Thus, for example, all e-mails to info@firma.de, pmustermann@firma.de, or webmaster@firma.de land there. When downloading e-mails, the POP3 connector checks the To and Cc lines and on the basis of this information, forwards the messages to user mailboxes or distribution groups.

Bear in mind that in a global mailbox the names of recipients in the Bcc (Blind Carbon Copy) line cannot be read. The original Bcc e-mail is sent to the mailbox that receives all e-mails that cannot be delivered for the domain—by default, the administrator's mailbox.

Configuration of the POP3 Connector

To configure the POP3 connector, click on Internet and E-Mail in the server administration and then on Administer POP3 E-Mail. Then open the POP3 Connector Manager. To create a new POP3 account, click on Add. You now require the following information: username and password for the account, name of the POP3 server, and whether secure password authentication (SPA) is necessary. Next specify whether this is a user mailbox or a global mailbox and enter the Exchange mailbox to which the e-mails are to be forwarded. Click on OK.

You can also set global options for the POP3 connector. On the Schedule tab specify the interval at which e-mails should be retrieved from the mail server. There are pre-defined schedules for this, but you can also create your own schedule. Using Retrieve now you can retrieve mail immediately outside the scope of the plan.

On the Troubleshooting tab you will see an overview of the service status and the number of failed e-mails.

Under Service logging you can specify the degree of detail (minimum, medium, maximum, or none) for entries in the application log. Under Undeliverable Pop3 E-mail you can also indicate the mailbox to which all e-mails that cannot be forwarded to a valid user mailbox can be forwarded.

Adding more Connectors

In addition to the connectors installed by default, you can add some more. To do this, take the following steps:

1. Insert CD 2 of SBS 2003 in the CDROM drive and double-click the Setup.exe file in the EXCHSRVR65\SETUP\I386 folder.

2. In the installation wizard click on Next, say yes to the license agreement and enter the license number. In the Component Selection window click on the arrow in the Microsoft Exchange column under Action and then on Change.

3. Under Microsoft Exchange Services for Messaging and Collaboration you can select the following additional connectors:

   • Microsoft Exchange Connector for Lotus Notes
   • Microsoft Exchange Connector for Novell GroupWise
   • Microsoft Exchange Calendar Connector

4. To install, select the appropriate entry under Action. Then click on Next and follow the wizard's instructions.

Outlook Web Access

In addition to using Outlook on a local computer within the SBS network, you can also access your e-mails from a remote workplace via Outlook Web Access (OWA). This access takes place via a web browser. For this reason the client operating system is immaterial for OWA. It can be any Windows, Macintosh, or Linux/Unix client.

To access e-mails over the Internet, enter the following address in the web browser: https://External Name of the SBS/Exchange/. This opens a special Internet-based version of Outlook. It is this version that is referred to as OWA.

You can also make an OWA connection with a remote connection diskette. The prerequisite for this is that you should have completed the RAS wizard in the task list of the server administration.

In the server administration, open the Create remote connection diskette link under Internet and E-mail. Follow the wizard's instructions to copy the connection manager to a diskette. Insert this diskette in the desired clients and run the setup.exe file to install. Under Network Connections you will now find the new entry Set up connection with Small Business Server.

You can now connect remotely to the SBS network. To start OWA, enter the following address in an Internet browser: https://Name of the SBS/Exchange/.

Special Configuration for Exchange Server with more than 1 GB RAM

If Exchange Server 2003 is running on a machine with more than 1 GB RAM, and if there are mailboxes and/or public folders on this server, you must modify the boot.ini file to ensure optimal usage of the virtual memory. Additional start parameters for the operating system must be included in this file. Otherwise, the store.exe process, which uses 20 MB of memory when the system has just been (re)started, is seen in Task Manager to be using up to 500 MB in the course of the day. This can significantly slow down the server. It is not possible to free this memory without restarting the server—which is clearly not desirable for the server. That is why the modification in the start parameters is required.

For each process, 2 GB of virtual address space is allocated for the user mode and 2 GB for the operating system by default. If you enter the parameter /3GB in boot.ini, 3 GB is allocated to the user mode and only 1 GB to the operating system. Allocating only 1 GB of memory reduces the risk of memory fragmentation in the virtual address space of store.exe.

Modifying boot.ini

The boot.ini file is modified by adding the two parameters /3GB and /USERVA=3030. For a Small Business Server 2003 the entry could look as follows:

```
[boot loader]
Timeout=30 Default=multi(0)disk(0)rdisk(0)partition(1)\WINDOWS
[Operating Systems]
multi(0)disk(0)rdisk(0)partition(1)\WINDOWS="Windows Server for Small
Business Server" /fastdetect /3GB /USERVA=3030
```

SBS 2003—like Windows Server 2003—reserves 2 GB of virtual address space for the kernel and allows user-mode processes (like the Exchange 2003 information storage process store.exe) to use 2 GB of virtual address space. A specific amount of virtual memory is assigned to a process when it starts. This amount can increase during operation. By default, the memory usage of a process is much smaller than the address space allocated for that process. On an Exchange Server 2003 with more than 1 GB RAM a modification is made so that 3 GB of memory is available for user-mode processes.

Take the case of an Exchange Server 2003 with over 2 GB RAM. If the /3GB parameter is not set, a memory overflow is created if the virtual address space of store.exe reaches 2 GB. In this situation Task Manager shows that only 1.5 GB of memory is in use. This is however not correct, and the server actually has no more free memory.

The /USERVA parameter is a new parameter of Windows Server 2003. This makes it possible to distribute memory allocations for the user mode and kernel mode in a better way.

Fax Services

After the e-mail services of Exchange Server, fax services are the second communication option. Fax services enable fax clients to send and receive faxes. For this, the faxmodem installed on the SBS 2003 is used. This modem should be a class 1 faxmodem.

It is possible to install the fax services even if no modem is attached to the SBS 2003. However, using these services is obviously *not* possible in this situation.

Functional Model of the Fax Services

During the installation of the fax services a default fax printer is set up on SBS 2003. This shared printer is used for sending and receiving faxes. When the user wants to send a fax via the fax printer, the printer sends a command to the fax device to send the fax.

The fax services consist of three separate components. These are the fax service, fax (local), and the Microsoft fax console.

- **Fax service**: The fax service is the central component of the server. The fax service manager is called via Start/Programs/Accessories/Communication/ Fax/Fax Service Manager.

- **Fax (local):** With the help of fax (local) you can perform all administrative tasks, make advanced settings, and monitor the fax service. You can call these components from the server administration of SBS 2003.

- **Fax client console**: This MMC is also for administration. Here, you can monitor fax queues as well as send and receive faxes. You can call this MMC via Server Administration/Fax (Local) by clicking on Administer fax tasks.

Administering Fax Devices

You can add more faxmodems to SBS 2003 even after installing SBS 2003. Optimally, you should install at least two modems there, one to send and one to receive. When you install a new fax modem, it is automatically recognized by SBS 2003 if it is Plug & Play enabled. Otherwise you can add the device via Control Panel/Hardware.

All fax devices recognized by the fax service are displayed in the server administration under Devices and Service Providers/Devices. To see newly installed devices there, you must restart the fax service. Recognition of all the devices is possible only when the service is started.

The moment you add a new device it is configured by default for sending faxes, but not for receiving them. To specify whether a fax device should send and/or receive faxes, open the Properties of the device and configure the settings on the General tab.

If you have selected the Receive Faxes option, you must specify the number of Rings before answering for automatic receiving of faxes.

Furthermore, for a fax that is configured for sending, you must enter the TSID (Transmitting Subscriber Identification). For faxes that are configured for receiving, the CSID (Called Subscriber Identification) is entered. By default your company name is entered in both cases.

Regulating Access to a Fax Printer

Access to the fax printer can be regulated in the same way as access to a normal printer. To deny some users or groups access to the fax server, open the properties of Fax (Local) and then the Security tab. Here, you can add new users and groups or remove them and even configure rights for these individually. The following four default rights are assigned to a fax printer:

- Fax
- Administer fax configuration
- Administer fax documents
- Special rights

To configure special rights for a fax printer, click on Advanced and then on Edit. The following special rights are available for a fax printer:

- Submit low priority faxes
- Submit normal priority faxes
- Submit high priority faxes
- Display fax jobs
- Administer fax jobs
- View service configuration
- Administer service configuration
- Display archive for incoming messages
- Administer archive for incoming messages
- Display archive for outgoing messages
- Administer archive for outgoing messages
- Read rights
- Change rights
- Take over ownership

Incoming Faxes

This section shows you the settings that you can make for incoming faxes. Of particular importance in this context is the configuration of routing guidelines for incoming faxes.

Stopping Faxes from being Submitted

You can stop faxes from being submitted on the SBS at any time. To do this, select Properties from the context menu of Fax (local) and switch to the General tab. Mark the Disable submission of new outgoing faxes checkbox.

Routing Policies for Incoming Faxes

Routing policies are the processing methods for incoming faxes. In SBS 2003 you can print faxes, forward them by e-mail, save them in a folder, or add them to the document library of the SharePoint Services.

To specify the desired routing policy for the faxmodem, open the path Devices and Service Providers/Devices/Device Name/Methods for incoming faxes under Fax (local). To configure one of the policies, select its properties and enter the appropriate values, such as e-mail addresses to which the faxes should be sent or the folder in which the faxes should be saved. After you have configured a method, select Enable from its context menu. Each of these methods can always be disabled later.

Since you can select several methods, you must specify priorities for them. To do this, open the path Routing incoming messages/Global Methods under Fax (local). The default priorities are as follows:

Priority 1: Forward via e-mail

Priority 2: Save in folder

Priority 3: Print

Priority 4: Save in a document library

From the context menu items Up and Down you can create your own priority list.

Further instructions for configuring routing guidelines can be found in Chapter 2.

Outgoing Faxes

This section gives you more information about configuration settings for outgoing faxes.

If you want to prevent a faxmodem from sending fax messages, switch to the General tab under the properties of Fax (Local). Here, select the Disable sending new outgoing faxes checkbox. This means that users can no longer send new faxes to the Outgoing folder. If you select the Disable transmission of outgoing faxes checkbox, faxes that are already in the Outgoing folder will not be sent. Further settings for outgoing faxes can be made on the Outbox tab under the properties of Fax (local).

If you have selected the Include banner checkbox, the transmission information is printed on the margin of outgoing faxes. If the Allow use of personal cover pages option is selected, users can use cover sheets in their personal folders in addition to the standard cover sheets. Further instructions about cover sheets can be found in the *Fax Cover Pages* section later in the chapter. If the Automatically delete faxes older than checkbox is enabled, faxes that cannot be sent for the specified number of days are automatically deleted from the Outgoing folder.

Under Fax transmissions you can specify how often a failed fax should be resent. You can specify the waiting period under Retry after. Under Discount rate start and Discount rate stop enter the times between which cheaper tariffs for sending faxes are applicable. If you specify a period for the sending of faxes, all faxes are sent only in this period. At all times outside this period, **no** faxes are sent. This can lead to problems if faxes cannot be sent within this period due to overloading of the fax devices. Renewed attempts at sending are only made when the period kicks in again on the next day.

If a fax transmission begins within the discount period but exceeds the time limit, the transmission continues but the cheaper tariff is no longer applicable.

In defining the interval you should always consider if the fax capacity is adequate to send all waiting faxes within the pre-defined time. If this is not the case, you should increase the fax capacity or disable the schedule. Although you will not get the advantage of cheaper tariffs, you can be sure that all faxes will be sent immediately.

You can also configure receipt confirmations for outgoing faxes. These settings are made on the Receipts tab.

If the Enable message boxes as receipts checkbox is selected, users get a pop-up informing them about the successful sending of the fax.

If you want a confirmation by e-mail, select the Enable SMTP e-mail receipts delivery checkbox. Then enter the sender address, the SMTP server address, and the port in the appropriate fields. Then click on Authentication... to specify the authentication type for the SMTP server. You can choose between Anonymous Access, Standard Authentication, and Integrated Windows Authentication. In the last two cases, you must also enter the username and password.

Finally, you can also specify the maximum number of users to whom a fax can simultaneously be sent.

1. To do this, open the fax service manager via Start/Programs/Accessories/ Communication/Fax. Stop the fax service by clicking the relevant icon.

2. Open the registry with the `regedit` command and navigate to the key `HKEY_LOCAL_MACHINE\SOFTWARE\Microsoft\Fax\RecipientsLimit`. Enter the value here.

3. Restart the fax service via the fax service manager.

Working with Multiple Fax Devices

If several fax devices are installed on the SBS 2003, you can configure further options for the fax service. Different devices can be combined into groups that follow specific usage rules.

By default all fax devices can be found in the All Devices group under Fax (local)/ Outgoing Routing/Groups. To create a new group, click on New in the context menu of Groups and give the group a name. Within a group you can change the order of devices via the Up and Down context menus. You can also remove devices from a group.

Under Fax (Local)/Outgoing Routing/Rules you can specify how the various devices are to be used. To create a new rule, select New/Rule from the context menu of Rules (see screenshot overleaf).

First specify the country code under Country/region code; for USA this would be 1. If you do not know the country code, click on Select... and select the desired country. Then you can either enter a specific area code within the country or select all area codes via All areas. Under Target device you can specify an individual device or one of the device groups just created.

Monitoring Fax Services

You can monitor the fax services via the fax client console. The faxes can be monitored at four different stages. In the Incoming folder, faxes that are being received are shown. The Inbox shows faxes that have already been received. Under Outbox you will see faxes that are currently being sent, and the Sent Items folder contains faxes that have already been sent.

Each of the four folders has a Status column. One of the following status messages can be displayed in this column:

- Sending: The fax is being sent. The send process consists of dialing, initializing, and transmitting. This is displayed under Advanced Status.

- Outstanding: The fax is in the queue until a faxmodem becomes available to send it.

- Halted: A fax in the queue was halted either by the administrator or the user.

- Will be repeated: The sending of the fax will be repeated once the recipient's telephone line is free.

- Number of repetitions exceeded: The maximum number of send attempts has been exceeded. The maximum number can be set on the Outbox tab in the properties of Fax (local).

Archiving of Faxes

You can enable archiving for all incoming and outgoing faxes. If this is set up, faxes can be archived in specific folders.

To set up archiving for incoming faxes, select the Properties of Fax (local) and switch to the Inbox tab. Select the Archive all incoming Faxes in the following folder checkbox and enter the name of a folder. To archive all sent faxes, switch to the Sent items tab and select the Archive all sent Faxes in the following folder checkbox. To change the folder, click on Browse.

Additionally, you can also specify whether there should be an entry in the event log if the content of an archive folder exceeds a certain size.

In the Inbox and Sent Items tabs, select the Generate warning in event log checkbox. Specify the maximum size under Upper limit for quota. If this is exceeded, there is an entry in the event log. Under Lower limit for quota enter the value that must be reached for the event warning to stop appearing. To prevent continuous growth of the archive folder, you should enable the Automatically delete older faxes after option. Enter the number of days for which a received or sent fax should remain preserved in the archive folder.

Fax Cover Pages

Fax cover sheets are server-based cover pages. When a user wants to send a fax, he or she can select one of the cover pages and add it to the fax he or she is sending.

Four pre-configured cover pages are available by default in the server administration under Cover Sheets—Urgent, Info, Standard, and Confidential. All cover pages have the extension .cov (cover). The templates for the cover pages are in the \Documents and Settings\All Users\Application Data\Microsoft\Windows NT\MSFax\Common Coverpages folder.

To create a new cover page, select New/Cover Page from the context menu of the cover pages. This starts the cover page editor (see the following figure). If you want to change an existing cover sheet, choose Edit from the appropriate context menu.

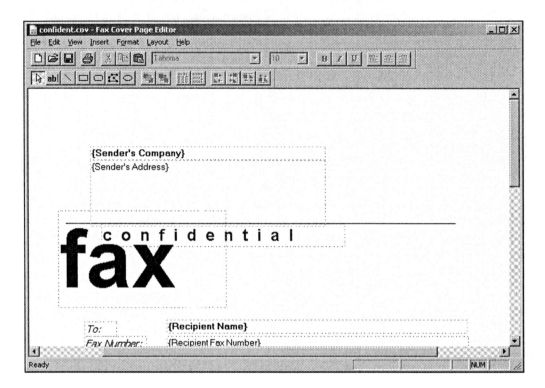

5
Windows SharePoint Services 2.0

The installation of SharePoint Services version 2.0 takes place automatically in the course of the SBS 2003 installation. The installation files can be found on CD 3 of the SBS 2003 installation media.

Since SharePoint Services installations made after 24 November 2003 can be problematic, you should always use an updated version of SharePoint Services. Customers also have the option of obtaining an error-free version of CD 3 free of charge from Microsoft. Use the order form at `https://microsoft.order-4.com/sbsrtmcd/` for this. More information about installation problems with SharePoint Services can be found in Chapter 13.

Task of the SharePoint Services

The Microsoft SharePoint Services constitute an innovation in SBS 2003 as compared to its predecessors. These services offer an HTML-based central administration as well as centralized access to documents, calendars, project data, presentations, and lists for collaborative work and communication on projects.

The central website for accessing these services is `http://companyweb`. This site is created automatically during the installation of SharePoint Services and set as the home page for Internet Explorer. Initially, it only has some sample data. This is how the companyweb page looks after installation:

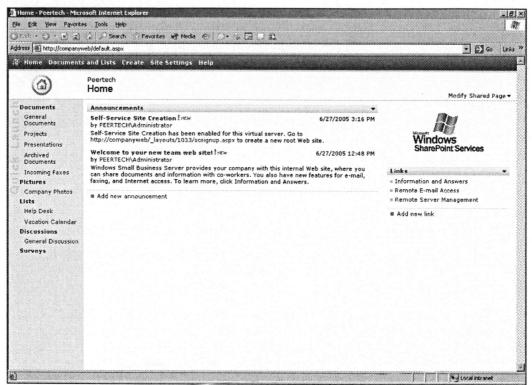

Figure 5.1: The website http://companyweb immediately after installation

To be able to use all the functionalities of SharePoint Services, users must deploy Microsoft Office XP or Microsoft Office 2003. Older versions of Office can cause problems. Office documents placed on the website cannot be edited or saved with these versions. Only viewing the website and making contributions is possible, since this only requires a web browser.

Features of SharePoint Services

You can make the following information available on the website:

- Documents for shared use by a team
- Information about tasks to be completed, important events, or project-related information
- Publication of contacts and their telephone numbers within the project or the help desk
- Discussions for team members
- User surveys

As soon as any of the above information is added to the website by an administrator or users, new links are automatically generated on the site so that the page is always in the most current state. Optionally, notifications about all changes on the website can be sent to one or more persons.

Additionally, the page is highly customizable for users. So the information can be sorted in accordance with specific criteria such as date, author, or subject. Uninteresting information can be blanked out and pre-defined views configured for specific users.

The following content areas are available by default on the website:

Content area	Description
Documents	General Documents: The files in this are displayed along with their properties—for example, change date and person who made the last change—and a hyperlink to the file is also given.
	Projects: The documents here are classified according to projects and can likewise be edited and saved.
	Presentations: Company presentations can be stored and edited in this area.
	Archived Documents: Archived documents that are not currently required are stored in this area.
	Incoming Faxes: You can collect all incoming faxes here. For this, the relevant option in the task list of the fax wizard must be enabled.
Pictures	Company Photos: You can make user photos available here, for example those of a company picnic, or other photos that are meant to be available for all users.
Lists	Helpdesk: Data and information about helpdesk personnel can be entered here.
	Vacation Calendar: The vacation calendar gives a quick overview of the vacation days of colleagues and can be linked with Outlook.
Discussions	General Discussions: Team members can conduct discussions here in the style of a newsgroup.
Surveys	No surveys are provided by default. A survey directed at users can be created quickly with the help of a wizard.
Announcements	Current announcements and instructions for the team.
Hyperlinks	Hyperlinks that are interesting and important for team members for their work are displayed here.

The contents of the website can be modified via a web browser by adding or removing specific content. You can also select different views for the website with the help of a web browser. However, if you want to change the layout of the company website, you need an HTML editor such as FrontPage 2003, which comes with the Premium Edition of SBS 2003.

From the security point of view you can give users different rights for access to the website. Some users can only be given read rights while others can add documents or even edit the website configuration.

The Structure of the SharePoint Services

The pre-configured website http://companyweb is based on the Windows SharePoint Services. This website uses Internet Information Services (IIS) and a database created by MSDE (Microsoft SQL Database Engine) or SQL Server. The contents of the website, such as documents, lists, settings, etc., are stored in MSDE, while the website itself on the virtual server Companyweb is stored in IIS. Further instructions about the virtual server can be found in the section *Managing the Virtual Server*.

Document Libraries

Document libraries are the central location for documents within a website. A document library can be further classified using subfolders. When a user opens a library via a website, the files contained in it are shown as hyperlinks and can be opened and edited. When the mouse pointer is placed on the link, the user gets more information about the document.

Other users can also be given e-mail notification about changes in documents. The fax library, in which all incoming faxes are stored, is a special case.

Incorporation of New Sites

For a better overview—especially with extensive constructs—it may make sense to add new sites to the Companyweb website. These sites can be configured to have different rights or the same rights as the main site.

Uninstalling the SharePoint Services

There are several options for uninstalling the SharePoint Services. You can either uninstall them directly from the server or just from the virtual server.

If you want to remove the SharePoint Services from SBS 2003, go to Control Panel/ Software/Windows SharePoint Services and click on Remove. This does not remove the Microsoft SQL Server Desktop Engine (MSDE). This component must be removed separately. The content of the website is also not deleted when uninstalling SharePoint Services. You can also opt for this procedure if you want to or have to repair the SharePoint Services.

If you want to remove the SharePoint Services from the virtual server, you can either use the HTML administration page or the command line.

To uninstall from the administration page:

1. In Server Management click on SharePoint Central Administration.

2. In the Configure Virtual Server area, click on the link Configure Virtual Server settings and click the desired server from the list. By default you will find the following entries there: Companyweb, Microsoft SharePoint Administration, and Default Web Site.

3. In the Virtual Server Settings window, click on the Remove Windows SharePoint Services from virtual Server link in the Manage Virtual Server area.

4. You will see the Remove Windows SharePoint Services from virtual Server dialog. If you select the Remove without deleting content database option here, only the SharePoint Services folders are removed from the virtual server, while the content database remains intact. Therefore it is possible to connect either the same or another virtual server to the database later. If you select the Remove and delete content databases option, both the folders of the SharePoint Services as well as the content database are deleted from the virtual server. In this case the websites can only be restored via a backup. Make your choice and then click on OK.

If you want to uninstall via the command line using the service program `stsadm.exe`, perform the following steps:

1. If you want to delete only the SharePoint Services folders but retain the database, use the following command:

```
Stsadm.exe -o unextendvs -url http://Name of the virtual server
```

2. If you want to delete the folders and the database, use the following command:

```
Stsadm.exe -o unextendvs -url http://Name of the virtual server
                          -deletecontent
```

By uninstalling the SharePoint Services using one of the methods just described, you can ensure that the uninstallation proceeds cleanly and you can reuse the server for other websites or applications.

Administering the SharePoint Services

This section describes the most important administrative tasks that you can carry out under the SharePoint Services.

Administration Points of the SharePoint Services

An HTML-based administration area is available for the administration of the SharePoint Services. The administration can be done locally as well as from a remote computer. You must always have administrator rights to do this. The central administration pages and the website administration pages are available to administrators.

Central Administration Pages

The central administration page is accessed via the Server Management under Internal Web Site/Central Administration. On these central pages you can configure settings for the web server as well as the virtual server. Essentially, the default values of the server are specified here. The values specified here are passed on to all newly created virtual servers. The following figure shows the main page of the central administration.

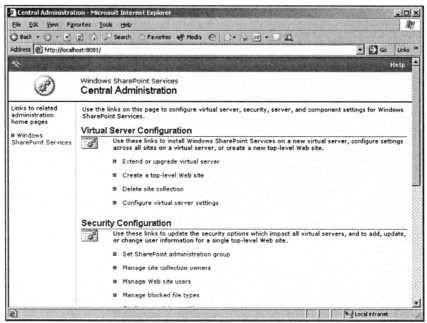

Figure 5.2: The main page of the central administration

To access these sites you must either belong to the local administrators group or the SharePoint administrators group. The central administration pages are called via the start menu or directly from a web browser.

If under Start/Programs/Administration in SBS 2003 you click on Microsoft SharePoint Administration, what you get is not the administration page of the Microsoft SharePoint Services but, incorrectly, the administration page for FrontPage Server Extensions 2002. It is not possible to start the administration web page via this menu entry.

Instead, go to Start/Programs/Administration and open SharePoint Central Administration. This opens the correct page.

To open the central administration page from a web browser, enter the address `http://Servername:Port number` or `http://localhost:Port number`. The port number is the one specified during the SharePoint installation. The default port is 8081.

Website Administration Pages

The settings for the individual websites are configured via website administration.

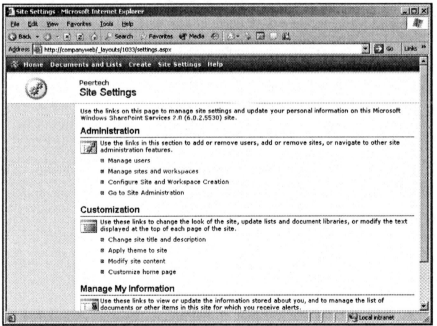

Figure 5.3: The configuration page for the website settings

You can access these on each website from the Web site settings menu. The configurations made here refer only to the current website. You can, for example, edit the title, content, or design of the current site.

Website Groups

Website groups are used to assign and administer rights for the website. For a user to have any access to the website, he or she must be a member of at least one of the various website groups. There are different website groups in all with different levels of rights. The following table shows the rights of the individual website groups.

Website group	Description
Guest	A guest can have read access to certain pages or lists but is not able to see the whole website. This website group cannot be deleted or modified. Moreover, you cannot add users directly to this group. Users to whom you grant access to certain document libraries or lists via list rights automatically become members of the Guest website group.
Reader	A member of this group may view pages and entries and also create higher-level websites via the Self-Service Site Creation feature. However a reader cannot add content to the websites. If a reader creates a site via the Self-Service Site Creation feature, he or she becomes the owner as well as a member of the administrator website group for this website.
Contributor	In addition to the rights of a reader, a contributor has the following rights: adding, deleting, and editing elements, adding, removing and updating personal web parts (see the section *Editing a Site*), administering personal views, browsing directories, and creating website groups common to all websites.
Web designer	In addition to having the rights of a contributor, a web designer can perform the following actions: administering lists, adding and modifying pages, canceling checks, and applying and defining style sheets, designs, and margins. A designer may change the structure of the website and create document libraries or lists.
Administrator	An administrator has the rights of the other groups and can additionally administer website groups and create new SharePoint websites. This website group cannot be modified.

Website groups are defined for each individual SharePoint site. To change the settings for all SharePoint sites or the virtual server, the user must be a member of the administrator group of SBS 2003 itself or a member of the SharePoint administrators group. Membership of the website administrators group is not sufficient for such tasks.

You can change the rights of a website group or add new website groups with user-defined rights. If you withdraw certain rights from website groups, bear in mind that some rights are mutually dependent. If you delete a right on which other rights depend, the dependent rights are deleted. If you add a right for which other rights are required, these are automatically added.

The rights of both the guest and administrator website groups cannot be edited.

If a user creates a new website, he or she automatically becomes a member of the administrator website group. As a result of this he or she is shown as the website owner. Under some configurations it is necessary to have a second user. This user also automatically becomes a member of the administrator website group. The owner of a website can be changed via the central administration on the Web Site Collection Owner or through the command line program stsadm.exe using the siteowner parameter.

Various methods are available to you for authenticating users. The authentication method for the SharePoint Services is based on the IIS authentication methods. The desired method is specified at the time of setting up the web server. The methods available are:

- Anonymous authentication
- Standard authentication
- Integrated Windows authentication
- Digest authentication and advanced digest authentication
- Certificate authentication (SSL)

Editing the Contents of the Company Website

This section describes various tasks for modifying the company website and its contents.

Adding Data to the Company Website

The company website makes little sense if it has no documents and files for editing. An import function is available to import pre-existing files, for example, from a file server.

1. In the Server Management open Internal Web Site and then the link Import Files. A wizard is launched.

2. In the File and Document Library Path dialog select the data source via Browse. Under Copy files to the default path is Companyweb/General Documents. This target path can also be changed via Browse. Then click on Next and close the wizard. The selected files are copied to the selected document library.

Creating a New Document Library

When importing files, you can only select a pre-existing document library. To create a new document library:

1. Open the page http://companyweb and in the Create menu, select the Document Library entry from Document Libraries.

2. In the New Document Library dialog, first enter the name and description of the new library.

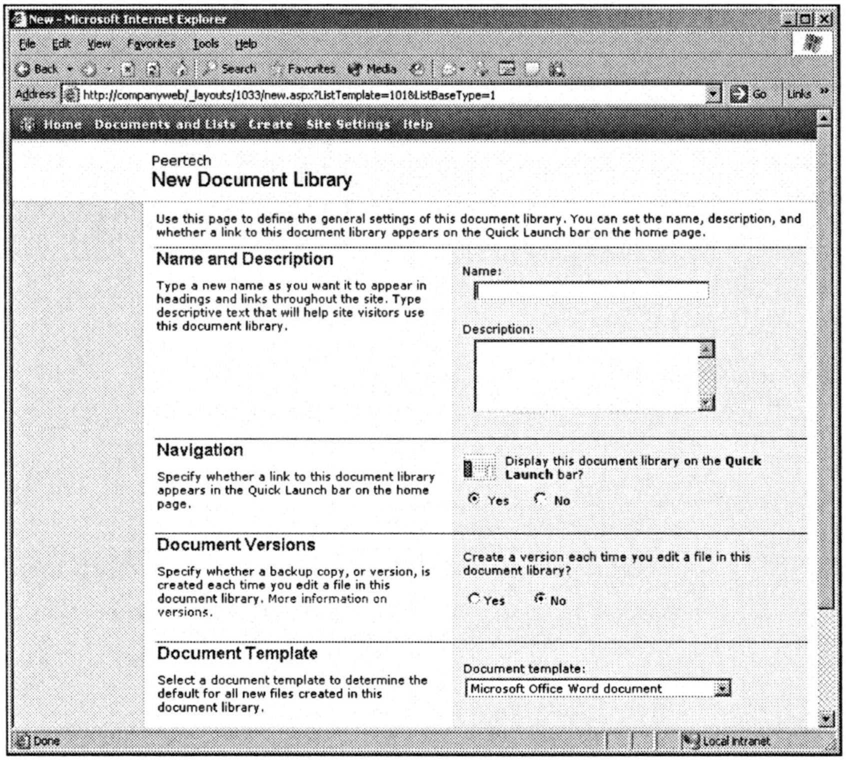

Figure 5.4: Creating a new document library

Under Navigation you can specify whether a link should be created in the shortcut bar on the left side of the website.

Under Document Version you can specify whether a new version of the file should be created or a backup copy. See the *File Versioning in SharePoint Services* section for further information about versioning in SharePoint Services.

Finally, under Document Template specify whether a template such as an Office Word Document or an Office Excel Calculation Table or No Template should be used. Then click on Create.

3. After creating the new library, you will see the dialog box with the name of the newly created library. Documents are assigned to the new library here.

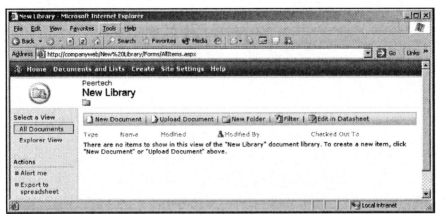

Figure 5.5 : Assigning documents to a document library

To populate the library with new documents, you can use either the New Document or Document Upload menu. In the first case a SharePoint-compatible application such as Office XP or Office 2003 must be installed. In Document Upload you either give the name of the desired document or click on Browse. If an existing file with the same name is to be replaced, select the Overwrite existing files checkbox. To add the document, click on Save and close.

Other Libraries

You can also create form, picture, and fax libraries in a manner analogous to a document library. In the form library you can add XML-based documents. The pre-requisite is an XML-compatible editor such as Office InfoPath. Shared pictures are stored in a picture library. All incoming faxes are collected in a fax library. Further information about the fax library can be found in the section *Forwarding Faxes to the Document Library*.

Creating a New Site

1. To create a new website, click on Create and then on Web Sites and Workspaces under Web Sites.

2. As with a new document library, enter the name and description of the new site here. Next enter the URL of the new site. The http://companyweb/ path is already entered. The third step is to specify the rights for the new site. You can either take over the rights of the higher-level site or select Use own rights. If the rights of the higher-level site are inherited, the user rights can

later only be changed by a person with administrator rights. Then click on Create.

3. You then come to the Template selection page. Here you can select a template such as Team Site or Blank Web Site. Then click on OK. The new site is then created. To go back to the higher-level site from here, click on the Up to site name link in the upper right corner.

Editing a Site

After you have created a site, you can edit it at a later point in time. This applies to the Companyweb site as well. To do this, use the Web site settings menu. Under Administration you can:

- Manage users: Here you can add users to websites, remove them from these groups, and edit users that have been added to the current website.

- Manage sites and workspaces: Websites and workspaces are displayed here. New sites and workspaces can be created and existing ones edited.

- Change Web Site and Workspace creation: Here you can see which website groups are allowed to create websites and workspaces. These settings can also be changed here.

- Web Site Administration: This link takes you to the administration of the top-level website (see the following figure). The settings made here are passed on to the subordinate websites.

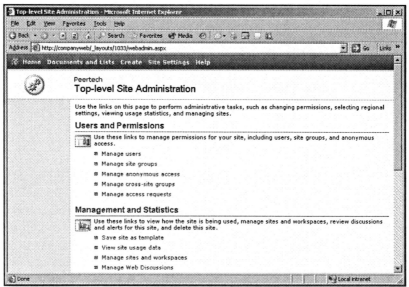

Figure 5.6: The administration of the top-level website

Under Modification you can do the following configurations:

- **Change Web Site Title and Description:** Here the title and the optional description of the site can be edited.

- **Apply Design to Website:** Here you can choose a design for the website from a pre-defined list of designs and examine it using the preview function.

- **Change Web Site Content:** Here you can modify the following areas of the website: document library, list, discussion round, and survey. Click on the desired link. You can then change the general settings of the element, store it as a template, edit the rights, or delete the element. Even the columns and views of the selected element can be changed.

- **Update Homepage:** You can edit the web parts of the site via this link (see Figure 5.7). Web parts are the editable areas of the site, e.g. General Documents, Announcements, Vacation Calendar, etc. You can add selected web parts to the right or the left part of the website.

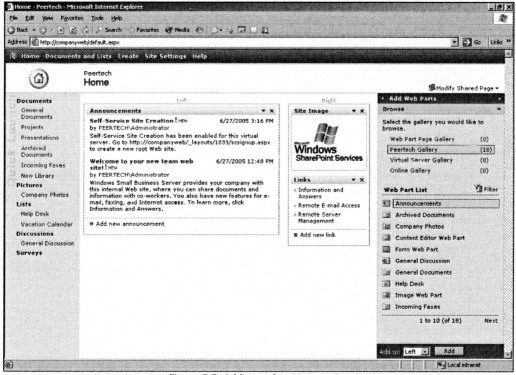

Figure 5.7: Adding web parts to a site

Editing Web Parts

Web parts can be edited by clicking on the arrow in the title bar of the web part on the desired website and then on Edit Item; e.g. if you were to do this Announcements, you'd see the following screenshot:

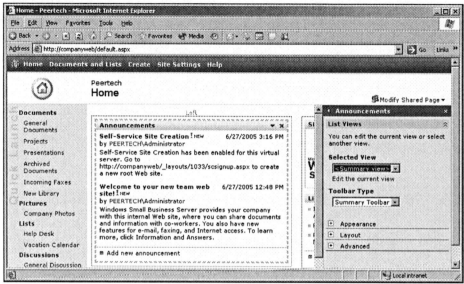

Figure 5.8: Editing web parts

Configuration of E-Mail Notification

E-mail notification is used to inform users when documents, document libraries, or lists are changed or new objects are added or deleted. To configure this notification:

1. In the Server Management open Internal Web Site/Central Administration. Navigate to the Server Configuration section and click on Configure Default E-Mail Server settings.

2. Configure the settings for the SMTP server, the From address and the Reply-to address here (see Figure 5.9). The default SMTP server is the SBS 2003 itself. Then click on OK.

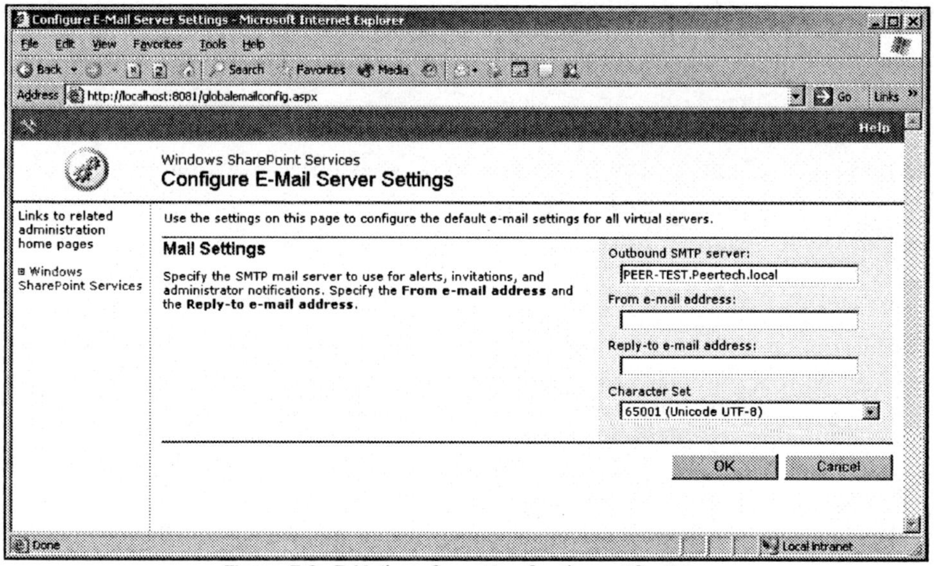

Figure 5.9: E-Mail configuration for the notifications

Selecting the Notifications

To make sure that a user does not get too many or unwanted notifications, a selection of the desired notifications and their options can be made. Click on the desired element (for example General Documents). Under Actions click on Notifications.

The following notification options can be set here:

- The e-mail address to which the message should be sent.
- The type of changes for which notification should be sent. Possible changes are All changes, Added entries, Changed entries, Deleted entries, or Web discussion changes.
- The notification frequency. Here you can choose whether the e-mails should be sent immediately or you want to receive daily or only weekly notifications of selected changes.

Displaying Notifications

Although the notifications are sent to the specified e-mail address, they can also be viewed on the website. To do this, click on Site Settings and then in the Manage my Information area on My notifications on this web site. New lists or libraries for which you want to receive notifications can also be selected. Existing notifications can also be deleted here.

Forwarding Faxes to the Document Library

All incoming faxes are stored in the Incoming Faxes document library. Information about each fax can be found in the various columns such as date of receipt, number of pages, and size. The faxes are shown as hyperlinks and can be sorted by the various columns.

The prerequisite for displaying faxes in the document library is that you have also selected storing in the document library as an output option in the task list for the fax device. If you are using several fax devices, storing in the document library must be activated for each of the devices.

File Versioning in SharePoint Services

As already described in the context of creating a new document library, you can specify whether you want to create a backup copy or a new version of an edited file. To be able to do this, you will now be given a brief insight into the file versioning mechanism of SharePoint Services.

If when creating the document library you have enabled the Create a new version each time you edit a file in this library option, the Version history entry is added when you click on the arrow next to the document. You have the option of selecting and editing an older version of a document.

If versioning is enabled, new versions of the document are created in the following cases:

- The user opens and edits the document and saves it for the first time. New versions are not created for subsequent saves—this is done only when the user restarts the application and saves the file.
- The user checks out a file, edits it, and checks it back in.
- The user restores an older version of the file and does not check it out.
- The user uploads a pre-existing file. The existing version now becomes an older version.

When a file is deleted from the document library, all existing versions of the file are automatically deleted.

Upgrading the Servers and the Virtual Server

You can upgrade a server to SharePoint Services at any time. This process upgrades the server itself *and* the virtual default server. To upgrade, run the setupsts.exe file from the installation CD of SBS 2003 and follow the instructions of the wizard.

To upgrade other virtual servers, you must use the command-line program stsadm.exe. For this take the following steps:

1. Open a command line and switch to the folder C:\Program Files\Common Files\Microsoft Shared\Web Server Extensions\60\Bin.

2. Next enter the following command, where URL stands for the URL of the virtual server to be upgraded:

```
Stsadm.exe -o upgrade -url <URL>
```

If you want to upgrade a virtual server on which the FrontPage 2002 server extensions have been installed to SharePoint Services, the FrontPage 2002 server extensions must first be uninstalled. If you want to preserve the contents of the website, migrate these with the help of the smigrate.exe tool to the SharePoint website. You will find this program in the folder Program Files\Common Files\Microsoft Shared\Web Server Extensions\60\Bin.

Managing the Virtual Server

There are one or more virtual servers on SBS 2003, which is simultaneously an HTTP server. Outside the SBS 2003 environment, a virtual server can also be located on any other web server. Each virtual server can have its own pages and run its own programs. Furthermore, each virtual server can have its own IP address and domain name. The default virtual servers on the SBS 2003 are companyweb, default website, and Microsoft SharePoint Administration.

If the SharePoint Services are installed on the virtual server, one speaks of an extension of the virtual server. An extension is the basis on which a SharePoint-based website will be created. This extension is done automatically in a normal installation of the SharePoint Services.

The contents of the virtual servers are stored in databases. When a server is extended, the content database and the configuration database are accessed. The contents of the various websites are included in the content database. These include settings for the usernames, rights, and the documents and lists of the document libraries. By default a server needs only one content database. But if you are running a server farm, a sufficient number of content databases must be available. The configuration database is responsible for managing the connections between the servers and the content databases.

Furthermore, the server settings are stored here. Only one configuration database is required per server (and even per server farm).

Extending Virtual Servers

An extension can make sense if you want to make room for new user websites. You can either add the new contents to a new virtual server or add website collections or other content databases to an existing virtual server. If you want to provide for a large number of possible connections to a website or direct several URLs to the same website, first connect to an existing content database. The list of existing content databases is automatically generated by the configuration database. The content databases are shown as virtual servers.

When extending a virtual server you must give the following information:

- Account and e-mail address of the owner of the higher-level default website of the virtual server
- Application pool to be used
- Content database to be used

Optionally, you can also enter the following information:

- Alternative URL (if the default website is not to be created in the root folder of the virtual server).
- The website template to be used.
- The language for the higher-level default website. One can only choose from the languages that are installed on the server for the SharePoint Services.
- If quotas are to be used, you can enter the quota template.

When extending the virtual server you can proceed in two ways. The way you will take depends on whether you are creating a new content database or using an existing one. The two scenarios are described in the two sections after the next section.

Creating the Virtual Servers in IIS

Before you can extend a virtual server, you must first create it in IIS. To do this:

1. Open Administration/Internet Information Services Manager and expand the server to which you want to add the new virtual server.
2. From the context menu of Web sites select New/Web site.
3. A wizard appears. Click on Next and enter a description for the new website.

4. Next enter the following information:
   - o The IP address for this website, or accept All unassigned, the default setting.
   - o The TCP port (Default is Port 80).
   - o You must not make an entry under Host header as the hosting is handled by the SharePoint Services.
5. Next, enter the path to the base folder for the site. Disable the checkbox Allow anonymous access to this web site.
6. Specify the access rights for the website. You should retain the two selected settings Read and Run Scripts (e.g. ASP). The SharePoint Services automatically add the right Run (e.g. ISAPI applications or CGI) to the corresponding folders. Then click on Next and Finish.

Extending the Virtual Server and Creating a Content Database

If you want to extend the virtual server and also add a new database in the process, perform the following steps:

1. Open the SharePoint central administration and click under Configure virtual server on Extend or upgrade virtual server.
2. In the server list click on the desired server. In the next window click on Extend and create content database under Set up options. Enter the required information such as website owner, language, and application pool to be used. Then click on OK.
3. The extension of the virtual server follows. The new page is created in the root folder of the virtual server. Finally, you get the dialog for configuring the settings for the higher-level website.

Extending the Virtual Servers and Linking with an Existing Content Database

If you want to extend the virtual server and set up a connection to an existing database in the process, perform the following steps:

1. Open the SharePoint central administration and under Configure virtual server, click on Extend or upgrade virtual server.
2. Click on the desired server and in the next window on Extend and assign to another virtual server.

3. You will see the Extend and assign to another virtual server window. Switch to the Server assignment section and enter the name of the virtual server or host to be used in the Hostname or virtual Servername in IIS field.

4. In the Application pool section you can decide whether you want to use a pre-existing application or create a new one. For a new application pool you must specify a name, a username, and a password. Then click on Send.

After a virtual server has been extended in this manner, it prepares the contents of the same database as the other virtual servers that use the database. If you create a new higher-level website for the virtual server, this website is simultaneously hosted by all other virtual servers that use the same database.

6

Internet Security and Acceleration Server 2000 (ISA)

ISA Server 2000 is the successor to Microsoft Proxy Server 2.0. It is sometimes also referred to as Proxy Server 3.0. As compared to its predecessor, it has a greatly improved firewall function in addition to the proxy functionality. ISA Server can either be used only as a proxy server or firewall, or in a combination of the two roles. In its firewall function ISA server uses the Active Directory services of SBS 2003 for administration.

This chapter first gives you an overview of the various configuration and implementation scenarios of the server, and then discusses the installation and base configuration. Building on this foundation, the chapter goes on to discuss configuration specifications, the interplay with other servers, and the proxy function. The function, installation, and configuration of the firewall client of SBS 2003 are also discussed.

ISA Server 2000 has in the meantime found its successor in ISA Server 2003. Whether, to what extent, and when the ISA Server 2000 of SBS 2003 will be replaced by the new version of ISA Server 2004 has not been made known yet.

The Version of ISA Server in SBS 2003

The version of ISA Server supplied with SBS 2003 premium edition is functionally equivalent to the standard edition of ISA Server 2000 with Service Pack 1. Additionally, all patches published between the release of the Service Pack and SBS 2003 have also been integrated in this version. Some setup files have also been modified as compared to the standard version of ISA server.

Scenarios and Bases for the ISA Server

The installation type of the ISA server depends on how the network is secured or is to be secured. The most common scenarios are the use of a firewall, a demilitarized zone (DMZ), or even a DMZ with two firewalls.

Deployment of a Firewall

A firewall is equipped with two network cards. One connects to the Internet, and the other connects to the local network. Thus two separate physical networks are established. The firewall serves as a router for the clients and protects the local network against unauthorized access via various filter mechanisms.

Although the ISA server firewall *can* inspect packets even at the application level, a modified packet can still pierce the firewall and cause damage due to the existence of security holes.

Building a DMZ

This procedure is more secure than using a firewall. In this scenario the firewall has three network cards (in the case of a DSL connection—if you have an ISDN card or an analog modem, this takes the place of the third network card). The first network card is used to connect to the Internet. The Internet is also referred to as the public network.

Computers that may be accessed directly from the Internet are connected to the second network card. This area is known as the **demilitarized zone (DMZ)** because access takes place via the firewall making an attack difficult.

All clients and servers that may not be accessed from the Internet are connected to the third network card. These computers are also protected by the firewall. This is also called a private network.

To ensure that the security of the DMZ is also passed on further, routing is implemented between the private network and the DMZ, and between the DMZ and the public network. All client requests are forwarded via the DMZ. Direct routing between private and public networks is not possible. Internet access for users can be via a proxy server. This can either be installed along with the firewall or set up in the DMZ. The IP address of the proxy server must be entered in the configuration of the clients' Internet Explorer.

A DMZ with Two Firewalls

This scenario is applied in environments that are highly security-critical. Here the DMZ is protected by one firewall between the DMZ and the public network, and a second firewall between the DMZ and the private network.

As compared to the solution with just one firewall, access to the private network is made considerably more difficult by the second firewall. In the scenario with just one firewall, an attacker can get into the private network if he/she penetrates the DMZ and the firewall.

What Dangers the ISA Server can Identify

These days there are a number of dangers lurking on the Internet. Most attacks are aimed at collecting unauthorized information, blocking servers or their services, or modifying specific data. The most frequent dangers are listed below.

Reading Unencrypted Data

Sending unencrypted data over the Internet represents a very high risk because this data can always be intercepted and read. This problem has of late been minimized as there are add-ons available for a number of protocols that enable encrypted transmission of data. The problem with encrypted communication, however, is that a firewall can no longer recognize manipulated IP packets due to the encryption. The ISA server can, however, use the encryption of the server. It can thus decrypt the data at the firewall for checking purposes and, after the check is done, again encrypt and send it.

IP Half Scan

In this form of attack, packets are sent to the server with a forged sender. The server tries to verify these packets. Since it does not receive a reply from the forged sender, it keeps trying, and gets into an endless loop since it simultaneously receives a number of these forged packages. Even this form of attack can be identified with the help of IP packet filtering.

Land

In a land attack, a packet is sent to the server, which gives the target address as the forged sender address. This results in an endless loop that overloads the server. This form of attack can also be identified via IP filtering.

WinNuke

This form of attack is also referred to as Windows out-of-band. TC packets are primarily sent to the NetBIOS interface of the server to bring the server down. This attack is easy to identify via IP packet filtering. You should reflect whether you need the NetBIOS protocol at all in your network. In Active Directory NetBIOS has been replaced by DNS and is thus no longer required. Check whether some applications do require this protocol.

Ping of Death

With a Denial of Service (DoS) attack, a server is attacked in such a way that it can no longer respond due to overload. This is the so-called **ping of death**. Here the ping command is modified so that IP packets with non-permissible sizes are sent. One solution is to change the settings so that servers in the internal network can no longer accept ping commands. However there can be other DoS attacks on ports that you use for the communication between the servers in the network. ISA Server, on the other hand, uses a filtering mechanism to filter out IP addresses in a targeted manner. Via the ISA SDK (Software Development Kit) you can make further changes to be able to react to new packet characteristics.

Port Scans

A port scan is done using a so-called port scanner. These scanners analyze *which* ports are used by the server so as to be able to gain entry into the system. These scanners are especially used when the servers are configured not to use the default ports. On one hand ISA Server can be configured via filters to allow sending of data to only specific ports and IP addresses. On the other hand, ISA Server can also determine the originating IP address when a port scan is identified.

SMTP Relaying

Here, an outside SMTP server is used for sending mass e-mails. In SMTP relaying, a person sends to the SMTP server a message meant for several recipients in domains other than that of the SMTP sever. This mass mail is then sent via the misused SMTP server in such a way that it appears to be the sender; even the costs for the mass-mail dispatch are not borne by the actual sender. The protection against this is to only allow e-mails meant for this server to be sent through it. Only users in the same e-mail domain can send e-mails over the Internet.

Operating Modes of ISA Server

ISA Server can be implemented in three different operating modes. In two of these modes the server is deployed either as a firewall or as a proxy. However, it is precisely in small and medium-sized companies as in an SBS 2003 environment that you will you will use the third operating mode: the integrated mode. In this mode, the proxy and the firewall are installed together on one computer—in our case, therefore, on the server of the SBS network.

The Installation of ISA Server 2000

This section describes the installation of ISA Server. To gain a better understanding, we will first give an overview of the different components of ISA Server 2000.

The Components of ISA Server

ISA Server consists of various services and configuration tools. The core components of the ISA Server are the **ISA-Services**. These are always installed, but their content depends on whether you deploy the server as a firewall, a proxy, or both.

Add-in-Services are another component. These consist of the **H.323 Gatekeeper Service** and the **Message Screener**. The **Message Screener** serves to filter file attachments in accordance with a filename or specific text inside an e-mail. With the help of this tool it is possible to respond to a specific virus and keep it away from the network until a solution is offered by the anti-virus manufacturer. The **H.323 Gatekeeper Service** is used in audio and video conferences via NetMeeting. The installation of these two components is optional.

Apart from the services, ISA-Server offers the **ISA Management Console** for the central administration of the servers, and the **H.323 Gatekeeper Administration Tool** for administering the Gatekeeper Services.

The Installation of ISA Server

After you have made the preparations, ISA Server can be installed.

1. Insert the SBS 2003 Premium Technologies CD in your drive and start the installation of ISA Server via the appropriate link.

2. After the warning to close all open programs, the Microsoft Product ID of your copy of ISA Server is shown to you. Make a note of this—you may need it later for support purposes. You need to then concur with the license agreement. It is not necessary to enter a license number. The system then checks if there is a pre-existing installation of ISA Server or any of its components.

3. Then specify whether you want to carry out a default installation, a complete installation, or a custom installation. Only in the last case can you select the components to be installed. The default installation folder is \Program Files\Microsoft ISA Server. You can, however, choose another installation folder. The installation of ISA Server requires only 17 MB. Click the button for the desired installation type.

    The installation path relates only to the program files. The storage location for the proxy cache will be determined later (see step 7).

4. If you have opted for the custom install, you can now select the desired components. To install additional components for Additional Services and Administration Programs, click Change option. If you have selected all the components to be installed, click Next.

5. Next, select the operating mode of ISA Server. You can choose between Firewall Mode, Cache Mode, and Integrated Mode. In our example the server is installed in integrated mode. The integrated mode is presupposed in the rest of this chapter as this is the mode that is offered in the SBS environment. Then click Next.

6. You will then see a dialog box informing you that the IIS web service (W3SVC) was stopped. After the ISA installation is completed, IIS must be configured in such a way that it no longer uses the default ports 80 and 8080 as these are now used by ISA Server. Confirm this message with OK.

7. Next, specify the storage location for the proxy cache.

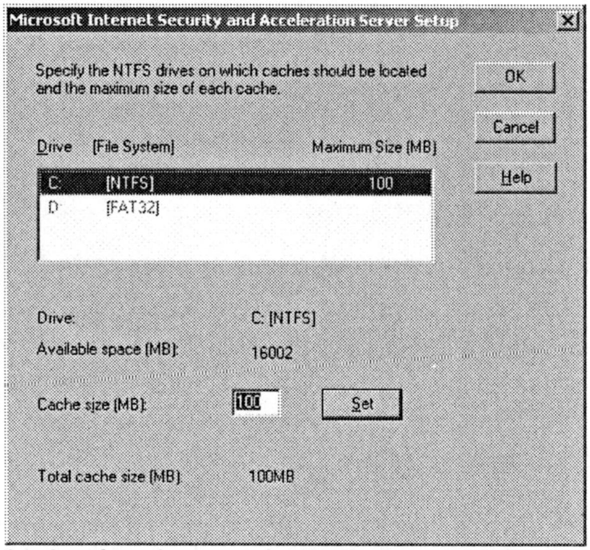

Figure 6.1: Specifying the storage location for the cache of the proxy server

The cache must be on a drive with the NTFS file system. You can also distribute the cache over several drives. This improves the performance of ISA Server. Check each drive you want to include, enter the maximum size of the cache in the appropriate field, and click Set. Then click OK.

To perform administrative tasks on the cache later, use the Cachedir.exe program. You will have to copy this program manually from the Support/Tools/Troubleshooting folder of the CD into the installation folder of ISA Server.

8. Next you have to tell ISA Server about the IP address ranges of the private and public networks.

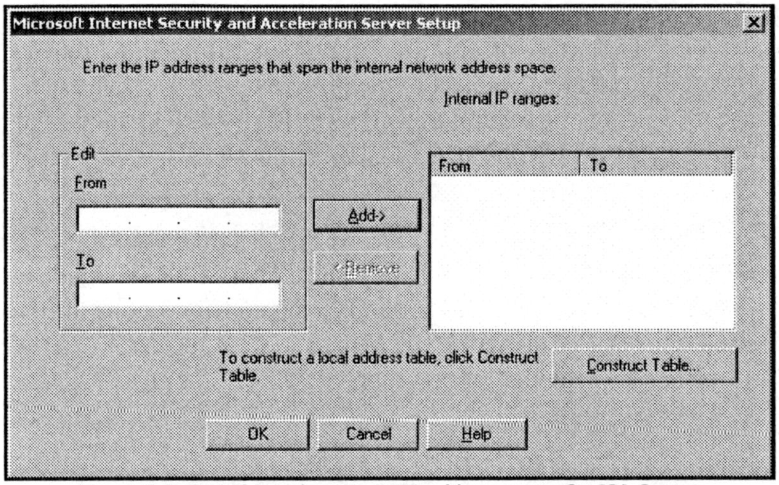

Figure 6.2: Specifying the private IP address range for ISA-Server

Enter the address range of the private network in the From and To fields and then click Add. This way you can even add several private networks. The information entered by you here goes into the **Local Address Table** (LAT) of ISA Server. IP addresses not found in this table are treated as public IP addresses. To create this table, click Construct Table. You will see the Local Address Table dialog:

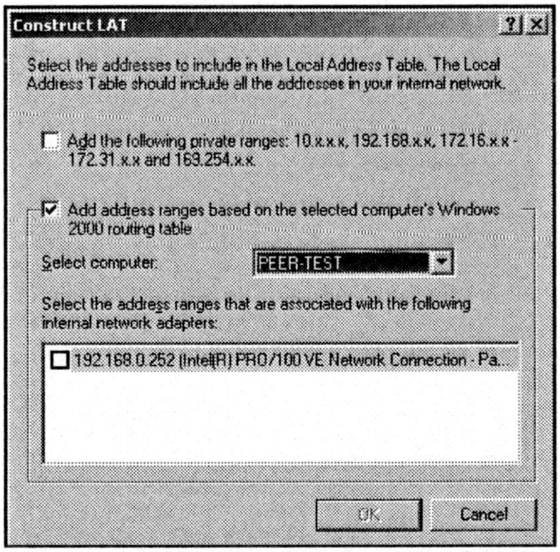

Figure 6.3: Additional configuration options for LAT

9. In this dialog box you can add more address ranges to the LAT. Via the upper checkbox you can add address ranges that are reserved as private network addresses. This includes the ranges 10.x.x.x, 192.168.x.x, 172.16.x.x

to 172.31.x.x, and 169.254.x.x. The second checkbox lets you add address ranges on the basis of the Windows routing table. Remember to select only those network cards that connect to the private network. Then click OK. A message will now appear telling you the LAT has been created. The installation is then carried out.

The "First Steps" Wizard

After completing the installation you have the option of starting the First Steps wizard. This wizard helps create security guidelines and cache configurations for the network. The configuration options for this will be described soon in the *The "First Steps" Wizard and the Base Configuration* section of this chapter.

Changing the Configuration of IIS

If a web server is already running on the SBS 2003 before the installation of ISA Server, this will be stopped before the installation of ISA Server as already mentioned. The reason for this is that ISA Server itself uses the ports of the web server. To reactivate the web server, you must first assign a new port to the virtual web server and then restart the IIS services. When pages on the web server are called, ISA Server takes the requests instead of the web server and forwards these to the web server.

Installed Services of ISA Server

After the installation, the following new services are available on the server. There can be variations depending on the choice of components. The following table describes the services of ISA Server 2000:

Service	Description
Microsoft Firewall	This is the service for the firewall component of ISA Server.
Microsoft H.323 Gatekeeper	Service for the Gatekeeper, which acts as the interface between the private and public networks for services using the H.323 Standard (e.g. NetMeeting).
Microsoft ISA-Server Control	This is the central service of ISA Server and controls all the other services.
Microsoft Scheduled Cache Content Download	This service is responsible for forward caching. It checks files to see if they are current and reloads them if required.
Microsoft Web Proxy	This service is responsible for the intermediate storage of data transmitted via HTTP or FTP.

Administration of ISA Server

This section familiarizes you with the extensive administration options of ISA Server. For the base configuration, administrators not conversant with ISA Server should use the "First Steps" wizard. Further configuration of the server is done via the ISA Administration Console. This is also introduced in the next section.

The "First Steps" Wizard and the Base Configuration

This wizard walks you through the base configuration options of ISA Server. All the steps in the task list under the point Set up Internet Connection are worked through once again. A detailed description has already been given in the *Network Task: Setting up an Internet Connection* section in Chapter 2.

Control and administration of ISA Server are done via the ISA Management MMC under Programs/Microsoft ISA SERVER:

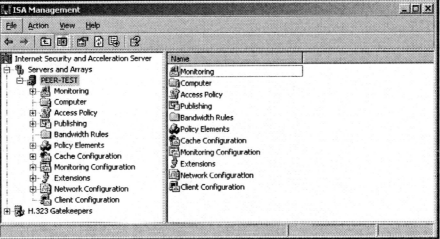

Figure 6.4: The administration console of ISA Server

Before you go any further, set the View option of this console to Advanced.

You must perform some basic administrative tasks after the installation. These include configuring the routing and setting up a dial-up connection (if available).

The Routing Configuration

By default the forwarding of packets from the private network to the Internet is disabled. You can activate this routing function by taking the following steps:

1. Open the Properties of Access Policy/IP Packet Filter and switch to the General tab.
2. Check the Enable Packet filtering and Enable IP Routing checkboxes.

Enabling the routing function is only meaningful if the function is required. If the ISA Server is deployed as a proxy server, this is not necessary as the clients send their requests to the proxy server, which in turn forwards them to the target server.

If you have configured routing under ISA Server, the routing function of SBS 2003 may not be enabled anymore. The routing function of SBS could otherwise disable the security mechanisms of ISA Server.

You should therefore check in the Routing and RAS MMC whether any additional interfaces have been entered.

Configuring a Dial-Up Connection

If a dial-up connection has been set up on the SBS, the corresponding entry must be made for ISA Server. To do this, take the following steps:

1. Open Policy Objects/Dial-Up Entry and select New/Dial-up Entry.
2. On the New Dial-Up Entry page (see the following figure) enter a name and a description. Select the connection from Network Dial-Up Connection. Under Network Dial-Up Account click Set account, enter the username and password for the dial-up account, and click OK.

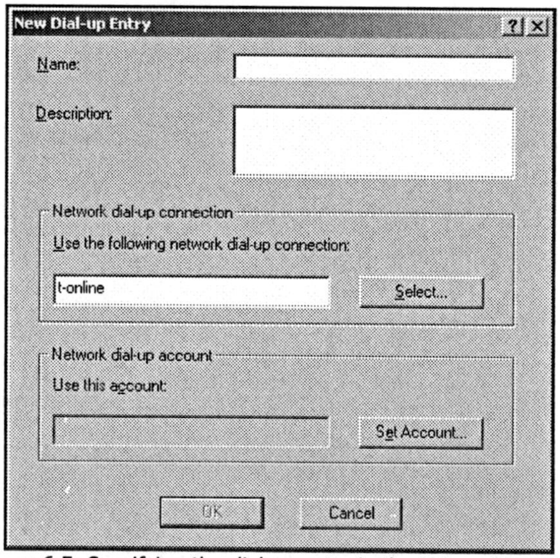

Figure 6.5: Specifying the dial-up entry in the ISA configuration

Routing and Dial-Up Connections

The last step is to set up routing for the dial-up connection. This is necessary even if the dial-up connection is just a backup for a temporarily unavailable always-on connection.

1. Open Network Configuration/Routing. Select Properties from the context menu of Default Rule.

2. Switch to the Action tab (see the following figure). You can usually retain the Retrieving them directly from the specified destination setting. It is only necessary to specify settings for an upstream server if the ISP uses a web proxy since it does not allow access to all Internet servers. This is, however, not the case as a rule. If this is indeed the case, you must enter the web proxy of the ISP as an upstream server.

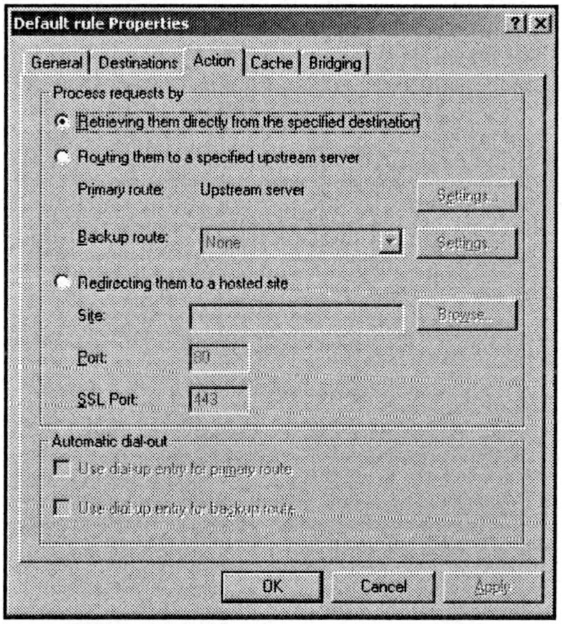

Figure 6.6: Configuring the routing function

Finally, under Automatic dial-out, specify *when* the route should be used. If the route is conceived only as a backup, check the second checkbox. If it is the main route, select the upper checkbox.

The Filter Functions of ISA Server

The most important function of ISA Server is to monitor the data traffic between the local network and the Internet. Different filters and rules are used for the monitoring and control functions. Initially these filters/rules are configured in such a way that all connections over the ISA Server are denied. This means that the administrator must configure all permitted connections as exceptions. If all connections were allowed to begin with and the administrator's task was to configure the non-permitted ones, the danger of security holes being overlooked would be too great.

The available filter and rule functions are protocol, site, and content rules, and IP packet and application filters.

Protocol Rules

Protocol rules are used when clients use the proxy client and the ISA Server is configured as proxy server. The proxy server is then entered as the default gateway for the clients. A protocol rule specifies *which* protocols the client may use.

1. From the context menu of Access Policy/Protocol Rules select New/Rule and enter a name for the rule.
2. Specify whether response to client requests with the protocol of the rule should be permitted or denied, and then click Next.
3. In the Protocols dialog specify the protocols for which the rule should be applied. If you have selected the Selected Protocols option there, you can select the protocols from the list (see the following figure). Then click Next.

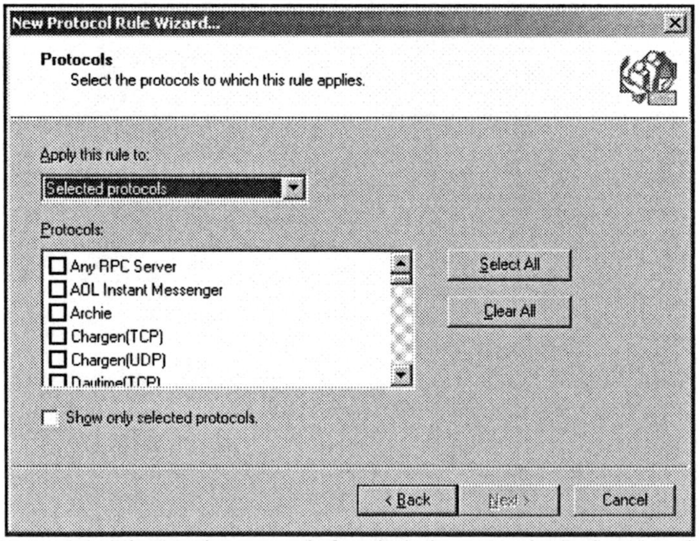

Figure 6.7: Selecting the protocols for which the protocol rule should apply

4. Next, decide whether this rule should be applied "Always" or in accordance with the "Normal Working Hours" or "Weekend" schedules. Precise tuning of the two options is, however, not possible. Click Next.

5. Specify the client type for which this rule should apply. You can select the All requests option, or specific computers or users and groups. If you select the All requests option, click Next and complete the wizard. Otherwise select the computers or users to whom the rule should apply, and close the wizard.

Site and Content Rules

This type of rule is used to restrict a user's access options on the Internet. You can restrict access to specific sites or deny the download of certain file types. For the latter, so-called content groups must be created. This procedure is described in the *Creating Content Groups* subsection.

1. Select New/Rule from the context menu of Access Rules/Site and Content Rules and give it a name.

2. Specify whether response to client requests should be allowed or denied (by default it is denied). You can even enter a URL at which you inform the user (in a polite way) that he or she may not visit the requested site from the company network. Then click Next.

3. Next, specify whether the rule based on the called target should apply in accordance with a specific schedule or to specific clients. It is also possible to have user-defined rules. The following options are available:

Target

*   All destinations: The rule is applied to all target servers.

*   All internal destinations: The rule is applied to all servers in the internal network. Server membership is obtained from the LAT.

*   All external destinations: The rule is applied to all external servers, i.e. all servers outside the local network.

*   A given destination set: Here, a selection is made from so-called destination sets. In a destination set, various IP addresses are combined into a group. The creation of a destination set is described in the following subsection. For example, after the installation of SBS 2003 the Small Business Exchange OWA Destination Set is available to you.

*   All destinations other than the selected set: This is the converse of the previous option. The rule is applied to all servers outside the selected set.

Time

The following schedules are available: "Always", "Normal Working Hours", and "Weekend". Further fine-tuning of the schedules is not possible.

Clients

Here you can specify whether the rule should apply to all requests or only to specific computers or users and groups. You can subsequently select these.

If you have selected user-defined in the Rule Configuration dialog, you can make the settings for destination, time, and clients one after the other.

Creating Destination Sets

To create a new destination set:

1. Select New/Define from the context menu of Policy Objects/Destination Sets.

2. In the New Destination Set dialog enter a name, and a description (optional) for the destination set. Click Add to select the elements of the destination set.

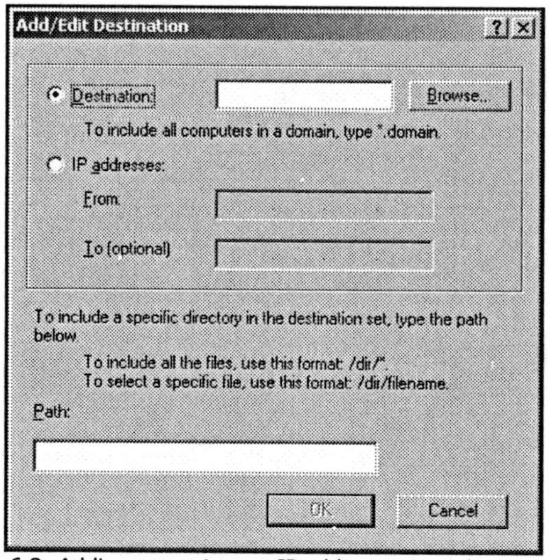

Figure 6.8: Adding computers or IP addresses to a destination set

You can select computers based either on domains or IP addresses. Click OK once you are done.

Existing destination sets can also be edited or deleted.

Creating Content Groups

By creating content groups you can prevent users from downloading certain file types. To create a content group, take the following steps:

1. From the context menu of Policy Objects/Content Groups select New/Content Group and first enter a name.

2. From the Available types list (see the following figure) select the file types and click Add. If a file type is not available, you can enter it manually in the text field.

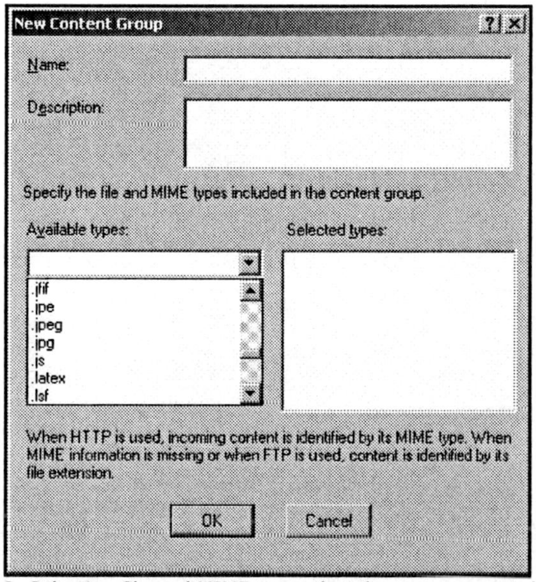

Figure 6.9: Selecting file and MIME types that the user may not download

Apart from file types, you can also select certain mime types. Thus, for example, the MIME type **audio/midi** indicates that the file in question is an audio file. This is specified more precisely by the type midi.

To delete specific types from the list, click Remove.

IP Packet Filters

IP packet filters are used to filter data sent to or from the ISA server or routed through it. To activate IP filtering, take the following steps:

1. Open the Properties of Access Policy/IP Packet Filters and switch to the Packet Filters tab.

2. On this page you can specify the principles for the filtering. Via **Enable filtering of IP Fragments** you can ensure that even packets that can become a malevolent data packet once the fragments are reconstituted are filtered (even though individually they're not dangerous). If you check **Enable Filtering of IP Options**, even IP headers, which are also referred to as IP options, are filtered so that no harmful packets can get into the network even via this route. Via **Log Packets from Allow Filters** you can ensure that even packets that are allowed to pass the filter are checked. Click OK.

As you can see under IP Packet Filters, some default IP packet filters have already been set up by ISA Server. The status of a filter can be seen from the symbol next to it. The predefined filters allow DNS requests and ICMP (for the ping function).

1. To create a new filter, select **New/Filter** from the context menu of **IP Packet Filters**.

2. First give the filter a name. Then specify whether the filter should allow or prevent the transmission of data. Click **Next**.

3. On the **Filter Type** page, specify whether you want to set up a user-defined filter or a predefined filter. In the predefined filter list you can choose from the most important filters:

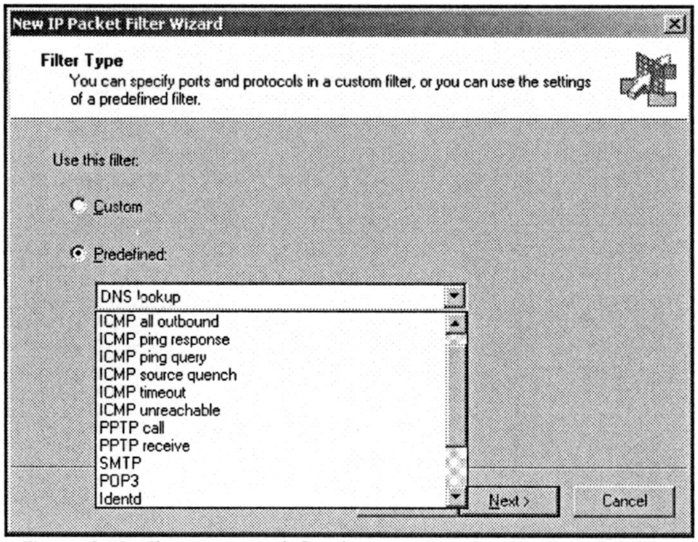

Figure 6.10: Choosing pre-defined connections for the IP packet filter

If, however, you want to set up a user-defined (custom) filter, enter the protocol, the number, the direction, and the local and remote ports.

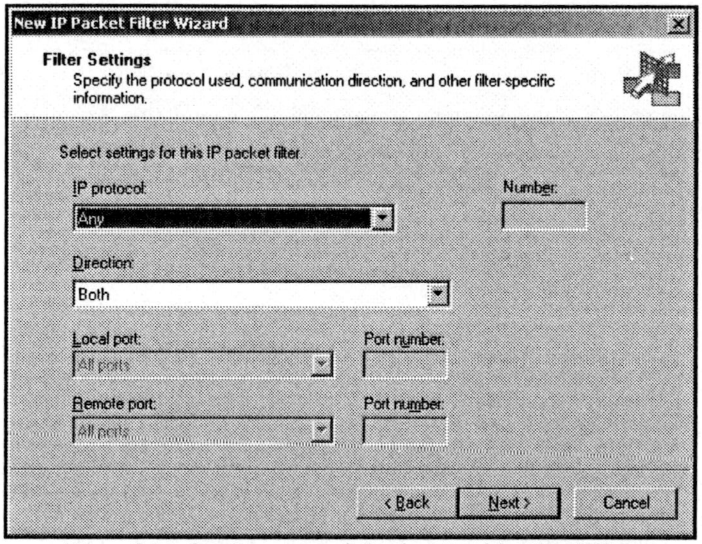

Figure 6.11: Creating a user-defined protocol for the IP filter

The filtering is based on IP addresses and ports—the following table gives you an overview of the most important protocols, and the corresponding numbers:

Number	Protocol	Number	Protocol	Number	Protocol
0	HOPOPT	46	RSVP	95	MICP
1	ICMP	47	GRE	96	SCC-SP
2	IGMP	48	MHRP	97	ETHERIP
3	GGP	49	BNA	98	ENCAP
4	IP	50	ESP	100	GMTP
5	ST	51	AH	101	IFMP
6	TCP	52	I-NLSP	102	PNNI
7	CBT	53	SWIPE	103	PIM
8	EGP	54	NARP	104	ARIS
9	IGP	55	MOBILE	105	SCPS
10	BBN-RCC-MON	56	TLSP	106	QNX
11	NVP-II	57	SKIP	107	A/N
12	PUP	58	IPv6-ICMP	108	IPComp
13	ARGUS	59	IPv6-NoNxt	109	SNP

Number	Protocol	Number	Protocol	Number	Protocol
14	EMCON	60	IPv6-Opts	110	Compaq-Peer
15	XNET	62	CFTP	111	IPX-in-IP
16	CHAOS	64	SAT-EXPAK	112	VRRP
17	UDP	65	KRYPTOLAN	113	PGM
18	MUX	66	RVD	115	L2TP
19	DCN-MEAS	67	IPPC	116	DDX
20	HMP	69	SAT-MON	117	IATP
21	PRM	70	VISA	118	STP
22	XNS-IDP	71	IPCV	119	SRP
23	TRUNK-1	72	CPNX	120	UTI
24	TRUNK-2	73	CPHB	121	SMP
25	LEAF-1	74	WSN	122	SM
26	LEAF-2	75	PVP	123	PTP
27	RDP	76	BR-SAT-MON	124	ISIS
28	IRTP	77	SUN-ND	125	FIRE
29	ISO-TP4	78	WB-MON	126	CRTP
30	NETBLT	79	WB-EXPAK	127	CRUDP
31	MFE-NSP	80	ISO-IP	128	SSCOPMCE
32	MERIT-INP	81	VMTP	130	SPS
33	SEP	82	SECURE-VMTP	131	PIPE
34	3PC	83	VINES	132	SCTP
35	IDPR	84	TTP	133	FC
36	XTP	85	NSFNET-IGP	255	Reserved
37	DDP	86	DGP	-	-
38	IDPR-CMTP	87	TCF	-	-
39	TP++	88	EIGRP	-	-
40	IL	89	OSPFIGP	-	-
41	IPv6	90	Sprite-RPC	-	-
42	SDRP	91	LARP	-	-

Number	Protocol	Number	Protocol	Number	Protocol
43	IPv6-Route	92	MTP	-	-
44	IPv6-Frag	93	AX.25	-	-
45	IDRP	94	IPIP	-	-

After you have configured the filter, specify the IP addresses to which it should apply. You can choose between all IP addresses of the external server interfaces (default), only one external IP address, or a specific computer on the network. Click Next once this has been done.

4. Next, choose which remote computers the filter should be applied to. The default setting is All Remote Computers. You can, however, specify just one remote computer. Click Next and complete the wizard.

To find out via the IP packet filter whether an attack is taking place, check the Enable Intrusion detection checkbox under Access Policy/IP Packet Filters on the General tab.

Switch to the Intrusion Detection tab (see the following figure) and check the checkboxes for the attacks to be identified via the ISA server.

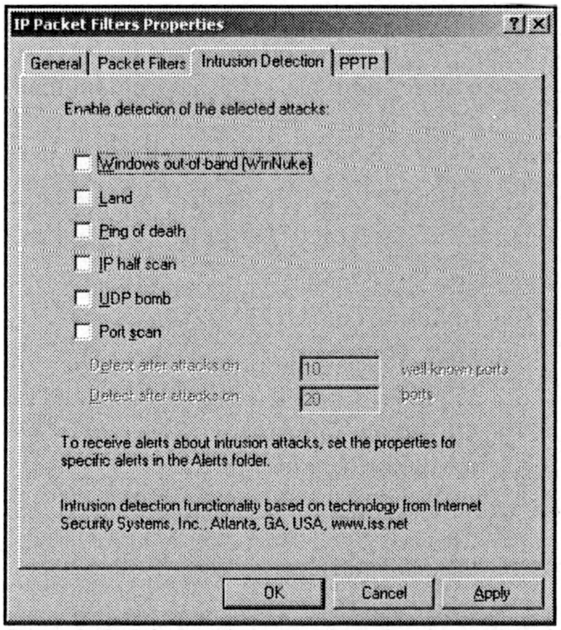

Figure 6.12: Selecting the types of attack to be monitored

The various types of attacks have already been described in the *What Dangers the ISA Server can Identify* section earlier in the chapter. Just a few words here about the settings for the port scan. If this option is selected, you can set the number of intrusions before an attack is deemed to have occurred. Ports 1 to 2048 are the so-called well-known ports. This is the area that is used most often by the server-based services. That is why a smaller value is set here than for the remaining ports.

Application Filters

Application filters are used to protect the services that are responsible for the transmission of specific packets. Thus, for example, the HTTP, DNS, or SMTP services can be protected. ISA server has a number of predefined application filters. You can find these under Extensions/Application Filters. Here you can also see whether a filter has been enabled or not. If it is disabled, you will see a symbol with a red arrow in a white circle. You can enable or disable a filter from its context menu. Filters other than the predefined ones here can be obtained from third parties. You can get an overview of these other filters at http://www.microsoft.com/isaserver/partners.

Let's now move on to the possible settings for these application filters.

DNS Intrusion Detection Filter

DNS intrusion involves sending such large quantities of data to the DNS server that the DNS buffer overflows. If no buffer limit has been set programmatically, other buffer areas can also be overwritten, leading to a collapse of the server. The DNS intrusion-detection filter can identify the following intrusion attempts on the DNS server:

- DNS Hostname Overflow: Excessively long hostnames are deliberately sent in DNS requests.
- DNS Length Overflow: The default length of an IP address is four bytes. A greater length is used for the attack.
- DNS Zone Transfer from Privileged Ports (1–1024): In a zone transfer the DNS database of one server is transferred to another and compared. If the port lies in the 1 to 1024 range, a regular DNS server makes this request. This can be checked with the help of a filter.
- DNS Zone Transfer from Higher Ports (Above 1024): If one of the higher ports is used, the request usually proceeds from a client.

FTP Access Filter

This filter is important for pure text-based FTP clients for which no proxy settings can be made. The ISA server is deployed as a **transparent proxy**. As for a web server, FTP requests to Port 21 are first sent to the ISA server, which then forwards them to the FTP server. No other options are available for this filter.

H.323-Filter

This filter is primarily responsible for controlling services such as Microsoft NetMeeting. If you do not use these services, the filter does not have to be activated. If due to a firewall there is no routable connection between two networks, you must use the gatekeeper. This then functions as a NetMeeting proxy. Select the desired computer via Browse. You can also specify whether incoming and/or outgoing calls are permitted and which media (audio, video) should be transferred.

HTTP Redirector Filter

This filter forwards requests to the web server since these are received by ISA Server. You can specify how the forwarding is to be done via the options. The default option is Forward to local Web Proxy Service. Via the appropriate checkbox you can specify that, in the event of the failure of the proxy server, routing should take place directly to the web server. If this checkbox is not enabled, there can be no access to the server. If you do not want to use the proxy functionality, enable the Send to requested Web server option. If all access to the web server only takes place via the proxy server, check the Reject http requests from firewall and SecureNAT Clients checkbox.

POP Intrusion Detection Filter

This filter checks data sent to the POP server to make sure that the internal buffer of the POP server is not flooded with excessively large quantities of data. No further options are available for this filter.

RPC Filter

This filter is not used to protect against attacks. If this filter is enabled, servers that use the RPC protocol (Remote Procedure Call) can be published. There are no further options for this filter.

SMTP Filter

This filter is disabled by default; it takes up a lot of computing power on the ISA server because both the commands to the SMTP server and the contents of the SMTP mail are inspected. If you enable this filter, the firewall service must be restarted. You can decide whether this service should be automatically restarted right away or you will restart it manually later. The changes come into effect only after the firewall is restarted.

This filter has the most extensive settings. You can search e-mails for specific content via the Keywords tab. To do this, click Add and enter the keyword. Then choose whether the keyword should be sought in the message header text field or subject text field. Then specify via Action whether the e-mail in question should be deleted, preserved, or forwarded. If you have selected several keywords, you can also specify the priority of the processing sequence.

Via Users/Domains you can filter out specific senders and thus block them. You can enter special e-mail addresses under Sender Name and block all the e-mail addresses of an e-mail domain under Domain Name. These e-mails are no longer forwarded to the Exchange Server and thus do not have to be filtered out using the spam filter there. On the Attachments tab, click Add to specify the file attachments that should not be transmitted. Here you can enter an attachment name, a file type, or a size limit. Furthermore, you can specify under Action whether the message in question should be deleted, saved, or forwarded. If you have selected multiple criteria, you can specify an order of priority.

Under SMTP Commands you can enable, disable, and edit the SMTP commands that are required for the communication between client and server. To do this, double-click the relevant command and choose whether this command is enabled or not. You can also give the maximum length of the command in bytes. This prevents the appending of additional "malicious" parameters to a harmless SMTP command.

SOCKS V4-Filter

An application can access a server either directly by using TCP/IP or via a proxy server. For the second option, ISA Server acts as a SOCKS V4 proxy server. This makes it possible for mail clients, for example, to be used via the proxy server. You can specify a port for the communication via Options.

Streaming Media Filter

In Streaming Media, an audio or video file is not completely downloaded before it is played but is played during the course of the download. ISA Server supports the MMS protocol for Windows Media Player, RTSP for Real Player G2 and Quick Time, and PNM for Real Player. Windows Media Services must also be installed on the server.

To permit the transmission of split media files, select the Divide Active Data Flows with a local WMT-Server. The default setting prohibits the transmission of data. If the media services are not directly installed on the ISA server, you must also give your username and password to use these services.

The Monitoring Function of ISA Server

After the filters and policies have been configured on ISA Server, the intrusions identified must be registered and evaluated so as to be able to trace the attacker.

The settings for this are made under Monitoring Configuration/Alarms. There you will find an extensive list of predefined alarms. To configure a specific alarm, double-click it. The configuration is then done via the Events and Action tabs.

Under Events (see the following figure) you can specify an event other than the current one under Event. Furthermore, you can also enter the Number of Occurrences and/or the Number of events per Second before the alarm is triggered. If the actions are repeated, you can specify whether these should be executed immediately, after resetting the alarm, or after a certain interval.

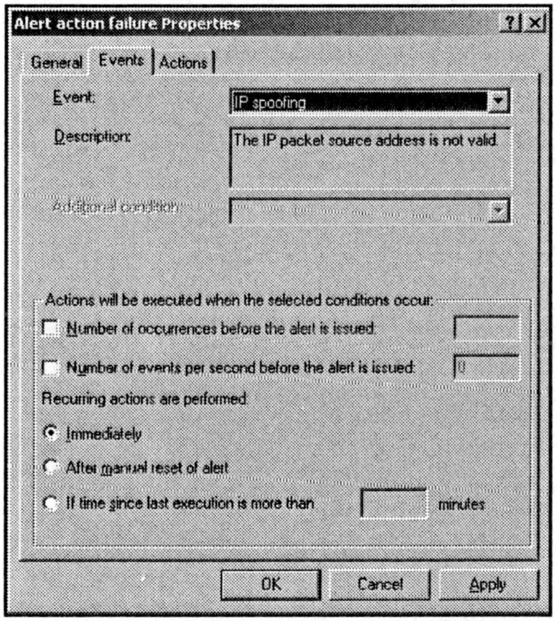

Figure 6.13: Specifying the events to be monitored

On the Actions tab (see the following figure) you can then specify which actions should be executed after the alarm is triggered:

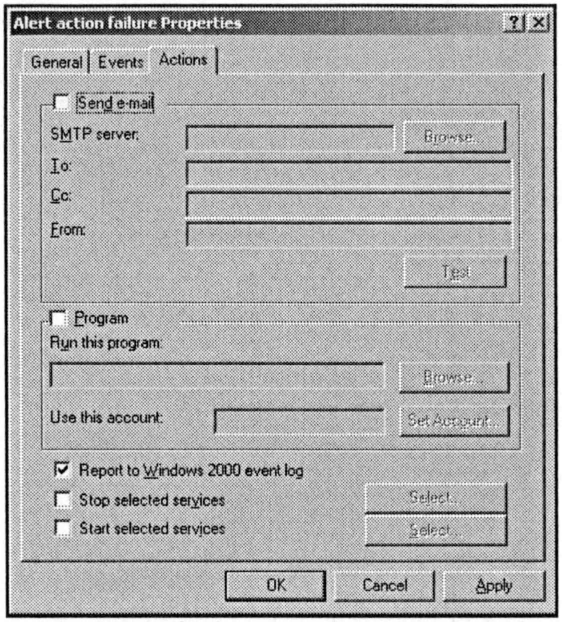

Figure 6.14: Settings for the actions after an intrusion is identified

You have the option of sending an e-mail. Enter the SMTP server and the recipient or recipients. Additionally or alternatively, you can also run a program. If another account is required for this program, you can enter this information here.

In addition to the predefined alarms, you can also create new custom alarms. To do this, select New/Alarm from the context menu. Enter the desired information in the wizards as just described.

To view elapsed alarms for which no special action has been configured, switch to Monitoring/Alarms. Here you will find the alarms and messages of ISA Server. These are also written to the Windows event log.

The Interplay between ISA Server and other Servers

After you have become acquainted with the system-immanent settings of ISA Server, you must get to know the interplay between ISA Server and other servers. Here you will learn about the settings that need to be made on ISA Server so that the internal servers can be accessed from outside. It is precisely in the SBS 2003 environment that you must configure ISA Server appropriately for, say, the Exchange Server, a web server, or a even a terminal server. This is also referred to as publication of servers.

From a purely theoretical perspective, you can always assign a reserved public IP address to each server that is meant to be accessed from the Internet. The address conversion between private and public addresses is regulated by **Network Address Translation (NAT)**. In this case the ISA Server would only function as a router. The cost of reserving several IP addresses is, however, an argument against this. It makes more sense to reserve a public IP address only for the ISA Server. All requests are first sent to the ISA Server, which then forwards them to the individual servers.

Publishing Web Servers

A request to an internal web server or FTP server first comes to the ISA Server, which then forwards it to the web server. From the outside, the ISA Server appears to be a "normal" web server that accepts requests on ports 80 and 443 (HTTP and HTTPS). This prevents a direct connection from being established between an external client and the web server.

Since the ISA Server acts as a proxy server here, you should have selected the cache component during the installation. The pure firewall functionality is not sufficient for this task.

For this forwarding to work, you must set the IP address of the web server and FTP server to that of the ISA Server in the DNS settings.

Base Configuration

1. Open Properties from the context menu of Server Name and switch to the Incoming Web Requests tab.

2. Specify under Identification whether the settings should apply to all IP addresses of the server or only to some. Specify which TCP and SSL ports should be used. You should deviate from the default values 80 and 443 only if the server is not a public server and only authorized users know the changed ports. In this case the change in ports can actually contribute to security. SSL encryption can, however, only be enabled if a certificate has been installed beforehand.

You can specify via Configure how many simultaneous connections are allowed. Consider whether you want to retain the default setting, which provides for no limit, in view of possible bandwidth restrictions. Furthermore, you can specify when a connection should be terminated after the client and the server have stopped exchanging data. By default the disconnection takes place in two minutes.

If users need to be authenticated on the web server, check the Request Identification of non-authenticated Users tab. Authentication is required if, for example, you want to use filters to allow access to only certain users.

To edit the authentication settings, check the entry under Identification and click Edit. You will then see the Add/Edit Listeners dialog:

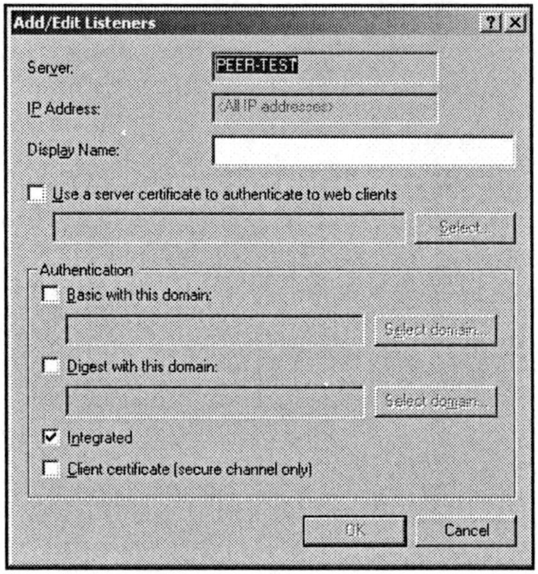

Figure 6.15: Configuration of the authentication methods

In the Display Name text field, enter a name for the relevant interface, e.g. Public, Private, or DMZ if you are using three network cards for accessing the LAN, WAN, and DMZ.

You can either select a certificate as the authentication type or one of the following three: basic authentication, digest authentication, or integrated Windows authentication. If you have enabled SSL encryption beforehand, you must check the checkbox and select a certificate. If you have selected one of the other forms of authentication, the ISA Server asks you for a username and password before the request is forwarded to the web server.

Configuring Forwarding

By default no forwarding of requests to the web server is allowed. There is just a rule that denies all requests. Forwarding must first be allowed by creating a new rule. To do this, take the following steps:

1. Select New Rule from the context menu of Publication/Web Publication Rules and give the rule a name.

2. Specify whether this rule should apply to all destinations, all internal destinations, all external destinations, a destination set, or to all destinations outside the set. The description of these options is already known to you

from the configuration of site and content rules described earlier in the *Site and Content Rules* section. Click Next.

3. Specify whether the rule should apply to all requests or only to certain computers. You can then select these computers. Click Next.

4. On the Rule Action page, specify whether the request should be denied or forwarded to an internal web server. In the second case, enter the name and address of the web server. Also specify the ports for HTTP, SSL, and FTP. Click Next and complete the wizard.

After you have created some rules, you can change their processing priority via the Up and Down context menu items.

Publishing Exchange Server

1. To publish a mail server—in our example we are assuming the Exchange Server of SBS 2003—select Secure Mail Server from the context menu of Publication/Server Publication rules.

To be able to do this configuration, you must first connect to the Internet if you have a dial-up connection so that an IP address is assigned to you by your ISP.

---

2. Next choose whether the Incoming and Outgoing SMTP, Exchange/Outlook, POP3, IMAP4, and NNTP protocols should use the default authentication or SSL-based authentication. For SMTP you can additionally activate the content filter. Click Next.

3. Select the external IP address through which the mail server can be reached. The mapping between internal and external addresses is done with the help of LAT. Next enter the IP address of the mail server. Since under SBS 2003 Exchange Server runs on the same computer as ISA Server, select the Localhost option.

During the preparation for the mail server, an IP packet filter is set up for the mail services on the ISA Server. If the mail server were on a separate machine, a server publication rule would be created for the mail server.

Publishing Other Servers

For all servers other than the web, FTP, and mail servers, you must yourself create a rule if you want to publish them. These additional servers could be a terminal server and an SQL server.

1. Select New/Rule from the context menu of Publication/Server Publication Rules and give the rule a name.

2. In the Address Allocation window, enter the IP address of the internal server and the external IP address of the ISA Server. The external IP address must be one that is not assigned as internal in the LAT. Click Next.

3. Select the protocol that you want to publish on the server. You can only select from the predefined entries here. The entries in this list are based on the application filters (see the *Application Filters* section earlier in this chapter). Only when new filters are added can more protocols be selected here. Click Next.

4. Finally, decide whether the rule applies to requests from all clients or only certain computers. Click Next and complete the wizard.

The Firewall Client of SBS 2003

The firewall client is installed on the clients along with the other distributable applications. When a firewall client is installed, it secures the client machine's Internet usage.

All requests from the firewall client are forwarded to the firewall service of the ISA Server. The firewall service decides whether the client can be granted access or not. The requests from the firewall client can be examined using application filters, for example. A request for an HTTP object is forwarded to the web proxy service (of the ISA Server) via the HTTP redirector service. Finally, the web proxy service forwards the requested object to the client.

Installing the Firewall Client

After the installation of ISA Server 2000 is completed, you must distribute the firewall client for Internet access to the client computers.

1. Create a share folder for the installation files of the firewall client. To do this, go to the \Program Files\Microsoft ISA Server\Clients folder in Windows Explorer.

2. Click on the shared folder Clients. You will see the Share Properties dialog.

3. On the Security tab click Add. Select the Domain Users user group and click Apply.

To prepare the firewall client for the client computers, take the following steps:

1. On the SBS, open Server Management and double-click Client Computers.

2. Select Set up Client Applications.

3. In the Available Applications dialog click Add.

4. In the Application Information window, enter Firewall Client under Application Name and then the path \\SBSServername\MspcInt\Setup.exe. You can also find the file via Browse. Follow the remaining instructions of the wizard.

5. When you are asked whether you want to assign this new application to clients, confirm with Yes. The wizard for allocating applications appears.

This wizard can only be used for allocating applications to clients under Windows XP and 2000. From all other operating systems you will have to manually connect to the shared folder \\SBSServername\MspcInt\Setup.exe and install the firewall client manually.

When a user logs on to a client computer, he or she finds an icon for the installation of the firewall client on the desktop. Double-clicking this icon starts the installation of the firewall client. The connection for this purpose is made automatically via the ISA Server.

The Proxy Function of ISA Server

Apart from its firewall function, ISA Server can also be used as a proxy. This function has only been discussed here briefly. In contrast to the firewall, there are not too many settings here. The proxy server function consists in providing accelerated Internet access for the clients. This cache contains frequently requested objects so as to reduce the network traffic.

Configuring the Proxy Server

To configure the proxy server, switch to the Outgoing Web Requests tab. As you did with incoming requests (see the *Installing the Firewall Client* section on the previous page), check whether the settings should be configured globally for all internal IP addresses or separately for each individual IP address. If you change the values for the TCP and SSL ports here, make the corresponding changes in the client browsers.

The configuration of the authentication and connection settings is analogous to that for incoming web requests. Refer to the *Installing the Firewall Client* section for more information on this topic.

The Cache Function of the Proxy Server

Various types of caching are available. The method used most often is Forward Caching, in which the objects used most often by network users are cached. The other way round,

ISA server also offers the option of Reverse Caching. This is used when users from outside, e.g. Remote Desktop users, access the resources of the local network.

In all ISA Server 2000 offers five different caching methods. In addition to the methods already mentioned—Forward Caching and Reverse Caching—they are Planned Caching, Distributed Caching, and Hierarchical Caching. We will now describe these methods in detail.

Forward Caching

As already described, Forward Caching is used when internal clients access the Internet. You will find the Internet objects most often requested by users on the ISA Server. This caching offers the clients a speed gain as their browser can process objects that are read from the hard drive of the ISA Server faster than data that is to be obtained directly from the Internet. In addition to the faster response time of the Internet browser, this method also minimizes the bandwidth used for the Internet connection.

Technically speaking, Forward Caching works as follows: Client A visits an Internet site and requests a certain Internet object. The web proxy service on the ISA Server determines whether this object already exists in the cache. If the object is not stored in the cache, the ISA Server requests it directly from the Internet server in question. This server sends the object to the ISA Server. The ISA Server stores this object in its cache and forwards it to the client. Now client B visits the Internet site and requests the same object. The ISA Server again checks its cache and finds the desired object there. It directly hands the object to client B without having to request it again from the Internet.

Reverse Caching

Reverse Caching works in the same way as Forward Caching, except that in this case a client accesses the web contents of an internal server from outside.

Planned Caching

You should use Planned Caching when you want to download most frequently accessed contents into the cache of the ISA Server.

Distributed Caching

Distributed Caching does not play a significant role in the context of the use of ISA Server in an SBS 2003 network. This method is used when you use several ISA Servers. In this case the different ISA Servers are brought together into a single logical cache. The **Cache Array Routing Protocol (CARP)** is used for this purpose.

Hierarchical Caching

As with Distributed Caching, Hierarchical Caching plays a limited role in our context and is mentioned only for the sake of completeness. This method further refines Distributed Caching. The various ISA Servers are combined into a hierarchy, and this enables users to access the cache that is nearest to them geographically.

Configuration of Caching

After this overview of the various caching methods, let's move on to the configuration. We will only go into the configuration of the caching methods relevant for SBS 2003—Forward and Reverse Caching. (For more information refer to the help documentation for ISA Server 2000.)

1. To configure the settings, open the Properties of Cache Configuration. Switch to the Http tab.
2. By default HTTP caching is enabled with the installation of ISA Server. If you do not want to use this function, uncheck the Allow http caching checkbox. Otherwise you can specify the frequency with which objects in the cache are refreshed on this page.

The following steps are required only if the object does not have its own validity period (time to live, or **TTL**) on the web server from which it is requested.

You can either specify a special validity period or select the Often, Normal, or Seldom options. With Often, the object is loaded afresh from the web server with each request, with Seldom, only a few transmissions take place. The client user, however, has the option of forcing an update via the ISA Server by using the reload function of the web browser (Internet Explorer). The key combination *Ctrl+R* is used for this purpose.

Configuration for OWA

This section describes the configuration you need to do on the ISA Server to gain access to Exchange mailboxes via Outlook Web Access (OWA).

SBS 2003 provides a wizard to help you with the settings. To start the wizard, enter the command iwc under Run.

The ISA Server must be so configured that it generally accepts incoming web requests on its external interface. To ensure this, take the following steps:

1. In the MMC of the ISA Server click Servers and Arrays. Select Properties from the context menu of the ISA Server.

2. Switch to the Incoming Web Requests tab. Click on Configure Listeners individually for each IP Address.

3. Click Add. Select the server from the list of available ISA Servers. Here you can enter the IP address and port that will be used for responding to HTTP requests. Confirm your entry with OK and switch back to the ISA MMC.

The second step is to set up the destination set through which the clients can be referred to the folders used on the OWA website. The following steps are required for this:

1. Expand the ISA Server and click on the Policy Elements entry.

2. Expand the Policy Elements item and select New. Then select Set from the context menu of Destination Set. Give the new destination set a name (for example, OWA).

3. In the Destination field, enter the URL to be used by the external clients for OWA access. This URL resolves the Internet DNS name of the external IP address of the ISA server. The URL must be entered without the http:// or https:// prefix.

4. In the Path field enter /exchange* and click OK.

5. Enter /exchweb* for the Exchweb folders and /public* for the public folders in the Path field. Confirm each entry with OK.

Next, configure the web publication rule to use the policy element just created. To do this, the following steps are required:

1. Expand Publication and select New and then Rule from the context menu of Web Publication Rules.

2. Enter, say, OWA Rule as the name of the new rule and click Next. In the Destination Set field click on the previously created OWA set and then click on Next.

3. Select Every Request so as to make sure that this rule is applied to each web request, and then click Next.

4. Click Forward request to internal web server (Name or IP Address). Then enter the internal IP address and *not* the server name—in the SBS environment, ISA Server runs on the same server as OWA. If, however, the two services are running on different servers, you can give the server name. Under SBS 2003, however, there is a risk that the server name will be resolved to the external IP address so that OWA is available only to the internal network and not to external clients.

5. Check the Send original host header instead of the one given above to the publication server checkbox. Click Next followed by Finish.

6. Expand Monitoring in the ISA MMC and then click on Services.

7. Stop and restart the web proxy and firewall services.

8. To test server access, enter the address http://URL/exchange in a browser. Replace URL with the address you entered in the Destination field while setting up the destination set (step 3 in the previous procedure).

If OWA is used over SSL connections (Secure Sockets Layer), first create a new server publication rule that uses the HTTPS server protocol definition. Then enter the internal OWA server and the external address of the ISA Server. The OWA server must use the ISA Server as its default gateway.

To host OWA on the ISA Server, socket pooling must be disabled on it. Socket pooling is by default enabled in IIS 5.0 and later, forcing IIS to listen to all IP addresses on port 80. To disable socket pooling, take the steps described in the section that follows.

After socket pooling is disabled, the OWA site can be configured to process HTTP requests on the internal interface. The following steps are required for this:

1. Open the IIS MMC. Select Properties from the context menu of the website that hosts the OWA site.

2. Select the internal IP address of the ISA Server from the list of IP addresses. Then specify the port that the OWA site should listen on. The default here is port 80. This step is necessary because IIS and ISA Server run on the same server under SBS.

3. Furthermore, the automatic search feature should not be enabled on the ISA Server when port 80 is used to respond to requests. To disable this, open the ISA MMC and select Properties from the context menu of the server. Switch to the Automatic Search tab and disable the Publish automatic search information checkbox.

Set up a web listener, a destination set, and a web publication rule as described earlier.

Disabling Socket Pooling

If socket pooling is enabled (which is the default situation in IIS 5.0 and later), IIS listens to all IP addresses. In a situation where a domain has multiple networks, socket pooling can sometimes become a security risk:

1. At the command prompt change directory to \Inetpub\Adminscripts.

2. Enter the following command:
    cscript adsutil.vbs set w3svc/disablesocketpooling true

    You should get the following output:

    disablesocketpooling : (BOOLEAN) True

3. Stop and restart the IIS administration service. The web publishing service must be restarted as well.

Publishing the http://Companyweb Folder

This section describes the publication of the internal website http://Companyweb when the ISA Server is deployed. The aim should be to allow external clients to access this site by entering the address https://FQDN of the SBS 2003:444 or alternatively the address https://FQDN of SBS 2003/remote via the Remote Workplace feature.

Before publishing the company website, you should create a protocol definition and a server publication rule. You must also add a certificate to the company website. You finally need to make some registry changes for the Remote Workplace so that it can also be accessed from the Internet.

Creating a New Protocol Definition

To create a new protocol definition on ISA Server 2000, take the following steps:

1. Open Start Menu/Programs/Microsoft ISA Server/ISA Administration.
2. Expand Policy Elements and select New followed by Definition from the context menu of Protocol Definitions.
3. On the wizard's welcome page, enter a name for the protocol definition (say Companyweb 444) and click Next.
4. In the Primary Connection Information dialog, enter the value 444 under Port Number. The protocol type must be TCP. Select Inbound from the Direction list and click Next.
5. In the Secondary Connections check No under Do you want to use secondary connections? and click Finish.

Publishing the Company Web

To publish the company web via ISA Server, take the following steps:

1. Open Start Menu/Programs/Microsoft ISA Server/ISA Administration.
2. Expand Publishing and select New and Rule from the context menu of Server Publication Rules.
3. Give a name for the new rule (for example Companyweb) and click Next.
4. Under IP Address of the internal server enter the internal network address of the SBS 2003. Then under External IP address of the ISA Server enter the IP address for the network device that makes the external connection. The external address should always be a static IP address. Otherwise you will have to change the publication role each time a dynamically assigned address changes. Then click Next.

5. In the Protocol Settings dialog, select the Companyweb 444 (this must be the protocol you have created as described in the previous section) entry from the Apply rule to this protocol list. Then click Next.

6. On the Client Type select the desired client type from the Apply the rules to requests from list. If the server is accessed by clients over the Internet, select the All requests option. Click Next and then Finish.

7. The ISA Server 2000 firewall service must then be stopped and restarted. To do this, open Servers and Arrays/Name of the ISA Server/Monitoring in the ISA MMC and click on Services. In the right window pane click on Firewall, and from the context menu select Stop and then Start.

If the ISA Server is behind an additional firewall, you must make sure that port 444 is open on it.

Issue of a Web Server Certificate

Next, you must add a web server certificate for http://Companyweb via IIS. The following steps are required for this:

1. In the start menu open Administration/Internet Information Services (IIS) Administration.

2. In the left window pane click on the name of the IIS, and on the right, double-click Internet Pages.

3. Select Properties from the context menu of Companyweb.

4. Click on Directory Security and then on Certificate. On the welcome page of the wizard that appears, click Next.

5. On the Server Certificate page, click Use existing certificate and then on Next.

6. Select an installed certificate from the Available Certificates window and then click Next. The name of the certificate must be the same as the name you chose when running the wizard for configuring e-mail and the Internet connection in the task list. Do not click on Publishing. This certificate is used for internal purposes only. The certificate that you assign to the website must conform to a URL so that users can connect to the server over the Internet.

7. In the SSL-Port dialog, enter port number 444 and click Next.

8. You will be shown a summary of your entries. If these are appropriate, click Finish and then OK.

Configuration of the Remote Web Workplace

To make the `http://Companyweb` page available in the Remote Web Workplace, you must make a few changes in the registry:

1. Open the Registry Editor with the `regedit` command and navigate to the key `HKEY_LOCAL_MACHINE\SOFTWARE\Microsoft\SmallBusinessServer\RemoteUserPortal\AdminLinks`.
2. Set the value of the Help Desk key to 1.
3. Change the value of the STS key likewise to 1.
4. Next, open the key `HKEY_LOCAL_MACHINE\SOFTWARE\Microsoft\SmallBusinessServer\RemoteUserPortal\KWLinks`.
5. Set the value of Help Desk and STS to 1 under this key as well, and close the Registry Editor.

If you restart the e-mail and Internet connection wizard after making the changes in the registry, the changed values are again set back to 1 and 0. You must edit the registry again.

7
SQL Server 2000

Like ISA Server 2000, SQL Server 2000 is available only in the premium version of SBS 2003. You will find SQL Server 2000 on the Windows Small Business Server Premium Technologies CD.

SQL Server can be used as a database for your business applications. You can, however, update the copy of MSDE (Microsoft SQL Server Desktop Engine) used by the SharePoint Services. It is also possible to use only MSDE instead of SQL Server if the company's requirements do not exceed its functional scope.

Without databases, it is virtually impossible to manage information and tasks within an organization. By structuring the data, you can ensure effective access to it for all areas and employees of the organization.

The implementation of the database environment consists of several steps. If no database has been implemented in the organization so far, you must first formulate a plan for the database to be installed. The more careful you are with this plan, the more effectively can you use the data later. After the planning stage, SQL Server is installed and the individual databases created. To ensure that the database is always current, it needs to be maintained, updated, and administered.

Implementation Considerations

What follows is an overview of MSDE and SQL Server 2000 features. Since SQL Server comes only with the premium edition, the question naturally arises whether this component is at all necessary and the additional cost justified. This is of particular importance because, in contrast to SQL Server, Microsoft provides MSDE free of cost and the SharePoint Services, for example, can use it.

SQL Server or MSDE

The Microsoft SQL Server 2000 Desktop Engine (MSDE 2000) uses SQL Server technology as its database module. As a background program, MSDE supports transactional desktop applications but does not have its own user interface or other control and administration programs. The user's communication with MSDE takes place via the application in which it is contained. MSDE is available as a self-extracting archive. This ensures ease of integration and distribution.

MSDE is not bound to a license and may be freely distributed. It functions as an embedded database for applications that require a database module. MSDE can be used under the following operating systems: Microsoft Windows 98, ME, NT 4.0 SP5 and later, 2000, XP, and 2003. Because of its compatibility with SQL Server and the fact that it shares a common code base, an application can easily be ported to SQL Server if it no longer meets MSDE's requirements.

MSDE has the following features (and some limitations) compared to SQL Server 2000:

- **Functional scope**: MSDE is a database module at the local level. Joint access to it is possible. However, there is a limit of five simultaneous working accesses. For more than five simultaneous accesses, there is a noticeable fall in the performance and increase in the processing time of the database. This is because of the monitoring of the system. This is also the main argument in favor of using SQL Server. If you continually need more than five simultaneous accesses, you should stop using MSDE for performance reasons.

- **Support of multiple instances**: MSDE supports up to 16 database server instances per computer.

- **Size of the database**: MSDE supports a database size of up to 2 GB per database. You can also have multiple instances of MSDE on one computer, each of whose databases can have a size of 2 GB.

- **Remote administration**: MSDE can be administered locally as well as remotely. However, remote administration of MSDE isn't possible in a multi-server environment, where transactions take place between several servers.

- **Data Transformation Services (DTS)**: MSDE can run Data Transformation Services packages, but it cannot design them because it does not have a DTS designer.

- **The osql.exe service program**: Interactive Transact SQL instructions and scripts can be run at the command prompt using this program. The output is also at the command prompt.

System Requirements

To run MSDE, the following minimum requirements must be met:

- **Operating system**: Windows 98, ME, NT 4.0 SP5 or later, 2000, XP, or 2003
- **Hardware**: 166 MHz or faster processor, at least 32 MB RAM (recommended 64 MB), and 44 MB free hard disk space

Organization of the Database

You can decide whether you want to implement a client-server database model or whether you want the database entirely on a server.

Database on a Server

In this model, the database is located on the server. When a user wants to access the data, the database is transmitted over the network to the client. On the client, a database driver (Jet Engine) can help with evaluations of the database. In this model, the server only provides the data while the client works with it.

Client-Server Database Solution

The model just described can only be used to a limited extent for complex databases. In the client-server model, on the other hand, the relational database is located on the server, while the database application is distributed between the client and the server. For communication between the client and the server, the database uses **Structured Query Language (SQL)**. To receive specific data, an SQL query is launched from the client. The server then takes over the task of filtering the data from the database and returning it to the client in the form of tables.

The database program on the individual clients constitutes the front end, while the database on the server is the back end. The server manages the database, and a database product such as Microsoft Access can be deployed as the user interface.

In contrast to the database on a server model, the client-server model offers the advantage of greater reliability and scalability. SQL Server 2000 is a relational database management system (RDBMS). The areas of application of SQL Server include web applications such as e-commerce or B2B, Online Transactional Processing solutions (OLTP), and data warehousing over OLAP services.

Client Access to the Database

Of particular importance when deploying a database server is the possibility of integrating it with a wide spectrum of client operating systems. Even a relatively small environment such as a company running Small Business Server does not necessarily have a homogenous client structure.

SQL Server 2000 offers access to its instances for the following client operating systems: Windows 9x, ME, NT, 2000, XP, Apple Macintosh OS, OS/2, and Unix/Linux.

These clients can use different application types. These include, for example, ODBC applications, OLE DB consumers, or DB library clients. In the case of clients running Apple Macintosh OS, OS/2, or UNIX/Linux, you must remember that these operating systems do not support the graphical programs of SQL Server (e.g. SQL Server Query Analyzer). Third-party ODBC programs are required for this purpose.

The Design of the Database

If you do not have a database in your company yet, careful design and planning will play an important role in the later success of the database. When planning the database, keep also in mind the programs that are to be used on the client side for accessing it.

When planning the database, you should first determine the information that should go into it. This data is then stored in individual tables in the database. It should be ensured that no information is duplicated in the database; redundancy of the contents is not advised. Meaningful integration of this wealth of data takes place via the linking of tables.

All in all, the implementation of the database consists of the following steps:

1. Analysis of the data to be included in the database. This analysis depends on the special business processes and requirements of the company.
2. Conception and modeling of the database. In this context, one speaks of **Entity Relationship Modeling (ERM)**.
3. Logical design of the database. What tables the database should contain and what links there should be between these tables is determined here.
4. Once the planning and design stages are completed, the database is created physically on the SQL Server. All tables and other database objects are created and populated with data one after the other. Subsequent exhaustive testing of all database functionality is a mandatory task.
5. The last step is the installation of the database in a production environment. This should, however, only be done after the database is tested.

The Installation of SQL Server 2000

The version of SQL Server that comes with SBS 2003 is equivalent to SQL Server 2000 Standard Edition.

This chapter describes various installation scenarios for SQL Server 2000. When installing SQL Server 2000, you must decide whether you want to install a new instance of SQL or update the existing MSDE instance SHAREPOINT of the SharePoint Services.

After installing SQL Server, you should also install Service Pack 3a. This update provides important security e.g. against the Slammer worm.

Installing a New Instance of SQL Server 2000

To run a new instance of SQL Server 2000, take the following steps:

1. After the Premium Technologies installation CD auto-starts, click on Install Microsoft SQL Server 2000.

2. You will see the SQL Server 2000 SP2 and below dialog. Click Continue, as the problem indicated will be resolved after installing Service Pack 3.

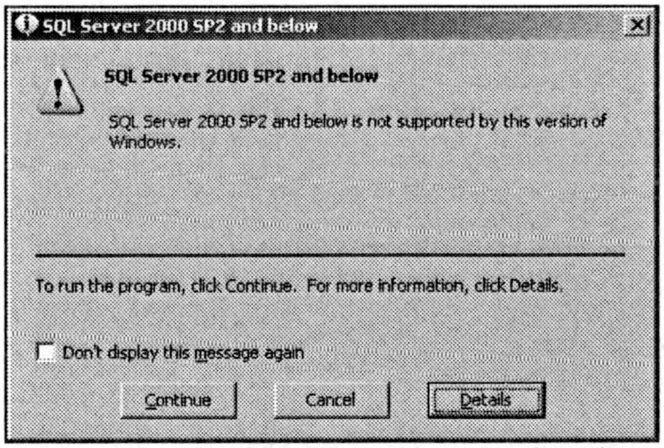

Figure 7.1: Warning about installing SQL Server 2000 without the Service Pack

3. After the welcome message, you will see the Computer Name dialog (see Figure 7.2). Here you can decide whether the new instance should be installed on the local computer or on a remote computer. In our example, we select the local computer and click Next.

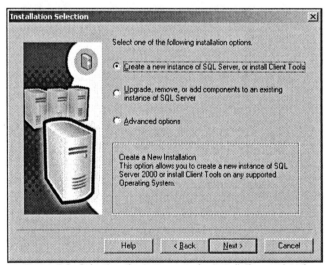

Figure 7.2: Selecting the server for the installation

4. In the Installation Selection dialog (see Figure 7.3), select one of the three available options. The options are Create a new instance of SQL Server, or install Client Tools; Update, remove, or add components to an existing instance of SQL Server; and Advanced options. The last option is interesting because it allows you to create a response file for an unsupervised installation. Click Next.

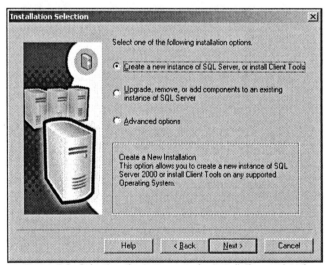

Figure 7.3: Selecting the instance to be installed or updated

5. After you decide to install a new instance, enter your name and optionally the name of your company. Then click Next and accept the license agreement that is displayed.

6. Enter the 25-digit license key for SQL Server 2000 and click Next.

7. In the Installation Definition dialog (see Figure 7.4), select the installation type. You can choose between Client Tools Only, Server and Client Tools, and Connectivity Only. The second option installs the server along with the client tools so that administrative tasks can be performed. Click Next.

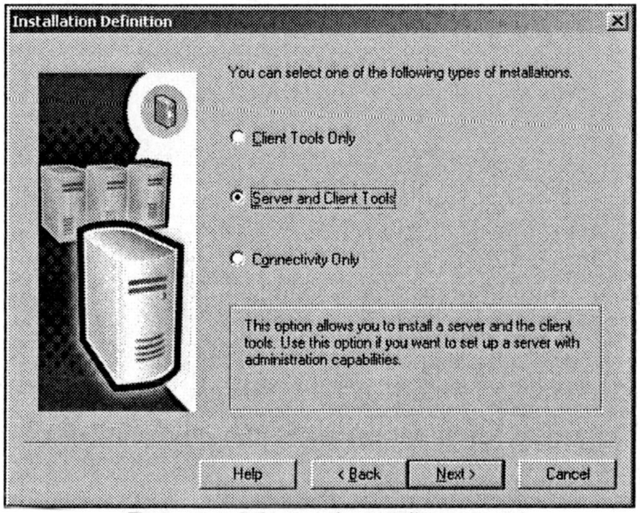

Figure 7.4: Selecting the installation type

8. Next, you must specify in the Instance Name dialog (see Figure 7.5) whether you want to carry out a default installation. If you want to give the new instance a name (maximum 16 characters), uncheck the Default checkbox and enter the desired name in the Instance Name text field. The name must start with a letter, a number, or one of the characters &, _, or #. The name should not be Default or MS SQL Server. With SQL Server 2000, it is possible for the first time to install multiple SQL instances simultaneously on one machine. Click Next.

SQL Server 2000

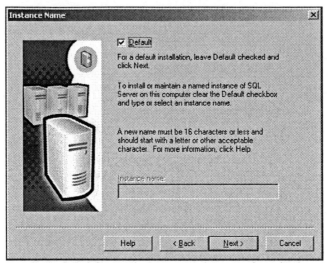

Figure 7.5: Selecting the instance to be created or edited

9. Finally, in the Setup Type dialog, specify whether you want a typical, custom, or minimum installation, and choose the directory in which SQL Server should be installed. Whenever possible, install the program files and data files in two separate folders. It is best to change only the destination folder for the data files. You can then click Next and, if you have opted for a custom installation, select the desired components.

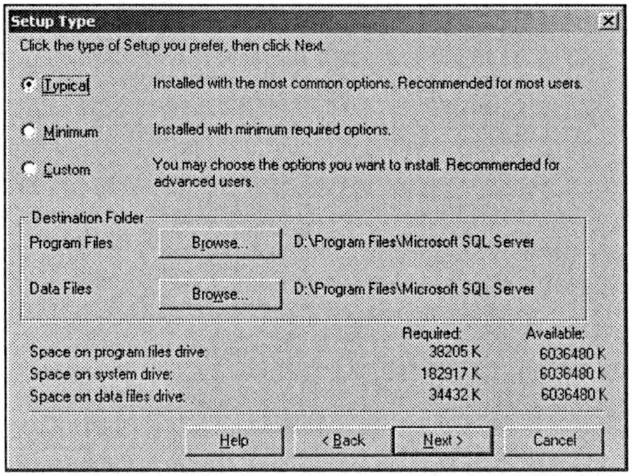

Figure 7.6: Determining the setup type and the installation folder

10. You will now see the Services Accounts dialog. Decide whether you want to use the same account for the SQL Server and SQL-Server Agent services, or Customize the settings for each service. You can use either

254

the Local System account or a Domain User account. Enter the account name, password, and a domain for this and click Next.

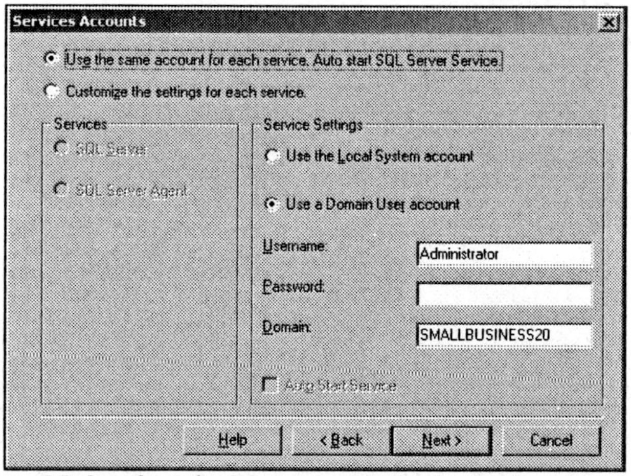

Figure 7.7: Specifying the Services Account for the SQL Server services

11. Next, under Authentication Mode, decide whether you want to use the Windows Authentication Mode. This is the default setting. In this way, user accounts under Windows NT, 2000 XP, and 2003 can authenticate themselves on the server. You can also use the Mixed Mode, which includes both Windows Authentication and SQL Server Authentication. You must use this setting if you have clients running Windows 9X or ME—these cannot run Windows Authentication. In this case, you must enter the account name and password for the system administrator login. Then click Next.

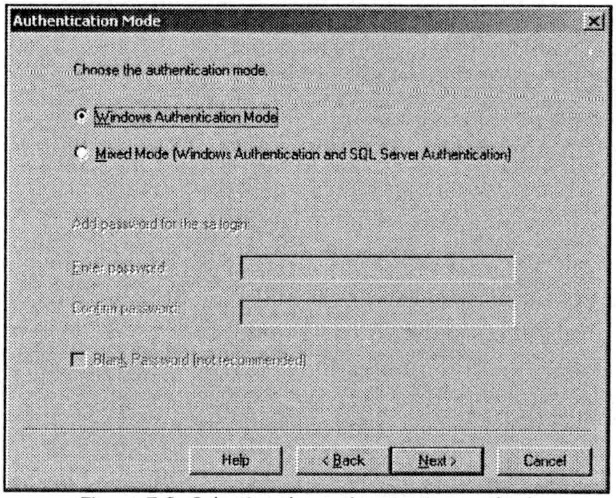

Figure 7.8: Selecting the authentication method

12. In the Collation Settings dialog, specify the language setting that should be used for the sort order of the data sets under Collation designator. Retain the default setting Latin1_General. Under Sort order, you can specify additional sorting options. If, for reasons of compatibility, you need to work with previous SQL versions, use the SQL Collation option. Click Next.

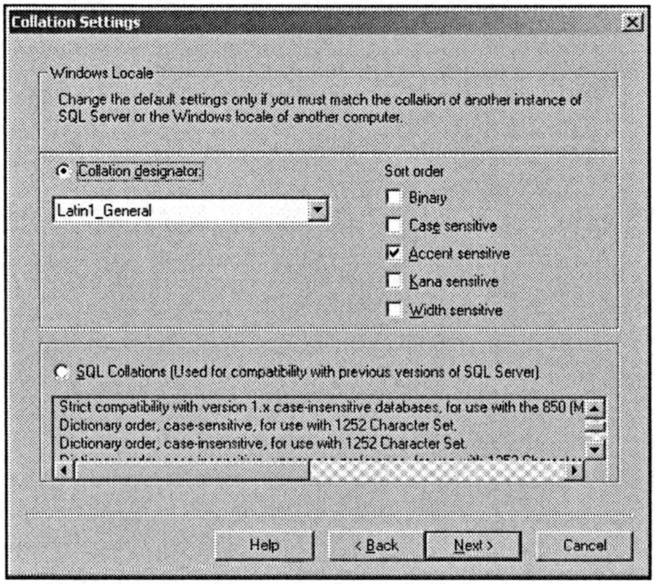

Figure 7.9: Specifying sort orders and collation designators

You need to specify sort orders at the time of installing SQL Server 2000 only if you do not wish to use default settings for the sorting. This is the case if one of the following scenarios applies to your SQL environment:

- o You want to install a new instance, but there is already an older version of SQL Server.
- o An application depends on an older version of SQL Server because it is not compatible with SQL Server 2000.
- o SQL Server uses a language other than the one used by the clients that connect to the database.

13. Under Network Libraries (see Figure 7.10), select the connections that should be used for communicating with the SQL Server. The two options selected by default are Named Pipes and TCP/IP-Sockets. The TCP port 1433 is recommended as the communications port there. You can also add other

libraries such as AppleTalk ADSP or NWLink IPX/SPX. Click Next to start the installation.

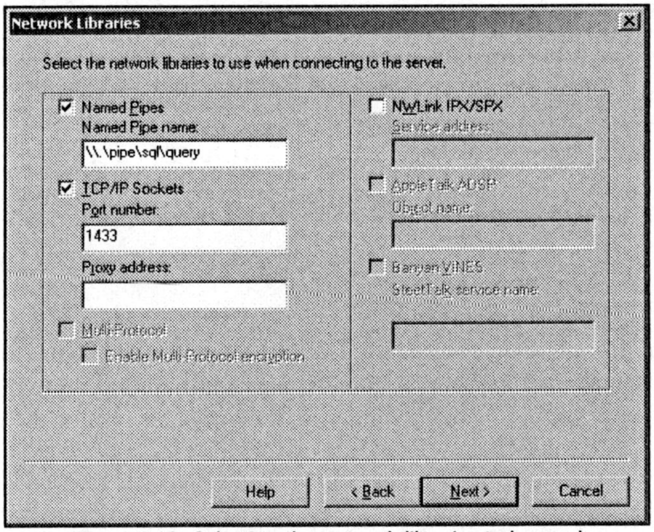

Figure 7.10: Selecting the network libraries to be used

Installing Service Pack 3a for a New Instance

To install SQL Service Pack 3a, take the following steps. The Service Pack should be installed in all cases.

1. On the auto-start page of Premium Technologies, select Install SQL Server 2000 Service Pack 3a.

2. After the welcome message, accept the license agreement and then click Yes.

3. In the Instance Name dialog, make the same choice as you made for the default name or a custom name for the SQL instance in step 8 of the SQL installation. Then click Next.

4. In Connect with the server, specify the authentication mode for the connection. This depends on the decision made in step 11 of the installation. Then click Next.

5. If the setup determines that the password for the user sa (system account) is blank, you can specify a new password in the SA Password Warning dialog. Then click Next.

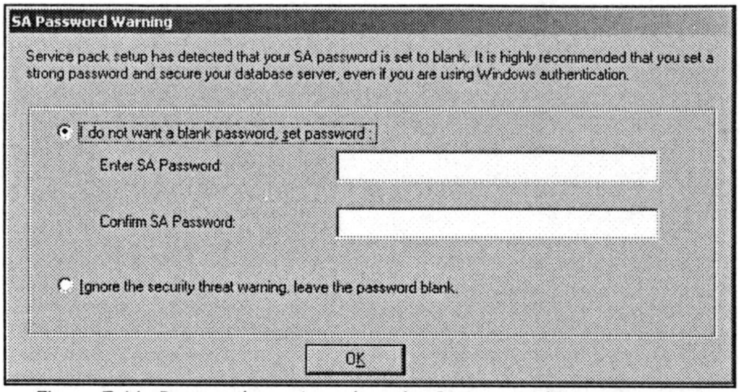

Figure 7.11: Password warning when the SA account has no password

6. In the next dialog, you can see the Enable cross-database ownership chaining for all databases checkbox. It is recommended that you do *not* select this option but instead enable ownership chaining for the individual databases after installation. Click Next.

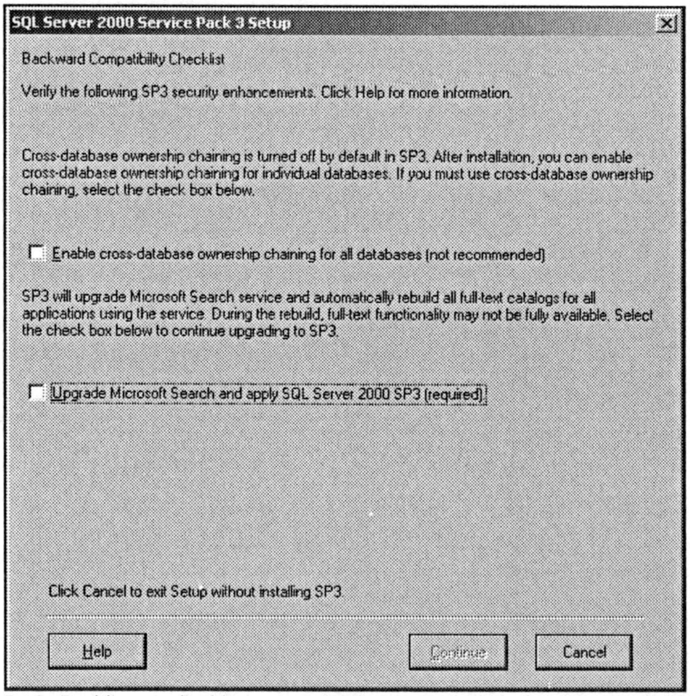

Figure 7.12: Enabling or disabling cross-database ownership chaining for all databases

7. Next, specify whether SQL Server should automatically send error reports to Microsoft after serious errors. To enable this, use the relevant checkbox and

click OK followed by Next. This begins the installation of Service Pack 3a. The installation progress of the various update scripts is displayed.

8. In the course of the installation, you will be prompted to back up the **master** and **msdb** databases since their contents are going to be updated. The server must then be restarted. Click on Finish to do this.

Problems with the Service Pack Installation

*   If in the course of installing Service Pack 3a you get the message that the scm.exe file is in use, you must restart the server and again select the installation menu for Service Pack 3a.

*   You may get the following error message: Error in running a script: sp3_serv_uni.sql(1). To end the installation of Service Pack 3a, click OK. You must then restart the installation of the Service Pack.

*   If during the installation of the Service Pack there is an error message Setup initialization error: Source \SQL2000_SP3a\x86\Setup\Sqlspre.ini, there is a problem in copying the setupsql.ini file to the %Temp% folder. This means that an earlier version of this file in the %Temp% folder has been marked as write-protected. The setup program cannot overwrite this file. To continue the installation, delete the existing version of the setupsql.ini file from the %Temp% folder or at least remove the write protection.

Updating the MSDE Instance Used by SharePoint Services

The updating of the MSDE instance SHAREPOINT is largely identical with the installation of SQL Server 2000.

1. First carry out the installation as described in the *Installing a New Instance of SQL Server 2000* section up to step 7.
2. In the Instance Name window, disable the Default checkbox and enter the instance name SHAREPOINT in the name field.

However you may not update the SBSMONITORING instance used for monitoring Small Business Server. An update of this instance is not supported.

3. In the Existing Installation dialog, accept the default setting Update the existing installation and click Next.
4. Next, you will see the Update dialog. Check the Yes, the programs should be installed checkbox here. Click Next, and when asked to confirm the installation of additional components, click Yes.
5. In the Select Components dialog, check the Full text search checkbox under sub-components. Additionally, you can also select Online Documentation of

SQL Server 2000. Click Here on this page and Next on the next page for the installation to begin.

Installing Service Pack 3a for the SHAREPOINT Instance

The installation of the Service Pack for the SHAREPOINT instance is also similar to the installation of the Service Packs for a new installation.

1. First follow steps 1 and 2 described in the *Installing Service Pack 3a for a New Instance* section earlier in the chapter.

2. In the Instance Name dialog, uncheck the Default and enter the name SHAREPOINT in the text field.

3. Follow the subsequent steps described in the *Installing Service Pack 3a for a New Instance* section.

4. After completing the installation, open Start/Programs/Microsoft SQL Server/Enterprise Manager. Double-click Microsoft SQL Servers and select New SQL Server Registration from the SQL Server Group context menu. Under Server Name enter Name of the Server\SHAREPOINT. Select Windows Authentication as the Authentication Method.

If you get an error message when updating the SHAREPOINT instance, check if the MSSQL$SHAREPOINT service has been stopped. If this is not the case, you must manually stop the service and restart it after the update is complete.

Sorting Settings for SQL Server 2000

As mentioned under step 12 in *Installing a New Instance of SQL Server 2000* section, you should only change the default sort order if one of the following reasons is applicable:

- You are using an older version of SQL Server. You are using the SQL sort order for reasons of backward compatibility.

- An application depends on an older version of SQL Server as it is not compatible with SQL Server 2000. The documentation of this application should give information about the required sort orders.

- An existing SQL Server uses another region schema or a different sort order.

If the SQL Server uses a language different from the clients that connect to its database, you must also enter sorting markers for the sort order to be selected.

Checking the Sort Orders of other SQL Servers

To check the sort order of other SQL Servers, use the Query Analyzer program from the SQL Server program group.

1. Under SQL Server enter the name of the server to be checked.

2. After the connection with this server is established, key in the following lines in the Query Area:

```
Sp_helpsort
Go
```

3. Press the *F5* key to run the command. The results are shown in the results area of the query window.

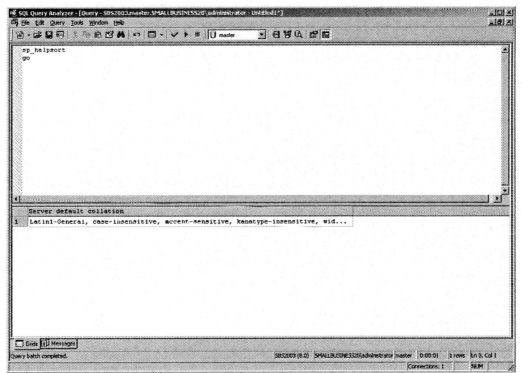

Figure 7.13: Querying the collation settings of an SQL Server

---

Remember that several processes between the SQL Servers can fail if the sort orders on these servers differ from each other.

The sort order can always be changed later. To do this, however, it is necessary to create the databases afresh and re-enter the data in them.

The Databases of SQL Server

During the installation of SQL Server six different databases are created with their corresponding protocol files. The following table lists the databases and protocol files of SQL Server:

Database name	Database file	Protocol file	Size after installation
Master	Master.mdf	Mastlog.ldf	17 MB
Model	Model.mdf	Modellog.ldf	0.76 MB
Msdb	Msdbdata.mdf	Msdblog.ldf	12 MB
Tempdb	Tempdb.mdf	Templog.ldf	8.1 MB
Pubs	Pubs.mdb	Pubs_log.ldf	1.8 MB
Northwind	Northwind.mdf	Northwnd.ldf	3.3 MB

The first four databases mentioned above are system databases. The individual databases have the following functions:

- **Master**: The master database contains all the system-level information of SQL Server. This includes system configuration, login accounts, initialization information, and storage locations for all databases.

> For the functioning of SQL Server it is very important that you regularly back up the master database and can restore this backup when required. Further instructions about backing up the database can be found in the *Backing Up and Restoring the Database* section later in this chapter.

- **Model**: This serves as a template for all newly created databases. When a new database is created, the contents of the model database are copied and the rest of the new database is filled with blank pages. The model database also serves as a base for the Tempdb database.

- **Msdb**: This database is used by the SQL Server Agent for the planning of orders and warnings and the logging of operators.

- **Tempdb**: This database contains all temporary tables and temporarily stored procedures. It is created anew each time SQL Server is started. When SQL Server is shut down, the temporary database becomes blank as the temporary contents are automatically deleted when the client connections are closed. The database has an initial size of 8 MB when SQL Server is started. This size can, however, increase as SQL Server is running.

- **Pubs** and **Northwind**: Both these are sample databases that allow you to familiarize yourself with SQL Server.

The Structure of a Database

A database contains a number of different objects. You can see all these objects when you open any database in the **Databases** container in Enterprise Manager (see the section that follows).

Components	Description
Diagrams	The relations between the individual tables of the database are represented graphically.
Tables	The contents of the tables are the actual objects of the database. As in an Excel table, the data is arranged in columns and rows.
Views	A view is a table built on the basis of a specific query.
Stored procedures	These are pre-compiled Transact SQL instructions. A procedure consists of a set of SQL commands. Procedures are created for displaying information as well as for managing the server. Thus, for example, you can check the integrity of a database with the help of a procedure.
Users	Users identified by the system for security reasons.
Roles	Roles and groups with specific rights.
Rules	Rules are bound to columns. Nonetheless, they are displayed as independent components.
Defaults	A default value can be defined for columns and is applied when the user does not specify a value for the column.
Custom data types	Custom data types, e.g. as required by a specific application, can be defined.
Custom functions	These are sub-routines consisting of one or more Transact SQL instructions. Users can compile their own Transact SQL instructions and are thus not restricted to the integrated functions.
Full-text catalog	These are used to browse the database.

Administering SQL Server

This section familiarizes you with the most common administrative tasks and tools.

Enterprise Manager

The central administration of SQL Server is done through Enterprise Manager. This is called via Start/Programs/Microsoft SQL Server/Enterprise Manager. In this management console, you can create databases, manage procedures and indexes, edit users and rights, and back up databases.

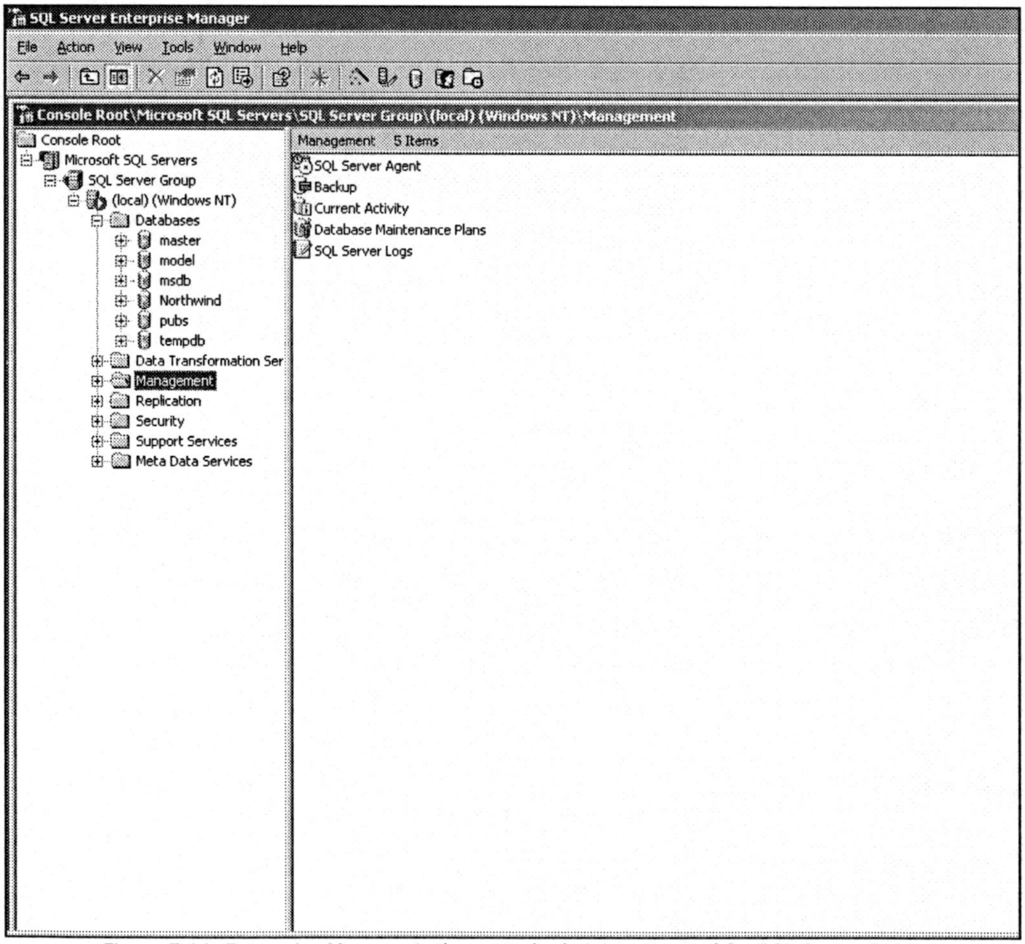

Figure 7.14: Enterprise Manager is the central administrative tool for SQL Server 2000.

The console structure under SQL Server has the following containers:

Container	Description
Databases	The databases contain the tables and objects.
Data Transformation Services	The Data Transformation Services (DTS) consist of a number of graphical programs and objects for extracting and consolidating data from various sources.
Management	Here you will find various graphical programs and programmable utilities for administering SQL Server.
Replication	Here you will find various administrative objects for the distribution of data objects and data to other databases. This makes it possible to distribute data to other locations. The distribution can take place via a LAN or a WAN.
Security	Access and permissions for the SQL Server are configured here.
Support Services	This container has all the different service programs for the SQL Server.
Meta Data Services	An object-oriented repository is realized with the help of the Meta Data Services. This makes it possible to integrate with information systems or other applications that use metadata.

You must first register SQL Server before you can administer it with Enterprise Manager.

4. To do this select New SQL Server Registration from the context menu of a server or a server group.

5. Click Next in the registration wizard, followed by Add to choose from the list of Available Servers.

6. In the Select Authentication Mode, decide whether Windows Authentication or SQL Server Authentication should be used and click Next.

> When prompted to enter a username and password, check the Prompt for the SQL Server account information when connecting checkbox; this ensures that login information is not stored in the registry.

7. In the Server Group list, check one or more of the checkboxes. You can activate the service via Display SQL Server state in console. Show system databases and system objects displays all these objects. Via Automatically start SQL Server when connecting, an instance of SQL Server is automatically started.

To be able to connect to an instance via Enterprise Manager, the service must first be started. A correctly running service can be recognized by the green arrow near the server icon. To stop the service, select Stop from the context menu of the server. Optionally, you can also send a message to the clients that are connected to the SQL Server so that they can log off. After allowing a reasonable amount of time for logging off, select Stop from the context menu of SQL Server Agent. Then select Stop from the context menu of the server.

Starting Services and Instances

After the installation of SQL Server you can start and stop its services and instances even at places other than Enterprise Manager.

You can start, stop, or continue an instance of SQL Server or the SQL Server Agent Service via the SQL Server Services Manager. This is possible for local as well as remote computers.

Via Control Panel/Services you can start, stop, or continue an instance of SQL Server or the SQL Server Agent Service on the local computer. To do this, use the following commands:

```
Net start mssqlserver
Net start sqlservr
Net start SQLServerAgent
```

If you want to start a specific instance, use the following commands:

```
Net start mssql$Instancename
Net start SQLAgent$Instancename
```

Alternatively, you can also run the SQLSERVR.EXE file.

Installing an Existing Database

If an existing database is going to continue being used under SQL Server 2000, you must first install this database. To do this, in Enterprise Manager select Restore Database from the context menu of Databases. Here you can select the database to be installed under Restoring the Database. Further information about restoring databases can be found in the *Restoring the Database* subsection under *Backing Up and Restoring the Database*, later in the chapter.

Service Programs of SQL Server

Apart from the main administration via Enterprise Manager, SQL Server also has a few service programs. You'll find these under the start menu entry of Microsoft SQL Server.

SQL Server Network Utility

You can edit the network settings with the help of the SQL Server Network Utility.

Thus, for example, you can enable and disable network protocols and edit their properties, force protocol encryption, or enable a WinSock proxy.

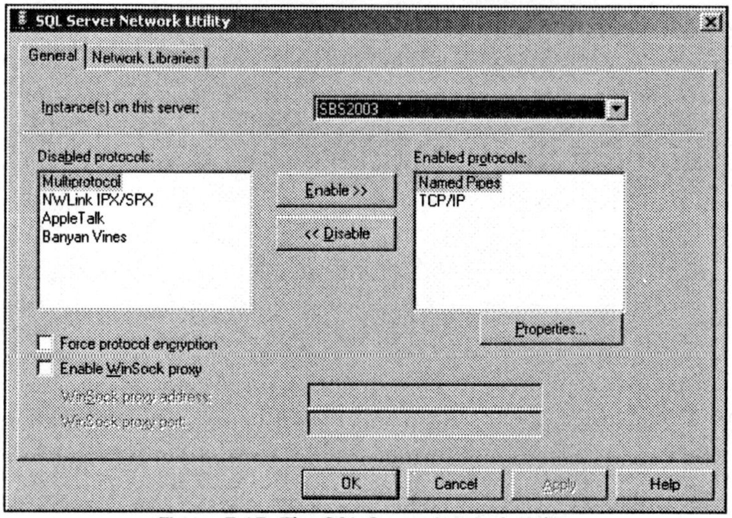

Figure 7.15: The SQL Server Network Utility

SQL Server Client Network Utility

Via the SQL Server Client Network Utility, you can configure network libraries for the clients to access SQL Server. Furthermore, you can specify the network protocols and access methods for the clients.

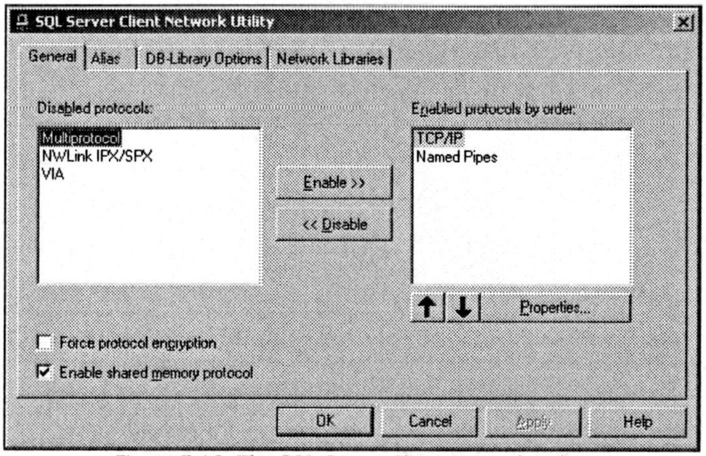

Figure 7.16: The SQL Server Client Network Utility

Permissions for Database Access

By issuing appropriate permissions, you can protect the database both against damage caused inadvertently by users due to wrong usage and against damage caused by willful malicious access. To control security, SQL Server 2000 uses authentication on the one hand and permissions for accessing individual database objects on the other.

Authentication on the Database

For authentication on the database, SQL Server uses Windows NT authentication and SQL Server authentication. You specify the form of authentication to be used at the time of installing SQL Server. To change the settings made there, open Extras/Server Configuration Properties in Enterprise Manager. You can change the setting on the Security tab.

In Windows NT authentication, SQL Server uses the username and password of the operating system. Once the user has been successfully authenticated with the operating system, he or she need not enter any further login information for accessing the database. To be able to access the database, however, the user must have permission in his or her account to access the SQL Server.

SQL Server Authentication is also known as mixed-mode authentication. In this form, SQL Server first checks the operating system account of the user. If this does not permit access to the server, the SQL Server login is used. If the user has such a login, he or she can gain access to the database. You must always use the mixed mode for clients of the Windows 9X and ME operating systems, as these do not support Windows NT authentication.

Permissions on the Database

Once a user has been authenticated, the permissions determine what actions he or she can carry out on the database. There are two kinds of permissions—object permissions and instruction permissions.

The object permissions regulate the way in which users may access objects in the database (Tables, Columns, Views, and Procedures). The following object permissions are available:

Permission	Available for objects
DELETE	Tables, Columns, Views
EXECUTE	Procedures, custom functions
INSERT	Tables, Columns, Views

Permission	Available for objects
REFERENCES (DRI)	Tables
SELECT	Tables, Columns, Views
UPDATE	Tables, Columns, Views

The various permissions have the following meanings:

Permission	Description
DELETE	Existing datasets of the database can be deleted.
DRI	Foreign keys can be created to refer to the database.
EXEC	Procedures can be executed.
INSERT	Datasets can be added to the database.
SELECT	It is possible to read the contents of the database.
UPDATE	Existing datasets can be modified.

The instruction permissions on the other hand do not apply to "normal" users of the database. These permissions determine who may edit the database in what way. Such permissions are, for example, CREATE DATABASE, CREATE VIEW, or BACKUP DATABASE.

Permissions through Roles

To simplify the issue of permissions to individual users, roles are used in SQL Server 2000. These roles can be compared in principle to groups used in the user administration of Windows. A distinction is made between server roles and database roles.

Database Roles

The database roles regulate the permissions for the database. A database role is only valid for the database for which it has been issued. In all there are ten predefined database roles (you can define your own database roles in addition to these):

Database Role	Description
Db_accessadmin	Access to the database is regulated via this role by adding or deleting users.
Db_backupoperator	This role permits you to backup the database.
Db_datareader	This role gives unlimited reading rights for the database.

Database Role	Description
Db_datawriter	This role gives unlimited writing rights for the database. These include adding, updating, and deleting data (INSERT, UPDATE, and DELETE permissions).
Db_denydatareader	This role completely denies reading (SELECT permission) of the database contents.
Db_denydatawriter	This role completely denies writing (INSERT, UPDATE, and DELETE permissions) to the database.
Db_ddladmin	Database objects can be created, modified, or deleted with this role. DDL stands for **Data Definition Language**.
Db_owner	This role identifies the owner of the database. He has all the permissions contained in the remaining roles.
Db_securityadmin	This role allows you to give out instruction and object permissions.
public	This role automatically applies to all users who have some permission relative to the database.

Server Roles

In contrast to the database roles, server roles are used for issuing permissions for specific tasks on the SQL Server. You will find the roles in Enterprise Manager under Security/Server Roles. The following server roles are available:

Server Role	Description
Bulkadmin	This role permits the execution of bulk add operations.
Dbcreator	This allows the creation and editing of databases.
Diskadmin	Disk files are administered via this role.
Processadmin	This role enables the control of SQL Server processes.
Securityadmin	This role can issue permissions for the database and logins to the server.
Serveradmin	Via this role it is possible to administer the server and its settings, and also to shut down the server.
Setupadmin	This enables replication configuration on the server.
Sysadmin	This is the highest permission level. It comprises all the permissions of all other roles.

In contrast to the database roles and even user groups, you cannot create any server roles in addition to the eight listed here. Even the permissions of the individual server roles cannot be modified.

Configuring Permissions for a User

After you have been introduced to the theory of the various authentication methods, permissions, and roles, this section describes the configuration of permissions for a user.

1. Select New Username from the context menu of Security/Username in Enterprise Manager.

2. On the General tab, specify the form of authentication that the user should employ.

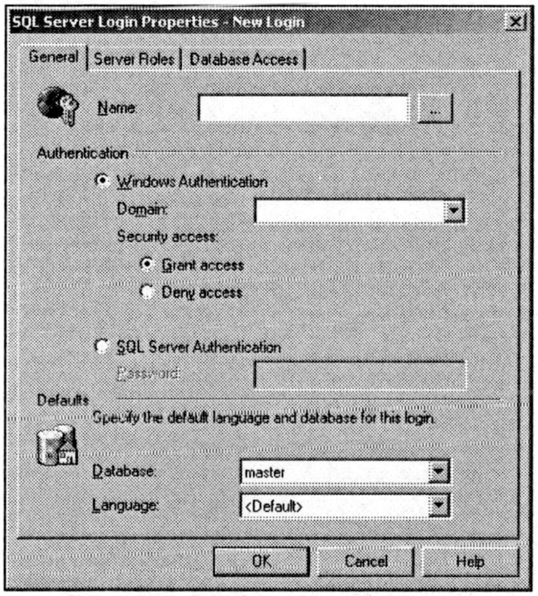

Figure 7.17: Specifying user authentication

Specify the domain under the Windows Authentication option. Its name is automatically added to the Name field, where you then add the username. The password is not given in this case as the user has already given at the time of logging on to the domain. Remember that this form of authentication is only possible for clients running Windows NT, 2000, XP, and 2003. For older client operating systems, use SQL Server Authentication. Select SQL Server Authentication, enter the user's name under Name, and then his or her password. You can also enter a default database and the preferred language for the user.

3. Next, you can specify the server roles for the user. To do this, switch to the tab of the same name. As a rule, none of the server roles is issued to a normal user. It is, however, possible to assign a server role to a user later.

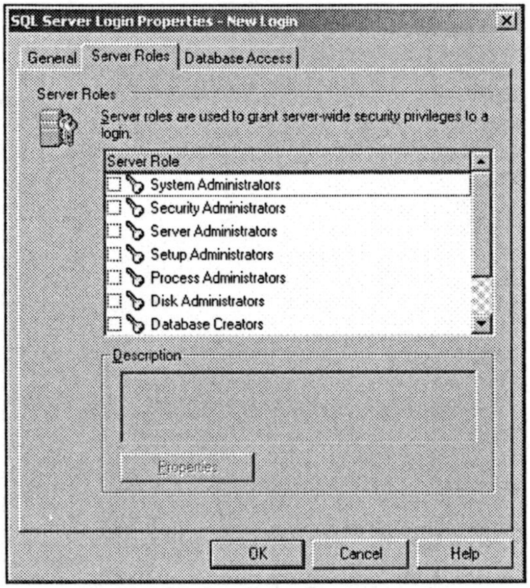

Figure 7.18: Specifying the server roles

4. Then switch to the Database Access tab.

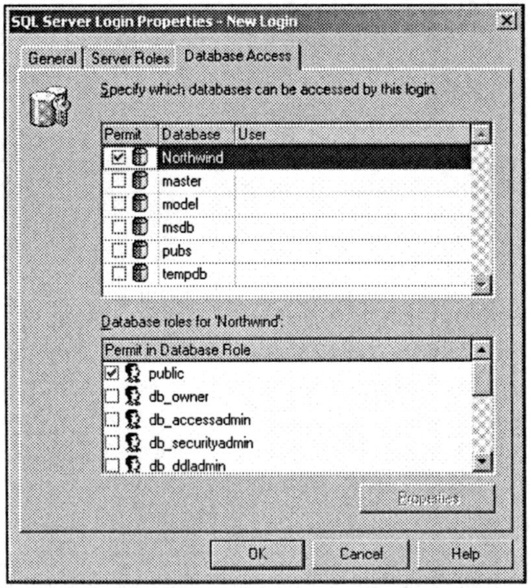

Figure 7.19: The choice of database roles for a database

First check all databases to which the user should have access. Once you have checked a database, you can select the database roles to be assigned to the user for the database under Database roles for Database Name. Once a database is selected, the username for the database is automatically selected. By default the same name that you have given in step 2 is used. If you want to change this, double-click in the User column.

By default, you should assign the database roles db_datareader and db_datawriter to a user. If you have not assigned a database role to a user, you will get an error message. It is, however, still possible to create this user.

If you have selected Windows Authentication, the system simultaneously checks whether the user in question exists in the domain. If this is not the case, the user cannot be created for access to SQL.

Further Configuration Options for Permissions

This section introduces you to additional configuration options for issuing permissions.

Creating and Adding a Database User

If you have created a database but have not yet assigned a user to access it, no database user is set up to log on to this database. To create a user, select the desired database and select New Database User from the context menu. On the General tab, select a username under Username. Here you will find a list of all users for whom a SQL Server login is configured. As soon as you select a username, it is entered without the domain name suffix in the Name field. You can also change this name. Then you can select the various database roles for the user.

When a user is newly created, the Permissions button next to the Username field is not yet clickable. To assign special permissions via this button, you must first confirm the creation of the user with OK and then close and reopen the window.

Creating Additional Database Roles

As you have already learned in the *Permissions through Roles* section, you can create your own database roles in addition to the pre-defined ones. To do this, highlight Roles in the desired database and select New Database Role from the context menu.

In the Name field, enter the name for the new database role. You must then decide whether this role should be a **standard role** or an **application role**. A standard role always relates to only some users. The users to whom this role should apply can be selected via Add. An application role, on the other hand, is provided with a password. Any user who knows the password can receive this role.

Issuing Permissions

Permissions can be defined for a role as well as for a user. However, always keep in mind that the configuration of permissions for a user requires considerably more administrative input than the configuration of roles. If you regulate permissions via roles, you do not have to assign permissions to individual users.

To assign permissions to a user, select the database user and click Properties. Then click Permissions. This brings up the Database User Properties window.

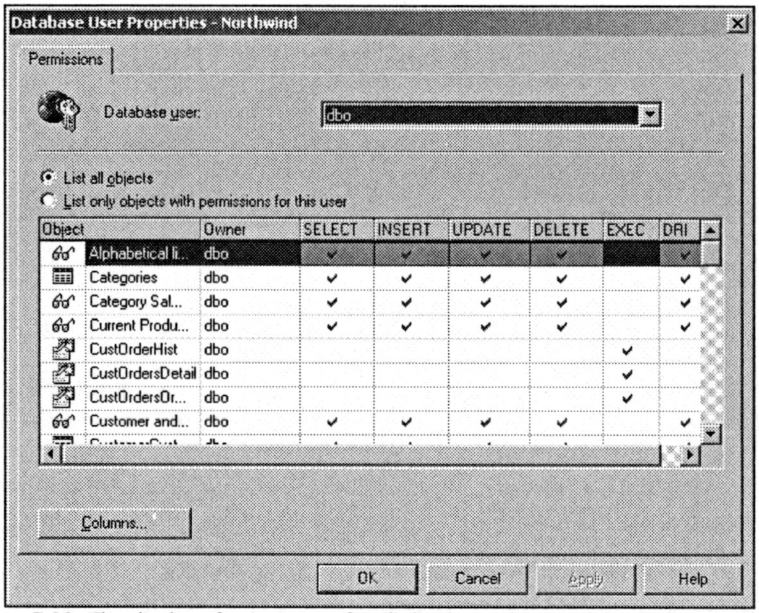

Figure 7.20: The display of permissions for all database objects of the desired database

Here you will see all the database objects belonging to the selected database. For each object you can assign the SELECT, INSERT, UPDATE, DELETE, EXEC, and DRI permissions. A permission is only selectable if it is available for the object in question (see the table under the *Permissions on the Database* section).

To further fine-tune the SELECT and UPDATE permissions, click Columns. You will see the various columns of the table and can now assign permissions for each individually.

As regards the issue of permissions, there are three possibilities: Granted, Neutral, and Withdrawn. The granting of a permission is marked by a green check, and its withdrawal by a red cross. It is possible to withdraw a permission from a user even if it's available to him or her by virtue of his role membership. A neutral permission is not directly assigned to a user. A user can receive such a permission via membership in a particular role.

To assign permissions to a database role, follow the steps just described. All you have to do is select a role instead of a user. Remember that the permissions for the default database roles cannot be changed. The only exception is the Public role. Otherwise, permissions can only be assigned to self-defined database roles.

Backing Up and Restoring the Database

To minimize the time between the failure of a database and its restoration, you must work out an effective backup strategy. Whether the problem that has occurred is a hardware issue or a database issue is irrelevant to begin with.

To ensure the most effective restoration of data, you should on the one hand use various backup media, and on the other, combine the various backup options of SQL Server 2000 meaningfully with one another. Furthermore, with the help of a current backup, you can quickly put up a copy of the database on a second server. You must always include the **master**, **msdb**, and **model** databases in the backup. Backing up the **model** database is, however, necessary only when changes have been made. If the SQL Server also serves as a replication distributor, you should also regularly back up the **distribution** database.

> The backup of the SQL Server can be done during actual operation. It is not necessary for users to log off the server.

If you are backing up the database to transfer it from one SQL Server to another, you should reduce the size of the backup file with a compression program. The compression of the backup file is very effective.

Types of Backup

In addition to the normal backup, SQL Server also offers a differential database backup and a transaction log backup. You can also carry out a file and file-group backup.

Complete Database Backup

With this option, a complete backup is carried out. In this backup, the state of the database when the backup was taken is preserved. Since the backup also contains the transaction logs, you can delete the transaction logs after a complete backup is done.

Differential Database Backup

In a differential backup, only the changes in the database since the last complete backup are stored. This type of backup is particularly relevant for large databases as you can save time and disk capacity in this way. To restore the database to the state before the backup, you must also carry out transaction log backups.

Transaction Log Backup

A transactional log backup contains all the data that has been completed since the last complete, differential, or transaction log backup. With the help of this backup you can restore the state of the database up until the time of the backup. All non-active transactions are stored and then removed from the log to free up disk space for other use.

File and File-Group Backup

This procedure is used for very large databases whose size makes a complete backup very difficult. For this reason, the database is broken up into a number of small parts, which are then backed up. This method is only available if the database consists of several data files (MDF files).

Creating a Backup

As a backup destination, SQL Server supports a file on the hard drive or a tape drive. It makes sense to first back up the database to a file and then store the file on the tape drive in the course of the backup of the SBS.

To simplify your administration of the backups, SQL Server offers the option of creating backup media. When you select a backup medium, you do not have to enter the complete backup destination with its full path each time. You only select the name you have given to the backup medium.

To create a new backup medium, take the following steps:

1. In Enterprise Manager, open the Administration folder under the SQL Server. From the context menu, select New Backup Medium.
2. Give the backup medium a label under Name. Under Filename the folder you specified as the backup folder is entered by default. You can also select another folder or a tape drive.

If you select a network folder, the SQL Server service must have the appropriate permissions there. However, this is not the case if the server is started under the local system account.

Now whenever you want to take a backup, this backup medium will be displayed to you.

The Backup Wizard and Manual Backup

The database can be backed up either manually or by using the backup wizard.

The Backup Wizard

After you have created a backup medium, you can carry out a backup with the help of the backup wizard. To do this, take the following steps:

1. In Enterprise Manager, select Wizards from the Tools menu. In the Select Wizards dialog check Backup Wizard under Administration and click OK.

2. After the welcome screen, select the database to be backed up under Database, and then click Next.

3. Next, give a name for the backup. The backup can later be found under this name in Enterprise Manager. Additionally, you can also give a description for the backup. Then click Next.

4. Select the desired backup method. The various backup methods have already been described in the *Types of Backup* section. In our example, we will select the option Database backup – Backup entire database. Then click Next.

5. In the Select Backup Destination and Action dialog (see Figure 7.21), you can specify whether a Backup device, a Tape, or a File should be used as a backup destination.

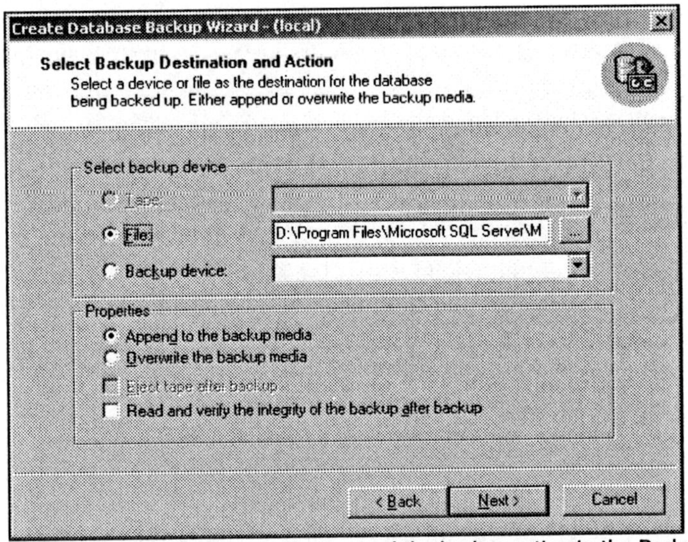

Figure 7.21: Specifying the backup destination and the backup action in the Backup Wizard

6. Additionally, you can also select the following backup options:
    - Append to the backup media: With this option, several backup sets are created on the medium. Previous backup sets are not overwritten in this process.
    - Overwrite the backup media: This overwrites an existing backup set. The set can no longer be restored.
    - Eject tape after backup: This option is available only if you have selected a tape as a backup medium. After the backup, the tape is ejected to prevent overwriting.
    - Read and verify the integrity of the backup after backup: With this option, the readability of the backup file and the conformity of its contents with the data to be backed up is verified after the backup. This integrity testing can take some time if the database is large.

7. You can verify the backup set, create a schedule, and define an expiry date for the backup set. If you want to set up a backup cycle, enter a name under Media Set Name. Also enter the backup date. This prevents the premature overwriting of a backup file. Until the expiration date a new backup file is created each time. This file is differentiated by the date or a number. If the time stamp has expired, the files are overwritten from the first onwards.

8. You can create a schedule for the backup. To modify the schedule, click Change under Schedule. In the Edit Schedule dialog, enter a name for the schedule. Make sure that the Activated checkbox is checked so that the schedule is applied. To create a schedule, select one of the following options:
    - Start automatically with the SQL Server Agent: The backup starts automatically with the SQL Server Agent service.
    - Start when CPU(S) is (are) free: This option is meaningful when you use hardware that is sufficiently loaded even under standard usage. This ensures that the backup will be carried out only when there is not much data traffic on the SQL Server.
    - Once: Specify a one-time backup by entering the time and date.

The one-time backup auto starts the moment you close the backup wizard if the time and date are not entered.

    - Recurring: Via Change you can specify a recurring backup schedule. You can adjust the backup interval in accordance with your firm's requirements.

> The schedule for the recurring backups can only be applied if the SQL Server Agent service is running. To prevent complications, you must specify the Automatic start type for this service. If the service is not running when you create the backup schedule, you will be reminded of this. The time-controlled backup tasks can also be seen in Enterprise Manager under Administration/Tasks.

9. Finally the wizard shows you a summary of the entries that you can still change. Then click on Next.

Manual Backup

If you don't want to use the wizard, you can take the backup manually. To do this, select All Tasks/Backup Database from the context menu of the desired database in Enterprise Manager. All these tasks can be performed on the General tab. The other settings of the wizard such as verification of the backup and the expiration date of the backup set can be found on the Options tab.

Modifying Backup Tasks

All time-controlled backups can be found in Enterprise Manager under Administration/Tasks. Here you have the option of modifying backup tasks by a double-click.

On the Notifications tab, you can specify whether and in what way the notification about a backup should be sent. You can choose between e-mail, pager, net send command, and an entry in the Windows event log.

Restoring the Database

A database is restored after an error on the database or on the server, and when it is being transferred to another server.

1. To restore the database, select the desired database in Enterprise Manager and select All Tasks/Restore Database from the context menu.

2. In the Restore Database dialog, you will see all available backups of the selected database on the General tab under Parameters. The latest backup is always inserted automatically. If you have selected the From Media option, you will see the Select Media button through which you can select a backup file. You can also use this option to restore the database on another server. It is also required in the case of such a serious problem on the SQL Server that the history of existing backups is no longer available.

SBS 2003 Administration

This chapter discusses the daily administration of SBS 2003 and its wide spectrum of tasks. Apart from the various administrative tasks to be performed, you will learn about the various consoles and tools that simplify the administration of SBS 2003.

The Server Management Console as Central Administrative Instance

The server management console is the central switchboard for the administration of SBS 2003. Many management components can be found in this console (see the following figure). You will find this console under Start/All Programs/Server Management.

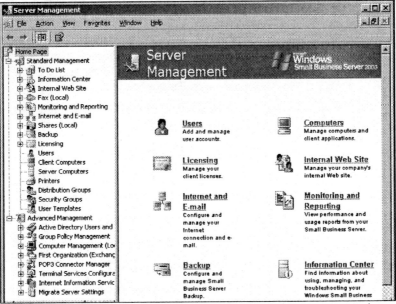

Figure 8.1: The server management console as central management tool

The following table gives you an overview of the various management components:

Management components	Description
Standard Management:	
To Do List	Tasks contained in this list are indispensable for the configuration of SBS 2003 and must be carried out after the installation and base configuration.
Information Center	Here you will find links to the documentation and web resources of SBS 2003. These include Windows Help, the resource pages at http://www.microsoft.com, and links to the Windows SBS community.
Internal Web Site	Programs for managing the internal website. These are described in detail in the *Internal Website* section.
Monitoring and Reporting	Tools for viewing and configuring server performance and usage reports, event logs, and monitoring. Further details can be found in the *Monitoring and Reporting* section later in this chapter.
Internet and E-mail	Configuration of the firewall, e-mail, phone, and modem options, as well as those for Internet and Remote Access. These tools are described in *Monitoring and Reporting* section.
Shares (local)	Viewing and managing all the shares set up on the SBS 2003. A detailed description can be found in the *Shares (local)* section.
Backup	Tools for viewing and changing the backup plan and backup status. Further information can be found in the *Backup and Restore* section.
Licensing	Tools for viewing and editing the SBS 2003 Client Access Licenses (CALs).
Users	Tools for the management of user accounts.
Client computers	Tools for the management of client computers.
Server computers	Tools for the management of server computers.
Printers	Tools for the management of printers and print jobs.
Distribution Groups	Tools for the management of distribution groups.
Security Groups	Tools for the management of security groups.
User Templates	Tools for the management of user templates.

Management components	Description
Advanced Management:	
Active Directory Users and Computers	The computers and users of Active Directory are managed here.
Group Policy Management	Tool for creating and managing group policies.
Computer Management (Local)	This will open the computer management console.
First Organization (Exchange)	This will take you to the Exchange settings, which you can also access via Exchange Management.
POP3 Connector Manager	Configuration of the POP3 connectors for the management of POP3 e-mails.
Terminal Services Configuration	This will take you directly to the configuration and management of the server's Terminal Services.
Internet Information Services	Configuration of Internet Information Services (IIS 6.0)
Migrate Server Settings	The settings of one server can be transferred to another; see the *Migrating Server Settings* section.

Server Management for Power Users

The Server Management for Power Users management console has a limited number of management components for users to whom certain areas of server management have been delegated by the administrator. Only users belonging to the Power Users group can access this console.

For a member of the Power Users group this console is available at Start Menu/All Programs/Management. To view this console as an administrator, open %Systemdrive%\Documents and Settings\All Users\Application Data\Microsoft\ SmallBusinessServer\Administration\mysbsconsole.msc.

An important difference as compared to the server management console is that the actual console structure is not available here (see Figure 8.2). This prevents the user from accessing advanced management features. Thus, for example, the deleting of users and computers is not possible.

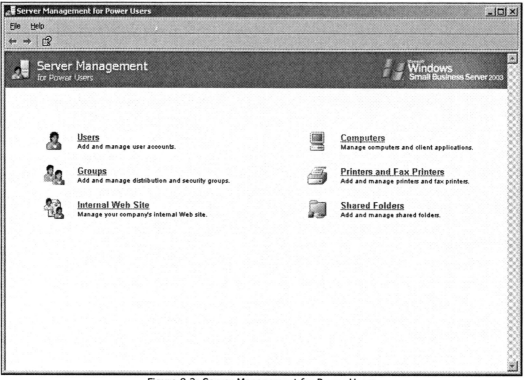

Figure 8.2: Server Management for Power Users

The following management components are available in this console:

Management components	Description
Users	Addition and management (except deletion) of user accounts.
Computers	Management (except deletion) of computers and client applications.
Groups	Addition and management (except for deletion) of security and distribution groups.
Printers and Fax Printers	Addition and management of printers and faxes.
Internal Web Site	Administration of the internal company website.
Shared Folders	Addition and management of shared folders.

User Management

Under User Management you will find links to the most commonly used user-related administrative tasks. These include Add User, Add Multiple Users, Change User Permissions, Configure Password Policies, and Configure Redirection of the My Documents Folder options, as well as those for changing mailbox quota and disk quota settings, offering remote access, and managing computers.

In the Name column of the MMC you will see the Administrator and Guest accounts as well as all the user accounts of the SBS 2003 domain. The storage location of the first two accounts mentioned in Active Directory is Domain Name\Users, and that of the SBS user accounts is Domain Name \MyBusiness\Users\SBSUsers. You will find the users there when you open the Active Directory Users and Computers MMC.

Adding a User

We will now walk through the creation of a new SBS 2003 user account along with the other related configurations.

To create a user account, take the following steps:

1. Open the Add User link.

This configuration step consists of a number of tasks. A user account, mailbox, and home folder are created for each user. Furthermore, the user's membership in the security and distribution groups is specified. SharePoint access and disk quotas are also configured. Finally, a client computer is assigned to the user.

2. Before you create the user you must select a user template for him in the Template Selection dialog (see Figure 8.3). The following user templates are available by default:
   - User Template: In this template, access to the Internet, e-mail, network printers, fax devices, and shared folders is permitted. This template should be used for normal user accounts.
   - Mobile User Template: This template contains all the permissions of the User Template. Additionally, a VPN or dial-up connection can be made to the SBS 2003.
   - Power User Template: This template contains all the permissions of the Mobile User Template. Furthermore, users based on this template can manage users, groups, printers, faxes, and shared folders. They can also make a remote connection to the server. A local connection to the server is not possible.

o Administrator Template: This template gives unlimited access to the server and domain management.

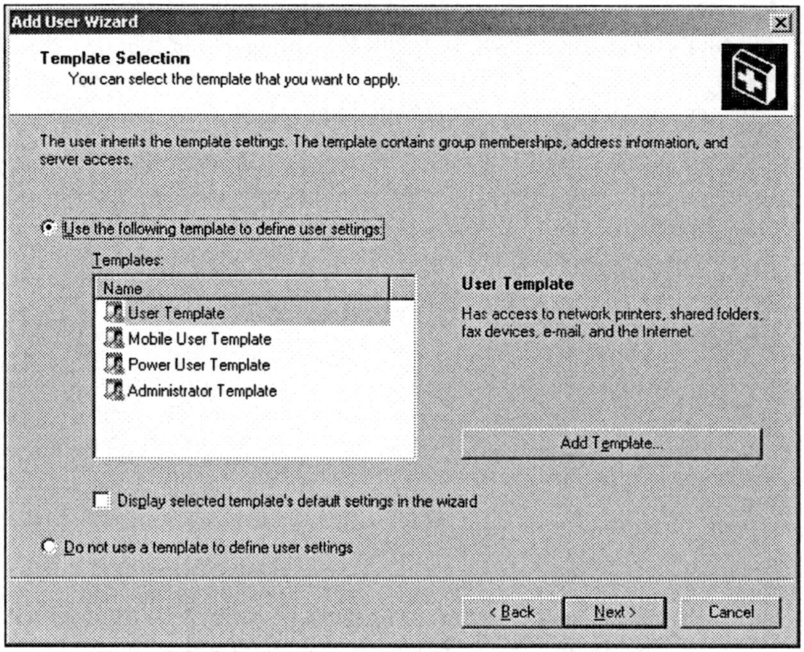

Figure 8.3: Selecting the user template to be applied to the user

Apart from these predefined templates, you can also create templates your own. This procedure is described in the *Adding New User Templates*. Furthermore, you can change the user template for any user later.

After you have selected the appropriate template, click Next.

3. In the User Information dialog (see Figure 8.4) you can create a new user for the template via Add. If you have already created some new users for the selected template, you will find them listed under Users.

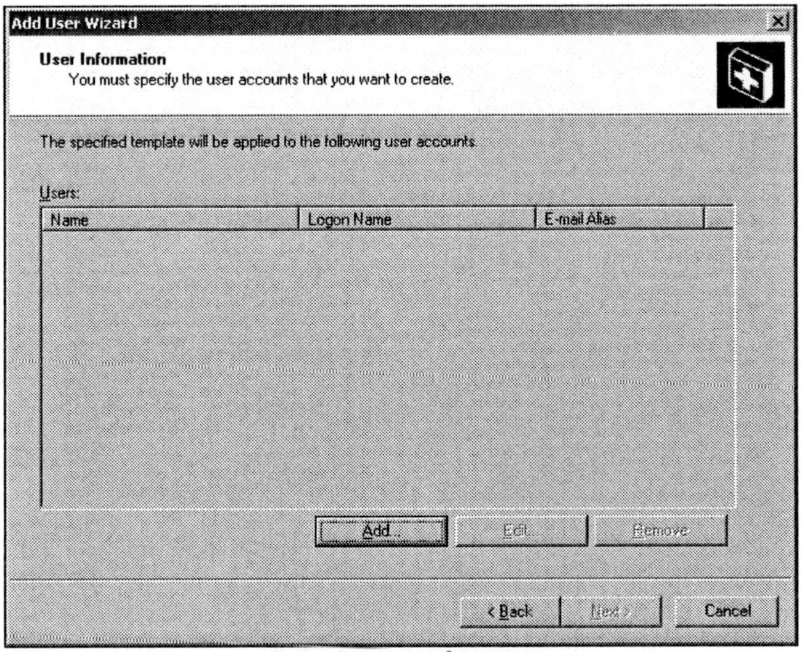

Figure 8.4: User information

4. After you have clicked on Add, fill in the appropriate fields in the Specify the user information dialog (see Figure 8.5). For the Logon name field you can choose one of the four available formats from the drop-down list. In our example you can choose between Pmustermann, MustermannPeter, PMustermann, and PeterM. These suggested values are an advantage over Windows Server 2000 and 2003 in that you, as the administrator, can quickly achieve a uniform structure in the issue of usernames. No name structure was suggested in the previous versions.

5. The value selected here is also entered in the e-mail alias field by default, but you can change this. Once you have made all the entries, click OK.

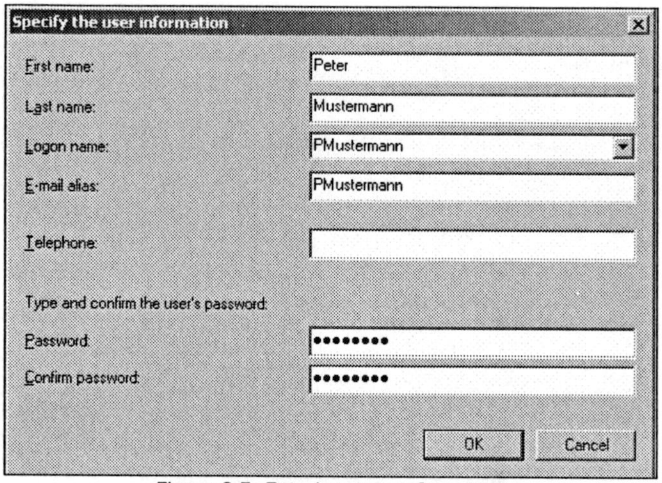

Figure 8.5: Entering user information

6. In the Add User Wizard (see Figure 8.6) you can also set up a computer for the user. If you select the Set up computers now option, the computer is configured in the next steps. Then click Next.

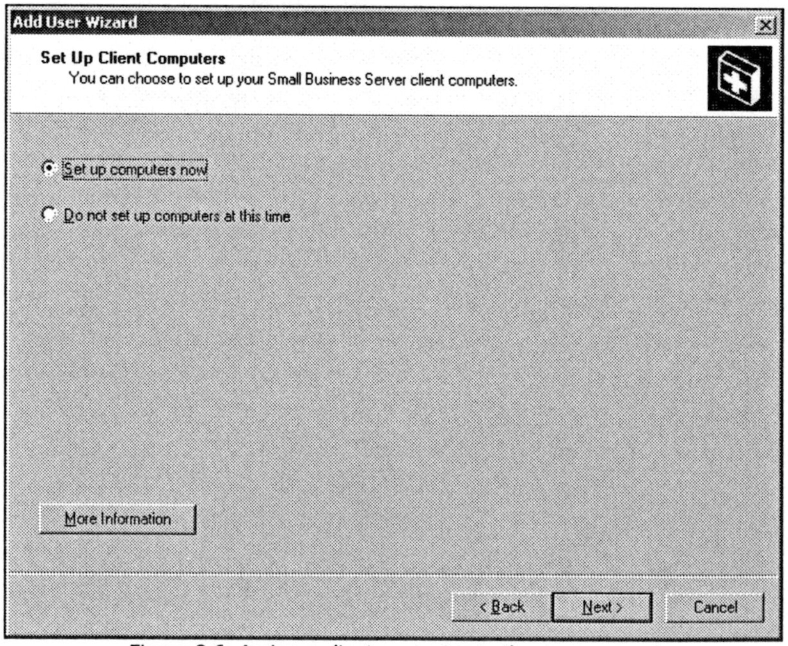

Figure 8.6: Assign a client computer to the user account

7. In the Client Computer Names dialog (see Figure 8.7) enter the name of the computer and then click Add. For the computer name, the valid characters that can be used are letters A to Z (capitals or lower case), digits 0-9, and - (hyphen). All information that you provide via the wizard is applied to all computers in the Accounts will be created for list. You can also remove computers from this list. The default name of the computer account is always Username01, in our example PMustermann01, but it can be deleted and replaced by another one. Then click Next.

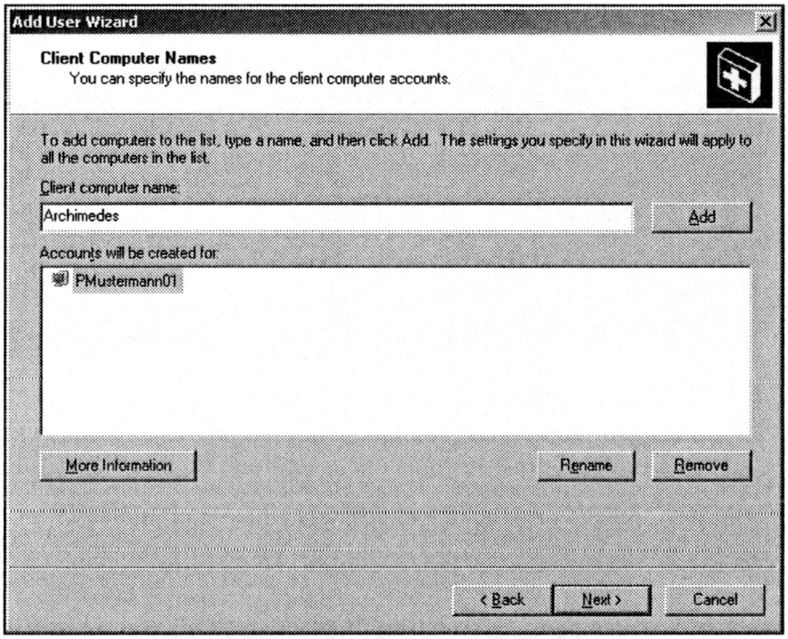

Figure 8.7: Specifying the computers for the user

8. Next, the applications to be installed on the computer are selected in the Client Applications dialog (see Figure 8.8). The following applications are installed by default: Client Operating System Service Packs, Internet Explorer 6.0, Outlook 2003, and the Shared Fax Client. You can change and extend this selection.

> Unchecking the checkbox for an installed application does *not* uninstall the application from the client computer.

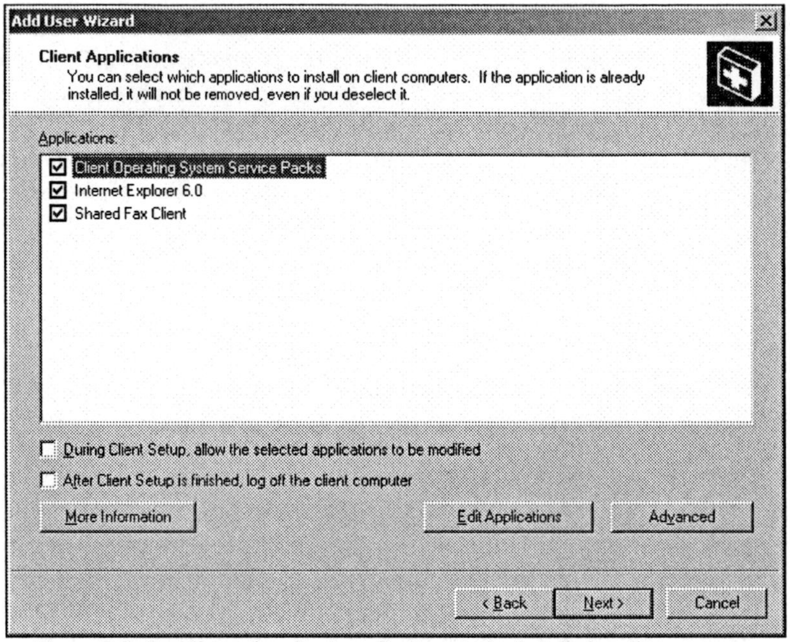

Figure 8.8: Specifying the client applications to be installed on the computer

If you have selected Outlook 2003 for the installation and there is already a previous version of Outlook on the client computers, disable the COM add-ins on the clients. Take the following steps under Outlook on the clients for this:

- o From the Tools menu select Options and switch to the Other tab.
- o Click on Advanced Options and then on COM Add-ins.
- o Uncheck the checkbox for the Add-in.

9. In the Client Applications dialog check the During Client Setup, Allow the selected applications to be modified if you want to allow the user to change the installation path or to not install an application. You should activate the After Client Setup is finished, log off the client computer checkbox if the user is not able to wait till the setup ends and you don't want anyone to have unauthorized access to the computer after installation ends.

10. If you click on Edit Applications, you will see the Available Applications dialog (see Figure 8.9). All applications that are available for installation are listed here. With Add you can make other applications available for installation on the clients.

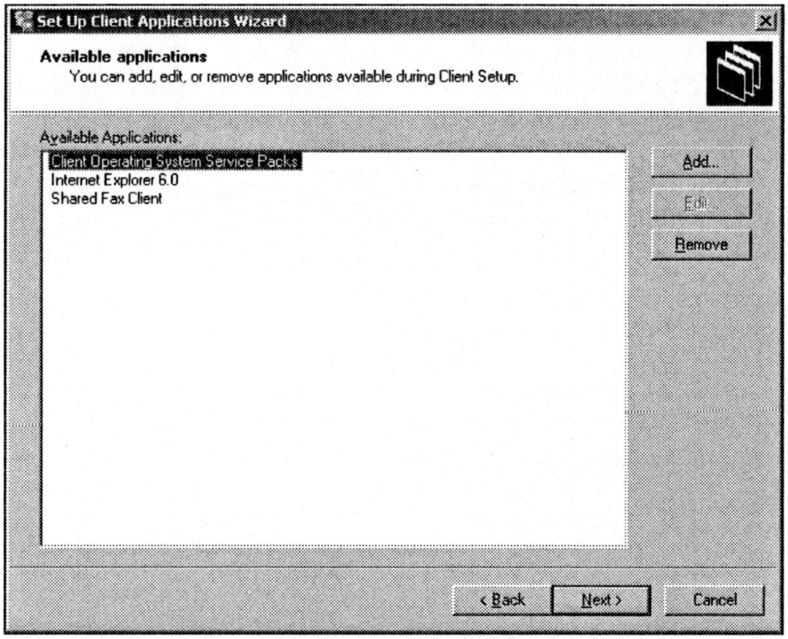

Figure 8.9: Applications available for client installation

If you decide to add another application, you will see the Application Information dialog (Figure 8.10).

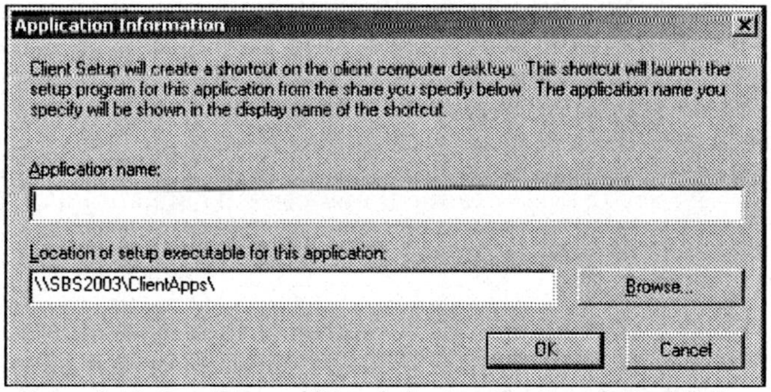

Figure 8.10: Specifying additional client applications for installation

Before you can add an application here, you must copy the installation program to a shared folder. It is best to copy these applications to the default folder \clientApps on the SBS2003. Domain users must have Read and Execute permissions for the shared folder so that they can proceed with the installation.

11. In the Application Name text field enter a name for the application and use Browse to select the path to the application. A link to this application is created on the client's desktop. Then click OK. You come back to the Available Applications dialog. The added applications can always be edited here. The Edit function is not available for the default applications. It is also possible to delete applications from the list. Then click Next to end the wizard for adding new applications.

12. You now return to the Client Applications page. If you click on Advanced on this page, you will see Advanced Client Computer Settings dialog (Figure 8.11).

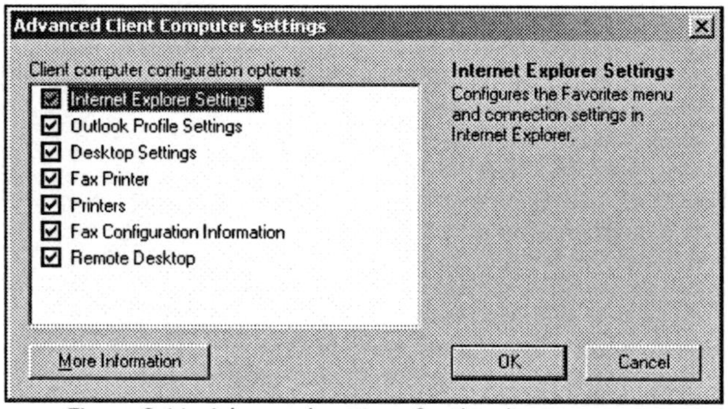

Figure 8.11: Advanced settings for the client computer

For each of the listed options, you can accept the default setting for the client computer by checking the relevant checkbox.

The default settings for the various options are:

- Internet Explorer Settings: The internal company website (http://Companyweb) is set as the home page. There are links to various internal websites in Favorites. If ISA Server is installed, Internet Explorer is set up for using the proxy server.

- Outlook Profile Settings: Outlook is configured for using the Exchange Server. The account information and the Exchange Server settings are used in the profiles for new users. If profiles already exist on the computer, the Exchange profile of the SBS is added and set as the default. The fax mail transport is also configured. This makes it possible to send faxes from Outlook and other e-mail applications. If remote access is configured for the client computer, manual synchronization of Outlook folders is configured under Outlook.

- Desktop Settings: Shortcuts and links are created in the Network Neighborhood folder.

- Fax Printer: A fax printer that uses the connection to the fax server is set up on the computer.

- Printers: The printer published in Active Directory is added by SBS as the default printer for clients. If a local printer is connected to the client or if several printers are published in Active Directory, no default printer is set.

- Fax Configuration Information: The fax information saved on the SBS is passed on to the clients. This includes, for example, the fax cover sheet with the sender information so that users do not have to enter this information for each new fax.

- Remote Desktop: Remote Desktop and Remote Desktop Support are enabled for the clients. Via Remote Desktop users can set up a session with their client computer. Remote Desktop Support makes it possible for other users to connect to the client and help in troubleshooting.

If checkboxes are disabled, you can configure the settings manually on the client. Click OK.

Next, you will see the Mobile Client and Offline Use page (Figure 8.12):

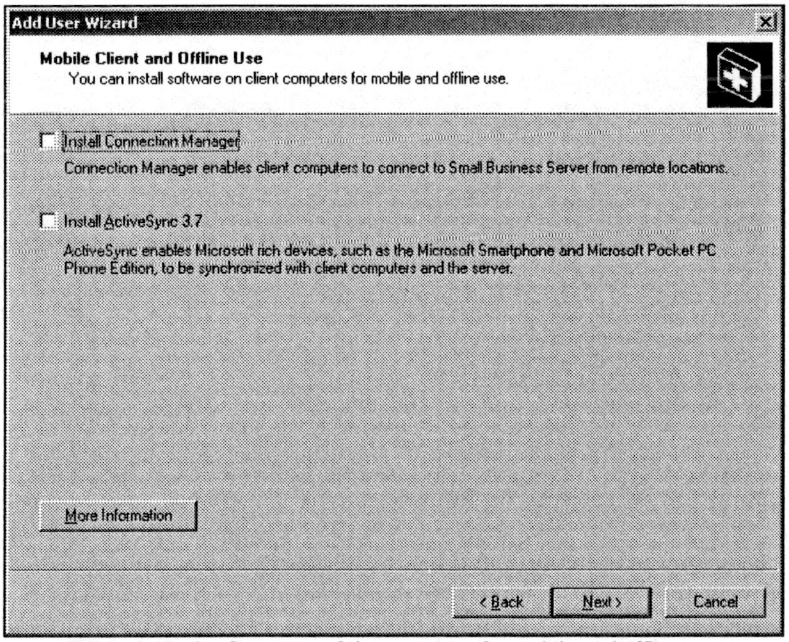

Figure 8.12: Configuration of the computer for mobile and offline use

You can install the Connection Manager and Active Sync 3.7 here.

- Connection Manager: Users can make a remote connection with the SBS 2003 with the help of the connection manager.

- ActiveSync 3.7: Via ActiveSync users can synchronize mobile devices, e.g. Microsoft Smartphone or Microsoft Pocket PC Phone Edition with the client computer and server.

> To allow users to use the remote connection, you must first close the wizard for the RAS connection in the task list. Furthermore, the user must be added to the Mobile Users Template (see step 1 in this section).

13. Finally, click Next. You will now see the Completing the Add User Wizard dialog (see Figure 8.13). If you are satisfied with the settings, click Finish. Click Back if you wish to make changes in the configuration.

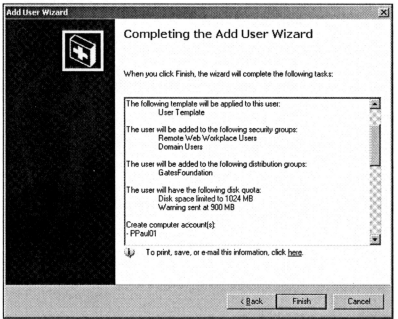

Figure 8.13: Completing the Add User Wizard

While the settings are being configured for the user, you will see an information dialog (see the following figure). To complete the configuration of the client computer including its network configuration and application deployment, log on to the client and enter http://SBSServername/ConnectComputer in a browser, and then click OK to confirm.

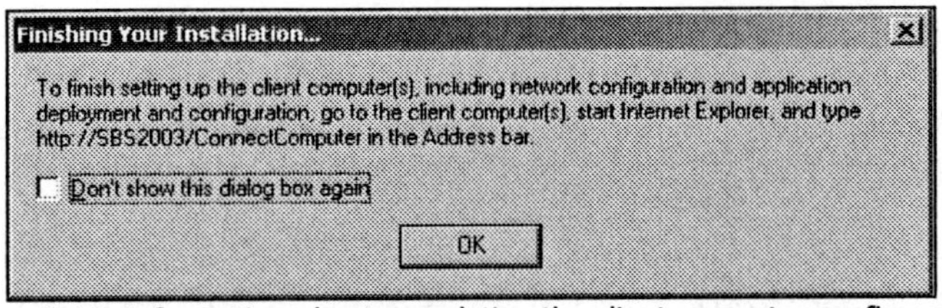

Figure 8.14: Information about completing the client computer configuration

After the user account is created, you will be asked if you want to rerun the wizard to create a new user. If you select No here, another information dialog lets you know that you can now configure the transmission of POP3 e-mail for the user accounts. Confirm this dialog with OK.

Properties of User Accounts

After creating the new user object, you will find it in Server Management under the Users link and also in the Active Directory Users and Computers MMC in the Domain name/MyBusiness/Users/SBSUsers container. Each user account has a predefined set of properties, which you can configure individually for each user. To access a user's properties, select the entry with the same name from the context menu (Figure 8.15).

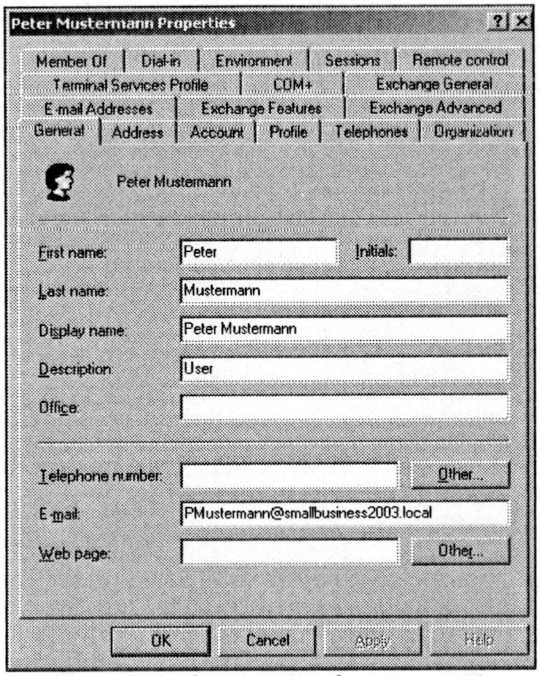

Figure 8.15: The properties of a user account

The properties are divided into 17 categories. A tab is available for each category. The meaning of the various tabs is explained in the following table (a local user account has only three tabs: General, Profile, and Member of.). The most important of these properties are introduced in detail later.

Tab	Description
General	Here you can enter the name of the user, an optional description as well as information about his or her office, telephone number, e-mail address, and website. Only the First Name, Last Name, and Display Name fields are mandatory. The rest are optional.
Address	Enter the address (street, PO Box, city, state, zipcode, and country/region) here. These entries are also optional.
Account	Here you will find the username and other options for the user account. These are explained separately later. Furthermore, you can also restrict the log on hours and the computers from which the user may log on.
Profile	Here you can enter the path to a user profile, a log on script, and a home folder for documents.
Telephones	Here you can enter additional phone numbers for the user (private, radio phone, mobile, fax, and IP telephone).
Organization	Here you can enter company-related information such as title, department, company, and manager.
E-mail Addresses	Edit the e-mail reply addresses for the various address types such as SMTP or X400.
Exchange Features	View and change the status for mobile services such as OMA or synchronization, and protocols such as OWA, POP3, and IMAP4.
Exchange Advanced	Here you will find advanced Exchange settings such as inclusion in address lists, mailbox permissions, and advanced attributes.
Terminal Services Profile	Here you can enter a user profile and the home folder for Terminal Services sessions.
COM+	Determine the COM+ partition group.
Exchange General	Settings for the e-mail alias, delivery options, receive restrictions, and disk quotas.
Member Of	Here you can specify which groups the user should belong to. By default he or she only belongs to the domain users group. If a user belongs to several groups, you can change the default setting via "Set primary group".

Tab	Description
Dial-in	You can configure the options for RAS access here. By default no RAS access is allowed.
Environment	You specify here whether network drives and printers should be connected automatically when the user logs in, and which programs should run when the Terminal Services are started.
Sessions	Options for terminal sessions are set here.
Remote control	You can enable or disable the remote control for the Terminal Services as well as switch the user permission for the monitoring on and off.

Adding Multiple Users

Adding multiple users comprises the same settings as were described in the last chapter. For this process, choose Add multiple users from the Users context menu.

The process of adding multiple users is similar to that of creating a new user, which we just saw. You begin by choosing a template for the users to be created (see Figure 8.3) and then adding a number of users to this template. You can then follow the subsequent steps described.

Changing User Permissions

After you have created a user, you can change his or her permissions on the basis of the user template.

1. To change the permissions, select Change User Permissions from the Users context menu.

2. In the Template Selection dialog (see the figure that follows) first select the new template for the user. You can then select one of the following options: Replace any previous permissions granted to the users or Add permissions to any previous permissions granted to the users. In the first case, all existing permissions of the user are overwritten by the permissions of the new template. The second option adds the permissions of the new template to the permissions already granted to the user. Click Next.

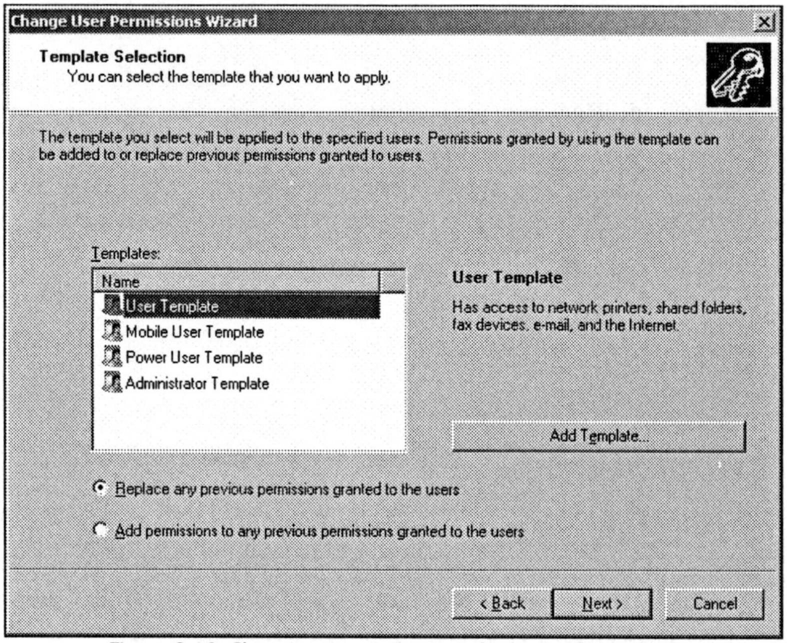

Figure 8.16: Changing permissions on the basis of templates

3. You can select the users whose permissions are to be defined by the new template. Mark the desired users in the left pane and click Add. Click Next, and complete the wizard.

Configuring Password Policies

1. After you have created a new user and have closed the information dialog for POP3 e-mail in this process (see Figure 8.15), you will see a new dialog asking you to configure the password policies. Confirm with Yes.

    The Configure Password Policies dialog will appear (see Figure 8.17). Alternatively, you can also click the Configure Password Policies link after opening Users in Server Management.

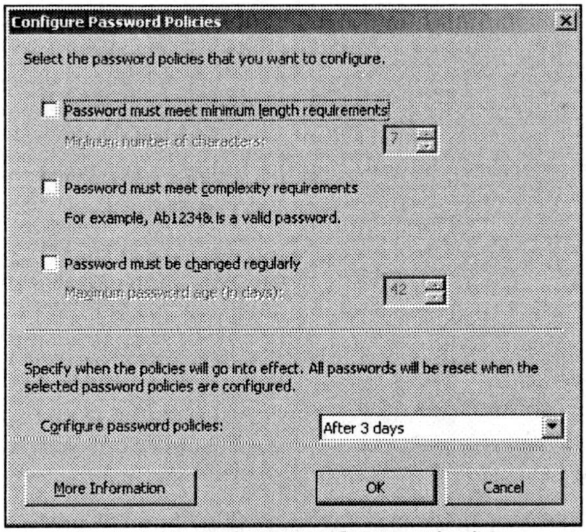

Chapter 8

Figure 8.17: Configuration of password policies

2. For security reasons, specify the requirements for passwords via the password policies. Check Password must meet minimum length requirements and select the minimum number of characters. Passwords that are shorter than the prescribed length are not accepted. The minimum length is seven characters.

3. If the Password must meet complexity requirements checkbox is enabled, the password must have at least three of the following categories of characters:
    o   Uppercase letters A to Z
    o   Lowercase letters a to z
    o   Digits 0 to 9
    o   Special characters such as %, #, or $

    Furthermore, the password should not resemble the username, even in part.

4. If the Password must be changed regularly checkbox is enabled, you can specify the number of days after which the password must be changed. The longest validity period for a password is 42 days.

5. Finally, under Configure password policies specify when the policies should come into effect. By default this happens in three days. You should retain this interval initially so that you don't have to use complex passwords in the

course of client configuration. After completing the client configuration, set the value to Immediate.

6. Click OK to apply the settings.

If you want to make further password settings for a user later, switch to the Account tab in his or her Properties. There you will find the following entries under Account Options:

Password option	Description
User must change password at the next logon	The user is asked to change his password at the first login. The responsibility for the password thus lies with the user.
User cannot change password	In this case only the administrator can change the password. This option makes sense when you consider, for example, the guest account, which can be used by several users.
Password never expires	The password can be changed any time, but changing it isn't mandatory.
Account is disabled	The account has been created but cannot be used.
Store password using reversible encryption	The passwords in the password database are encrypted by default. The default encryption is not reversible. When using reversible encryption the password database must be well protected against attacks from outside. You must enable this option for users with Apple Macintosh clients, as these clients only work with reversible encryption.
Smart card is required for interactive logon	The user must authenticate himself with a smart card via a card reader.
Account is trusted for delegation	This user is permitted to give other users or groups part of the domain namespace for administration.
Account is sensitive and cannot be delegated	The delegation of administrative tasks cannot be handed over to this account by any other user.
Use DES encryption types for this account	You can enable support for Data Encryption Standard (DES) with this account. DES supports various encryption mechanisms, e.g. MPPE 40, 64 and 128 Bit, or IPSec in various stages.
Do not require Kerberos preauthentication	Enable this option only if the Kerberos implementation of Windows 2000 is not used for the account, but, say, a Unix implementation is used that uses a different time mechanism for issuing ticket-approving tickets through the Key Distribution Center (KDC).

You can also specify whether the account should expire at a certain point in time or not (this last is the default). This is meaningful if some employees are engaged only temporarily. If the account should expire at a certain time, check the relevant box and select the desired date from the calendar element.

Specifying Logon Hours for a User

Furthermore, you will find the Logon Hours button on the Accounts tab. Here you can specify when the user may log on to the domain. By default the user can log on at any time on any day of the week. To restrict his or her logon hours, take the following steps:

1. Click on the Logon Hours button. You will see that the hours are not restricted.

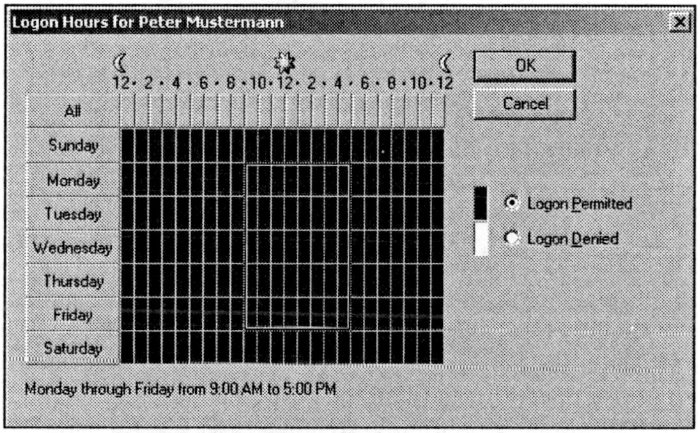

Figure 8.18: Restricting the logon hours for a user

2. Now mark the hours for which a logon is not allowed and click the Logon Denied radio button for these (the background for the hours then becomes white). In our example the logon hours are selected to be restricted to working days from 9:00 AM to 5:00 PM. For a normal office employee, these hours should suffice. Then click OK.

Restrict Logon to Specific Computers

Via the Logon button on the Account tab you can specify the computers from which the user may log on. If a user works only at a fixed workstation or from his or her laptop, you can assign only this computer to him or her. By default he or she can log on from any computer.

To restrict the logon workstations, take the following steps:

1. Click on the Logon button. You will see that the All Computers option is enabled (see Figure 8.19).

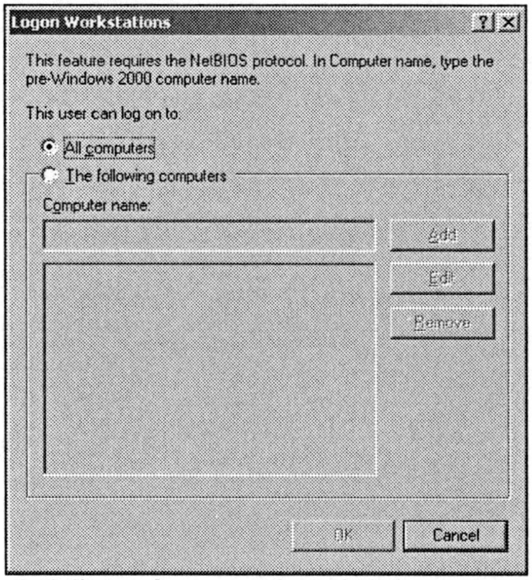

Figure 8.19 Choice of computers from which the user may log on

2. To restrict the logon process to one or more computers, select The following computers, enter the name of the computer in the Computer name text field, and click Add. Repeat this until all the desired computers are included in the list. To remove computers from this list later, mark the desired computers and click Delete. You can also change the name of a computer in the list via the Add button. Once you've configured this, click OK.

> You can set valid logon hours for *all* workstations, not for each one individually.

Also remember the following: the more restrictive you make the logon hours and workstations for the users, the less the probability of the account being misused.

Day-To-Day Work with User Accounts

In addition to the creation and configuration of accounts just described, day-to-day work with accounts also includes many other activities. These additional administrative tasks include the enabling (and disabling), renaming, and unlocking of accounts. To disable an active account or enable an inactive account, select Enable Account or Disable Account from the user's context menu. An account should be disabled until it is needed. If, for example, you have in the middle of the month created accounts for employees who are joining only next month, enable these accounts only on the first of the next month. Disabled accounts are always marked by the symbol of a white cross in a red circle.

Even for renaming of accounts select the appropriate entry from the context menu. Renaming an account makes sense when a new employee is to inherit all the settings of his or her predecessor except for the name.

If a user is to be deleted, use the context menu item Remove User.

The context menu has one more item: Change Password. Even if you have allowed users to set their password (see the previous table), as administrator you can always reset a user's password in the event that he or she forgets it and cannot logon any more. To reset the password, select Change Password from the context menu, enter the new password, and conform it. You can even set a blank password in this way. Inform the locked-out user about this temporary password and request him or her to remember it better the next time. If the option is enabled, the user can now change the password set by the administrator at the next logon.

Managing User Profiles

We now move on to the fundamentals of user profiles and home folders. Various folders with data and configuration settings for a user are stored in a user profile. User profiles also ensure the consistency of user settings. A home folder is an alternative storage location for the My Documents folder.

First we will learn about the various types of user profiles. Then we will learn how user profiles and home folders can be set up and configured.

Types of User Profiles

A user profile contains all the personal settings and files of a user. One also speaks of desktop settings on the local computer. A new user profile is automatically created when a user logs on to a computer for the first time. By default profiles are created for the users at the time of installation—Default User and All Users—and for the account name of a new user. The use of profiles ensures that several users can work on one computer with their own personal settings, and changes made by one user to his or her settings have no effect on other users. Let's say user 1 wants to have large icons on the desktop and chooses this option. At the next logon, user 1 will have large icons while user 2 will continue to have the default Windows icons. A profile always contains the settings and data that were present at the time of the last successful shutdown of the computer.

A profile is thus a snapshot of the last state before shutdown. If the computer is not shut down properly, the profile can be damaged to the extent that not all changes are recorded in the profile.

The contents of all profiles are identical—they only differ as regards the storage location and the changed options. The local user profiles are found in the %System%\Documents and Settings\%Username% folder, e.g. C:\Documents and Settings\Administrator. On a computer updated from Windows NT to Windows 2000/XP, the profile can be found in %Systemroot%\Profiles\%Username%. Profiles stored on the server are located in a network share on the server. A profile contains the personal folders and individual settings such as the screensaver, the color scheme, view options in Windows Explorer, Favorites, etc. This information is stored in the following folders of the profile:

Folder	Content
Application Data[1]	Personal settings for applications are stored here, e.g. Office dictionaries or Office templates. All applications compatible with Windows 2000/XP store the personal settings here instead of the program folder.
Cookies	Information about Internet sites visited.
Desktop	All elements of the current desktop such as links or data stored on the desktop.
PrintHood[1]	Links to objects in the Printers folder.
My Documents	My Documents is used as a default folder for personal documents. Microsoft applications such as the Office package also use this path. The My Pictures sub-folder is also located here. It is the storage location for all the graphical items of the user.
Favorites	Has links to Internet sites selected as Favorites.
Local Settings[1]	This folder contains four other folders: Application Data, e.g. Outlook Archive, Temp for all temporary files, Temporary Internet Files for transitional Internet data, and History for an overview of Internet sites visited.
NetHood[1]	Has links to network items such as currently connected network drives.
My Recent Documents[1]	Contains a list of recently opened documents and folders.
SendTo[1]	Contains links to items found under Send to in the context menu of an object.
Start Menu	Contains links to all entries and elements of the start menu.

Folder	Content
Templates	Contains templates for document types that can be opened on the computer.
NTUSER.DAT1[1]	Stores registry settings such as screensaver, preferred color scheme, view options for Explorer and the folders, although the links are all in the folders already mentioned.

> The folders marked with [1] are visible only if you have selected Show hidden files and folders in Windows Explorer under Tools/Folder Options/View. These hidden objects are never displayed by default.

In all there are three types of user profiles: local, server-based, and mandatory. The following table gives an overview of these various types.

User profile	Description
Local	This type of profile is created when a user logs on to a computer for the first time. The settings stored in this profile are only valid for the local computer.
Server-based	Server-based profiles are not stored locally but on a server. They are always available. The computer from which a user logs on is irrelevant here. Any changes that the user makes are also stored on the server. A server-based profile must be set up by the administrator.
Mandatory	This profile is also stored on the server. Thus it is available irrespective of the computer from which the user logs on. However, the user's changes are not stored in this profile. The user always gets the settings that the administrator has defined once and for all for him or her, or for an entire group of users.

In contrast to server-based and mandatory profiles, a local profile does not have to be explicitly created. It is created automatically each time a user logs on. The base settings of the Default User folder in Documents and Settings are used for this purpose and are given a new name.

Checklist for Creating User Profiles

The following checklist gives an overview of the steps you need to carry out for the setup and configuration of server-based user profiles up to the specification of quota limits.

These steps have not been described chronologically here but are placed in the overall context of the chapter.

- Select a file server and create several shared folders on it to save user profiles. Using a central storage location also simplifies data storage.

- Set up the server-based user profiles. Consider *which* settings would be meaningful for *which* user groups.

- Specify the user folders for which you want to set up the redirections. These redirected folders appear as local folders to users in contrast to folders and, in contrast to folders in a server-based profile, do not load the network.

- If required, enable the option for making files and folders available offline. The user can then access the data even when not logged on to the network.

- Set limits on the maximum size of the contents of the user profiles by defining disk quotas.

- Plan which options in the group policies and other configuration settings you want to define as default functions, and which as advanced functions. Classify your employees into groups based on their functions and assign default or advanced functions to them as needed.

Setting Up a Server-Based Profile

The server-based profile is stored on a server in the network and is thus always available. The personal settings are available to each user on any machine he or she uses to log on, and are not limited to his or her local machine. Windows copies the profile data to the client computer when the user logs on. The profile is fully copied when the user logs in for the first time. On subsequent logons, a check is carried out to determine if any changes have been made to the profile. If this is the case, only the changes are copied to the client. Changes that are made on the client during the user's session with the profile are written to the server during the log-off process. The ideal storage location for the profiles is a file server that is backed up regularly. Do not put the profiles on the domain controller as the copying of profiles is network-resource intensive and can lower the performance of the domain controller.

You can create a server-based profile not just for an individual user but also for a complete user group. This makes sense if, for example, all members of a group are meant to receive the same settings. The users get only the entries and links that they need for their work. Even the required network resources, for example a specific drive for data and a particular printer, can be made available to them automatically. All this involves the creation of mandatory server-based user profiles.

To set up a new server-based profile for a user, take the following steps:

1. Create a new folder on the fileserver and share it. You can call the share Profiles.

2. Select the desired user object and open the Profile tab from Properties. In the Profile Path field, enter the path in the following format: \\Servername\ Sharename\Username, e.g. \\Borussia\Profile\pmustermann.

> Instead of the username, use the variable %username%. Windows can replace this variable with the name of the user account. This will save you work and you can copy the profiles more easily. When the user logs on for the first time, the profile folder is automatically created with his or her username.

To create a server-based profile for a group of users, take the following steps. (This is also referred to as a standard server-based user profile.)

1. In Server Management create a new user account under User. This will serve as a profile template. Give this user a username, e.g. Template.

2. Log on with this template name, and make all the settings and changes to the desktop that you want. Then log on again as administrator.

3. Create a new folder on this fileserver and share it. You can call the share Profiles. All user profiles are stored in this folder.

4. From the computer on which you have made changes to the profile, copy the profile folder from %System%\Documents and Settings\Username to the share on the file server. This is done as follows:

    o   In Control Panel, open System and select User Profile. Here you will see a list of all users who have logged on to this computer.

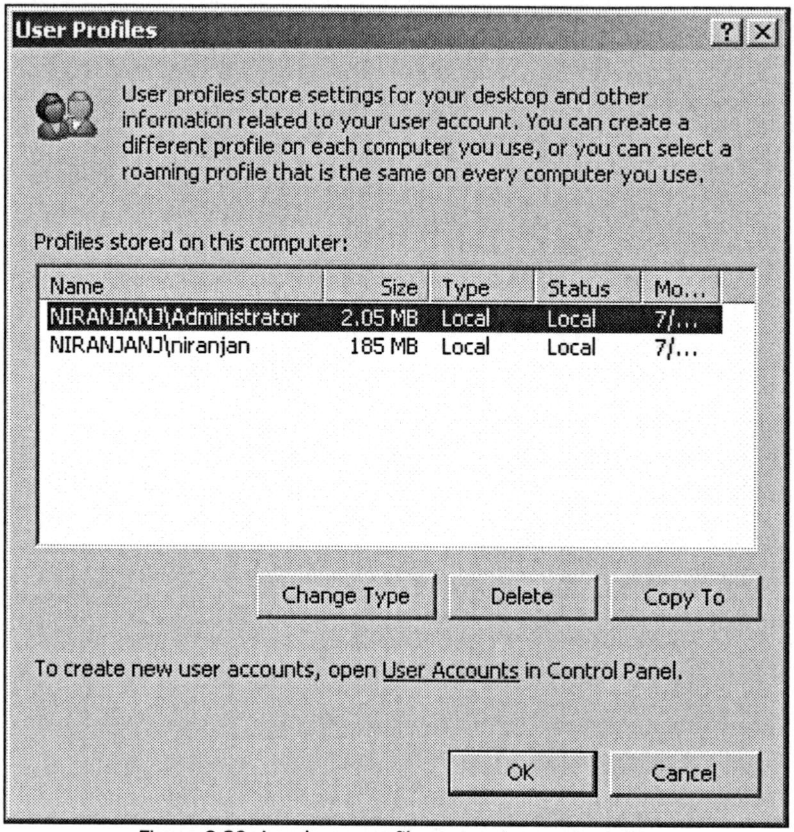

Figure 8.20: Local user profiles present on a computer

○ You will also see the template profile of the form COMPANY\
Template. Choose this profile and click the Copy to button.

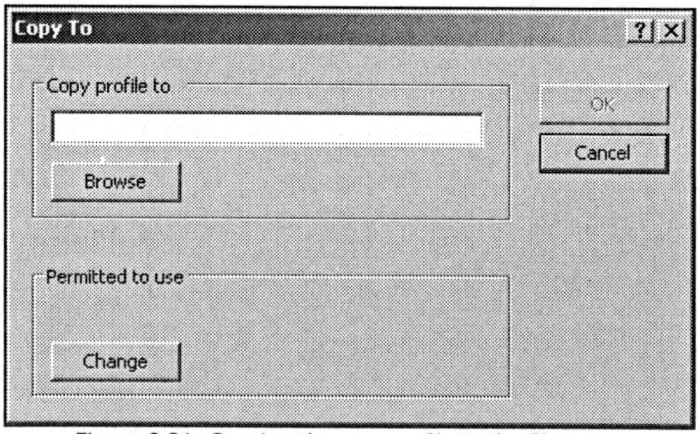

Figure 8.21: Copying the user profile to the fileserver

o To add users who will use this profile, click on the Change button. You will see a list of all existing users and groups and can select the desired objects. Confirm this with OK.

5. Finally, enter the profile path in the account properties for all users.

In future all users that you have selected for the use of this profile will receive it as the default profile when they log on. Their changes will be saved in the \%username% folder for each user.

The advantage of server-based profiles is that the user can log on from any computer in the network and still receive his or her personal settings. A disadvantage is the network traffic that this generates. You should also not create a server-based user profile for users who access the network through slow RAS connections such as a telephone line.

Creating a Mandatory Profile

With a mandatory profile a user cannot make permanent changes to his or her desktop. He or she can only temporarily change settings. However, these settings are not saved and are thus not available at the next logon. With this method you, as the administrator, have full control over the desktop settings of your users.

A mandatory profile is write-protected. To create a mandatory profile:

1. In the profile folder of each user, find the file NTUSER.DAT (this file is hidden by default). To see it, select the Show all files and folders option under Tools/ Folder Options/View in Windows Explorer. The user's desktop settings are stored in this file.

2. To write-protect this file, it must be renamed. Rename it to NTUSER.MAN. The .MAN file extension stands for mandatory. The user can now change his or her settings only for the period that he or she is working. The changes are not carried forward the next time he or she logs on.

Setting Up Home Folders

A home folder is an alternative to the My Documents folder for personal documents. A home folder can be accessed by a user using any Microsoft operating system from MS DOS to Windows XP. The home folder is not part of the user profile. You can either keep the home folders of all users centrally on a fileserver thus simplifying the administration and backup of data, or assign a local home folder to each user.

To set up a home folder, take the following steps:

1. If you opt for a server-based folder, you must create a share on the fileserver in which all home folders can be stored. For access permissions to the share select only the Users group and remove the All group.

2. Now open the Profile tab in the user's account properties (Figure 8.22).

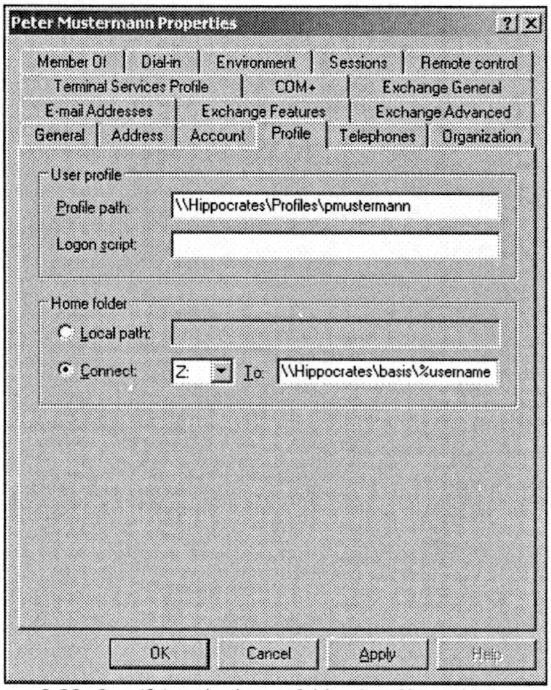

Figure 8.22: Specifying the home folder (profile path) for a user

3. Since you have opted for a server-based home folder, select the Connect radio button and choose a drive letter. You should use the same unused letter, say Z, for all users. Then enter the path in the format \\Servername\ Share\Username. Instead of the username, you can also use the variable %username%.

4. If you want to use a local path as the home folder, select the Local Path radio button and enter the path. A local path only makes sense if the user logs on from only one computer. If he or she attempts to log on from another computer in the network, the local path is of course not found. In this case you must separately organize the backup of the home folder on each separate computer. In most cases a server-based home folder is a better solution.

Redirecting the My Documents Folder

The My Documents folder is the default storage location for the user's documents. Applications such as Word and Excel save and open their files in this folder. The following five components can be redirected via folder redirection:

- My Documents folder
- My Pictures folder
- Application Data folder
- Desktop folder
- Start menu folder (this option is only available to Terminal Server users)

To redirect the My Documents folder, take the following steps:

1. In Sever Management open Users and click on the Configure "My Documents" Redirection link in the right pane.

2. In the Client Documents Redirection dialog (see Figure 8.23), you can configure three types of redirection:

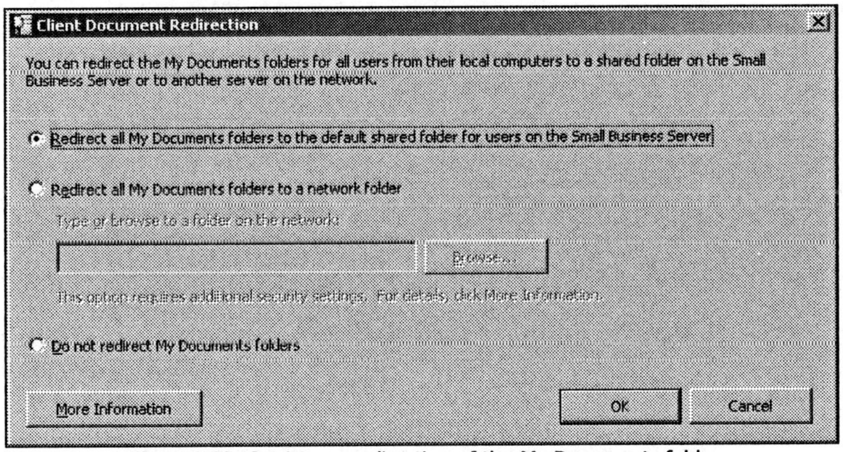

Figure 8.23: Setting up redirection of the My Documents folder

The first option is enabled by default. This redirects the contents of the My Documents folder to the default user folder of the SBS user. If you select the option Redirect all My Documents folders to a network folder, select any network folder via Browse. The third option disables folder redirection. Confirm your choice with OK.

As an alternative to this procedure you can also configure folder redirection via a group policy. More information about this can be found later in this chapter.

Changing Mailbox and Disk Quota Settings

To give the user a specific amount of disk space, you can set limits for both the mailbox size and the disk quota for the user's data on the server. For mailboxes, limits can be set for each user separately or for all at once. A disk quota applies to all users.

Specifying the Mailbox Size for a Specific User

1. To change the mailbox size for a particular user, select his or her properties in Server Management under Users.

2. Switch to the Exchange General tab. Click on Storage Limits.

3. In the Storage Limits dialog (see the following figure) disable the Use mailbox store defaults checkbox.

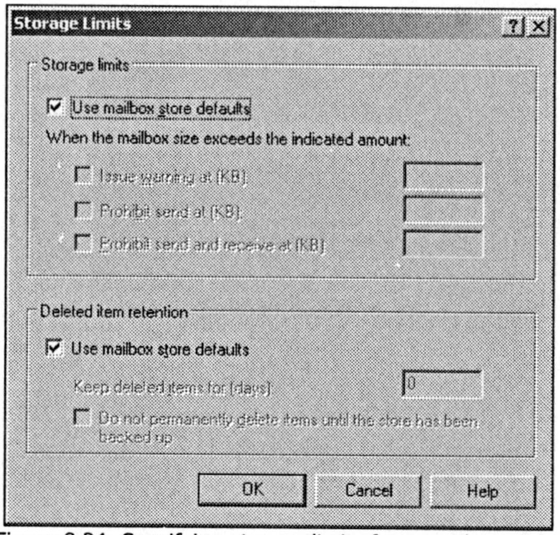

Figure 8.24: Specifying storage limits for a user's mailbox

4. To specify new values, enter the desired values under Issue warning at (KB), Prohibit send at (KB), and Prohibit send and receive at (KB) and click OK. You can also specify the number of days for which items deleted under Outlook should be kept on the Exchange Server.

Specifying the Mailbox Size for all Users

If the mailbox size limits are meant to apply to all users of the SBS domain, take the following steps:

1. In the Server Administration open Advanced Administration and double-click Exchange Domains.

2. Click on Server, the name of your server, and First Storage Group. Under Mailbox Store select Properties from the context menu.

3. Switch to the Limits tab (see Figure 8.25) and enter the desired values for Issue warning at (KB), Prohibit send at (KB), Prohibit send and receive at (KB), Keep deleted items for (days), and Keep deleted mailboxes for (days).

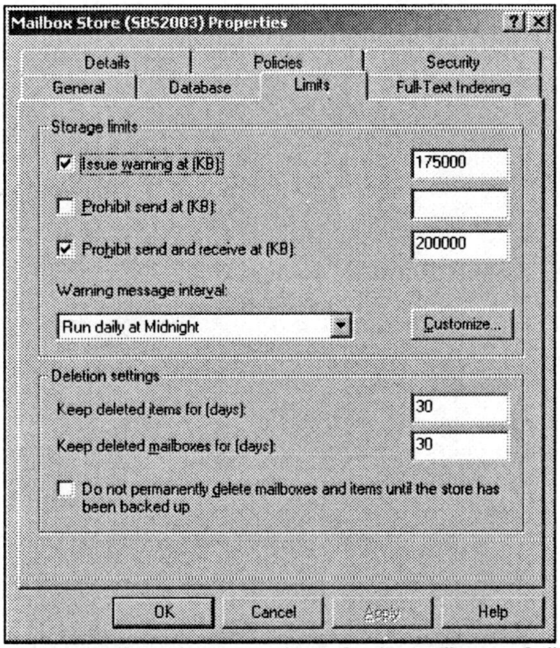

Figure 8.25: Specifying the storage limits for the mailboxes of all users

The default value for Send warning at is 175 MB and that for Prohibit send and receive is 200 MB.

4. Using Customize you can configure the intervals or the schedule for issuing warnings. Click OK once you are satisfied with the settings.

Setting Up Disk Quotas

With the help of disk quotas you can specify the amount of disk space a user may use on a particular drive. In this way you can ensure that the available disk space is distributed uniformly among all users.

You can enable disk quotas on drives on which the user profiles or home folders of users are located. You can configure a maximum size for the user folder and threshold values for warnings that are issued when the quota is about to be exhausted. If the quota limit is reached, the user cannot store any more data in his or her user folder. In this way you can ensure that the user cannot store any amount of data, e.g. files that are never used, in his or her folder and use up hard drive space on the server. The user is thus forced to examine his or her data repositories regularly, as files owned by the user count towards the disk quota.

You must set up the disk quotas before users access the disk. The quota settings will not apply to users who have already stored data on the disk before the disk quotas are activated; they will apply only to those who access the disk for the first time after the quota has been activated.

You can only set up disk quotas on drives with the NTFS file system. To apply quota settings to a network share, you must share the root of the drive in question.

The settings for disk quotas can be found on the Quota tab in the Properties of a drive. To enable a disk quota, make the following settings on the Quota tab:

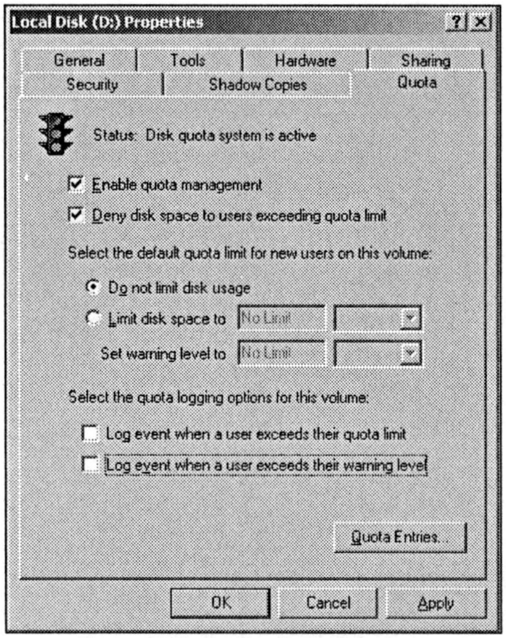

Figure 8.26: Configuring a disk quota

1. Disk quotas are disabled by default. To enable a quota, check the Enable quota management checkbox.

2. To effectively implement the application of quotas, check the Deny disk space to users exceeding quota limit checkbox. This ensures that users cannot store any more data when the limit is reached. Otherwise there would only be an entry in the event log and the user could continue adding data.

3. Select the limit disk space to radio button and enter the desired value.

> Remember to use the correct unit. The default is kilobytes (KB). A setting of 1000 KB, for example, would quickly lead to problems.

4. In the Set warning level to field, specify when the user should receive a warning that his or her disk quota is about to get exhausted. You should set the warning level to about 75% of the total quota.

5. Finally, you can specify with the help of the two checkboxes at the bottom whether there should be an automatic entry in the event log when either the quota limit is exceeded or the warning level is reached or both. Logging is disabled by default. Click OK.

Managing User Templates

In this section you will learn the work steps required to manage user templates. These include the adding, importing, and exporting of templates. User templates are only available in SBS 2003; there is no equivalent in Windows Server 2003.

By default SBS 2003 has four user templates: Administrator Template, Mobile User Template, Power User Template, and User Template, which we've already spoken about in the *Adding a User* section under *User Management*.

The advantage of user templates is that they already have a large number of pre-configured settings, e.g. in relation to permissions. When creating a new user, you must select one of the templates. In this way the user automatically receives all the settings that are valid for this template.

Adding New User Templates

To create a new user template, take the following steps:

1. In Server Management select Add Template from the context menu of User Templates.

2. Click on Next, and then in the Template Account Information dialog enter a name and optionally a description for the template (see Figure 8.27).

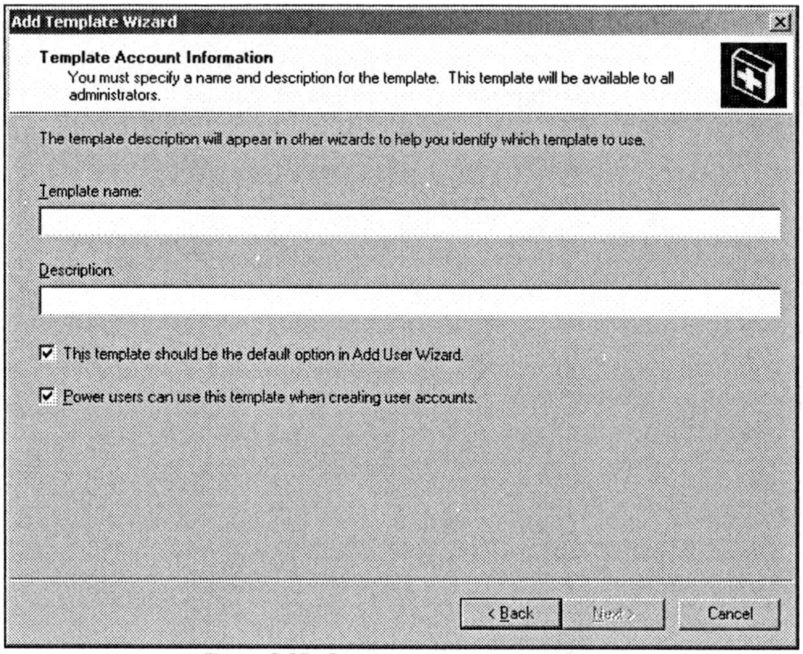

Figure 8.27: Creating a new user template

3. Additionally, you can specify via the relevant checkboxes whether the new template should be the default option in the Add User wizard and whether Power Users can use this template when creating user accounts. Click Next.

4. Next, you can select security group memberships for the users created with this template via Add and click Next.

5. You can select distribution groups. Again click on Next.

6. The selection of site groups for the SharePoint Services comes next. You have already seen a description of the individual site groups in Chapter 5. Mark the desired groups(s) and click Next.

7. Furthermore, you can specify address information for users who have been created with the template and click Next.

8. In the next step you can specify a storage limit for the user. This quota setting applies to the drive on the SBS 2003 that contains the user folder. The default storage limit is 1024 MB and the warning level is 900 MB. If you don't want to specify a quota, check the No storage limit checkbox and click Next. You can now complete the wizard.

Import and Export of Templates

You can exchange both the predefined and custom templates between multiple SBS 2003 servers using the import-export function.

Export

To export a template:

1. Choose Export templates from the context menu of the template
2. Click on Next in the wizard. In the Template Selection dialog, you will see all the existing templates on the left. Select the desired ones and click Add followed by Next.
3. Enter the destination path and filenames for the templates. The templates are exported as XML files. Click Next and complete the wizard.

Import

To import:

1. Choose Import templates from the context menu.
2. Click on Next in the wizard. In the Import Path dialog, select the XML file to be imported, and then click Next.
3. In the Template Selection dialog select the template(s) to be imported. This choice is useful if several templates are stored in the XLS file and not all are to be imported. Click Next and complete the wizard.

Management of Security Groups and Distribution Groups

In this section you will learn the fundamentals of user groups. To simplify the management of users, you can organize users into groups based on similarity in functions in a company.

Fundamentals of Groups

To begin with, a user group is nothing but a collection of several user accounts. By setting up groups, you enormously simplify user management as you are not assigning access rights and resources to individual users, but in one step granting or denying the appropriate rights to a group, and thus to all its members.

It is possible for a user to be a member of several groups or a group to be a member of another group. You can add user accounts, computer accounts, other groups, and contacts to a group.

Group Types and Group Zones

There are two different types of groups and three types of group zones. The two types of groups are **security groups** and **distribution groups**.

Users are put in a distribution group exclusively for processes that have nothing to do with access rights and security. A classic example is a distribution list for mass sending of e-mails. Only the security groups (the more important of the two types) serve the purpose of bringing together users to simplify the issue of access permissions. They have the base functionality of distribution groups—the bringing together of several users for a specific function—and, in addition, the option of controlling access to resources. In our context, only the security groups are relevant. Thus any future reference to groups should be taken to mean only security groups. In Server Management you will find links to manage both these types of groups.

The security groups are divided into three group zones: **global**, **domain local**, and **universal** groups. You can create these groups for one domain. Independent of these three group zones are the local groups that you set up on Windows 2000/XP Professional computers and member servers in the domain. These groups are available only on the local computer and should not be confused with the domain local groups.

The three group zones have the following properties with regard to the membership of their group members and access to network resources:

Group zone	Membership	Resource access
Global	Members of the local domain	To resources of all domains
Domain local	Members of any domain	To resources of the local domain
Universal (Universal domains are not available in the mixed mode of operation of Active Directory.)	Members of any domain	To resources of all domains

As you can see, the global groups are restricted as regards their membership, while the domain local groups are restricted in their access to resources. The absence of restriction applies to the other component in each case. Only for universal groups are there no restrictions.

Default Groups

There are several default groups under SBS 2003. Here, too, a distinction is made between domain controllers and Windows clients/member servers. Domain controllers can have three types of groups, viz. built-in, predefined, and special groups. On all other computers you can only set up pre-defined local groups. The following tables give you an overview of the default members of these groups, along with the deployment possibilities and permissions of the groups.

Built-In Groups

Built-in groups are domain local groups. They can be fond in the Built-in container of the SBS domain. Specific permissions required for them to work in Active Directory have already been granted to these groups.

Built-in group	Description	Default members
Administrators	Account for performing all administrative tasks in a domain.	Domain admins and organization admins
Users	Users can perform the tasks for which they have been granted permissions.	Domain users and authenticated users
Print operators	Account for setting up and administering network printers on domain controllers.	-
Guests	Members of this group can only perform the tasks that they are allowed to.	Guest IWAM_Computername IUSR_Computername TsInternetUser
Account operators	Account for setting up and administering user accounts and groups.	-
Performance log users	These users have remote access to plan the performance indicator logging.	Network service
Network configuration operators	These users have administrative rights for some network configurations.	-
Pre-Windows 2000 compatible access	To ensure backward compatibility, read access is given to all users and groups.	NT-system group All
Remote Desktop users	These users can log on remotely.	Remote operators

SBS 2003 Administration

Built-in group	Description	Default members
Replication operators	Account for supporting Active Directory replication.	-
Server operators	Account for backing up and restoring as well as joint access to the server.	-
Backup operators	Account for backing up and restoring all domain controllers with Windows Backup.	-
System monitor users	Members have remote access for monitoring the computer.	-
Terminal server-License server	This group is only available if a terminal server is configured.	-
Windows authentication group	Members have access to the (calculated) attribute tokenGroupsGlobalAndUniversal.	Domain controllers of the organization

Global Groups

There are also predefined groups belonging to the global zone. These groups can be found in the Users container of the SBS domain. New members can be added to these groups, and these global groups can also be added to domain local groups. The following built-in groups are available:

Predefined group	Description	Default members
Domain admins	Can perform administrative tasks on all computers of the domain.	Administrators
Domain users	All users are added to this group.	Administrator, Krbtgt, IWAM_Computername, IUSR_Computername, TsInternetUser
Domain guests	All guests are automatically added to this group.	Guest
Organization admins	Account for administrative tasks in the entire network.	Administrator

If you have installed other services, more pre-defined groups will be available, e.g. DHCP administrators and users, DNS add-ins, RAS and IAS servers, schema admins, etc.

Groups with Special Identities

Groups with special identities can be found on all computers running Windows 2000 and above, irrespective of whether they are domain controllers or not. However, you can neither add members to these groups nor make them members of other groups. These are groups with a purpose, and they hold members temporarily. These groups are not defined by the person who accesses a computer or a resource but by how the access takes place. That is why you will not find these groups in any container. The following table shows you the special identity groups:

Special Group	Description
Anonymous logon	Comprises all users who could not be authenticated by SBS 2003.
Authenticated users	Brings together all users with a valid domain account.
Creator user	The account of the user who originally created the resource or came to own it later.
Interactive	The account of a user who physically logs on to the computer.
All	Comprises all users who access the computer. This also includes the guest account. By default, this group has access to all resources.
Network	Comprises all users who are currently accessing any shared resource.
Dial-up connection	All current users of a dial-up connection.

There are predefined groups on any computer that runs Windows 2000 and above and is not a domain controller. The members of these groups can only perform their tasks on the local system. These group accounts are not valid in the domain. The following groups are predefined local groups: Administrators, Users, Guests, Power Users, Replication Operators, and Backup Operators. Except for the Power Users group, the descriptions given in the table apply to all these accounts. Power Users are only present in local groups. They can create new local accounts and modify them as well as make resources available for sharing.

Setting Up and Editing Groups and Group Properties

This section shows how to create a new group in SBS 2003 and configure its properties.

Creating a New Group

To create a new group, take the following steps:

1. In Server Management select Add Security Group from the context menu of Security Groups.
2. Click on Next in the wizard and enter the name and optionally a description for the group under Security Group Name. Click Next.
3. In the Group Membership window you will see all the users, groups, and templates on the SBS 2003 on the left. Highlight the desired entries and click Add. Then continue with Next. To complete the wizard, click Finish.

> You can create local groups on client computers and member servers via Start/All Programs/ Administration/Computer Management/Local Users and Groups.

Editing Membership Lists

To add members to the newly created group, select Properties from the context menu and then the Members tab. Click on the Add button. You can then select further members for this group. Conversely, you can also add this group as a member of other groups by switching to the Member of tab and selecting the desired group there via Add.

Deleting Groups

To delete a group, select Remove Security Group from its context menu. By deleting the group, you are not deleting the user accounts of the members. However, because the SID is also deleted when deleting a group, all permissions associated with the group are also deleted. If you create a new group with the same name, the settings of the old group are not inherited. A group can only be deleted if none of the members of the group has it defined as the primary group.

Changing Group Properties

You can also change the properties of the group zone and group type. As soon as you change the operating mode to uniform, for example, you can transform the groups into universal groups. A global group cannot, however, be transformed into a universal group if it is still a member of another global group. Even a domain local group cannot be transformed into a universal group when it is still a member of another domain local group. The group type of universal groups can no longer be changed. If Active Directory is running in mixed mode, the universal group option is not selectable. Also, you cannot transform a global group into a domain local group and vice versa. To change one of the properties, open the groups Properties. Make the desired changes on the General tab (Figure 8.28).

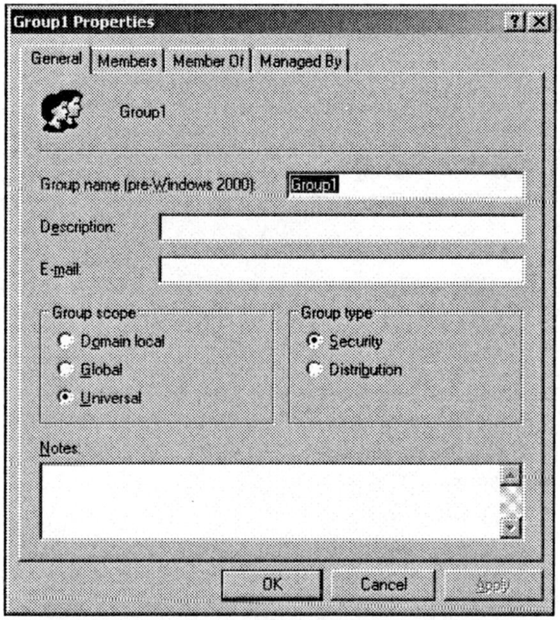

Figure 8.28: Changing group properties

Managing Client Computers and Server Computers

For managing the clients and servers, two links—Client Computers and Server Computers—are available to you in Server Management.

In the Active Directory structure, the new client computers are created in the container MyBusiness/SBSComputers, and the servers in the container MyBusiness/SBSServers.

In contrast to Windows Server 2003, the creation of computers in SBS 2003 is closely linked to the creation of users and also to the assigning of applications.

Client Computers

To create a new client computer, take the following steps:

1. From the context menu for Client Computer select Set Up Client Computer.

2. Enter a name for the computer there and click Add. In this way you can also set up multiple computers. Then click Next.

3. You can then select the applications to be installed on the computer from the client applications of SBS 2003 (see Figure 8.29). Click Next here.

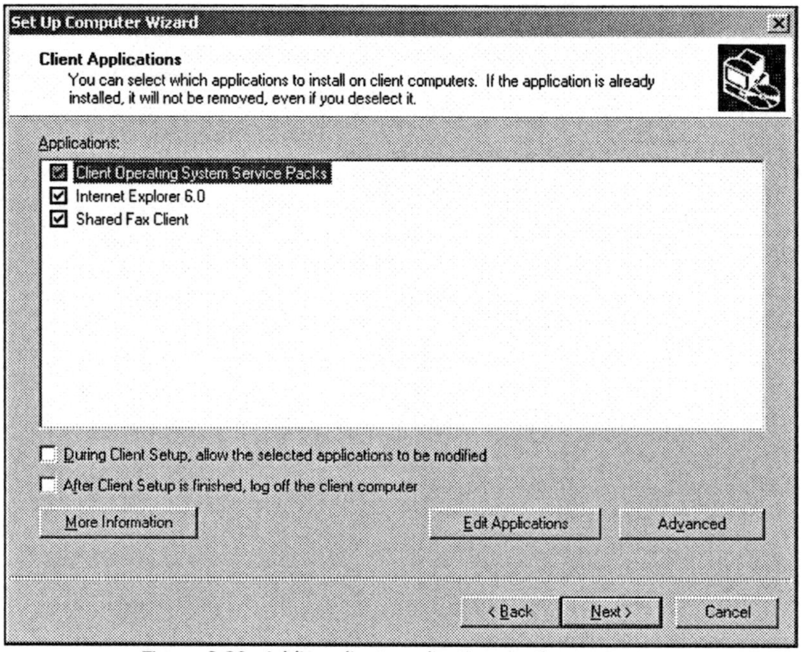

Figure 8.29: Adding client applications to the computer

The exact execution of this option has already been described in the *Task List for Concluding Configuration* section of Chapter 2 in connection with the task list after installation. More information can be found there.

Adding Applications

You can add applications to a client computer after it has been set up by using the Add Applications to Client Computers link. You first select all client computers via Add. You will then see the Client Applications window again (see Figure 8.29).

Settings of the Client Computer

To get a quick overview of the settings for individual client computers, click View Computer Settings link—all available computers are listed there. If you double-click one of the computers, you'll see its configuration settings under Assigned Applications, Client Setup Settings, and Client Setup Configuration Options (Figure 8.30).

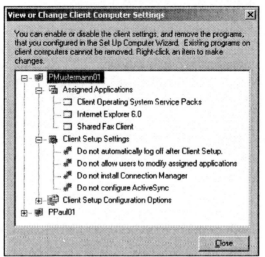

Figure 8.30: Viewing the various settings of a client computer

Further Management Options

The moment you click on one of the available computers, you get some more links for management. Apart from the options already described, you can view the event logs of the computer, start the computer management of the client, connect to this computer via terminal services to offer remote support, and remove the computer from the network. You can also call the same functions from the context menu of the computer.

Server Computers

Under the Server Computers link you only have the option of setting up server computers.

1. First enter the name for the server and then click Next.

2. Next, specify whether the server should have a fixed IP address or have one assigned to it via DHCP. Click Next. You can then complete the wizard.

As with the client computer, when you double-click the server you will see some more links. You can call the computer management, make a terminal services connection, view the event logs and services of the server, and remove it from the network. Here, too, you can call the same functions via the context menu.

Group Policy Management

In this section you will get to know about group policies. In Active Directory they are the central tool for controlling the configuration of users and computers. Group policies can be applied at location, domain, and organizational-unit level. For the user a group policy object represents a collection of company rules in respect of available resources, access permissions, and configuration of resources.

The desktop settings of a user can be configured via a group policy. You can assign software to him or her via this policy, or determine which objects he or she can (or cannot) see in the start menu. Under Windows NT, the system policy was available to you for this purpose, even though its scope was not as extensive.

Group policies are part of the IntelliMirror Technology. IntelliMirror is the generic term for controlling the client desktop under Windows 2000/XP/2003. Formulate policies for each client based on his or her function, location, and group memberships. The user gets the settings defined for him or her everywhere, irrespective of the computer on which he or she logs on. Intellimirror comprises the following functions: management of user data and settings, as well as the assigning, installation, and configuration of software.

In Windows Server 2003 the administration of group policies has been considerably simplified through the availability of the GPMC (Group Policy Management Console).

All the configuration steps in this chapter assume that the GPMC has been installed. If this is not the case, some of the options differ quite significantly.

The Windows NT System Policy and the Windows 2003 Group Policy

In Windows NT, user and computer configurations stored in the registry could be specified via the system policy editor. You could define a system policy through which the work environment of a user could be controlled. These configuration settings could then be applied to the user's computer.

In the NT system policy there were in all 72 options for the policy settings. Windows Server 2003, and thus also SBS 2003, have more than 700 group policies. These result from advanced features of the operating system such as Remote Desktop and the Software Restriction Rules, or relate to Windows Media Player or the start menu. Only one policy of a user or a computer in the domain could be processed through the NT system policy, whereas in Windows NT, several group policy objects in various levels of the Active Directory hierarchy can be connected with containers.

The Windows 2003 group policy has four administrative templates in all. Administrative templates are text files containing the appropriate values for the changed registry keys or even the default values. For each value, the corresponding position in the registry where the value is located is also given. The two files system.adm and inetres.adm are automatically installed in the group policy. They write the changes to four reserved areas of the registry. The keys in question are:

- HKEY_LOCAL_MACHINE\Software\Policies.

- HKEY_CURRENT_USER\Software\Policies.

- HKEY_LOCAL_MACHINE\Software\Microsoft \Windows\CurrentVersion\Policies.

- HKEY_CURRENT_USER\Software\Microsoft \Windows\CurrentVersion\Policies.

The files are Conf.adm (settings for NetMeeting), Inetres.adm (Internet Explorer), System.adm (system settings), and Wmplayer.adm (Media Player).

When a group policy is changed, the corresponding areas in the registry are deleted and written completely afresh. Changes can be made in these areas only if you have administrator rights. These administrative templates of the local group policy objects can be found in the %systemroot%\System32\GroupPolicy folder, and they can be manually edited. You can also create your own ADM files.

The administrative templates can optionally be installed in the group policies. They are, however, best called in the system policy editor (poledit.exe) for administering older versions of Windows. Do not use these three templates to administer 2000 or XP clients, as the settings of the system policy can remain permanently in the registry. The files in question are winnt.adm, windows.adm, and common.adm. User interface options for Windows NT are controlled through winnt.adm, options for Windows 9x through windows.adm, and common interface options for Windows NT and 9x through common.adm.

What GPO, GPC, and GPT Mean

We will first explain the three mysterious abbreviations that we will encounter again and again in the course of this section. GPO means **Group Policy Object**, GPC is a **Group Policy Container**, and GPT stands for **Group Policy Template**. Let us now breathe life into these terms.

A GPO consists of a number of individual group policies that you can assign to a user or a computer. All the settings and data of a group policy are stored in a GPO. The moment you implement a GPO for a user or a computer, it gets a GPC and a GPT.

The GPC contains GPO information such as version or status (enabled or disabled). The GPC has sub-containers for the policies for computers and users. All the properties of the policy that are not subject to frequent changes are stored in the GPC—thus virtually the description of the policy.

The settings for the policy are stored in the GPT. These include, for example, the scripts or the security settings. This data can change more frequently. The folder structure of the GPT is set up at the time of creating the GPO. The GPT data for domain-based group policy objects can be found in the %Systemroot%\SYSVOL\[Domain name]\Policies\ [GUID of the relevant GPO] folder. Additionally, the logon and logoff scripts for the GPO are stored in the \User\Scripts\ or \Machine\Scripts\ folders of SYSVOL.

On every Windows 2000/XP computer there is a local GPO—irrespective of whether the computer is a member of the domain or not. You will find this in the %Systemroot%\System32\GroupPolicy folder. Some of the functions such as software deployment or folder redirection are not available in the local GPOs in contrast to the domain-based GPOs.

Processing and Inheriting Group Policies

At the domain level, the GPOs can be applied directly at the sites, domains, and organizational units. When a computer is not connected to a domain, it has access only to its local GPO. If the computer is connected to a domain, then the settings of the local GPOs can be overwritten by the GPOs of that domain.

The group policies for the computers in Active Directory should be executed in the following order:

1. Local GPO
2. GPO of the site
3. GPO of the domain
4. GPO of the organizational unit

First, all the settings of the local GPO are examined. Then the settings of the GPO for the site are worked through. If a policy is defined only at the site level, it is added to the existing policy settings of the local GPO. In this way all the GPOs up to the level of the organizational unit are worked through. If you have set up a hierarchy of OUs and sub-OUs, the OU GPOs are worked through up to the lowest OU. This is also referred to as the LSDOU (Local – Site – Domain – Organizational Unit) sequence.

An individual GPO can be connected to several connectors such as sites, domains, and organizational units. On the other hand, one of these containers can also contain several GPOs. It is of course possible that a GPO is applied in only one container.

In Figure 8.31 you will see that the domain container is connected to two different GPOs (GPOs 1 and 2), while on the other hand the same GPO (GPO3) is connected to two different containers (organizational units 1 and 2). The individual site container is connected to only one GPO, GPO 4.

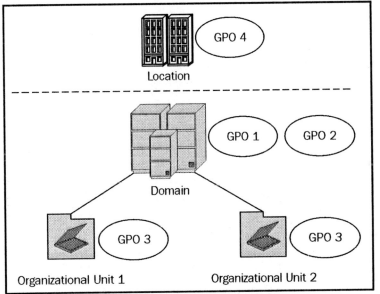

Figure 8.31: Linking options for GPOs

The model just described assumes that there is only one container for each hierarchy level, e.g. just one organizational unit with no additional OU sub-containers. If, however, there are more containers in a container (an OU is structured by further OUs, the default mode of inheritance also applies to group policies: the higher-level container passes on the configured policies to all users and computers of the subordinate containers. This, however, applies only to policies that are either enabled or disabled. Policies that are not configured are not passed on.

If you have configured some special policies in a subordinate container that are not mutually contradictory, these are added. If, however, the entries in the policies of the higher-level and subordinate containers contradict each other, the settings of the higher-level container are not passed on, and those of the subordinate container are used.

If a particular policy is not configured in a subordinate container but only in the higher-level container, the setting from the higher-level container is adopted.

Contents of a GPO

Each GPO is divided into two areas: computer configuration and user configuration. Only machine-related settings are made in the computer configuration. They are applied each time a computer starts. The identity of the user logging on to the computer does not matter in this context. Conversely, the user configuration pertains only to the user. It does not matter at which computer the user logs on. In both configuration areas you will find the sub-containers Software Settings, Windows Settings, and Administrative Templates.

Software Settings

Both configurations have only one default entry: Software Installation. Via this link you can create and configure new packages for software deployment (see the *Software Management and Deployment through Group Policies* section).

Windows Settings

Under Windows Settings you will find, for both configurations, the nodes Scripts and Security Settings. Additionally, the user configuration has Internet Explorer Maintenance, Remote Installation Services, and Folder Redirection. The following table shows you the meaning of the various nodes:

Node	Description
Scripts	Here you can define scripts for logging on and logging off users, and for starting and shutting down the computer. The scripts can either be batch files (`.cmd/.bat`) or Visual Basic, Java, or Perl scripts. When several scripts are used, their sequence can also be determined. When starting a computer first the start-up script, and then, when the user logs on, the logon script are processed. When shutting down first the log off script and then the shutdown script are processed. By default a maximum of ten minutes are given for the execution of the scripts. This limit can be raised if needed.
Security Settings	Here you can make detailed security settings for machines or

Node	Description
	users. These include account policies (password and account barring), granting of user permissions or monitoring policies. Furthermore, you can specify the start-up options for the Windows system services, configure security settings for specific registry keys and files, and specify the policies for public keys here.
Internet Explorer Maintenance	Here you can configure Internet Explorer for the client computer. These configuration settings could include a changed logo, modified toolbars, pre-defined connections with proxy settings etc., links that are automatically added, and even modified security filters.
Remote Installation Services	Here you can specify whether automatic or custom remote installations are permitted or not, and whether the computer should be restarted after the installation.
Folder redirection	Via folder redirection some Windows folders such as My Documents or Start Menu can be redirected from the default user profile to a central place in the network. Further information about this can be found in the *Folder Management through Group Policies* section later in this chapter.

The MMC nodes Software Settings (assigning, installation etc.), Remote Installation, and Folder Redirection are only available if a domain is set up with Active Directory.

Administrative Templates

Under computer and software configuration you will find the Administrative Templates node. Here you can configure the settings based on the HKEY_LOCAL_MACHINE (computer configuration) and HKEY_CURRENT_USER (user configuration) areas of the registry. The computer configuration refers to the following areas: Windows components, system, network, and printers. The administrative templates of the user menu cover the following additional areas: start menu and taskbar, desktop, and the control panel. The "printers" area is missing here. The following settings can be made in the individual areas:

Node	Description
Windows components	In the computer configuration you can adjust settings for the following Windows components: NetMeeting, Internet Explorer, TaskScheduler, and Windows Installer. Additional settings for Windows Explorer and the MMC are possible in the user configuration.

Node	Description
System	The following areas are available for the computer configuration: logon, disk quotas, DNS clients, group policies, and Windows file protection. The areas available for the user configuration are: logon, log off, and group policies.
Network	Here you can specify the settings for offline files and network and dial-up connections, e.g. the availability of network connection wizards or the enabling/disabling of LAN connections.
Printers	Printer settings, e.g. the publication in Active Directory, are undertaken here.
Start menu and taskbar	Here you can define the start menu on an individual basis. Specific program groups or menu entries can be removed or context menus in the taskbar disabled.
Desktop	You can configure settings for the Active Desktop (for example, the wallpaper), or add objects to it. Size or filters can also be set for the search dialog of Active Directory.
Control Panel	The Software, Display, Printers, and Regional Settings menu items can be configured here. The remaining items in Control Panel can even be made invisible if required.

Each individual policy of a user configuration (but not *all* in the computer configuration) has three tabs in Properties. On the Policy tab you can make policy-specific settings and enable or disable the policy. On the Explanation tab you will find the function of each policy that can be configure precisely explained, and so a detailed explanation of all policies is omitted here.

Each policy can have three possible values. It is either not configured, i.e. no value has been set for it, or a value has been specified so that the policy can be set to enabled or disabled. To set a value or to enable or disable a policy, select the appropriate checkbox in the properties of the policy.

If you have configured a certain number of policies in the administrative templates and want to see only these, you should select a different view option. By default all policies are shown, irrespective of whether they have been configured. Highlight the Administrative Templates in the computer/user configuration and select Show only configured policies from the View menu. This hides all the non-configured policies.

Executing Group Policies for Computers and Users

As soon as a computer for which group policies have been configured boots and its **Remote Procedure Call (RPC)** service starts, it will prompt for the group policies defined at the time of configuration. If the computer is not a member of the domain, only the local GPO will be executed. If several GPOs are defined for the computer at one level (say the site level), they are executed in the sequence of the defined list. Here the sequence of local, site, domain, and organization unit is maintained. Finally, the start-up scripts for the computer are executed. The computer-related group policies are executed, while the Applying Computer Settings message is displayed as the computer boots.

Then the login window appears. After the user is successfully verified, his or her profile is loaded. Then the GPOs are executed in the same sequence as that of the computer configuration. Finally, the login scripts for the user are executed. All these processes run in the background while the Loading Custom Settings window is displayed.

This is the default sequence of execution. However, exceptions can also be defined for this sequence. The three possible exceptions are No precedence, Disable, and Loopback. You can enable the first two options by switching to the Group Policy tab and then clicking Options.

These two options have the following meaning:

- No precedence: This option ensures that no property of the policies of this GPO can be overwritten and thus disabled. The execution of a policy marked with No precedence is enforced. If this option in selected for several GPOs, then this setting will be applicable to the highest object in the hierarchy. Thus if one GPO at domain level and one at OU level are set to No precedence, this option will be applicable to the OU-GPO, which is one level higher.

- Disabled: If this option is selected, the GPO settings are not implemented for the container in question. Disabling only works if the GPO is not set to No precedence.

A further option to control the GPO process is the Loopback option. To use this option, open the following: GPO/Computer Configuration/ Administrative Files/System/Group Policies. Here you will find the Loopback-Process Mode For The User Group Policy.

The loopback function is a logical choice when the user policy must be changed according to the computer (irrespective of the user). Laboratories and classrooms are an example of this. By default, all user settings are accessed from the GPO list of site, domain, and organizational unit—under the inheritance conditions configured by the administrator. To change this behavior, the Replace and Merge options are available when this policy is enabled.

Replace: When this option is selected, the GPO list of the computer is used instead of the GPO list for the user. The policy settings of the computer completely replace the user settings, which would normally have been used.

Merge: This option allows the use of the GPO lists of both the computer and the user at the time of login. However, the GPO list of the computer is attached to the GPO list of the user and is therefore processed second. If the two GPO lists conflict with each other, the GPO list of the computer overwrites the GPO list of the user as it is processed after the GPO list of the user.

Special Options for Group Policies

Apart from the execution sequence, there are a few special settings for the group polices for the user and computer configuration. These include the update interval or the synchronous or asynchronous application of the GPO. To select these options, click Group Policy/Computer Configuration/Administrative Files/System/Group Policies.

Computer Configuration

The following important options are available to you in the computer configuration:

- Disabling The Background Updating Of The Group Policy: If this policy is enabled, then the policies for the computer and user configuration will not get updated while the computer is running. The data will be updated only when the user logs off. If this policy is disabled, the policies for the computer can be updated at a definable interval.

- Update Interval Of The Group Policies For The Computer: You can set the interval at which the policies for the computer configuration should be updated in the background while the computer is running. It is possible to set the interval between 0 to 64,800 minutes (= 45 days). To ensure that all clients do not carry out their update simultaneously, a delay in the interval can be configured. The default interval is set at 30 minutes, but can be extended to 24 hours. In certain circumstances, the background update of a computer configuration policy is noticed by the user when the desktop automatically refreshes itself or when open menus automatically close. The same settings can be implemented for the domain controller via the Update Interval Of The Group Policies For The Domain Controller policy.

- Asynchronous Use Of The Group Policies For The Computer At Start-Up (only for Windows 2000): If this policy remains disabled, the user can only log on after all the group polices of the computer configuration have been updated. A dialog box for a Windows login is not displayed to the user

before that. This is the default and secure Windows 2000 boot process.
If this policy is enabled, the user can log on even if all the group policies are
not updated.

- Asynchronous Use Of The Group Policies For The User At The Time Of
  Login (only for Windows 2000): If this policy remains disabled, the user will
  have access to his or her desktop only after all the group policies for the user
  configurations have been updated. This, too, is the default Windows
  procedure. If this policy is enabled, the user has access to his or her desktop
  even if all policies have not been updated. If in this period a user starts an
  application to which changes have been made, there can be serious problems.

The aforementioned processing methods are carried out synchronously by default only
under Windows 2000. On the other hand, Windows XP Professional does not wait by
default, at the time of booting and login, for the network to fully start. Cached data is
used if a known user logs on the system. This considerably accelerates the boot process.
The group policies are thus processed asynchronously as soon as the network becomes
fully accessible. Only when a new user logs on to a computer with Windows XP are the
GPOs processed synchronously.

Furthermore, you can configure the registry, Internet Explorer, folder redirection, disk
quotas, scripts, or software installation options such as background update, identification
of slow connections, or update without changes.

Multiple Logins under Windows XP till a GPO is Activated

As mentioned previously, a fast user login can be carried out on Windows XP with the
help of a previously cached user login. If, meanwhile, the user settings have been
changed (for example, a new folder redirection), then this changed setting will not be
applied during the asynchronous policy processing at the time of the first login by the
user. Only after all the policies are worked through will the cached data and,
consequently, the login settings be updated. During this process the asynchronous
processing will be disabled for the next login process so that the changes can get applied.
Hence, the user will see the updated settings of the policies only at the time of his or her
second login, after the changes have been made.

The same happens when new software is assigned to the user via software installation. If
the user already has access to his or her desktop, the software cannot be installed during
the asynchronous process. In such a case, instead of the user, the *computer* is informed
that new software is to be installed. At the time of the user's next login, the computer
processes the user policies synchronously so that the new software can be installed.

This procedure is also carried out in Windows 2000, if the asynchronous processing of
the policy settings has been enabled.

In order to activate the changes in Windows XP and Windows 2000 by default at the time of the boot process and login, go to Computer Configuration/Administrative Templates/System/ Login and enable the Always wait for the network at the time of rebooting the computer and at the time of login policy.

Implementation Strategy for Group Policies

Before the group policies are generated, some thought must be given to the planning of the types of group policies needed, their implementation, and their allocation. Start creating GPOs only after careful planning before unleashing them on users and computers alike.

A few guidelines and hints are given in this section on how to implement the group policies. Most of these individual guidelines can be used in combination with each other.

Number of GPOs per User and per Computer

Decide how many GPOs are to be created in all and how should they be implemented at the various hierarchical levels. In the decentralized GPOs model, only one GPO is implemented on the basis of an organizational unit. This organizational unit contains a series of policy settings. No central GPO is defined on the basis of domain and site. If an organizational unit has users and computers that cannot use the same GPO, then the users/computers with identical security requirements within the organizational unit are merged together into a sub-organizational unit within the container. The advantage of this model is that at the time of login only one GPO is processed, and therefore the process is carried out faster. However, this model also increases the administration effort, as users/computers with identical security requirements have to be merged together into a sub-organizational unit.

Conversely, it is also possible to create a central GPO for a domain or a site that fulfills all the basic requirements of all the users. Options for user accounts and passwords are conceivable in this context. Besides this global GPO, specific GPOs can be created for individual organizational units. This procedure is logical if the organizational units are generated according to functional aspects. Thus, all the members of the finance organizational unit within this organizational unit will have access to similar GPO settings, but these will be completely different from the GPO settings of the members of the sales organizational unit. Thus, as far as possible, a specific policy setting will be available in only one GPO. If it becomes necessary to change this policy, then only one GPO will have to be edited, unlike in the previously mentioned model, where all the GPOs containing this policy have to be edited.

This model makes sense when a firm has different organizational units, each of which has to consider different security aspects. In this case, however, the login time of the clients will increase, as they will have to process a number of GPOs with only a few policies in each. As against this, the administrative overhead is less here.

Number of Policies per GPO

In this context it is necessary to define the different types of policies. You can create GPOs that only contain policies of either the user configuration or the computer configuration. The login time is slightly prolonged, as two different GPOs have to be processed. However, this division is suitable for conducting a quick search for errors. If it is assumed that the error is in the GPO of the policies of the user configuration, the user should, as a test, login under a different account to which no policies have been assigned. If this resolves the problem, the error lies in the user configuration, but if this does not, the error lies in the computer configuration.

A policy type can also be defined by specifying the scope of the policies that should be contained in a GPO. For example, you can create a GPO that contains only those policies that are required for software installation, or another GPO only containing policies required for the login process, etc. Obviously, it is possible for a GPO to contain policies from different areas. The more policies that a GPO contains, the less is the login time of the clients, and conversely, the higher will be the administrative effort in terms of editing the policy settings.

GPO Administration

By delegating the GPO administration, it is possible for the administrators to override specific domain-wide GPOs on an organizational-unit level. In the case of some GPOs, this option can also be withdrawn. If it's required that certain security settings of a domain-wide GPO should not overwrite the settings of the GPO of an organizational unit, the GPO of that organizational unit should be provided with the No precedence option. This procedure can be used for company-wide user account policies and password policies.

In order to give an administrator the option to implement specific organizational unit settings in his or her own organizational unit instead of applying only the domain-wide policies, he or she has to be given appropriate permissions to use the Block Policy inheritance option for the desired organizational unit. However, the inheritance of group policies can be disabled only when the No precedence option is *not* selected.

Special Logon and Log-Off Scripts

It is possible to assign computers and users scripts for booting and shutting down, and for logging on and logging off, through the group policies. The login script for a computer will run when it is booted and the login script for a user will run when he or she logs on. The logon and log-off scripts can be found in SYSVOL\User\Scripts.

These scripts can be run only by Windows 2000 and Windows XP clients. Clients using older versions of Windows can neither read out these scripts from Active Directory nor can they run them. These clients can only use the conventional boot and login scripts.

In contrast to the well-known login and log off scripts of Windows NT, which are mostly generated as batch files, scripts can now be generated in either VBScript or JScript. For instance: a script can be created to verify the group membership of a user while the computer boots. It can also identify whether the user is, for example, a member of the accounting group in the firma.de domain. With the help of such scripts it is also possible to assign specific drives and printers to the group members. For extensive reference material regarding scripting languages, go to http://www.microsoft.com/scripting.

With the help of a script it is possible to control the login behavior of a user. At the time of login, the script asks for the username and verifies whether the user is a valid Active Directory user. If he or she is, then the script further verifies whether he or she is a member of the user group defined in the script. If yes, then other options like mapping of the drives and printers are applied.

The script is written as a text file and is saved either with a .vbs extension if VBScript is used, or as a .js file, if JScript is used. Make sure you never open a script by double clicking on it as it will automatically start running with unforeseen consequences. To edit the script, open it in any text editor.

The following situation is an example illustrating the practical application of a logon and log-off script: When an administrator logs on to any workstation running Windows 2000 or Windows XP Professional and wants to manage the server from there, he or she must have access to his or her administrative tools. These tools must be accessible only for as long as the *administrator* is logged on to the computer. Another user who logs on to the same computer after the administrator must not have access to these tools. There is a great risk that the unauthorized user may misuse the administrative tools.

In a Windows NT environment, the administrator must install the administrative tools on every non-server computer and uninstall them at the time of logging off. For Windows 2000 and above, this time-consuming procedure is redundant. When the administrator logs in, the appropriate programs are installed, and with the help of a log-off script, the programs are uninstalled.

The application possibilities of the logon and log-off scripts as well as of the boot and shutdown scripts are manifold. As opposed to Windows NT, a decided advantage is that instead of only one script, any number of scripts can be implemented for a computer or a user. Let us assume that all the computers have access to the same standardized boot script, and a new DLL or a specific registry key is to be installed on all the computers. This installation can be controlled by a second boot script. Once the new DLL or the key is installed on all the computers, the second script can be deleted.

Scripts are also useful when the users are to be allowed to perform operations that are not normally assigned to them, for a limited period of time. If, for example, a group of users are getting trained in the use of Internet Explorer, it is possible, with the help of a second logon script, to give the users extended permissions for the period of the training and to lift the normally assigned restrictions like browser menus, auto-complete, or filter settings. When the training comes to end, the second script is deleted and the users again have access to only a limited number of functionalities.

The Group Policy Management Console (GPMC)

The GPMC is a new MMC in which all the settings pertaining to the group policies can be centrally configured, including backup and data retrieval from anywhere within the network, along with the import and export of GPOs and security settings. Furthermore, HTML reports of the GPO settings and their effects are also displayed. The administration of the security aspects is also simplified in the GPMC. There is also the additional possibility available of using **Windows Management Instrumentation** (WMI) filters. With the help of WMI filters, queries can be sent to the WMI database of a target computer. This database then evaluates these queries as either true or false. All operations that are configured through the GUI of the GPMC can also be script driven. However, the settings of the GPO cannot be configured via a script.

This centralization comes as a much better method than the original method of group policy administration. Although it was possible to link a GPO to a number of user groups, it proved to be complex as it was very easy to loose track of the places where the GPO was applied. Even the application of several GPOs at the site, domain, and organizational unit level became very complicated. It was not always easy to ascertain the exact effects of the GPOs on account the inheritance of the various polices and the prioritization of the GPOs of the same level.

In the absence of the GPMC, the administrator had to always have access to a number of tools for the creation and administration of the group policies—the Active Directory Users and Computers and Active Directory Sites and Services MMCs, RSoP (Resultant Set of

Policy), delegation wizard, and the ACL (Access Control List) editor. These programs
are now contained in the GPMC and can be centrally invoked. However, as soon as the
GPMC is installed, the administration of the GPOs cannot be carried out as before. If, for
example, you want to access the group policy editor through the Active Directory Users
And Computers MMC, a message is displayed stating that you should use the GPMC for
administrative purposes. The Group Policy tab in the properties of the domains or the
organizational units is no longer accessible. Only the GPMC can still be accessed.

The GPMC is already integrated in the SBS 2003. This console can be accessed via
Server Management.

In addition to direct access from the SBS 2003, the GPMC can also be installed on
another computer for remote administration, provided that the computer is running either
Windows XP Professional or Windows Server 2003. In case of Windows XP, the
following additional components need to be installed:

- Windows XP SP1
- Microsoft .NET Framework

SP1-Hotfix Q326469 will also be required. This is contained in the GPMC and will be
installed along with the GPMC. For use on another computer, the GPMC can be
downloaded from https://www.microsoft.com/downloads/details.aspx?
displaylang=en&FamilyID=F39E9D60-7E41-4947-82F5-3330F37ADFEB.

Besides these new core features, a wide range of administrative tasks in other areas can
also be carried out and simplified with the help of the GPMC. An overview of these
features of the GPMC is given in the following table:

Feature	Description
New group policy settings	Windows Server 2003 contains over 150 more GPO settings than Windows 2000. These settings relate, inter alia, to the following areas: Terminal Server, DNS, Error Reporting, and Roaming Profiles.
Web view of the administrative templates	As soon as a specific policy setting is selected, the web view displays the detailed information regarding the settings and their purpose. The web view can also be accessed from the Explanation tab of any setting.
GPO modeling	GPO modeling makes it possible to investigate the policy settings, security, and applications in a "what if" scenario. This function is very helpful at the time of restructuring or expansion. Before a change is implemented, numerous tests can be carried out in order to ascertain the consequences for a user or a group.

Feature	Description
DNS client	The DNS client settings of the SBS 2003, like dynamic registration of the DNS records or transfer of the primary DNS suffix, can be easily done through the group policy.
Network Connections	The GUI to set up the network connections can be made either inaccessible or accessible to specific users through the group policy.
Software installation at logon	With regard to software deployment, it is now possible to install the software assigned to the users when they log on rather than installing it only when the need arises.
Software Support URL.	For every installed software packet, the user can now directly access the support site of the manufacturer through the URL provided in Control Panel/Add/Remove programs. This helps relieve the load on the company's internal support department and help desk.
WMI filters	The software and hardware inventory data and also other configuration settings from the Registry, file system, drivers, Active Directory, Windows Installer, SNMP, Network, SQL, and Exchange are read out through the Windows Management Instrumentation (WMI). In WMI filtering you can specify whether a GPO should depend on a WMI filter. A WMI filter is a query of the WMI data. This filter can be used to decide for which user or computer a GPO should be used. This function is logical when a specific software package, requiring a certain amount of free space on the hard disk, is to be distributed to all the users of an organizational unit. In this case you can use a WMI filter that will only install the software for the users who have at least 500 MB free space on the hard disk.

Administration through the GPMC

After the GPMC is installed, the new entry Group Policy Management is added in the Start Menu/Administration. When this MMC starts, you are prompted to login with a valid domain user account, if the administration computer is merely a member of a workgroup. Figure 8.32 gives you an overview of the GPMC.

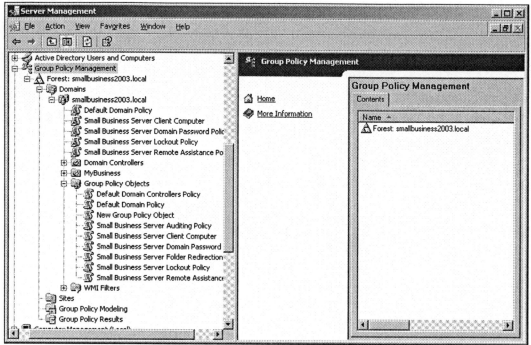

Figure 8.32: The Group Policy Management Console (GPMC)

In the MMC, the hierarchy of the network is represented—from the highest level of the forest via domains, sites, and organizational units right down to the individual GPOs. By default, only the current sites and domains are displayed. In order to add more objects to the MMC, select the options View Domains or View Sites from the context menu of Domains or Sites respectively. From the list select the sites and domains that should be displayed in the MMC.

Creating, Deleting, and Linking GPOs

In order to create a new GPO in the GPMC, select a domain and then click Group Policy Objects. Then select New from the context menu and enter a name for the new GPO. If the new GPO is to be linked immediately with the domain, select Create and Link Group Policy Object here. If an existing GPO is to be linked to a domain, a site, or an organizational unit, select Link Existing Group Policy Object from the corresponding context menu. After the GPO is created, select Edit from its context menu. The GPO editor will then open, through which all the settings can be edited, as described in an earlier section, *Contents of a GPO*. Keep in mind that the changes made to an existing GPO will affect all the containers to which the GPO is linked. When the changes are being implemented, the GPMC will display a warning, reminding the user of the changes being carried out.

The Scope tab (see the figure that follows) shows to which sites, domains, and organizational units the GPO is linked, for which user group the GPO is being used, and to which WMI filter the GPO is linked:

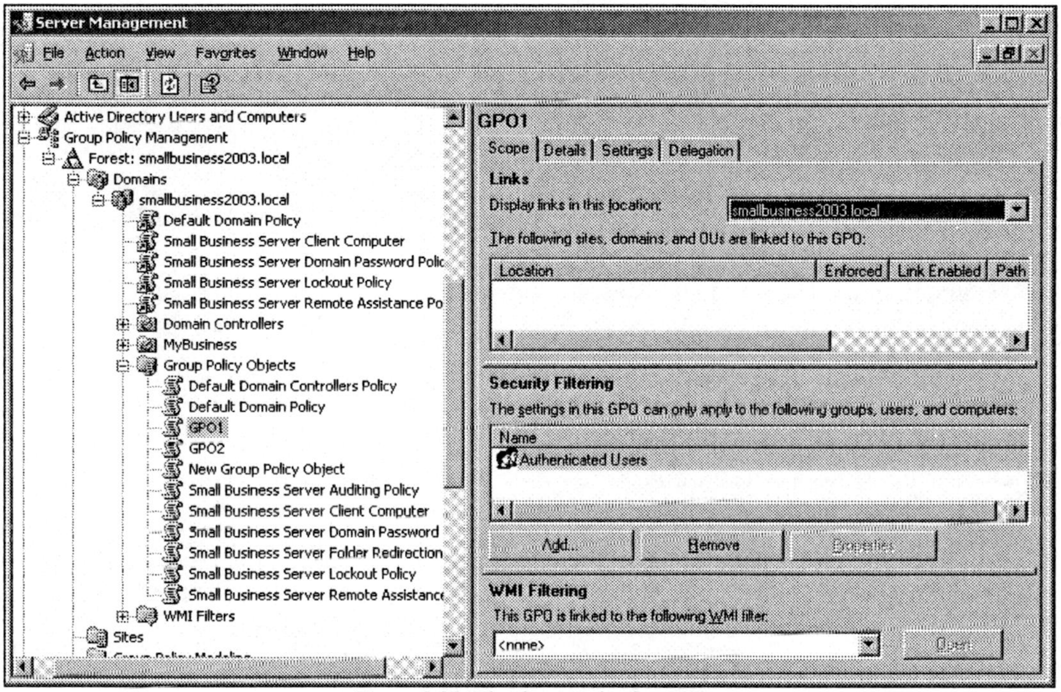

Figure 8.33: The Scope tab of a GPO

The Details tab gives information regarding the creation and the modification dates, the GUID, the owner, the domain, and the status of the object.

The Settings tab (see the following figure) shows which areas of the GPO are configured. A concise list of enabled and disabled policies is available for computer configuration and user configuration. The settings that are not configured are not displayed.

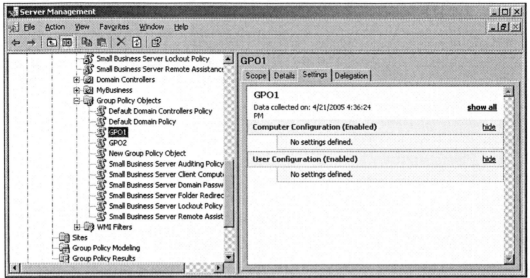

Figure 8.34: The Settings tab of a GPO

The Delegation tab shows which users and groups have which permissions for the GPO. The permissions of the users and the groups can be modified through the context menu.

Before a GPO is deleted, check via its Scope whether it has any existing domain local links. In order to do this, select the [Forest] entry from the View Links For This Directory drop-down list. It is now possible to delete all the existing links before the GPO itself is deleted. The Default Domain Controllers Policy and Default Domain Policy GPOs cannot be deleted.

The status of the group policies of all the GPOs can be set through the Group Policy Status context menu entry. You can enable the GPO and separately disable the user configuration settings, the computer configuration settings, or the entire GPO.

Backup of GPOs

The backup of a GPO involves backing up all the components of the GPO contained in the Active Directory and the file system contained in the SYSVOL folder. These components include the GUID of the GPO, the domains, the GPO settings, the access permissions for the GPO, and references to any linked WMI filters. However, the WMI filters themselves cannot be backed up at the time the GPO backup. The same holds true for IPSec policies that can be applied to a GPO. This is so because, for example, different permissions apply to a WMI filter than to the GPO itself. It could thus be the case that an administrator does not have access to the necessary permissions for a WMI filter or an IPSec policy when backing up or restoring a GPO.

Additionally, it would be unnecessary to save the WMI filter or the IPSec policies together with every GPO as they can be linked to several GPOs. For backing up the WMI filter use the export and import function of the WMI filter itself in the GPMC (see the *WMI Filters* section later in this chapter). A backup of the IPSec policies can be carried out through the import and export function of the IP Security Policies snap-in, which can be found in the relevant GPO itself.

When a GPO is backed up, an XML-based report is generated. This report contains a time stamp, an optional description, and the GPO settings. Every backup procedure is given a unique number. This makes it possible to store several backup files of the same GPO in the same storage location. The XML-based backup report can be read through the GPMC in HTML format. For a backup to be carried out, read permissions must be available for the GPO. Write access to the backup storage location must also be available. The following steps must be carried out to start a GPO backup:

1. Select Backup from the context menu of the desired GPO. The Back Up Group Policy Object window will be displayed (see Figure 8.35).

2. Specify the storage location via the Browse button. In the Description textbox, enter a brief description of the GPO (optional). Then click Back Up.

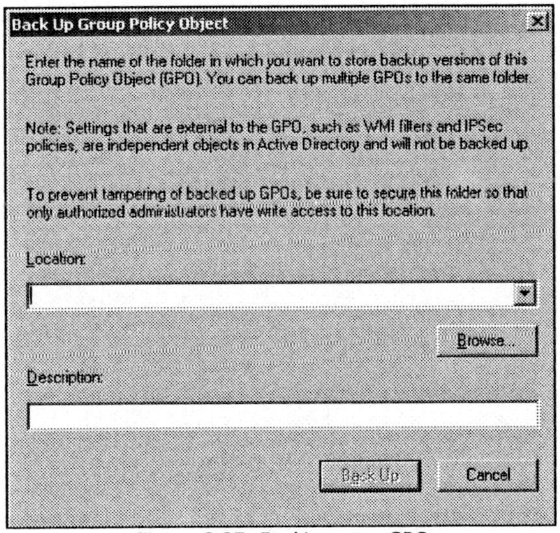

Figure 8.35: Backing up a GPO

Information about the backup status and its success or failure is given during the process.

To simultaneously back up several GPOs, click on the Group Policy Objects node in the GPMC. Then, in the Contents tab, select one or more GPOs. To select multiple GPOs, keep the *Ctrl* key pressed. The same dialog box as shown in Figure 8.35 will be displayed, and all the selected GPOs will be backed up.

In order to back up all the existing GPOs, select Back Up All from the context menu of the Group Policy Objects node. The same dialog box as shown in Figure 8.35 will be displayed again, and all the GPOs will be backed up. Scripts can also be used for GPO backup. The scripts can either be predefined ones or can be generated by the user. Predefined scripts are stored in the GPMC\scripts directory. The back up of a GPO can be carried out with the help of the BackupGPO.wsf script, while the back up of all the GPOs can be carried out with the BackupAllGPOs.wsf script.

Managing Multiple Backups

The backups are not only created in the GPMC, but can also be managed through it. The dialog box for backup management can be accessed by selecting Back Up Management either from the context menu of the Domain container or from the context menu of the Group Object Policy container. In the former case, all the backed up GPOs of the entire structure are displayed, and in the latter case only the GPOs of the updated domains are displayed. In both the cases, the management options remain the same (see Figure 8.36):

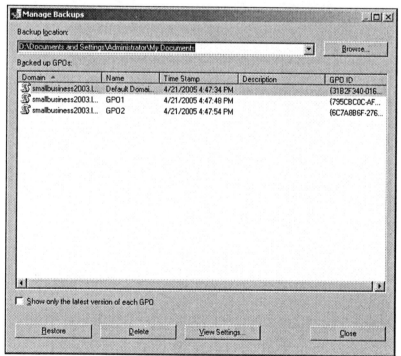

Figure 8.36: The management of multiple backed up GPOs

In the Manage Backups window, the path to the storage location where the displayed backups are stored can be seen in Backup location. Against every backed up object the domain name, the GPO name, the time of the backup, an optional description and a unique GUID of the GPO is given. If the Show only the latest version of each GPO option is checked, only the entry with the latest time stamp is displayed.

Three buttons are situated in the lower half of the window. Through these buttons, you can restore or delete a backed up GPO. Each of these two actions must be confirmed separately before it is implemented. It is also possible to display the GPO settings. For this, the default web browser of the user opens and shows the settings as an HTML page.

The management of multiple backups can also be script driven. For this, use the sample script QueryBackupLocation.wsf. This script is saved in GPMC\scripts.

Restoring GPOs

The restoration of a GPO must not be mistaken for the import or the copying of a GPO (see the *Copying of GPOs* section later in the chapter). When a GPO is restored, it goes back to its earlier status. This can become necessary if a GPO is to be rolled back to a functioning older status or if a GPO is accidentally deleted. When a GPO is restored, it retains its original GUID. Only its settings, permissions and its linked WMI filters are replaced. If the links of a GPO are also deleted with the GPO, then these links can only be restored manually. This process is not considered to be a part of GPO restoration. In order to restore the links quickly, refer to the GPO security reports in which the links of all the GPOs of the domain are listed.

> A backed up GPO cannot be restored if the domain is renamed in the meantime. In principle, all GPOs must be backed up as soon as a domain is renamed.

Restoring Existing GPOs

The following steps must be carried out in order to restore an existing GPO with its original settings:

1. Select Restore from Backup from the context menu of the GPO. This starts the restore wizard.

2. Enter the name of the folder in which the backed up GPO is saved, or use the Browse button to find the folder in which the backed up GPO is stored. Click Next.

3. After a backup folder is selected, all the GPO backups stored in this folder are displayed (see the following figure). For easier understanding, the timestamp and the optional description of the backups are also displayed. The details of the GPO can be viewed by clicking on the View Settings button. Select the desired backup and then click Next.

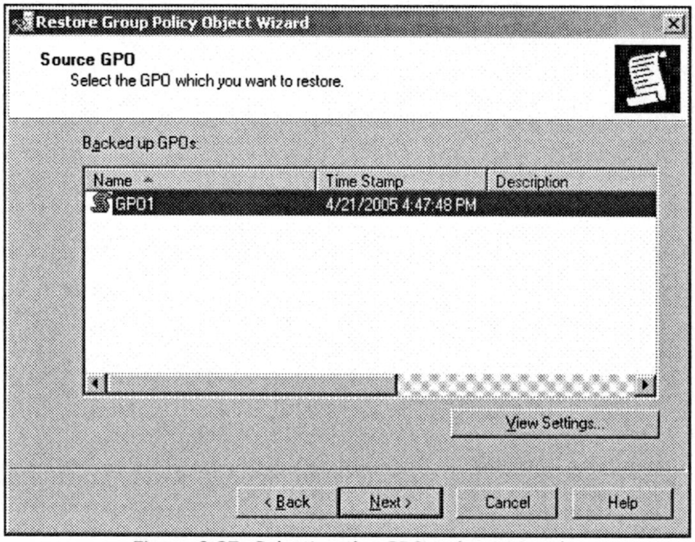

Figure 8.37: Selecting the GPO to be restored

4. A summary of the selected steps is generated. Click on Finish. This restores the backed up GPO with its settings, and the current values of the GPO are overwritten. The version number of the GPO is increased to the next value. This is necessary for the clients to which this GPO is applied to accept the restored GPO.

5. In order to restore a GPO, the user must have the permissions that allow him or her to delete, to change the security settings, and to edit the settings. The user must also have read access to the source directory of the backed up GPO. However, permission to create GPOs is not necessary.

Restoring Deleted GPOs

In order to restore an accidentally deleted GPO, open the Manage Backups window (see Figure 8.36). Select the desired GPO and click on the Restore button. If a deleted GPO is restored, then the version number of the backed up GPO is retained. In other words, the restored GPO has the same version number as that of the backed up GPO. In order to be able to restore a deleted GPO, you must have permission to create GPOs in the domain. The person who restores the GPO becomes the new creator-owner of the GPO.

Script-Driven Restoration of GPOs

A GPO can be restored through a user-generated script or through a predefined script from the GPMC\scripts directory. To restore a single GPO, use the RestoreGPO.wsf script. The RestoreAllGPOs.wsf script can be used to restore all GPOs.

Restoration of GPOs with Software Installation Settings.

When restoring GPOs, more attention should be paid to GPOs that contain software installation settings (see the *Software Management and Deployment through Group Policies* section). This is also applicable when such a GPO has been deleted and has to be restored. In this case, two different types of problems can occur:

- If there are GPO local relations that update an application in the restored GPO, then these relations are not retained after the restoration is complete. The application of the restored GPO loses its update. In these GPO local relations it is specified that an application should update another, the two applications not being distributed via the same GPO. However, the relations are retained if the application of the restored GPO is to update the applications of other GPOs.

- If the client computer has not been informed that a GPO was deleted—this is the case if the computer has not been restarted or the user has not logged in afresh after the deletion—and applications with the option Uninstall applications if they are outside the management area are given to it, published applications (see the *Installation* section under *Software Management and Deployment through Group Policies* later in this chapter) that are already installed are deleted at the next logon and assigned applications are uninstalled before a reinstallation.

> Normally, an application is uninstalled through the Uninstall applications if they are outside the management area option if the relevant GPO is no longer applied to either to the computer or the user.

This unwanted behavior is because a new GUID is assigned to the corresponding application when the Active Directory object representing the application is restored. Since the GUID of the existing application is different from the newly allotted GUID, Windows will view this application as two different applications. This problem can only be solved by using the original GUID of the application while restoring the GPO. This is the known as **tombstone re-animation**. Tombstones are objects of that have been deleted from Active Directory but are still not permanently removed from the directory. By default, all the deleted objects are permanently removed after 60 days.

At the time of GPO restoration, tombstone re-animation is automatically carried out by the GPMC. This re-animation can be successfully carried out if the following three requirements are fulfilled:

- The GPMC works with a domain controller that is running in Windows Server 2003.

- The time interval between the deletion and restoration of the GPOs does not extend beyond the defined tombstone interval. By default, the time interval is set to 60 days.

- The user carrying out the restoration has the permission for tombstone re-animation. By default, only the domain and organization administrators are given this permission. However, this permission can be given to any other person through the ACL Editor.

If the tombstone re-animation fails, a new GUID is assigned to the application that is thus identified as a new application and these problems appear.

Copying of GPOs

Whether GPOs should be copied between two domains or whether a GPO should be imported from one domain to another depends on the trust relationship between the domains. If the trust relationship exists, the GPOs will be copied or imported (see the following section). The latter case is also referred to as the migration of GPOs. Since in the SBS 2003 environment there can be no trust relationships between domains, GPOs cannot be copied. Thus, copying of a GPO from the test environment to the production environment is not possible. Therefore, in an SBS 2003 environment GPOs can only be imported or exported.

Import and Export of GPOs

The import of GPOs is also known as migration. At the time of GPO migration, various factors have to be taken into consideration; the data is complex, it's saved in different memory locations, and some of it is domain-specific. To migrate the domain-specific data correctly, the GPMC uses Migration Tables (see the *Migration Tables* section under *Group Policy Management*). The domain-specific data with new values for the GPO is entered in this table.

During import, the settings of a GPO are transferred into an existing GPO. These settings are sourced from the backup of the GPO. As in the case of copying, the destination GPO can either be located in the same domain or in another domain within the same forest, or it can be located in another domain of another forest. In this case, there need not be a trust relationship between the domains. All that is needed is access to the storage location of the GPOs in the source domain from the destination domain. The GPO to which the settings are transferred retains its security settings and the links to its WMI filters.

The following steps must be carried out to import a GPO:

1. From the context menu select Import Settings to start the wizard.

2. You can back up the updated settings, as they will be overwritten at the time of import. To select a backup, click on the Back Up button. A storage location can also be specified. Click NEXT.

3. Select the back up folder in which the GPO to be imported is located. If there are several GPOs, select only the desired GPO and click Next.

4. The wizard will examine the selected backup to determine if any UNC paths or security principals need to be transferred (see the following figure). If this is the case, the transfers will be carried out with the help of the Migration Tables. If there are no transfers to be carried out, click Next. A summary will be displayed. Click on Finish.

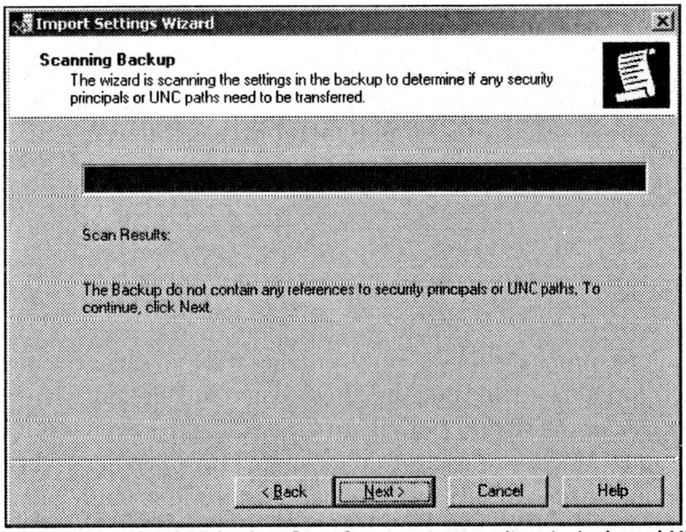

Figure 8.38: Checking the GPO backup for references to security principals and UNC paths

An import can also be script driven. To import a GPO the script ImportGPO.wsf is used, and to import all GPOs the script ImportAllGPOs.wsf is used. These scripts are located in the GPMC\scripts folder.

Creating HTML Reports

To generate an HTML report for a GPO, first select the GPO from an organizational unit or from a domain. Then click on the Settings tab in the details area.

From the context menu of the settings report, select Print or Save report. The reports are saved in the HTML format and can be displayed in Internet Explorer. To view this report, the computer must have Internet Explorer Version 6 or Netscape Navigator version 7. By using the Show/Hide option, you can determine what information about the GPOs should be contained in the report. If a higher security configuration is enabled in Internet Explorer, you will be asked for a confirmation at the time of displaying the report (since a script is about to be run). To avoid this confirmation, add about:security_mmc.exe to the list of safe sites in the Internet Explorer.

Migration Tables

Migration Tables are used for copying and importing GPOs between two different domains. These tables contain the domain-specific data of the GPOs. For different data types, for example UNC paths or global groups, both the source and the destination values are shown. With the help of these tables, the values of the source GPO are converted during the copying or importing process to a form that can be used for the destination GPO. The structure of a Migration Table is as follows:

Data Type	Source Value	Target Value
UNC path	\\Server1\Share1	\\Server2\Share2
Global Group	Domain1\Group1	Domain2\Group2

Let's say you want to migrate a GPO from Domain1 to Domain2. The security group Group1 is located in Domain1; only Group2 is located in Domain2. However, identical security settings are configured for both these groups, so that even Group2 can use the GPO. If a Migration Table is not used for the copying process, the security settings of Domain2 will be applied to Group1 even though this group is not located in the domain. These security settings cannot be used for Group2. This problem cannot be solved, even if there were a Group1 in Domain2. This is so because a group's unique SID is saved along with its name, and a Group1 in Domain1 and Domain2 cannot have identical SIDs. With local domain groups, the group is anyway valid only within the source domain and not in any other external domains. The Migration Tables can be modified for references to the following areas of security settings:

- Allocation of user rights
- Restricted groups

- System services
- File system
- Registry

Even existing UNC paths in the GPO cause problems if the values in a Migration Table are not modified. This happens when a UNC path, such as the path to the personal folders of the users, can be accessed only from Domain1, as Domain2 is located in another network segment. The users of Domain2 can no longer access these redirected folders. UNC paths can be modified to the following areas through the Migration Tables:

- Settings for folder redirection.
- Settings for software installation, e.g. software deployment points.
- References to scripts (e.g. logon and log-off scripts) that are saved outside the GPO. The scripts can be copied along with the GPO only if they are saved within the source GPO.

The above-mentioned problems can be avoided by using the Migration Table during the import or copy processes. The GPO is automatically searched for settings that contain, for example, the value \\Domain1\Release1 or Domain1\Group1, \\Domain2\Release2 or Domain2\Group2. This guarantees the functionality of the GPO in the destination domain.

Application of Migration Tables

A Migration Table is used while copying or importing a GPO as soon as it is determined that references to UNC paths are located in the security settings mentioned earlier (see Figure 8.38). Three different options are available for using the Migration Table:

- Do Not Use Migration Table: In this case all the references are copied to the destination GPO exactly as they are, and the function capability of the GPO in the destination domain cannot be guaranteed.
- Use A Migration Table: The values of all the source GPO references are set to the values for the destination GPO, as shown in the Migration Table. If some values for the destination domain are not specified, the values of the source GPO are applied.
- Exclusively Use One Migration Table: This option can only be used if, for all source GPO references, values for the destination GPO are entered in the Migration Table. If this is not the case, then the copy or the import process will not be carried out. This option ensures that the values for all references are changed.

Structure of the Migration Tables

The Migration Tables are XML files. They have the extension `.migtable`. The Migration Table Editor is integrated in the GPMC. Thus, changes must not be made in the XML file. The Migration Table Editor can be opened in one of the following ways:

- Select Open Migration Table Editor from the context menu of the container Group Policy Object.
- Select Open Migration Table Editor from the context menu of the container Domains.
- Start the `mtedit.exe` program from the GPMC installation directory.
- Double-click an existing `.migtable` file.

A sample file of a Migration Table is located in the `GPMC\Script` directory. Open the `SampleMigrationTable.migtable` file in the Migration Table Editor (see the following figure) or open it in any text editor like Notepad to view its XML code.

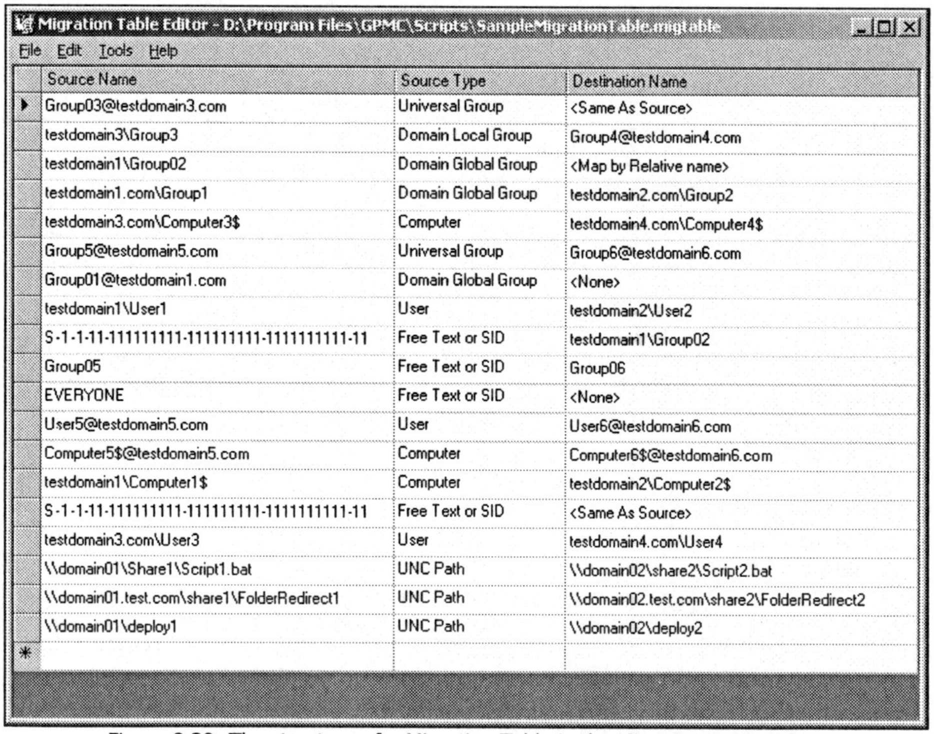
Migration Table Editor - D:\Program Files\GPMC\Scripts\SampleMigrationTable.migtable
File Edit Tools Help
Source Name | Source Type | Destination Name
Group03@testdomain3.com | Universal Group | <Same As Source>
testdomain3\Group3 | Domain Local Group | Group4@testdomain4.com
testdomain1\Group02 | Domain Global Group | <Map by Relative name>
testdomain1.com\Group1 | Domain Global Group | testdomain2.com\Group2
testdomain3.com\Computer3$ | Computer | testdomain4.com\Computer4$
Group5@testdomain5.com | Universal Group | Group6@testdomain6.com
Group01@testdomain1.com | Domain Global Group | <None>
testdomain1\User1 | User | testdomain2\User2
S-1-1-11-111111111-111111111-1111111111-11 | Free Text or SID | testdomain1\Group02
Group05 | Free Text or SID | Group06
EVERYONE | Free Text or SID | <None>
User5@testdomain5.com | User | User6@testdomain6.com
Computer5$@testdomain5.com | Computer | Computer6$@testdomain6.com
testdomain1\Computer1$ | Computer | testdomain2\Computer2$
S-1-1-11-111111111-111111111-1111111111-11 | Free Text or SID | <Same As Source>
testdomain3.com\User3 | User | testdomain4.com\User4
\\domain01\Share1\Script1.bat | UNC Path | \\domain02\share2\Script2.bat
\\domain01.test.com\share1\FolderRedirect1 | UNC Path | \\domain02.test.com\share2\FolderRedirect2
\\domain01\deploy1 | UNC Path | \\domain02\deploy2

Figure 8.39: The structure of a Migration Table in the Migration Table Editor

The following listing displays the XML code of a Migration Table. As an example, the code for the previous table is used.

```
<?xml version="1.0" encoding="utf-16"?>
<MigrationTable   xmlns:xsd="http://www.w3.org/2001/XMLSchema"
xmlns:xsi="http://www.w3.org/2001/XMLSchema-instance"
xmlns="http://www.microsoft.com/GroupPolicy/GPOOperations/MigrationTa
ble">
    <Mapping>
        <Type>GlobalGroup</Type>
        <Source>Domain1\Group1</Source>
        <Destination>Domain2\Group2</Destination>
    </Mapping>
    <Mapping>
        <Type>UNCPath</Type>
        <Source>\\Server1\Share1</Source>
        <Destination>\\Server2\Share2</Destination>
    </Mapping>
</MigrationTable>
```

There is at least one entry is in each the Migration Table. Each of these entries has three columns with the headings Source Name, Source Type, and Destination Name respectively (see Figure 8.39).

The Source Name column shows the name of the sources, for example, a group name or a UNC path that is referred to in the source GPO. The name type, for example a user name, must be identical in the source GPO and the destination GPO given in the Migration Table. The names can be entered in one of the following formats:

- User Principal Name (UPN), e.g. user1@domain.de.
- DNS Name, e.g. domain.de\user1
- SAM, e.g. domain\user1
- Free text, e.g. user1. Under Source Type, Free Text or SID must be entered.
- SID, e.g. S-1-11-111111111-111111111-1111111111-1112. Under Source Type, Free Text or SID must be entered.

The Source Type shows the domain-specific information of the source GPO. In the Migration Table the following source types can be entered:

- Users
- Computers
- Local Domain Group
- Global Domain Group
- Universal Group

- UNC Path

- Free Text or SID (this category is used only for security principles that exist as pure SID or text)

The Destination Name column shows how the names of the user, group, UNC path, etc., are to be treated when they are transferred to the destination GPO. Four options are available for this:

- The destination name corresponds with the source name: In this case the destination GPO uses the same reference that is in the source GPO. The same effect is achieved if no values are entered.

- <None>:The user, computer, or group is deleted from the GPO. This option cannot, however, be used for UNC paths.

- <Map by Relative name>: Here, the reference Domain1\Group1 will automatically become Domain2\Group2. Instead of the source GPO domain, the domain name of the destination GPO will be used. The user name, the group name, or the computer name is retained. This option cannot, however, be used for UNC paths.

- The destination name is given explicitly: The name of the source GPO is replaced with the name given in the destination GPO.

Creating a Migration Table

The Migration Table Editor has the option of automatically populating a newly created Migration Table with either the values of a GPO or the values of a backed up GPO.

1. Open an empty Migration Table by selecting Open Migration Table Editor from the context menu of the container Domain or Group Policy object.

2. An empty table with the three columns—Source Name, Source Type, and Destination Name—will open. Select Populate from Group Policy Object or Populate from backup from the Tools menu.

3. Select the GPO or the GPO back up; its references to security principles and UNC paths should be automatically entered in the Source Name and Source Type columns.

4. You can now make the desired entries in the Destination Name column.

5. After you have edited a Migration Table, you should examine the entered values. To do this, open Tools/Validate Table in the Migration Table Editor. A summary is displayed in the Validation Results window. Hints and warnings about entries that have thrown up problems during validation are shown under Details.

A Migration Table can also be created through scripts. The `CreataMigrationTable.wsf` script is used for this purpose. In doing so, the automatic entry function of the Migration Table Editors is used. The values for the new paths have to be entered manually.

Group Policy Modeling and Results

The deployment of group policies can be simulated through the group policy modeling wizard of the GPMC, as is done in Windows XP clients through Resultant Set of Policy (RSoP), and the results of the group policy settings can also be displayed. To be able to use this feature, at least one domain controller of the forest must run Windows Server 2003. Otherwise, the Group Policy Modelling node in the GPMC won't be accessible. The following steps are to be carried out in order to deploy a group policy and to simulate its results:

1. Select Group Policy Modelling Wizard from the context menu of the Group Policy Modelling node.

2. After the welcome message is displayed, select a domain controller on which the simulation is to be carried out (see Figure 8.40). The selected domain controller must be run Windows Server 2003 or SBS 2003. Click Next.

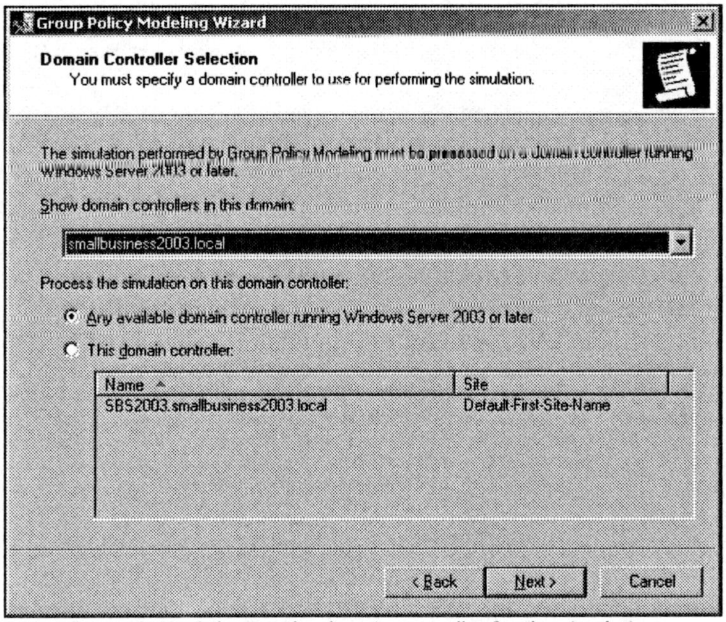

Figure 8.40: Selecting the domain controller for the simulation

3. Next, select whether the policy should be simulated for a particular user and/or computer, or for a container that contains the user information and computer information (see the following figure). Click on the desired checkbox and then select the container, the user, or the computer. Click Next.

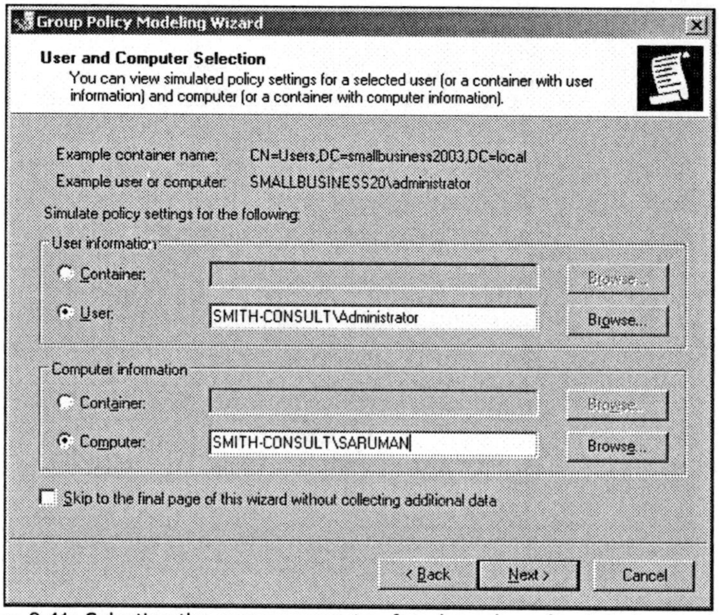

Figure 8.41: Selecting the user or computer, for whom the policy is to be simulated

4. Next, you can optionally enter the additional simulation parameters (see Figure 8.42). You can simulate a slow network connection (dial-up connection). Loopback processing can also be selected with its Replace and Merge options (see the *Executing Group Policies for Computers and Users* section, earlier on under *Group Policy Management*). Furthermore, even a particular site can be selected for the simulation. Click Next.

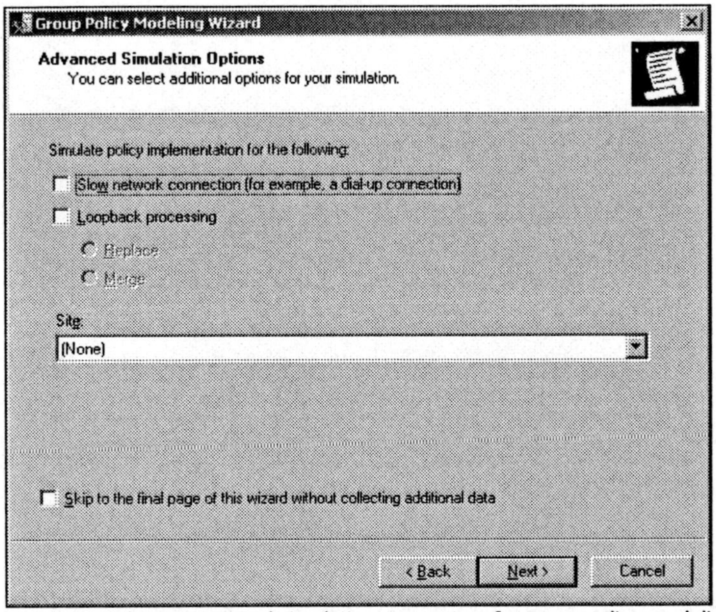

Figure 8.42: Selecting optional simulation parameters for group policy modeling

5. Even alternative Active Directory paths for the user and computer sites can be entered. The policy will be simulated with these settings. Click Next.

6. Next, the membership of the selected users with the security groups is ascertained. The Security Groups list displays the updated memberships. The memberships can be modified by clicking on either the Add or the Remove buttons. Then click Next.

7. As in the previous window, the group membership of a computer can also be modified. Then click Next.

8. Furthermore, you can also select WMI filters for users to be linked to the GPO (see the following figure). It is possible to select either all WMI filters linked with the GPO or just a few WMI filters. Then click Next. For more about WMI filters, refer to *The WMI Filters* section later in this chapter.

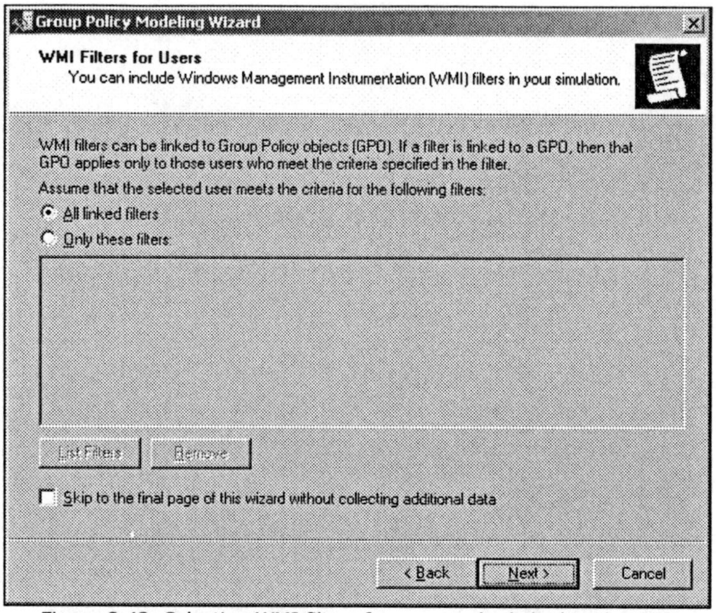

Figure 8.43: Selecting WMI filters for users to be linked to the GPO

9. A WMI filter can also be selected for computers. This selection functions in exactly the same way as described in the previous step. Then click Next.

10. A summary of the selections is displayed. To start group policy modeling, click Next, followed by Finish in the next window.

After you have completed the modeling wizard, a new entry is added in the Group Policy Modeling node. The Content tab of the node for all existing objects displays information about the domain controller used, the selected users and computers, and the execution date. Select any of the available objects to get the summary for this object (see the following figure). The Summary tab displays an HTML report of the user and computer configuration for group memberships, GPOs, and WMI filters. The Settings tab displays an HTML report of the simulated policy settings. The Query tab contains the parameters that were given to generate the simulation.

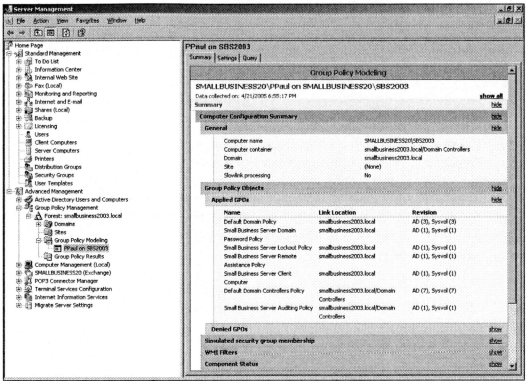

Figure 8.44: Group policy modeling in the GPMC

Via the context menu of the modeled object, you can run the same query again, run a new query based on the existing query, or generate a report.

Open the Resultant Set of Policy (RSoP) MMC by selecting Advanced View from the context menu. This MMC contains the same data as that contained in the HTML report.

However, the HTML report only shows the current value of a policy and the GPO that sets this value. If multiple GPOs are allocated, only the list of all the GPOs and their processing sequence will be displayed in the Group Policy Results MMC.

Group Policy Results

The group policy results are not only displayed for users and computers for whom group policy modeling has been carried out, but also for real users and computers. One is dealing here with real data that has been collected from an existing computer. No simulation is carried out on a domain controller. For this, the destination computer must have Windows XP or Windows Server 2003/SBS2003 installed on it. No group policy results can be obtained from computers running Windows 2000 Professional/Server.

In order to get the group policy results from a destination computer, the user must have local administrative rights for this computer. However, it is essential for the delegation of group policy result data that the Windows 2003 schema be available in the forest. Use the ADPREP program for this purpose. A domain controller under Windows Server 2003 environment is not essential. Take the following steps to display the group policy results:

1. Select Group Policy Result Wizard from the context menu of the Group Policy Results node.

2. Click Next when the welcome message is displayed. Then select the computer for which the group policy results are to be displayed. Either the current computer or any other computer can be selected. If you do not want to display any policy results for the computer, enable the Do Not Show the Policy Setting Results for the Selected Computer checkbox. Then click Next.

3. Select a user. You can either select the current user or any other user. If you do not want to display any policy results for the user, enable the do not show the user policy results checkbox. Then click Next.

4. A summary of the settings is generated. Click Next and then Finish.

   The newly created policy result set is available as a new node under Group Policy Results. By default, the name of this set is in the format username/computer name. It has three tabs: Summary, Settings, and Policy Events. The Summary and Settings tabs contain the same information as they did under group policy modeling. The Policy Events tab (see Figure 8.45) contains all the security-related events (information, warnings, and error messages) of the event log from the destination computer. For this the user must have permission to read the event log via remote access. All users have this permission in the Windows XP environment, but not in the SBS 2003 and Windows Server 2003 environments.

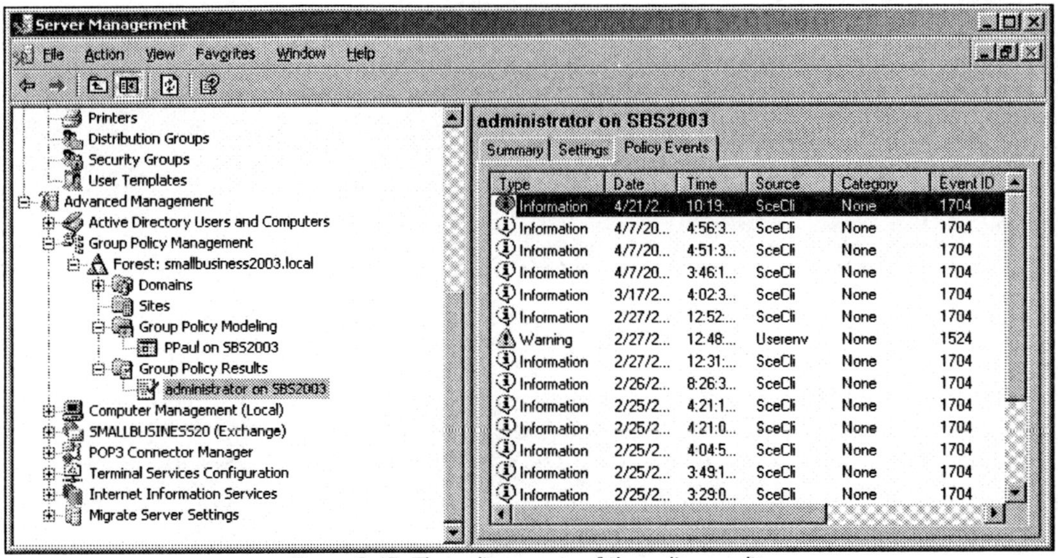

Figure 8.45: The policy events of the policy results

Task Delegation

The management of the group policies is a very extensive task, and does not necessarily have to be carried out by one person only; particular subtasks can be delegated to other people. For example, the creation of GPOs, their links and editing, or group policy modeling can be delegated. The following sections show how the delegation of the most important management tasks is carried out. As the GPO management becomes more extensive, you should give more thought to the delegation of tasks.

Creating GPOs

By default, all the members of the security group policy-creator-owner can create GPOs. You can either add more users to this group or directly grant this permission to users and groups via the GPMC.

As the policy-creator-owner group is a global domain group, a user cannot be added to this group if he or she does not belong to the domain. This problem can be resolved; users can be added through the GPMC. In the GPMC, open the Delegation tab of the Group Policy Objects node to add new users.

Even if a user has the right to create GPOs, he or she still doesn't have the right to edit or delete existing GPOs. A user can only modify and delete the GPOs created by him or her.

Access to Individual GPOs

For every individual GPO, the user can be assigned specific permissions.

Open the Delegation tab of the desired GPO.

The following table shows the various permissions.

Permission	Effect
Read	A user can only have read access to the GPO.
Edit settings	The user is allowed to read, write, create, and delete the secondary objects.
Edit settings, delete, modify security settings	The user is allowed to read, write, create, and delete secondary objects; delete, as well as modify their permissions; and take over ownership. These permissions make it possible to fully access the GPO.
Read (through security filtration)	This permission cannot be directly set. It is only displayed to users who are given the right to read and are displayed in the Security Filtration list in the Scope tab of the GPO.
Custom	Any combination of permissions can be assigned. By clicking on the Advanced button, the ACL Editor for setting advanced permissions opens.

Linking GPOs

For the settings of a GPO to be effective, it must be linked to a domain, a site, or an organizational unit. The users can be given permission to link GPOs, to edit the linking sequence, and to discontinue the inheritance of GPO settings. To do this, open the Delegation tab of the desired domain.

Group Policy Modeling and Group Policy Results

By default, the permission for group policy modeling is given only to the domain administrator, and the permission to read the group policy results is given only to users who have local administration permissions and remote access to the group policy results.

To change these settings, open the Delegation tab of the desired domain or organizational unit. Select Read Group Policy Results or Start Analysis Of Group Policy Modelling from the Permissions list box. By clicking on the Add button, more users can be given the desired permissions.

The permissions can be given directly from the ACL Editor by clicking on the Advanced button. The Read Group Policy Results option corresponds to the Create Policy Results Record (Planning) permission in the ACL Editor—the second option of the Create Policy Results Record (Logging) permission.

WMI Filters

The GPO can be linked to WMI (Windows Management Instrumentation) filters through the GPMC. In order to apply the GPO, the attributes specified via the WMI filter have to be fulfilled by the destination computer. If the attributes are not correct, the GPO will not be applied. Through WMI you can extensively query hardware and software inventory (for example data about RAM, CPU, free disk space, installed drivers, software configuration, etc.). Thus, through a group policy, it is possible to deploy the software to only those clients that, for example, have at least 128 RAM and 400 MB free disk space.

WMI filters can be used only for Windows XP and Windows 2003. It is not possible to have WMI filtering in Windows 2000, and basically the GPO is applied irrespective of whether the attributes specified via the WMI filter are fulfilled. Furthermore, a domain must have a domain controller running SBS 2003 or Windows Server 2003. Otherwise, the WMI Filter node will not be displayed in the GPMC.

Every WMI filter contains at least one hardware or software data query. The queries are coded in WQL (**WMI Query Language**). This language is very closely related to SQL. A query is always run for a specific WMI namespace, which is to be specified at the time of creation. By default, the namespace root\CIMv2 is queried. For more detailed information regarding WQL, go to http://msdn.microsoft.com/library/default.asp?url=/library/en-us/wmisdk/wmi/wql_operators.asp.

The query is evaluated as either "true" or "false" with respect to the destination client. In case of "true", the attributes defined in the filter are applied and the GPO linked to the filter is applied. Only one WMI filter can be used per GPO. However, the WMI filter can be linked to multiple GPOs. The WMI filters are saved based on the domain. Therefore, a GPO must always be in the same domain as the WMI filter, if they are to be linked. To create a new WMI filter, take the following steps:

1. In the context menu of WMI filter click on New (see Figure 8.46) and then click on the Add button. To link a GPO to a filter, select WMI Filtration from the Scope tab of the GPO, and select the desired filter.

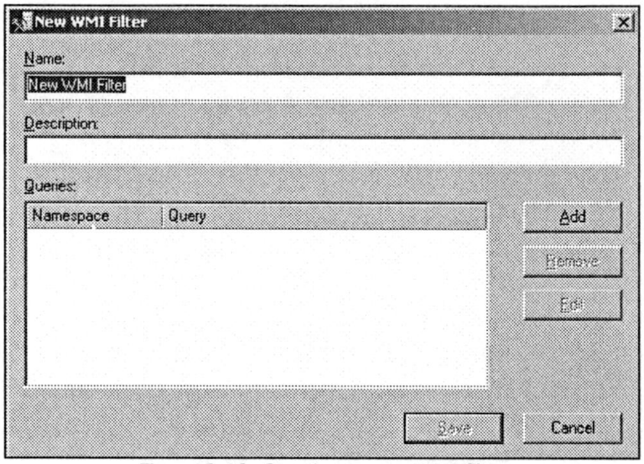

Figure 8.46: Creating a new WMI filter

2. Let's say you want to create a WMI filter for a GPO that is only to be used in the Windows XP environment. The following syntax is used (the root\CIMV2 namespace is already specified in the namespace field, as Figure 8.47 shows):

```
Select * from Win32_OperatingSystem where Caption = "Microsoft Win-
dows XP Professional"
```

3. If a software installation should be carried out only after at least one of two applications is installed, use the following syntax, confirm by clicking on OK, and then click Save.

```
Select * from Win32_Product where name = "MSIApplikation1" OR
"MSIApplikation2"
```

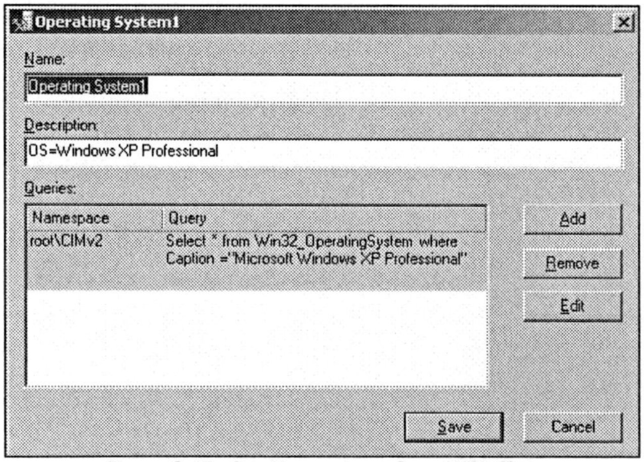

Figure 8.47: Creating a query for a WMI filter

In order to link the created WMI filter to a GPO, open the Scope tab of the GPO. Select the desired filter in the WMI filter section. Keep in mind that a GPO can be linked to only one WMI filter.

Delegating WMI Filters

Even WMI filter management can be delegated. There are two types of access permissions for a WMI filter: full access and edit. By default, full access is only given to the domain and organizational unit administrators, and the edit permission is only given to the creator of the filter. With this permission a user can create new WMI filters or modify and delete WMI filters created by him or her. WMI filters created by other users cannot be modified.

These permissions can be given to other people through the Delegation tab of the WMI filter. More users can be added by clicking on the Add button. After a user is selected, select Full Access or Edit from the Permissions list box.

Folder Management through Group Policies

Folders belonging to the user profile can be redirected to a central location in the network with the help of the group policies. These include folders like My Documents, My Pictures, Desktop, Start Menu, and Application Data, which are by default located in System Partition\Documents and Settings\%username% (for a fresh installation of Window 2000/XP). When Windows NT is updated, these folders are located in %Systemroot%\Profile, and when Windows 9x is updated, these folders are located in %Systemroot%\System\Profile.

The My Documents folder can grow very big in the course of time. It is thus logical to first redirect this folder when using server-based profiles. If this folder is not redirected, it will get copied back and forth as a part of the profile between the client and server every time the user logs in. When the folder is redirected, the profile will only receive the link to the redirected storage location of the folder within the network. If all the folders are forwarded to a central data server, data backup becomes easier as only one storage location has to be backed up. Even when server-based profiles are not used, the data can be forwarded by the local system partition to another local hard disk. Consequently, the data is available even when the operating system needs to be reinstalled.

1. Open the GPO of the site, the domain, or the organizational unit. This GPO must be assigned to the user for whom the folder redirection is being configured.

2. Open the User Configuration/Windows Settings/Folder Redirection node. Four folders—Application Data, Desktop, My Documents (with its subfolder My Pictures) and Start Menu—are displayed. Select Properties from the context menu of the folders that are to be redirected. We select the My Documents folder for our example. Other folders are similarly configured.

3. Multiple setting options are available in the Target tab of Properties. If the settings are still not configured, the No Administration Policies Are Specified warning is found in the Settings list box. The settings have two options: Basic – Redirect everyone's folder to the same location, and Advanced – Specify locations for various user groups. Both these options are configured separately and are thus described separately.

Basic – Redirect everyone's folder to the same location

For all the users of a site, a domain or an organizational unit, the selected folders are stored in a specific share on a file server.

1. If "Basic" is selected, you will see the following screen:

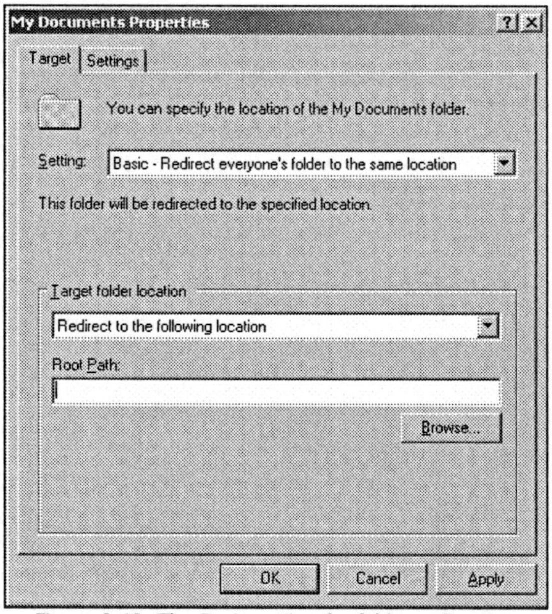

Figure 8.48: The Basic setting for folder redirection

2. Select the path to the folder to which the selected folder is to be redirected by clicking Browse. In either case, the variable %username% must be used. If, for example, you enter the path \\Archimedes\Data\%username%\My Documents, every user's personal folder and subfolders will be in the share on the file server. The path must always be specified as a UNC path.

3. Switch to the Settings tab. By default, the options Grant the user exclusive rights to My Documents and Move the contents of My Documents to the new location are enabled (see the following figure). If you enable the exclusive permissions option, only the user and the local system get full access to the folder; not even an administrator or another user can modify this folder. If you enable the second option, the selected folders will be moved to the redirected target folder and they will no longer be retained in their original memory location.

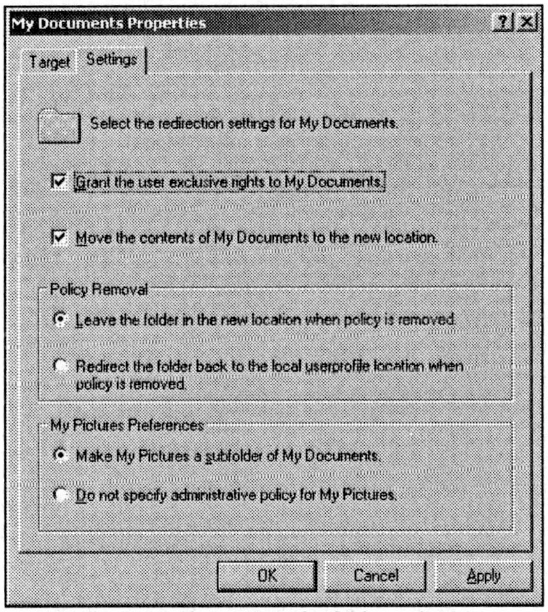

Figure 8.49: The settings for folder redirection

4. Furthermore, you can be determine how the folder should be handled after the policy has been removed. The folder can either remain at its new location, or it can be locally redirected again.

The following table gives an overview of the effects of these settings:

Status of the "Move the contents of My Documents to the new location" setting	Policy removal option	After removing the policy
Enabled or disabled	Retain folder	The folder remains at redirected memory location; the user continues to have access.
Enabled	Redirect Folder	The folder and its contents are copied to the local storage location of the user. The folder continues to exist on the server. The user has access to the local files, but can no longer access the files saved on network.
Disabled	Redirect Folder	The folder will be copied to the local storage location *without* its contents. If the contents are not separately copied or moved to the local memory location, the user will no longer have access to this data.

5. Only My Documents has the option for accessing the My Pictures folder, a subfolder of My Documents. If no policy is assigned, My Pictures will not be redirected as a subfolder of My Documents. In order to redirect My Pictures as a subfolder of My Documents, open the User Configuration/Windows Settings/Folder Redirection/My Pictures path in the GPO. Select Follow My Documents folder from the Properties.

Advanced – Specify locations for various user groups

For every user, the selected folders will be saved in a specific share on a file server. The folders will be redirected to different locations based on the security group membership of the users.

1. If "Advanced" is selected, the following screen is displayed:

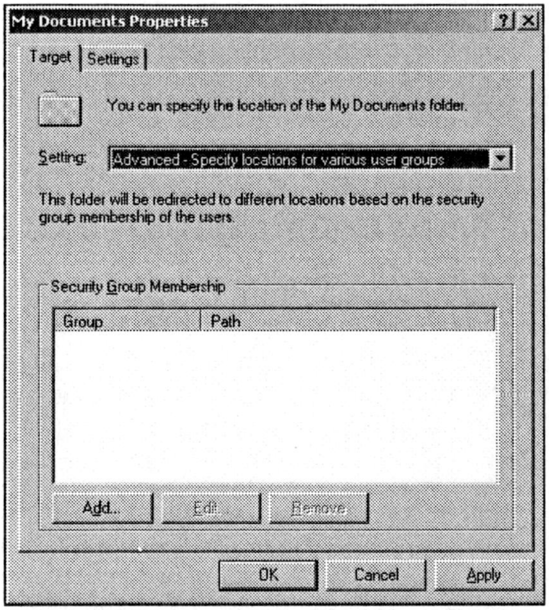

Figure 8.50: Advanced settings for folder redirection

2. Click Add. In the Specify Groups And Path dialog box select the security group for which you want to create a specific target folder. Alternatively, you can select the group by clicking on the Browse button. Enter the path to the share to which the folder has to be redirected. Use the %username% variable so that a folder can be created for each user with his or her user name. The path to the share should be specified as a UNC path.

3. Switch to the Settings tab of the selected folder (see Figure 8.49). The settings to be configured on this tab are identical to those described there.

Folder Redirection Problems in Windows XP

If the aforementioned folder redirection is applied to a user in a Windows XP environment, he or she may receive a warning that either there is no free disk space or there is very little free disk space available. This is because, by default, Windows XP buffers all the contents of the redirected folder locally. Thus, if the content of the redirected folder is bigger than the available disk space, the user receives this error message. Furthermore, the size of the share is locally occupied.

To resolve this problem, enable the group policy Do not make redirected folders automatically available offline. This group policy is not defined by default. Take the following steps in order to enable this policy:

1. Open the GPO that is used for the user and select the User Configuration/ Administrative Templates/Network/Offline files node.

2. Enable the Do not make redirected folders automatically available offline policy.

Software Management and Deployment through Group Polices

Through group policies you can not only manage the desktop environment of your clients, you can also assign users software for installation. Group polices can be used in this way, as long as no other third-party tool is installed in your company for software deployment. In this section you will find a theoretical overview of the planning schedule. The practical implementation is explained in the next section.

Several points are to be kept in mind and clarified before any software can be deployed. The entire software deployment process can be divided into four broad areas:

1. Preparation
2. Installation source
3. Recipients of the software
4. Installation

Preparation

In this phase general points are determined that are valid for all software deployment methods.

- First determine which software is currently installed and furthermore, which software should be deployed to the users.

- Subdivide this software into mandatory and optional programs. Standardize the workstations of the company in this manner.

- Next, ascertain which software consists purely of Windows Installer packages that can be assigned directly through the group policies. Programs that only have a conventional setup routine must be repackaged for deployment. The WinInstall LE program of Veritas Software is included with Windows 2000 Server for this purpose. However, this program is not included any more with Windows Server 2003 or SBS 2003. It can now be directly downloaded from OnDemand Software at http://www.ondemandsoftware.com/freele.asp.

- Furthermore, determine whether specific customizations and configurations of the software are required for specific users. For example, is it necessary to generate different office versions with varying features for different application areas? For further details refer to sections that follow.

Installation Source

Next, determine which computers should be the software deployment points from which software packages can be installed in the clients. At this juncture you must decide on the basis of the installed hardware whether you would like to use the SBS 2003 or a separate file server. Furthermore, you can specify whether you would like to use the group polices for software deployment at the site level or at the organizational-unit level.

Recipients of the Software

Next, decide whether the software should be deployed for a user or a computer, and specify the users and computers that are going to receive the software.

> Software deployment cannot be carried out for terminal server clients.

Installation

For a user, you can assign, publish, or announce software; for a computer, you can only assign it. When the software is assigned, the user will be notified when he or she logs on. The installation is carried out either when the user opens a document that requires the application or when he or she clicks on the relevant icon in the start menu or on the desktop. The software assigned to a user is installed on every workstation, irrespective of the computer on which the user has logged in. Software assigned to a computer will be installed when the computer is booted. Under SBS 2003 it is possible to fully install all the assigned software of a user when he or she logs on and not when the application is required for the first time. This has the advantage of providing a consistent environment—from the moment the user logs on, all the software packages are available to him or her.

The publication of software works only for users. In this case, no shortcuts are displayed on the desktop or in the start menu. The initialized software stores its publication information in Active Directory and not in the local registry of the computer. The application will only be installed when the user opens a file that requires the application or when he or she selects the published applications from Control Panel/Software for installation.

To install this software package, the software installation application uses the built-in Windows Installer technology. The following are the important file extensions of the Windows Installer technology:

- .msi: A .msi file is the central control file for the complete setup of an application that uses Windows Installer. In a database structure, this file contains all the features, as well as either the .cab files, copy instructions, etc., themselves, or links to them. The setup invokes the msiexec /i command internally in order to run the MSI file. An application can also contain multiple MSI files. These files are invoked mutually during installation. These files can either be native to a program or they can be generated by repackaging.

- .mst: A .mst file is also known as a transform file. This file contains an edited feature set for an application. Such a file is, for example, created for Office 2000 through the Office Resource Kit. The creation of an MST file is optional. If you do not add a transform file to an MSI file, even features that are selected manually during a default installation will be installed on the client.

- .msp: These are patch files or service pack files for an application that uses Windows Installer, e.g. Office 2000 SR-1A or SP2.

- .aas: Application Assignment Scripts. These scripts contain special commands for publishing or assigning a specific software package.

For further details regarding functionalities of Windows Installer Technology and the special package types, refer to the *Windows Installer Technology and Repackaging* section later in the chapter.

Furthermore, you must also consider a strategy for updating software or uninstalling software from a workstation, and then test the package deployment to ascertain whether all your requirements could be fulfilled.

Creating Software Development Points

First, an SDP (Software Deployment Point) must be defined for an application:

1. Create a share on a file server or on the SBS where all the subfolders of the applications to be installed can be placed. For the SDP share you must give read rights to the users who are meant to install the software from it. Administrators have permission to read and write so that they can even make changes to the software packages.

2. For every application, create a separate folder that contains all the necessary installation files, the .msi files, and the optional .mst or .msp files.

3. Copy all the components belonging to the application into this folder.

Administrative Setup

A few applications can be directly installed in the SDP via the administrative setup. In the following example the administrative setup for Office 2003 is described. Basically, the administrative setup process consists in copying the CD contents to the SDP. You have the option of personalizing the package with a CD key and a company name. The following steps are to be followed to carry out an administrative setup:

1. Insert the Office 2003 CD in the drive. The CD should start automatically. The welcome page is displayed. Stop the installation process here and switch to the command prompt.

2. From the command prompt change the current drive to the CD drive and type in the following command:

```
Setup.exe /a data1.msi shortfilenames=true
```

> It is possible that for some applications, there may be other MSI files on the CD, namely data2.msi, data3.msi, etc. If you are creating an administrative setup for one of these MSI files, replace the name of data1.msi appropriately at the command prompt.

The /a parameter prompts the Windows Installer to carry out the administrative setup instead of a normal installation. The shortfilenames=true parameter forces the Windows Installer to use short file names so that compatibility with different platforms is ensured.

> Some MSDN CDs do not support the above command for the administrative setup. In such cases, use the following command instead:
> ```
> msiexec /a data1.msi shortfilenames=true
> ```

3. After this command is entered, the graphical interface of the administrative setup is displayed.

4. Enter the CD key and the organization name, and then click Next.

5. You will see the end-user license agreement. Check the "Accept" checkbox here as a sign of your acceptance. Otherwise, you will not be able to complete the installation. Click Next:

6. Next, enter the path to set the SDP share as the destination of the administrative setup and click on Install now. This process will take a while as the entire CD contents have to be copied to the hard disk. A status bar will keep you informed of the progress.

7. Now, select all the objects and disable the Read-Only attribute via the Properties context menu.

This completes the administrative setup. All the files on the Office 2003 CD are copied to the SDP. If an installation is carried out now, it is carried out with the settings of a default setup. If additional customized setup settings are to be used, the creation of a .mst file becomes necessary. This procedure is briefly explained in the *Creating a .mst File (Transform File)* section later in the chapter.

Specifying the Installation Options

After you have initialized the application on the server, you can start configuring the settings for the GPO. For this, open the Software Settings/Software Installation node in user configuration or the computer configuration of the GPO, and select Properties from the context menu. On the General tab (see Figure 8.51) set options for the package:

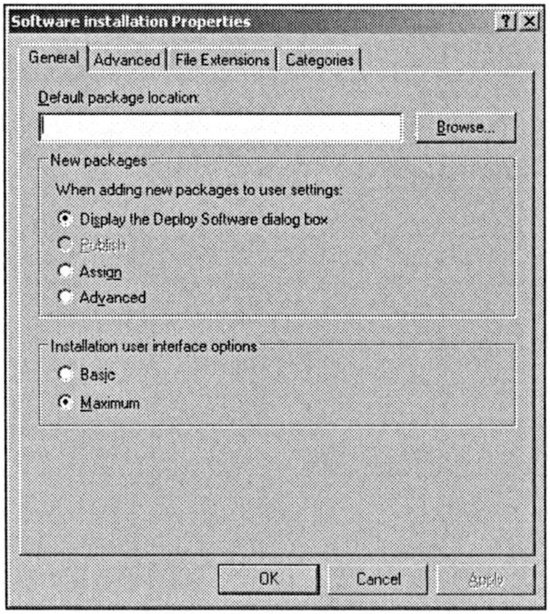

Figure 8.51: Software installation options

In the Default package location field, enter the path to the folders with the relevant .msi file of the application. In the New Packages section you have four options for adding packages to the user settings:

- Display the Deploy Software dialog box invokes the Deploy Software dialog box (see Figure 8.52), when a new package is added to the user settings. Through this dialog box, you can either edit the package settings or assign or publish the package.

- Publish: This option is disabled when the software settings of the computer configuration are open. A software package is only published with the default package settings.

- Assign: A package, with its default properties, is assigned to either a user or a computer.

- Advanced: Invokes the Package Setting Configuration dialog box at the time of assigning or publishing a package.

In the User Interface Options For Installation area you can determine whether a user should get only the default windows (Simple option) or all installation windows (Maximum option). A silent software installation is not provided for here.

If you enable the Uninstall applications when you are outside the management area checkbox, the application will be uninstalled if the concerned GPO is no longer applied to the computer or the user.

Assigning and Publishing Packages

The following steps are to be carried out for either assigning or publishing an application:

1. Open the Software Settings/Software Installation node in user configuration or the computer configuration of the GPO. Select New/Package from the context menu.

2. In the Open dialog box you will see the contents of the folder that you have selected as the Default package location (see Figure 8.51). Open the folder of the desired application and select the desired .msi file. In our example this is the Data1.msi file of the application Office 2003.

3. The Deploy Software dialog box will be displayed to you (see Figure 8.52) since this option was chosen in Figure 8.51.

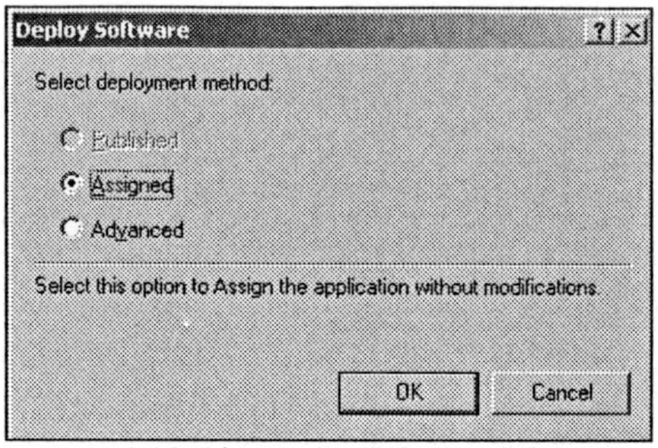

Figure 8.52: The Deploy Software dialog box

4. Here, you will find the options Publish (not for computer configuration),
    Assigned, and Advanced. If you want to assign the application without
    making any further modifications in its default configuration, select either of
    the first two options. If you select the third option, the (application-name)
    Properties dialog box will be displayed (see Figure 8.53). Here, for example,
    you can apply Transform Files to the default configuration on the
    Modifications tab.

These modifications must be immediately made on the package, before the package is
published or assigned for the first time, as the Transform Files are processed at the time
of first installation and not thereafter. Do not click OK before all the .mst files are
assigned. Otherwise you will have to assign the corresponding updates later.

The following table gives a brief summary of the differences between published and
assigned applications with reference to their availability, installation, etc.

Criterion	Application assigned to a computer	Application assigned to a user	Published application
Time of availability of the package	When the computer is rebooted	The user's next logon	The user's next logon
Installation method	Automatic installation	Installation via shortcut on the Desktop or in the Start menu	Application can be selected via Control Panel/Software
Uninstall option for the user	None; only with local administrative rights	Uninstallation and reinstallation possible	Uninstallation is possible; can be reinstalled any time via Control Panel/Software

5. After you have selected the desired `.msi` file, the package is created. You will now see the Properties page of the package (see Figure 8.53). You can now confirm (or change) the name of the package. For Office 2000 the name is Microsoft Office 2000 Professional.

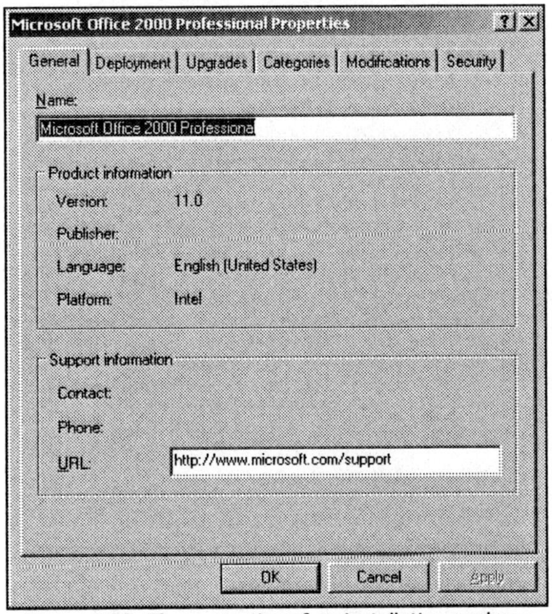

Figure 8.53: The properties of an installation package

General Settings for the Application Packages

As the next step, you can still configure a few general settings for the packages. These include the files types associated with the individual applications and also the combination of applications in specific application categories. Both these settings are applied by opening the Software Settings/Software Installation node in the user and computer configuration respectively and then opening Properties from the context menu.

File Extensions Tab

You can assign applications to specific file types; applications that are deployed within the GPO are automatically installed when a user clicks on a file with the relevant extension. You can also prioritize the installation of applications when several applications that can open one particular file type are deployed through a GPO. The File Extensions tab displays the list of all the available applications (see Figure 8.54). Select the desired file extension from the Select file extension list box. As soon as the user opens a document with the selected file extension, the selected application will be run.

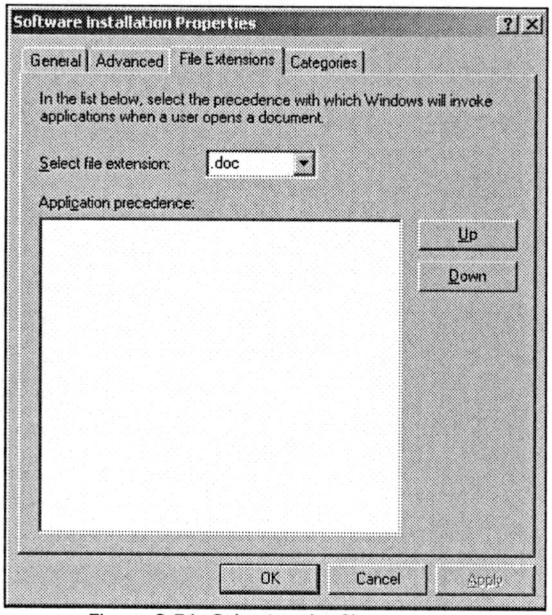

Figure 8.54: Selecting the file extension

If several packages are available in the GPO, you can select the application to be installed automatically by scrolling through the list by clicking on the Up and Down buttons.

You don't need to make these settings, but it makes sense to do so in any case, because otherwise the user will get the Open with window every time he or she opens an unknown file type. The user would then have to select a program from all the programs available on his or her computer to open the file. However, this can very quickly lead to problems if he or she doesn't know which program is suitable to open the file or no compatible program is installed on his or her computer as yet.

> If automatic installation is not specified for the applications, the Open with dialog box is displayed to users for whom these applications have only been published and not assigned.

Categories Tab

In the Categories tab you can set categories for the application packages in which the application packages are to be combined. Users will find their published applications under these categories in Control Panel/Software. For clarity you can set up categories like Office Packages, Graphics Suites, or Utilities.

To set up a new category, click on Add and enter a name. By clicking on Remove you can delete categories that are no longer required.

The categories created here are applicable to the entire domain and not only to the current GPO. Thus, these chief categories need to be specified only once.

Editing and Removing Application Packages

After you have prepared a package for deployment and configured all of its general options, you can configure special settings for each application. These include assigning categories, update and uninstall settings, and security settings.

The properties window of an available application package has six tabs: General, Deployment, Upgrades, Categories, Modifications, and Security.

General Tab

This tab displays the general summary (see Figure 8.53) containing information like version number, publisher, or language of the application packages.

Deployment Tab

In this tab you can set up options to initialize software or you can apply modifications to the default settings (see Figure 8.51). You can also toggle between Published and Assigned.

In the Deployment Options area you can specify settings for installation and deployment. The first option, Automatic Installation if the File Extension is enabled, is already enabled (and it cannot be disabled) when you have associated specific file extensions with particular applications, as described in the *Server Management for Power Users* section at the beginning of the chapter.

With the Uninstall this Application when User is outside the Management Area option you can specify whether an application is to be uninstalled when either the computer or the user is in a site or a domain or an organization unit for which the GPO containing this application has not been assigned. In this case, the application will be uninstalled either when the computer boots or when the user logs in.

Via the Do Not display this Package in the System Control under Software option you can hide a package that is not meant to be independently installed by the user.

In the User Interface for Installation area you can determine whether only the default window (for example, destination path) or all the windows and dialog boxes are to be displayed to a user.

By clicking on the Advanced button you can decide whether to ignore the language settings or not. For example, when the Windows operating system is in German and an application package is in English, you can specify whether the application package should be deployed despite the discrepancy in the languages or not. Furthermore, you can determine what to do with an application that is already installed on the computer but was not assigned through the group policy. You can uninstall these applications.

This setting will work only if, for example, you have already manually installed Office 2000 and you are now assigning it. You cannot uninstall any other unwanted software that is already installed on the computer, such as games.

Upgrades Tab

You can configure options in this tab to either upgrade or uninstall an application package. The upgrade package either contains a newer version of the application or an application that will replace the application that was used till now. Thus, Office 2000 can be replaced with the newer Office XP version. As described in the *Software Management and Deployment through Group Policies* section, the upgrade package will be deployed in Active Directory. The following steps need to be carried out to add an upgrade package:

1. From the list of packages under Software Installation in the MMC, select a package that is to be used for updating—not the package that is to be upgraded. From its Properties select the Upgrade tab.

2. Now click on Add to add the upgrade package to the original package. The window for adding the update will then be displayed. Here, you have to select whether the package to be upgraded is located in the current GPO or another GPO. If it is in some other GPO, find it through the Browse button. All the application packages available in the GPO are displayed in a list here.

3. Select the desired package. Decide what is to be done with the original package when the upgrade is installed. Using checkboxes, you can choose to uninstall the existing package, install the upgrade package, or upgrade the package by replacing the existing package. Select the first option when you are installing a completely new program package of some other manufacturer (you could select this option if you wanted to replace all Microsoft Office Applications with Star Office, for example). Select the second option if you

want to replace the existing application with a newer version of the same application (you can, for example, upgrade Office 2000 to Office XP). In this case, all the settings of the application are retained. Then click OK.

4. Enable the Upgrade Existing Packages checkbox in the Upgrades tab. This makes the upgrade process mandatory, so it is immediately applied to all users and computers.

Categories Tab

As we've already discussed, applications should be categorized for clarity. Select a suitable category from the Available Categories list and assign it to the application through the Select button. You can assign several categories to an application, but doing so will make the classification of the applications obscure, as the user will see the same application under different categories.

Modifications Tab

This tab will already be open, if you have selected Advanced as the software deployment method (see Figure 8.51). You can assign the default configuration modifications to the Windows Installer Package settings through the .mst files (transform files). Further details regarding *.mst files and an example showing how to create them are found in the *Creating a .mst File (Transform File)* section.

> The modifications that are applied through the .mst files must already be configured when the application is deployed. They must be configured before an application can either be assigned or published.

1. A default application can be modified by selecting New/Package from the context menu of the software installation. Select the desired .msi file from the list of available Windows Installer packages and then click on Open.

2. Select the third option from the Deploy Software dialog box. Select the Modifications tab in the Properties of (application-name) dialog box.

3. Click on Add to add an .mst file to the available installer package. Repeat this step if you want to add several .mst files. Selected .mst files can be deleted by clicking on the Remove button.

4. If you have selected several .mst files, you can determine their sequence for installing the modifications by clicking on the Up and Down buttons. Once this is done, click OK.

Security Tab

In order to correctly assign the application packages to the users, you must appropriately configure the security settings. All the users who are either assigned this application or for whom the application is published must be given read rights. The administrators must be allowed full access to the application, so that they can edit it.

Removing Application Packages

When certain applications are no longer needed, they should be removed. To remove an application, open the software settings/installation node in the user or computer configuration. From there select the application that is to be removed, and from its context menu select All Tasks/Remove.

The Remove Software dialog box will then be displayed. It lets you specify two different modes of uninstallation. You can:

- **Immediately uninstall software from users and computers**: In this case, the application will be permanently uninstalled from the computer. The software will be uninstalled when the computer is restarted or when the user logs on again. The application cannot be used any more and is not available for reinstallation. Even when the user opens a file with the associated file extension, the application will no longer be automatically installed. Remove an application in this way only after you have deployed a new application to the users/computers with the same functional scope as the older one.

- **Let users continue to use the software without letting them re-install it**: On selecting this option, the application will not be removed from the computer; however, its entry from Control Panel/Software will be removed so that the user cannot re-install it. This application cannot be re-installed by opening a file with the associated file extension either. This ensures that the application can be used until it is permanently uninstalled.

Every application can be redeployed through the All Tasks/Redeploy Application option in its context menu. The application will be re-installed on all computers on which it is already available. This procedure can become necessary if you have not assigned all or the correct .mst files to an application and, consequently, the application is deployed prematurely so that it is already installed on some of the computers.

Strategy for Configuring the Software Installation

This section describes some general strategies for implementing and configuring the software installation policy. If most users in the company use fixed workstations, you should assign the software to the computers and not to the users. In this way the software is installed automatically and the users cannot influence it in any way. Otherwise you should assign to the users all the software that they need for their work. This ensures that the application is installed via a desktop link or when opening a file of the specified type. You should only publish applications that the user does not compulsorily need for his or her work. Inform users about optional software that they can install via Control Panel/Software. This will forestall several queries to the help desk. To make it easy to locate applications under Software, you should classify them into categories.

Furthermore, you should assign or publish a Windows Installer package only once in a GPO. It makes little sense to assign the same application once in the computer configuration to computers and once in the user configuration to users. You will not get an error message if you do this, but the users' logon process to the computer will be unnecessarily prolonged. Before you decide to deploy new software, check if a Windows Installer package is available for the application. The repackaging can be very expensive in some cases. Even the deployment of resource kits for applications for creating .mst files can be an important factor for acquiring an application.

Windows Installer Technology and Repackaging

This section describes the fundamentals of the Windows Installer technology and repackaging. Both these topics are virtually indispensable as base knowledge for software deployment. Office 2000 was the first Microsoft application that used the Windows Installer as the default setup program. For the setup to proceed correctly, the Windows Installer must be available and running as a service on the destination computers. There are various versions of the Windows Installer. The following operating systems either have the installer natively or must have the appropriate version installed later:

Operating system	Natively available version of the Windows Installer	The following versions can be installed later
Windows XP/Windows Server 2003/SBS 2003	2.0	-
Windows 2000	1.1	Cannot take version 1.2, only version 2.0
Windows Me	1.2	2.0
Windows NT SP3	-	1.x
Windows NT SP6	-	1.x, 2.0
Windows 98	-	1.x, 2.0
Windows 95	-	1.x, 2.0

You will find installation packages for Windows Installer 2.0 at the following addresses:

- For Windows NT 4, SP6, and Windows 2000:
  `http://www.microsoft.com/downloads/details.aspx?FamilyID=4b6140`
  `f9-2d36-4977-8fa1-6f8a0f5dca8f&DisplayLang=en`
- For Windows 95, Windows 98, and Windows Me:
  `http://www.microsoft.com/downloads/details.aspx?FamilyID=cebbac`
  `d8-c094-4255-b702-de3bb768148f&DisplayLang=en`

The installation packages of Windows Installer contain the executables `instmsi.exe` and `instmsiw.exe`. `instmsi.exe` installs the Windows Installer service under Windows 9x, while `instmsiw.exe` installs it under Windows NT.

The installation is done on the basis of MSI files. The `.msi` file extension means **Managed Software Installation**. Each MSI file is a small relational database. The target situation after installation on the client is contained in it. This is the so-called post-install state. This state is not achieved with an installation script as is the case with a standard setup program, but by the application of certain rules. This defined target state is then stored on the relevant computer. If there are changes to the originally defined target state on the computer, for example through accidental deletion of files, the post-install state is restored by the Windows Installer. This automatic repair mechanism is not available with a standard setup.

If a Windows Installer installation is not completed successfully, there is an automatic rollback to the state before the installation of the unsuccessful MSI package. Another feature of Windows Installer technology is the installation of software on demand. This means that some less frequently used features are only installed when the user actually needs them the first time.

The Windows Installer technology even offers an option for the definition of various MSI packages: you can configure an MSI package, for example Office 2000, with special features through the use of MST files. The transform is used only once at the time of the first installation of the MSI package. After the installation of the base package, you cannot install any further transform files for updating. You can create as many transform files for an MSI package as you want. Although the creation of MST files is optional, it will surely be done in most cases.

To be able to deploy an MSI package, an administrative setup of the package in question must first be carried out. This is done with the /a parameter in the setup command. The contents of the application CD are copied to a specific location on the network from which the installation on the clients is then carried out. The standard MSI package contains all the features that are contained in a default installation. If you want to make changes to the base package, create one or more transform files with the help of a resource kit. These are assigned to the MSI package via the group policy and are applied to the client during the first installation.

Repackaging

The repackaging of applications can take place for a number of reasons. The most common reason may well be the modification of the setup. By default the user gets a number of dialog boxes during installation in which he or she can specify the installation path or features. This possibility should, however, be taken away from users in most cases. Ideally the installation program runs in the background without the user seeing a single dialog box. He or she does not have the option of intervening during this silent installation. The deployment of an application whose installation information is contained in a setup.exe file (not in an MSI file) also requires repackaging.

A number of third-party programs are available for repackaging. One of the most commonly used products is WinInstall LE 2003 from OnDemand Software.

In repackaging an application, a new Windows installer package is made from the changes that are made on the computer during installation, such as the addition or modification of files, paths, registry entries, etc. Most programs use a mechanism for this purpose that compares the state of the computer before and after the installation. The new package is built from the differences that are established in the process. Thus the application to be repackaged must not already be installed on the computer, otherwise the differences would not be recognized and the package would be faulty.

Creating a .mst File (Transform File)

This section explains the creation of a transform file on the basis of the example of Office 2003. As mentioned earlier, this step is optional, but will definitely be taken in most cases. To stick to our example of Office 2003, without modified transform files all users would get the default installation of the Office package. It is therefore possible that some users have installed too many unnecessary program components on their computer, while some features are not available to other users by default but are only installed when needed. For example, Word and Excel would suffice for users who are only responsible for correspondence, while users in the marketing department, for example, would need to have access to PowerPoint as well.

To create an MST file for Office 2003, start the Custom Installation Wizard. This is a component of the Office 2003 Resource Kit. You can download the Office 2003 Resource Kit from http://www.microsoft.com/office/ork/2003/default.htm.

Resource Kits are available for a number of applications. If no Resource Kit is available for a specific application, various packages with different feature sets can be created through repackaging.

When you start the Office Resource Kit wizard, up to 20 windows can appear, querying you for changes you want to make in the default settings. This collected data is stored in the transform file whose name you specify in the wizard. You can either create a new .mst file or edit an existing one.

> All options for individual modification in the Custom Installation Wizard are described in detail in the manual and the online help of Office Resource Kit. An explicit description of the individual dialogs is beyond the scope of this book.

Troubleshooting in Group Policies

This section gives an overview of commonly occurring problems in the context of group policies. For this purpose, we first present a listing of problems with solution approaches. At the end of this chapter, you will get references to possible malfunctions of group policies on migration from Windows NT.

A GPO snap-in cannot be opened and/or edited

- In order to be able to edit a GPO, the user must not only have read permission, but also have full access to the relevant object. Local Administrators can only edit the local GPOs, while by default a Domain Admin can also edit Active Directory-based GPOs.

- If you get the error message that the object could not be opened, check the network connection to the object. There could also be an error in the DNS configuration.

The local policy settings have no effect

- If other policies are defined at the location, domain, or OU levels, then they overwrite the local settings if they are not mutually compatible.

The policy settings in Active Directory have no effect

- If a user or computer does not receive the settings of the policy, it can be for a number of reasons. Check first whether the desired settings are actually configured and that the policy is not disabled by default.

- Keep in mind that the GPOs are processed in the sequence local, site, domain, and OU. If the configurations contradict internally, the setting with the higher priority will overwrite the subordinate one.

- The users or computers must be in one of the containers Location, Domain, or OU. Policies can be applied only to these three containers.

- Check if the GPO is also applied to the OU of which the user or computer is a member. Alternatively, you can apply the GPO even to a superior OU or the domain, if the settings are further inherited.

- Check whether several GPOs are defined within one OU and one is possibly given the option No precedence. This GPO compulsorily inherits its settings. Otherwise the settings of the GPO that is processed last are included. If the options No precedence and Disable Policy Inheritance have both been selected, the option No Priority is processed first.

- Even if the group policies are not based on the relationship of users and computers to certain security groups, you must still ensure that a user is not member of a group whose authorization Include group policy is set to Deny. Instead of that, the inclusion of the group policy must be allowed for at least one group and read permission must be granted for it.

- Check if the DNS server is entered correctly. The DNS server containing the complete resource entries must necessarily be entered. This is the DNS server that was set up first in the domain. If you do not use any DNS server under a Windows operating system, you must enter the server on which you have made the resources entry manually.

Special problems during software installation:

- If a public application is not available to the user under Control Panel/ Software, check if the corresponding policy was applied to the user (see previous problem statement). Are any published applications available at all in the applied GPOs? Besides, the client must not be a terminal server client.

- At the time of installation, if the user gets an error message that the application cannot be found in the source directory, check his or her permissions for the source directory share. The user must have read access to this directory. Also check the network connection to the source directory.

- If the user gets a message that the deployment of the package is not allowed from Active Directory or that the package cannot be prepared for deployment, the installation package is damaged. Also check the network connection to the source directory.

- After the installation of the package, you find an error message with one the following IDs in the events log: 102, 108, 303, or 1000, and the package is not correctly installed. This indicates that the appropriate permissions for the share are not set for the computer from which the package is to be installed. The complete processing of a group policy for a computer always takes place in the context of the system accounts of the machine. Also make sure that the computer also has read permissions for the share. Grant these permissions, for example, to the security group Domain computer.

- If errors occur during installation because the source package is in a DFS share, then you must check if the permissions are adequate at share level as well as at NTFS level. This is valid for all replicas of the DFS root directory and the shares of the DFS link.

- If the server containing the share for the installation package is in a forest different from the client that is to receive the package, you may receive an error message with the ID 1612 (possibly also 102) in the events log. The permissions for the share and the installation package contained in it are to be assigned to the computer. However, a computer in another forest can identify itself only through NTLM, and not through Kerberos. There is, however, no validation of the computer account. Computer accounts need Kerberos for authentication, so the installation package cannot be accessed. To solve this problem, you must assign the permissions to the corresponding users.

- If the software is not installed automatically as soon as it is needed for opening a certain document, the options for the software installation are not set to Install automatically.

- If an application is uninstalled and not all the components (such as links on the desktop or in the task bar) are removed, then these have been created by the user himself or herself after the installation. On uninstalling, only those components of the application that were introduced at the time of the installation are removed.

A very useful program for analysis of the individual group policy settings is the support tool GPResult.exe, which can be downloaded from http://www.microsoft.com/windows2000/techinfo/reskit/tools/default.asp. With GPResult, you have the option to see the effects of the GPO settings for a computer and/or logged-on user.

Monitoring and Reporting

In order to be able to configure the monitoring and reporting in the server administration, you must first shut down the item Configure Monitoring in the task list (see the *Administrative task: Configuring Monitoring* section in Chapter 2). If not, you will be first asked to repeat this step. Here you specify the e-mail address to which the warnings and performance reports should be sent and whether performance reports should be available on the company website for certain persons.

Setting Up Monitoring

To set up monitoring, open the Set up monitoring reports and warnings link in the server administration under Monitoring and Reporting.

1. In the Configuration mode window you specify whether an already existing monitoring function should be changed or the monitoring function should be installed anew. You should, however, use the second option only if the monitoring is not executed correctly, because in this process all the existing monitoring data are deleted. Then click Next.

2. Irrespective of whether you have selected the option to change or reinstall the monitoring function, you can edit one after the other all settings that you have already configured within the framework of the task list for the monitoring. You can also modify the following settings:

   • Whether usage and performance reports should be sent by e-mail, and the usage reports should be displayed in the server administration

   • The e-mail address to which the reports should be sent

   • The user for whom the performance reports should be displayed on the intranet

   • Whether performance warnings should also be sent by e-mail

3. Make the desired changes and complete the wizard.

The Server Performance Report

If you have selected the option during configuration of displaying the performance report in the server administration, it is reloaded every time and displayed if you click on Monitoring and reporting. There you will find entries for the following areas (see Figure 8.55):

   • Server Specification: Information about the operating system, processor, and RAM of the server.

   • Performance Summary: The current performance indicators for the hard disk and CPU loads as well as those for the previous month, and the rate of growth between the two values.

- Top processes: The five processes that have used up the most memory and caused the highest CPU loading are displayed.

- Backup: Information about the backup.

- Auto- started Services Not Running: All services are listed for which the start type is configured as Automatic, but which have failed to start automatically.

- Critical Alerts: A summary of the server's critical warnings.

- Critical Errors in the Event Logs: The critical warnings of the application, directory service, DNS server, file replication service, backup, and system event logs.

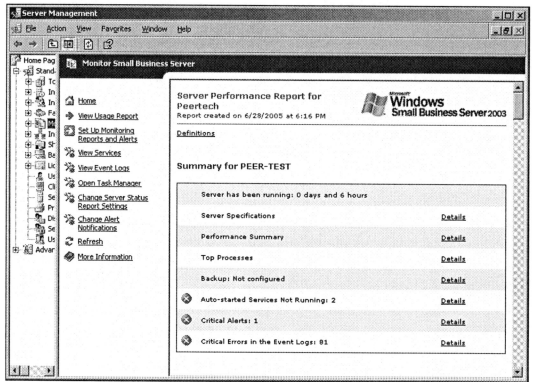

Figure 8.55: Overview of the server performance report

By clicking on Details in each case, you will get more precise information about the desired area. In the following example (see Figure 8.56) you can see the details of the Top Processes area.

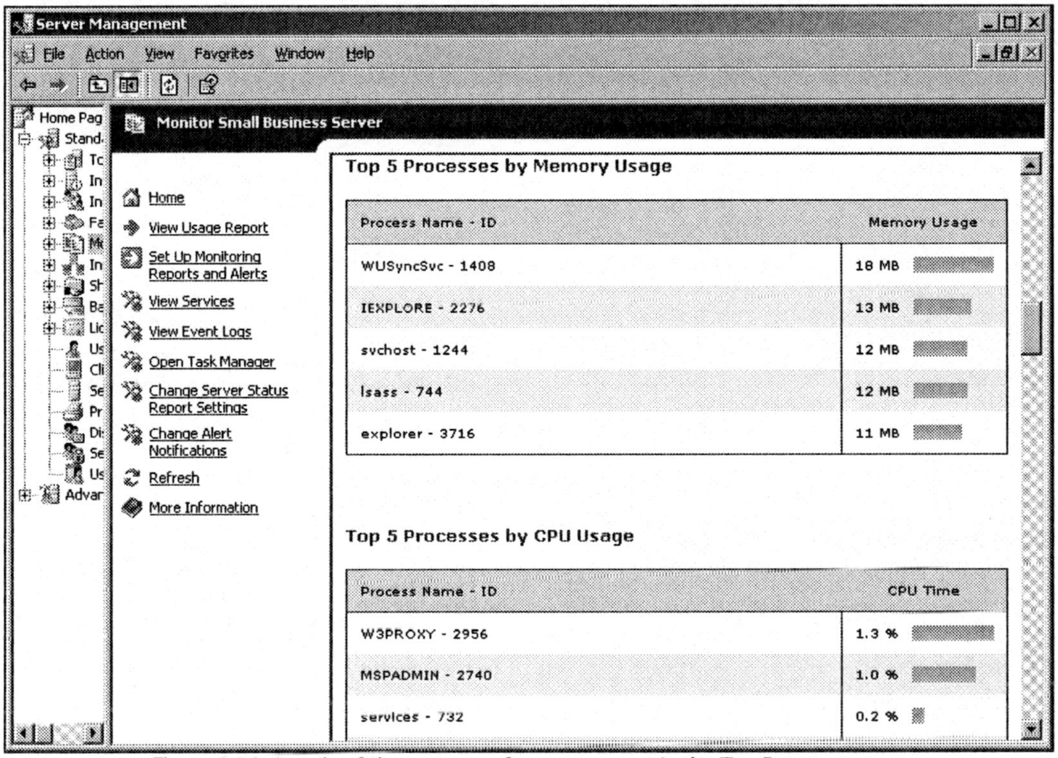

Figure 8.56: Details of the server performance report in the Top Processes area

The Usage Report

To view the usage report for the server, click on the corresponding link under Monitoring and reporting. A usage report always comprises the data for 14 days.

To create a new report, click on Create Report. Here you have to define the time frame and the scope for the report (see Figure 8.57):

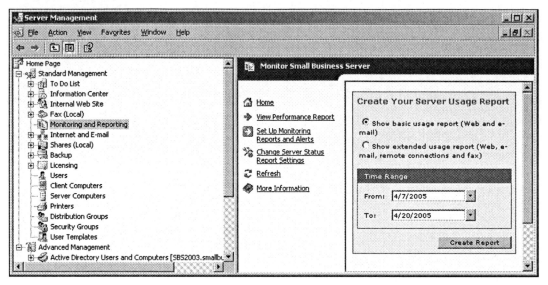

Figure 8.57: Creating a new usage report

Editing the Report Settings

The options for the performance and usage reports can be edited. For this, click on the Change Server Status Report Settings link.

In the Server Status Reports dialog (see Figure 8.58) you can add new reports, edit existing ones, or delete them, as well as force the sending of a report.

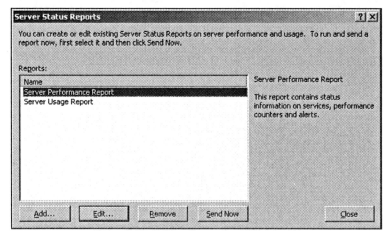

Figure 8.58: Editing the sever status reports

Of greatest interest is the editing of the reports. If you click on the Edit button, you get the properties window of the report with different tabs (see Figure 8.59).

- On the General tab, you can enter a new name as well as a description for the report.
- Under Content, you can select the log files to be sent with the report.

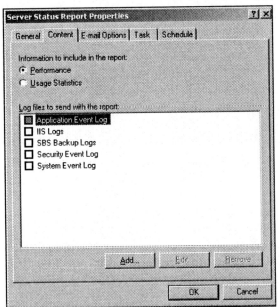

Figure 8.59: Selection of the information to be included in the report

- In the E-Mail-Options tab, specify the e-mail addresses to which the reports should be sent.
- In the Task tab, specify whether the task should be carried out automatically at the indicated time.
- Finally, under Schedule specify the schedule for executing the tasks.

Backup and Restore

Under Backup in the server management, you can configure the basic settings for backup through Configure Backup. These are the same settings that were made within the framework of the tasks list (see the *Administrative Task: Configuring Backups* section Chapter 2). These settings can now be modified here.

You can set the folder redirection of this user folder through the link Configure folder redirection for My Documents. This method has already been described in the course of the *User Management* earlier in this chapter.

The Show information about server restoration link takes you to an HTML page with additional information on the topic "Backup".

When you click on the SharePoint-Restore files link, you likewise reach an HTML page with some instructions. The restoring of SharePoint files has already been described in the context of SharePoint Services in the *Upgrading the Servers and the Virtual Server* section in Chapter 5.

Under Restore individual files, you can configure the new feature of shadow copying. This is described in detail in sections that follow.

Restoring Files with the Help of the Shadow Copy Feature

Windows Server 2003 and SBS 2003 use the new feature of volume shadow copying. For this purpose, the volume shadow copying service runs on the server (Volume Shadow Copy Service, VSS). A copy is stored for each file that the user registers on the server share. This automatic copying takes place according to a freely definable schedule. By default, the backup is taken twice a day. It is not important here whether the file is currently in use or not. These shadow copies are registered in the folder System Volume Information; no separate backup medium is necessary. Up to 64 backups can be registered per volume.

This makes it possible to restore a relatively new version of a file in the course of restoring. Users can themselves carry out this restoration of their files, for example if a file is damaged or was deleted unintentionally. The administrator is not needed for restoring an earlier data version, because the user can execute this step himself or herself.

Shadow copies can be configured only for shares on the server, and not for local drives on the clients. In addition, shadow copies can either be set up for all shares of the server or none at all.

> Do not make the mistake of thinking that the functionality of shadow copying replaces the conventional backup. As already mentioned, the data in the server shares is stored here—not system and system status files.

Client Configuration for Shadow Copying

In order that the clients can also use the shadow copying feature, they must be appropriately prepared. For that purpose, the shadow copy client (client for previous versions) must exist on the client.

The shadow copy client for Windows XP clients is supplied with SBS 2003. You will find the corresponding file on the SBS 2003 in the folder %Systemroot%\System32\Clients\twclient. You will find there the clients for the various process architectures x86 (folder x86), Athlon64, or AMD Opteron (folder amd64), as well as Intel Itanium (folder ia64). The installation takes place through the corresponding MSI file. For this purpose, you can either share the folder or install the file on the clients via the software deployment of group policies.

For Windows 2000 with Service Pack 3 and higher, as well as Windows 98 (here the Windows Installer must be installed in version 2.0), you can download the shadow copy clients directly from Microsoft.

Setting Up Shadow Copying on the Server

After you have made the functionality available for the clients, configure the server for the new feature:

1. Select the Properties context menu entry of the desired drive and switch to the Shadow Copies tab (see Figure 8.60).

    Here you will see for which drives the shadow copies are already activated and at what times shadow copies have been created. From the list, you can delete certain entries or even register a shadow copy outside the schedule by using the Create now button.

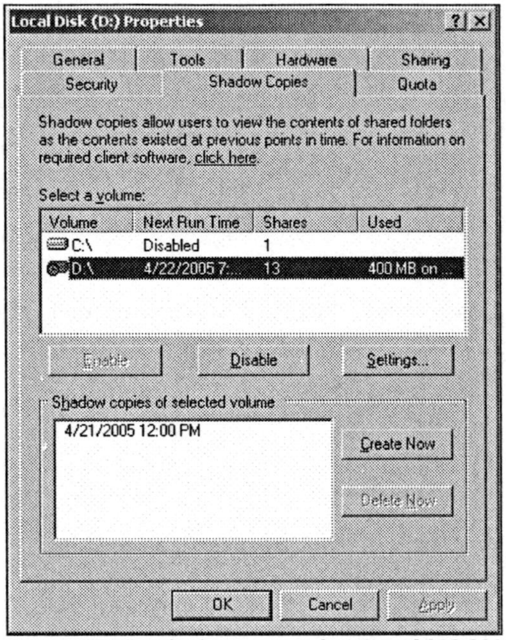

Figure 8.60: The shadow copying function of SBS 2003

2. By default this functionality is still disabled on the server. To activate shadow copying for a drive, select the drive and click on Activate. By default, the shadow copies of a drive are created on the same drive. You can, however, change this storage location. This is available if there is not enough space available on the drive (if the storage space is exhausted, new shadow copies can be created only if the oldest version is deleted) or you want to use another faster hard disk for the backup. To change the path, click on Settings and select the desired partition under the Storage area.

Changing of the drive is possible only if the shadow copying functionality has not yet been activated for the drive. Once the shadow copies are activated, the memory location cannot be changed.

3. To change the settings for the shadow copies, click on Settings. Here you can configure various options (see Figure 8.61).

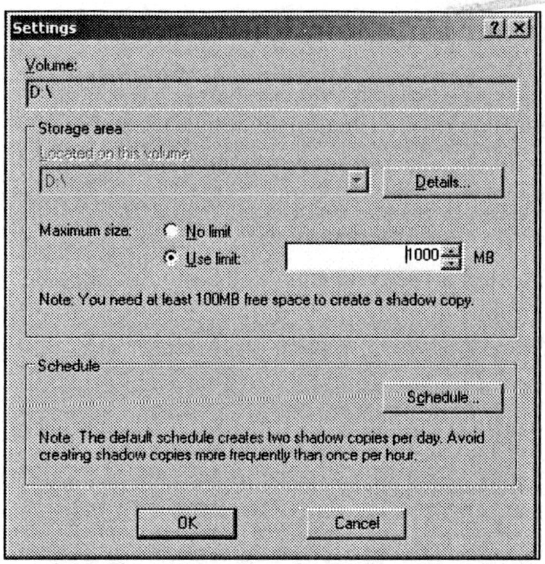

Figure 8.61: The setting options for shadow copies of a drive

Under Storage area you can see on which drive the shadow copies are created. You can specify via Details how much storage space is to be occupied by the shadow copies.

Furthermore, you can determine how much storage space should be made available on the drive for the shadow copies. The default setting is 10 per cent of the free storage space. At least 100 MB are needed for a shadow copy, so please think well about setting a limit, and if so, how much. If the storage space is exhausted, even though new shadow copies will be registered, the oldest version will be deleted automatically every time.

By using the Schedule button you can determine at what times a new shadow copy should be created. By default, shadow copies are created from Monday to Friday at 07:00 AM and at 12:00 AM respectively. You can adjust this schedule as you wish or even set up more schedules. Remember, however, that you should not create more than one shadow copy per hour.

Restoration by the User

After client and server have been prepared, the users can restore previous versions of their files. It is most advisable to show this method to the users once so that they can themselves later carry out restoring, and no longer put a load on the administrator.

Restoring an Earlier Data Version

The restoring of an earlier version is done through Windows Explorer:

1. Open the Properties of the file and switch to the Previous versions tab.

2. Under File versions, you will find all the versions of the file available in the shadow copies. For each version, the creation date is entered, so the user can determine which version to restore.

3. If you have selected a file, you can open and view the file using the View button, and can thus quickly find out the contents of the file. If you have decided to restore this version, click on Restore. This will restore the file to its original storage location and the existing file will be overwritten. If, on the other hand, you want to maintain the existing file and store the earlier version at another location, use the Copy button. You can choose another storage location here.

Restoration of a Deleted File

If an unintentionally deleted file is to be restored, navigate to the folder in which the deleted file is present, and through its Properties switch to the Previous Versions tab. You can view and restore the various versions of a file here.

> As soon as you restore the earlier version of a folder, all other files present in the folder are also automatically restored to the status existing on that date. Changes made to other files of the folder after creating the shadow copy are lost.

Administration of Network, Internet, and E-Mail

Under the Internet and E-Mail menu item, you will find in server management a series of settings for the network connection, Internet connection, as well as e-mail options.

Through two links, Connect to the Internet and Configure RAS, you can call the two wizards that you know from the task list of network tasks (discussed in Chapter 2).

The Remote Connection Diskette

Through Remote Connection diskette, you can create a configuration diskette that you use for the connection of remote clients to the SBS 2003 network. For this purpose, the setup.exe and sbspackage.exe files are copied to the diskette.

After the installation of the remote connection on the client, you will find, under the network connections, the new entry Create connection with Small Business Server. The registration on the SBS network can be done through this.

Problems in Remote Support via MSN Messenger

Suppose you would like to use remote support in MSN Messenger on an SBS 2003 and you get an error message: Your invitation could not be sent because you do not have the current version of Windows Messenger to run remote support. This indicates that the current version of MSN Messenger has not been installed on the SBS 2003. A version higher than MSN 6.0 should be present. Obtain the current version from the Microsoft Download Center at http://www.microsoft.com/downloads.

Editing Connection Passwords and Configurations

After you have created the connection type in the wizards for creating the Internet connection with the requisite data, you can change the passwords for the connections.

Depending on whether you have a dial-up connection or a broadband connection, you can edit the password for the connection through the corresponding link. You can also make settings for the network connections and for telephone and modem options.

If the SMTP connector for TURN authentication is configured, you can also change the e-mail password here.

Internal Website

The configuration settings under the Internal website link all relate to the companyweb website of the SharePoint Services. The administration of the internal website has already been described in this context Chapter 5 onwards.

Shares (local)

If you call the menu item Shares (local) in the server management, you will see a list of all shares available on the SBS 2003. In addition, you learn about the folder path, a description of the share, as well as the number of clients who are currently connected to the share. You can edit the shares through the respective context menu entry Properties.

Furthermore, you can create new shares through the Add a shared folder link. A wizard will guide you through this process. For further information on shares, refer to the Windows Help.

Changing Configuration Settings for the SBS 2003

In the course of the operating period of the SBS 2003, it can become necessary to modify a few configuration settings of the server. These include transferring the DHCP server services to the SBS 2003 or changing the dial-up connection settings.

Changing the Server IP Address

The IP address of the SBS 2003 is defined at the time of its installation. To change it subsequently, use the link Change Server IP address under Internet and E-Mail in the server administration for the appropriate tool (see Figure 8.62).

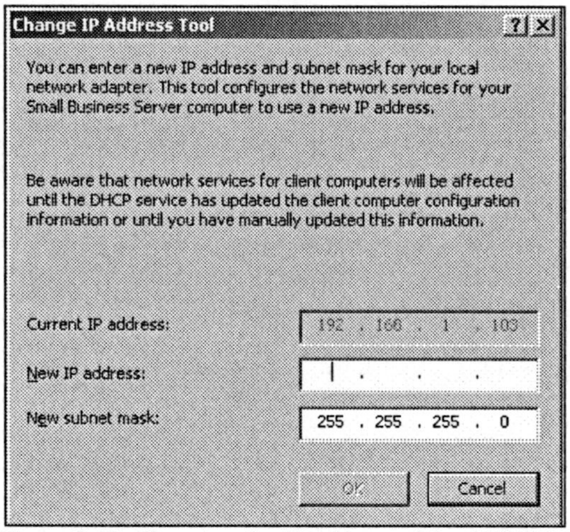

Figure 8.62: Changing the IP address of the SBS 2003

Only in this process is it ensured that the IP address is changed for all services and applications configured on the SBS 2003.

> Never change the IP address of the SBS 2003 through the properties of the network connection in the TCP/IP protocol. This will change only the address of the server, but not that of the services connected with the server. This is a way to preprogram functional errors.

Transferring the DHCP Service to the SBS 2003

During the installation you can decide whether the DHCP server service should be executed on the SBS 2003 itself or another device, for example an already existing router. Only by using the DHCP server service on the SBS 2003 can you ensure that all the necessary settings for the network are configured correctly. On many routers the DHCP range options cannot always be configured as required.

1. In order to transfer the DHCP service to the SBS 2003, you must first terminate the DHCP service on the router, because only one DHCP server is allowed to exist on the network. Before this, you should note the configuration of the old DHCP server.

> In order that the DHCP service can be executed on the server, it must have a static IP address.

2. Next install the DHCP service on the SBS 2003. For this purpose, open the link Add/remove Windows components under Control Panel /Software. Select the entry Network services and click Details. Activate the DHCP protocol checkbox and click OK. Click Next and the installation will be carried out.
3. Make the necessary settings and DHCP range configurations in the DHCP dialog box in the administration.

Changing the IP Address for the Internet Connection from Static to Dynamic and Vice Versa

If the dynamic IP address assigned by the DHCP server of the ISP for the network adapter of the Internet connection is converted to a static one, the status of the IP address must be changed. This is also the case if the change is carried out in the reverse direction.

To do this, on the SBS 2003 under Control Panel/Network connections select the connection to be reconfigured and click Internet protocol (TCP/IP). Then select either Static as the new setting and enter the IP address communicated by the ISP, or select Automatic if no static IP address exists any more.

If a router is used for creating the Internet connection, you need to configure the external interface on it according to the static or dynamic IP address.

Changing the Dial-Up Connection Settings

If the phone number for connecting to the Internet has changed while using a dial-up connection e.g. on changing the ISP, you must update the configuration accordingly.

The Advanced Management Menu Item

Under the Advanced Management menu item you will find other administration options for the SBS 2003 as well as its components.

Active Directory Users and Computers

Through this MMC you can control the structure of the SBS 2003 domains (see Figure 8.63). In contrast to a domain under a Windows Server 2000 or 2003, however, there are some differences with respect to the standard storage locations.

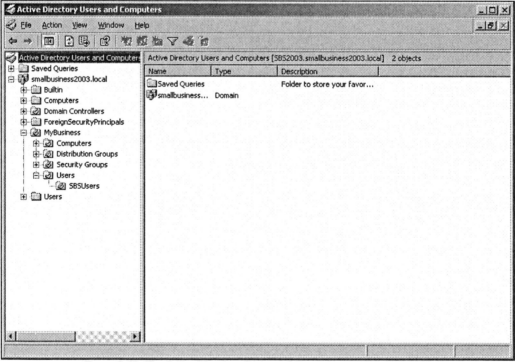

Figure 8.63: The Active Directory Users and Computers MMC in SBS 2003

The Active Directory of the SBS contains an additional organization unit: MyBusiness. Active Directory objects that are created on the SBS are stored in this OU. While the computer objects are created in the "normal" active directory in the Computers OU, these are located here under MyBusiness/Computers, and are classified additionally as client computers and servers into *two* OUs.

Furthermore, the security and distribution groups are located respectively in their own OUs, Distribution Groups, and Security Groups. In the conventional Active Directory, all group objects as well as the user objects are in the Users OU. Even the user objects are located not in the Users OU, but in MyBusiness/Users. The standard containers of Active Directory, Users and Computers, do not contain any objects.

Group Policy Management

This item calls the GPMC. Group policy management has already been dealt with in the *Group Policy Management* section.

Computer Management

Via Computer management (local) you can set various configuration options in the areas System, Data storages, and Services and Applications, which relate to the SBS 2003 only locally. This includes, for example, the hard disk management, the Device Manager, the events display, and the defragmentation program. You can find further information on these topics in Windows Help.

Exchange and POP3 Connector

Via the two management entries Exchange organisation name (Exchange) and POP3 Connector Manager, the management consoles for Exchange Server 2003 are called. The possible options have already been dealt with in detail in Chapter 4, under the sections *Administering Exchange Servers* and *The POP3 Connector and the SMTP Connector*.

Terminal Services Configuration

All of Chapter 10 is dedicated to the interaction between SBS 2003 and terminal services.

Internet Information Services

Through this item you can poll the Internet Information Services MMC for control of the IIS. The configuration settings most important for the SBS have been discussed already in the relevant chapters within the framework of the Exchange Server and ISA server. For further references to the IIS, please refer to Windows Help.

Migrating Server Settings

Server settings are migrated when the existing configuration of the SBS 2003 is to be used on another server. You can migrate the settings for Internet and e-mail, as well as import or export user templates and the Health Monitor configuration.

When exporting templates, remember that you must also create usergroups that are members of the template, and have been created on the source SBS, on the target SBS. You will find further instructions on import and export of user templates in the *Managing User Templates* section earlier in this chapter.

When exporting Health Monitor settings, the configuration is saved in a file with the .mof extension. This is an MS-Info file.

Update Management in the SBS Network through Software Update Services Server (SUS)

Installation of the current operating system updates and patches is an integral part of your network backup. Hence, Microsoft provides you with the SUS Server (Software Update Services). For the moment, the SUS version 1.0 SP1 is the latest available version. However, this version is available only in English and Japanese. The SUS version 2.0 released in the first half of 2005.

SUS 1.0, SUS 2.0, and their Alternatives

A comparison between versions 1.0 and 2.0 of the SUS Server, and a discussion of the purpose and the advantages of patch management and alternatives for SUS follow:

Why Patch Management?

When the SUS server—or any other product for automatic patch management—is installed in the network, the individual clients no longer have to source the update function of their patches, updates, and service packs from the Internet. The SUS centrally manages the automatic deployment of the updates to the clients. With the help of the SUS server, you can deploy updates to clients having the following operating systems:

- Windows 2000 Professional
- Windows 2000 Server
- Windows XP Professional (not Windows XP Home!)
- Windows Server 2003
- SBS 2003

Older Windows versions cannot be automatically supplied with the updates by the SUS Server. For an automatic update via the SUS Server, the clients have to be members of the SBS domain.

It makes sense to install SUS Servers in networks where there are a minimum of five clients. Otherwise, you should enable and configure the automatic Windows Update function of the respective clients (see the *Configuration of Automatic Updates without Using SUS Server* section). If you have installed the Systems Management Server (SMS) 2003 in your company's network, you can control the SMS as well as the entire deployment and the management of the patches. As no SMS is usually installed in an SBS environment, these methods are not considered at this stage.

Comparison between SUS 1.0 and SUS 2.0

Version 2.0 of the SUS released some time around the first half of 2005. You can directly register with Microsoft for the no-charge program of Windows Update Services.

The SUS 2.0 has a series of new and improved features over the earlier version. We have introduced these here so you can decide whether they are worthwhile for your company.

The biggest improvement made in this version is that you can automatically deploy patches, service packs, and updates for the operating systems Windows 2000 (from Service Pack 3 onwards), XP, and 2003, as well as for all Microsoft products. These include Microsoft Office (Office XP from SP2 onwards and Office 2003), Exchange Server (2003), SQL Server (2000), or the MSDE (2000). It goes without saying that the SUS clients can be automatically updated to this newer version. Even the deployment of Feature Sets for MSI-based applications is possible.

The scan function for missing patches and updates in a target system has also been improved. Furthermore, it is possible to uninstall the updates again, as well as to apply the installation or uninstallation of specific patches to/from a group of computers respectively. The administrator can also verify how often the individual users check their systems for new updates. Moreover, the administrator can specify the time frame by which the update must be installed at the latest or, if required, the installation be forced.

Even in the case of an incomplete patch file transfer to a client, only the remaining part of the file will be transferred in the future. This helps lessen the load on the SUS as well as on the network traffic. The data transfer between the SUS and the Microsoft Update Server, as well as between the SUS and the clients can be encrypted.

Even the reporting function has been considerably improved and expanded. Furthermore, the reports can be imported into an MSDE or SQL database.

Even the essential user intervention for the installation has been minimized. Hence, those patches that do not require a reboot are installed in the background without any user intervention. If several patches that require a reboot are installed, they will all be merged together for one reboot. Clients with the Windows XP SP2 environment will be rebooted only when the system has to be rebooted anyway.

Clients Inventory

Only when the conditions for the installation of a SUS Server in a SBS 2003 network, with respect to the number of clients and their operating systems are fulfilled, can you take an inventory of the individual clients. For the inventory, you have to note down the client name, its operating system and its version, and the installed Service Pack.

You will find this information under Client Computer in the Server Management of the SBS. In the right-hand side section of the window you will see a list of all clients. Double-click on the client whose settings you want to view. In the Operating System tab you will see information regarding the installed operating system and its version. To take the inventory of the server, click on Server Computer in Server Management and repeat these steps.

In order that the Windows 2000 clients can work together with the SUS Server, Server Pack 3, at the very least, has to be installed in them. If this is not the case, then install Server Pack 3, at the very least, on the clients.

Installation of SUS Server 1.0 SP1

Before you install SUS Server 1.0, download it from http://go.microsoft.com/ fwlink/?LinkId=22337. The self-extracting installation file is approximately 33 MB.

Before you can install the SUS Server on the SBS 2003 network, you should have completed the installation and processing of the to-do list. In particular, the configuration of the Internet connection must definitely be completed.

1. To download the SUS Server 1.0 SP1 follow the instructions given. Then click on Next and accept the license agreement.

2. Choose Typical or Custom from Choose setup type. Via Custom you can individually specify the installation path for the program files as well as the memory location for the patches and updates.

3. In the Language Settings window select the languages in which the updates will be downloaded later. Here you must disable the default setting All available languages and preferably choose the desired language(s) from the 31 available languages through Specific languages and Choose languages. Click on Next.

4. Next specify how the newer versions of the already verified updates should be dealt with. You have the choice of approving the new version either automatically (Automatically approve new versions of previously approved updates) or manually (I will manually approve new versions of approved updates). Click on Next.

5. From the Ready to install window, make a note of the URL from which the clients are to automatically install the updates later. This URL is `http://SBSServername`. Click on Install. When the installation is complete, click on Finish. To go to the administration page of the SUS, click on the link `http://SBSServername/SUSAdmin`.

After the installation is completed, the administration page of the SUS will be displayed. Click on Other Options and then on Set Options.

If an ISA Server is installed in the SBS network, you must configure the SUS for using the proxy server. To do this, click on Use a proxy server to access the Internet. Enter the URL in Use the following proxy server to access the Internet and the port number 8080 in Port.

With the help of the SUS Server you can deploy the client updates in different languages to different clients. To choose the languages, scroll down further in this window, mark the check box, and then choose the languages that you want to deploy in your network. Click on Apply and in the VBScript window and then on OK.

Downloading Available Updates on the SUS Server

After the installation and the configuration of the SUS Server, updates for the clients are now downloaded. To download a complete update set of one language, you will require approximately 600 MB free disk space. The following steps are to be carried out in order to start the download:

1. Open the administration page of the SUS Server from a browser, located at `http://SBSServername/SUSAdmin`.

2. Click on Synchronize Server from the console structure.

3. Click on Synchronization Schedule.

4. From Synchronize using this schedule, select a time schedule. By default, new updates are searched for at 3:00 a.m. In doing so, three repetitions will be executed if the download is not properly carried out. Click on OK.

5. Click on Synchronize now to start downloading the updates. The updates will first be deployed to the individual clients following your agreement to the same. The process is explained in the *Updating Clients through the SUS Server* section.

6. In the VBScript window click on OK to complete the download. You will get to the Approve Updates window.

At this stage, do not carry out any further steps!

Preparing Clients for Using the SUS Server

Even the clients, or more precisely their automatic update program, must be prepared for using the SUS Server to download updates, if the clients have one of the following operating systems:

- Windows 2000 Professional Service Pack 2
- Windows 2000 Server Service Pack 2
- Windows XP Professional without Service Pack

If the above-mentioned operating systems have higher versions of the Service Pack, or if the OS is Windows Server 2003, you need not update the automatic update program. On older operating systems the updates cannot be executed through the SUS.

Take the following steps to download an update on the client computer:

1. Log in as an administrator on the client computer.
2. Go to the Automatic Updates page: http:// microsoft.com/ windows2000/downloads/recommended/susclient/default.asp.
3. Here, select the desired language for the installation of **Automatic Update Client**. You must install the Update Client on all the running operating systems before they can use the SUS Server.

Settings for Automatic Updates Configuration

How and when the updates should be deployed and installed in the network is specified with a group policy (discussed next). More precisely, you have to configure the group policy objects (GPOs) **Basic SUS Config** and **Scheduled Install SUS Config**.

The GPO **Basic SUS Config** configures the updates in such a way that the user can decide when he or she would like to install the updates. Normally, this GPO is used on servers available in the network. However, it can also be used on the clients when it is left to the user to decide when he or she would like to install the updates.

A time-controlled download and the installation are configured using the **Scheduled Install SUS Config** GPO. At this juncture a time schedule is specified, and accordingly the client updates are downloaded from the SUS Server and installed.

Before the GPOs are applied, you must ensure that all the client computers on which the GPOs will be used are in the correct location. Typically, in an SBS 2003 network this location would either be the domain or the organizational unit. If the clients are located in a workgroup and not in a domain, these GPOs cannot be used.

To verify whether all the clients are in the correct location, open the Active Directory Users and Computers MMC under Advanced Management in the Server Management. Ensure that you have administrator rights when you carry out this process. Double-click there on the domain and select Computers.

1. In the right half of the window, you will find a list of all the available computers in the Computers container. This is the default storage location for the computer objects of the Active Directory in Windows Server 2000 and 2003 environments. However, in an SBS 2003 environment, no computers should be located here. Any such entries you find here must be moved.

2. To move the computers, select Move from the respective clients' context menus.

3. In the Move window, double-click on MyBusiness. Then double-click on Computer. If the computer is a client, then click on SBSComputers, if the computer is a server, click on SBSServers, and then click on OK.

Next create the **Basic SUS Config** GPO.

1. Log in as an administrator.

2. In Server Management double-click on Advanced Management and then on Group Policy Management.

3. Consecutively double-click on the Forest: (Your Domain Name), Domains, and Your Domain Name.

4. From the context menu of Your Domain Name select Create and Link Group Policy Object here. Enter the name Basic SUS Config in the text box and click on OK. The GPO will be displayed on the right-hand side, in the Detail section of the MMC.

5. From the context menu of **Basic SUS Config**, select Edit to open the group policy editor.

6. In the group policy editor open the following path: Computer Configuration/Administrative Templates/Windows Components/Windows Update. In the detail section, located in the right-hand side of the window, double-click on Automatic Updates Configuration.

7. In the settings window click on Enable. Select the option that downloads the updates automatically and lets you choose to install them. Then click on OK.

8. Double-click on Specify Internal Path for Microsoft Update Service. Click on Enabled. In both the Internal Update Service for Ascertaining Updates and

Intranet Server for Statistics text boxes, enter `http://SBSServername`. Make absolutely sure that you have entered the `http://` prefix.

9. Close the group policy editor.

Next, create the **Scheduled Install SUS Config** GPO in the manner described above.

This GPO for the scheduled installation of the updates cannot be applied to servers; it can only be applied to the clients.

1. Open the group policy editor as described earlier and click on Automatic Updates Configuration under Windows Update in the Detail section.

2. Click on Enable and select option 4: Download Automatically and Install according to the Time Schedule under Configure Automatic Update.

3. Under Planned Installation Day do not change the default setting 0: daily.

4. Under Scheduled Installation Time, select, for example, 5:00 a.m. Ideally, select a time when the users won't be at their workstations so that the installation can be carried out uninterruptedly. Then click on OK.

5. Double-click on Specify Internal Path for the Microsoft Update Service. In the settings window click on Enable. In both the Internal Update Service for Ascertaining Updates and Intranet Server for Statistics text boxes enter http://SBSServername. Make absolutely sure that you have entered the http:// prefix. Click on OK.

6. Double-click on Reset Planned Installations of automatic Updates. The associated settings window will then open.

7. Click on Enable and select 5 under Wait after System Boot (Minutes). Then click on OK.

8. Next, double-click on No automatic Restart for the planned Installations of automatic Updates. The associated settings windows will then be displayed.

9. Here, click on Disable and OK. Close the group policy editor.

Updating Clients through the SUS Server

After the GPOs are configured for the deployment of the updates to the clients, you must specify which of the updates you would like to permit to be downloaded and installed on the clients.

After downloading and installing the updates, you have to ensure that the updates have correctly come in. The SUS Server carries out only one download and one installation of the updates. These updates apply to the operating system and the language version of the client. When new updates are initialized by Microsoft, the processes described in the following subsections need to be repeated.

Testing the Updates

The individual updates need to be tested only when you are not sure, whether, for example, an update is compatible with an installed application or driver. Otherwise, you can proceed with the approval of the updates.

Approving the Updates

In a network, only the updates already approved by you are deployed. Carry out the following steps to approve updates:

1. Log in as an administrator on the SBS Server. Then open Start Menu/All Programs/Administrative Tool/ Microsoft Software Update Services.

2. Click on Approve Updates. Scroll through the list of available updates and mark the checkboxes of those updates whose installation you would like to allow. For a clearer overview of the updates, you can sort the updates according to installation status, operating system, name, and date through the Sort by drop-down list (see the following figure):

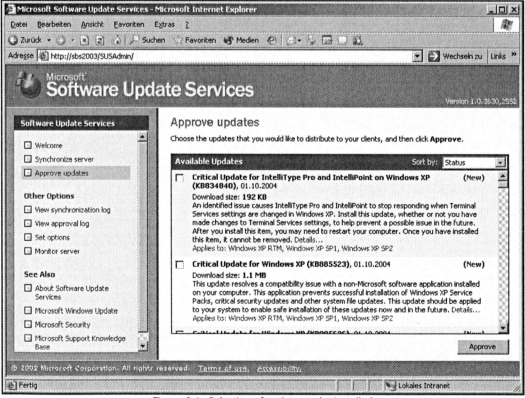

Figure 9.1: Selection of updates to be installed

3. After you have selected the updates, click on Approve and Yes to proceed. In the license agreement window click on Accept. The status window will then be displayed. Click on OK here and close the SUS Administration window.

Verifying the Installation of the Updates

After the SUS has been installed, the clients should download and install their updates from the SUS Server according to the schedule specified. If 48 hours later the installation has still not been carried out, refer to the *Search for Errors* section that follows.

The installation should always be carried out correctly when the users log off from their computers, close all applications, and save their data in the evenings. Of course, the users are not allowed to shut down their computers.

If you haven't created the **Scheduled Install SUS Config** GPO, follow the instructions to install updates in servers given in the *Installing Updates on Servers* section.

To verify whether the updates have been correctly installed on the clients, take the following steps:

1. Log in as an administrator on the client. Open Start Menu/Settings/ Control Panel/Software.
2. Under Add/Remove Programs you will see the list of updates installed on the client. Compare the contents of this list with the list of approved updates on the SUS Server.

Search for Errors: Updates not Deployed to the Clients

This section contains a few suggestions on dealing with the situation where an SUS Server is used and the updates do not get correctly installed on the clients.

Verifying Group Policy Settings (Windows XP)

Windows XP provides the tool **Resultant Set of Policy (RSoP)** in order to verify the group policy settings for the clients. This tool is not available in Windows 2000.

In Windows XP, enter the command rsop.msc under Run. The message Processing The Policy Results Report will be displayed briefly, and then the Policy Results Report window will be displayed.

In the MMC open the following entries: Computer Configuration/Administrative Templates/Windows Components and double-click on Windows Update.

If you have created the **Scheduled Install SUS Config** GPO, the following settings should be found in the client (both the GPOs have been created):

- Configure Automatic Updates
- Specify intranet Microsoft Update service location

- Reschedule Automatic Updates scheduled installations
- No auto-restart for scheduled Automatic Updates installations

If the **Scheduled Install SUS Config** GPO has not been created, but only the **Basic SUS Config** GPO has been created, then you will find the following entry in the client:

- Configure Automatic Updates
- Specify intranet Microsoft Update service location

If the settings displayed are not correct, verify the GPOs and recreate them as described in the *Settings for Automatic Updates Configuration* section. If you find that the updates are not installed even though the settings are correct, then you have to force the update of the GPO on the client.

Forcing Update of the SUS-Related GPOs (Windows XP and Windows 2000)

Enforcing GPO settings on a client is possible not only in Windows XP but also in Windows 2000 environments.

For this purpose, in Windows XP, open the command prompt and enter the gpupdate/force command.

In Windows 2000, open the command prompt and enter the command secedit /refreshpolicy machine_policy /enforce.

In both these cases, the GPO settings will be updated from the SBS Server to the clients.

If you have not created the **Scheduled Install SUS Config** GPO, it can take some time before the icons of the installed updates become visible on the clients.

Installing Updates on Servers

In an SBS 2003 network you have to manually install the updates on all the available servers, including the SBS 2003 itself. In this way you can specify the installation time yourself so that it does not overlap with the parallel execution of applications on the server. To carry out the manual installation, you have to log in as an administrator on the server. In the task bar, at the lower right-hand side, you will see the Windows Update Symbol when updates become available for the server. At this point in time, these updates have already been downloaded and can be installed.

Double-click on the symbol to start the installation.

Search for Errors: Updates not Deployed to the Servers

If after 48 hours, the update symbol is still not available, then take the following steps to rectify this error.

Verify the Group Policy Settings (Windows Server 2003)

Windows Server 2003 provides the tool **Resultant Set of Policy (RSoP)** in order to verify the group policy settings for the clients. This tool is not available in Windows Server 2000.

1. In Windows Server 2003, enter the command rsop.msc under Run. The message Processing the policy results report will be displayed briefly and then the Policy Results Report window will be displayed.

2. In the MMC open the following entries: Computer Configuration/ Administrative Templates/Windows Components, and double-click on Windows Update.

3. The following settings should be found on the servers:
   o Configure Automatic Updates
   o Specify intranet Microsoft Update service location

4. If the settings displayed here are not correct, verify the GPOs and recreate them as described in the *Settings for Automatic Updates Configuration* section. If you find that the updates are not installed even though the settings are correct, you have to force the update of the GPO on the server.

Forcing Update of the SUS-Related GPOs (Windows Server 2003 and 2000)

Enforcing GPO settings on a client is possible not only in Windows Server 2003 but also in Windows Server 2000. For this purpose:

- In Windows Server 2003, open the command prompt and enter the gpupdate/force command.

- In Windows Server 2000, open the command prompt and enter the command secedit /refreshpolicy machine_policy /enforce.

In both these cases, the GPO settings will be updated from the SBS Server to other servers. However, this process can go on for a few hours before the update symbol is displayed in the taskbar of the servers.

Further Updating

The SUS Server can automatically download all the updates that have been made available by Microsoft for the selected operating systems and language versions. At fixed intervals, you must go to the SUS administration page and see whether new updates are available, whose installation you have to approve. The best way of doing this is to register at http://www.microsoft.com/security/bulletins/alerts.mspx in order to automatically receive e-mails when Microsoft has made new updates available.

In order to ascertain which updates are available, open the SUS administration page. Through Approve Updates, you can determine which updates have been downloaded in the computer. The new updates are tagged with New in the list.

Testing Updates before Installation on Clients

In some cases it can be important to test the updates before they are installed on the clients. This is particularly the case when it cannot be determined whether the update is compatible with one of the applications running on the client.

For testing the updates, configure one or several test computer(s) and install the crucial applications on it/them. In any case you must have at least one test client for every installed operating system. The updates will be directly installed on these test clients from the Microsoft Windows Update page.

In the Windows XP test client you should additionally enable system recovery. If the installation of an update causes problems, you can reset the system status to what it was before the installation. Take the following steps to set a recovery point in Windows XP:

1. Select Start/Help and Support. In Select a Task click on Rollback Computer Modifications with System Restore.
2. Select the Create a Restore Point option and then click on Next.
3. Enter a name in Description of the Restore Point and then click on Create.

Alternatively, you can again uninstall updates in Windows XP, as in Windows 2000, through Control Panel/Software. However, some updates cannot be uninstalled from the operating system. You will find more information on this in the description of the respective updates.

For further questions regarding the compatibility of applications with specific updates, contact the manufacturer of the respective application.

Configuration of Automatic Update without Using the SUS Server

Even if the SUS Server is not used in a network, you can still configure automatic update for all the client computers with the Windows 2000 and XP operating system. Even servers with Windows Server 2000 and 2003 can be configured for an automatic update.

As the configuration has to be carried out separately for every client computer, it becomes very time consuming when you have more than a handful of clients. To configure an automatic update for Windows XP:

1. Open the Automatic Updates tab from the Properties of the workstation (see the figure that follows).

2. To enable automatic update, check the Automatic (Recommended) entry. Then you will have several options on how the automatic update should be carried out.

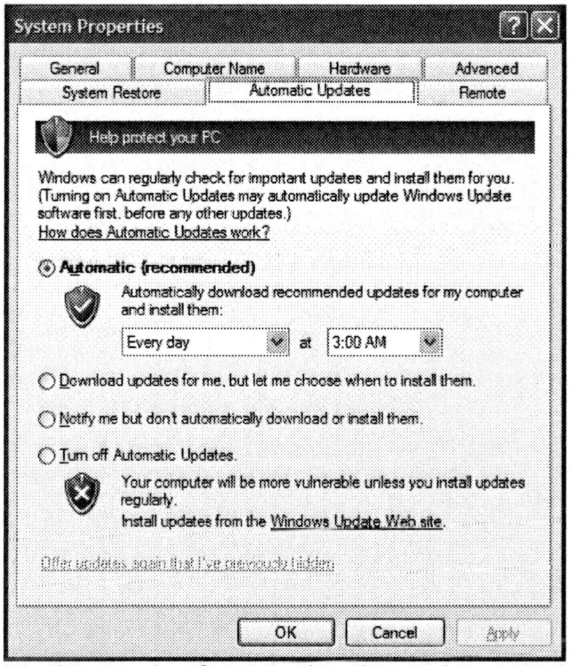

Figure 9.2: The manual configuration of Windows Updates in Windows XP

- Download updates for me, but let me choose when to install them: When the system finds a new patch while scanning the Windows Update page, the patch gets automatically downloaded. However, installation will take place only on the date specified by you through the calendar element.

- Notify me but don't automatically download or install them: This is the default setting when you select automatic update. At this point, a symbol of the globe will be displayed in your system tray when a new update is available. To start the download and the installation, double-click on this icon.

- Turn off Automatic Updates: The automatic download and installation of patches can be stopped through this option. If you have selected this option, you must ensure that you keep the client regularly updated through the Internet with the latest updates from the Microsoft Update page. You will find the link to this page under Windows Update Web site on this tab.

10

Terminal Server in an SBS 2003 Environment

This chapter describes the implementation of Windows Server 2003 terminal server in an SBS 2003 environment. In order to host user desktops in a SBS environment, you have to install an additional Windows Server 2003, Windows Server 2000, or NT Server 4.0, and configure this as the terminal server. It is not possible to directly operate the terminal server in application mode in a SBS 2003 environment.

> It is highly recommended to install the terminal server only after the task list of SBS 2003 has been processed.

Purpose of a Terminal Server

Like its predecessors Windows Server 2000 and NT, Windows Server 2003 can be installed as a terminal server. As a terminal server, the server provides the terminal server clients with the Windows Desktop and Windows-based applications from a central site. The terminal server client does not have to be a Windows client. Even Macintosh-based and Unix-based clients (to some extent with add-ons) can have terminal sessions.

A user can only see his or her own current session when connected to the terminal server.

During a session between the terminal server and its client, the user interface is transmitted to the client from the server. The client sends the server only the keyboard and mouse click inputs. Thereby, the data to be transmitted between the client and the server is maintained at a minimum level. The terminal server and its clients use the **Remote Desktop Protocol (RDP)** to transmit this data. The administration of the client inputs is carried out on the server, and requires no disk space on the client computer. Besides using the terminal server in a local network, the clients can also access the terminal server through the Internet. For this the Remote Desktop Web Access is used.

For more details on this topic refer to the *The Remote Desktop Web Connection* section later in the chapter.

Thus, the implementation of a terminal server has the advantage that with respect to the hardware of a conventional client, the hardware requirements for a terminal client are considerably less. This saves the cost of purchasing the hardware and also the time and cost of installing and maintaining the clients.

One more purpose of using the terminal server is to host special applications. In this way, the administration of the programs and data in the network can be carried out centrally from one place within the network. In this case, however, you also have to ensure that the application is compatible with the terminal server.

Terminal Server in the SBS Network

Besides the additional Windows applications, the components of SBS 2003, namely Outlook 2003 or the fax services, can also be carried out on the terminal server (for further details refer to the *Installation of Client Applications* section later in this chapter). When a terminal server is deployed in a SBS network the following configuration results:

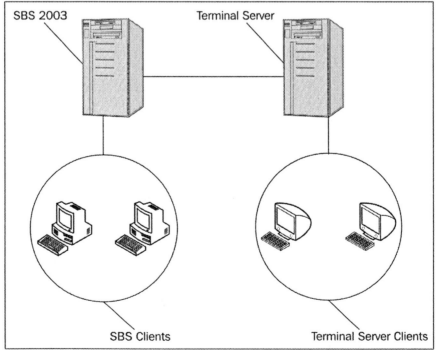

Figure 10.1: The deployment of a terminal server in a SBS Network.

The terminal server is installed on a server other than the SBS 2003 itself. Thus the conventional SBS clients can directly access their SBS Server, but run their applications themselves. They store their data on the SBS and receive their configuration and security settings from it. The terminal server clients establish a connection with the terminal server and run their applications with its help. Through a configurable folder redirection (refer to the *Redirecting the "My Documents" Folder* section later in the chapter), the terminal server clients can also store their data on the SBS 2003.

Typical Scenarios for the Implementation of a Terminal Server

Some typical examples of the use of terminal servers are:

- **Locations with low Bandwidth**: At locations where there is no broadband connection, or in case of a very expensive one, the terminal server improves the performance of remote users—only a small quantity of data needs to be transferred through the slow connection.

- **Use of thin clients**: Thin clients are computers that do not have their own hard disk. They are designed to be implemented on terminals and, as compared to conventional client computers, are much cheaper to purchase and maintain. Thin clients are suitable, for example, to be used by those people who essentially store data inputs in the data banks. In doing so, the terminal server runs the actual database applications.

- **Users on other operating system platforms**: If you have users that almost exclusively work in an environment other than Windows (for example, graphic designers who work in a Macintosh environment, but who nonetheless require access to a Windows-based application from time to time), you need not separately provide hardware to these users so that they can use the Windows software. They can access the required applications from their systems through the terminal server.

- **Software under development**: If a piece of software still under development is hosted on the terminal server, you can ensure that the updated version is always available to the users, as every update for the application will always be transferred to the server with very little administration cost.

Planning and Initialization of the Terminal Server

After you have completed the installation and configuration of the SBS 2003, you can begin with the planning and initialization of the terminal servers for the SBS domain. This planning and initialization phase can be divided into the following steps:

1. Determining the demands made on the terminal server and the network
2. Setting up the additional server as the terminal server
3. Opening an administrator account and a computer account for the terminal server in SBS 2003 and establishing a connection
4. Setting up the terminal server license server
5. Redirecting the "My Documents" folder
6. Installing the client applications
7. Configuring the terminal server clients

These steps are discussed more fully in the following sections.

Demands Made on the Terminal Server and the Network

The area of application of the terminal server naturally depends on the requirements of your company. This will also affect your planning for the server, for example, the hardware requirements. The following is a listing of typical areas of application:

- **Users for limited task areas**: When you have users who only carry out a specific task and should not have access to other resources, a terminal server-based workstation is indicated for such users.

- **Administrative management tasks**: If there are administrators or persons who carry out administrative tasks only from time to time and who only have user rights for their conventional tasks on the local client, it is possible to install administrative tools for which administrator or domain-administrator rights are required on the terminal server. Thus the user needs to have administrative rights only on the terminal server. This can make a lot of sense from a security perspective.

- **Use of applications that are bound to an operating system**: If you use a specific application that can run only in a specific operating system, which in turn is not installed on the clients, then you must consider accessing this application through the terminal server. This scenario comes into play, for example, when an application can run only on Windows NT 4.0 but you would like to upgrade the desktops of the users to Windows 2000 or XP.

- **Applications with a big central data pool**: It is logical to access even those applications that regularly access a specific central data source through the terminal server. Thus, the network traffic will be relieved of the individual accessing of data, which will now be centrally accessible from the terminal server instead of being sent to the individual users.

- **Use of older hardware**: If you are still using old hardware that is unsuitable or is suitable only to a limited extent for Windows 2000 or Windows XP, you can use this hardware in the same way as you use thin clients for accessing applications on the terminal server. This may possibly save you the cost of purchasing new hardware.

Furthermore, the question arises whether the terminal server should host only individual applications or the complete desktop of the clients. When a user logs on, his or her entire desktop with all his or her settings are provided by the terminal server.

Setting Up the Server as a Terminal Server

After the new server is added to the network, you must configure this server as the terminal server. To do this, carry out the following steps:

1. Select the Start/Programs/Administration/Server Configuration Wizard entry and click on Next in the welcome page and the instructions for preparation page. On the configuration options page, select Custom Configuration. You can then yourself select the components that you want installed. Then click on Next.

2. In the Server Role window (see Figure 10.2) select the Terminal Server entry. Then click on Next.

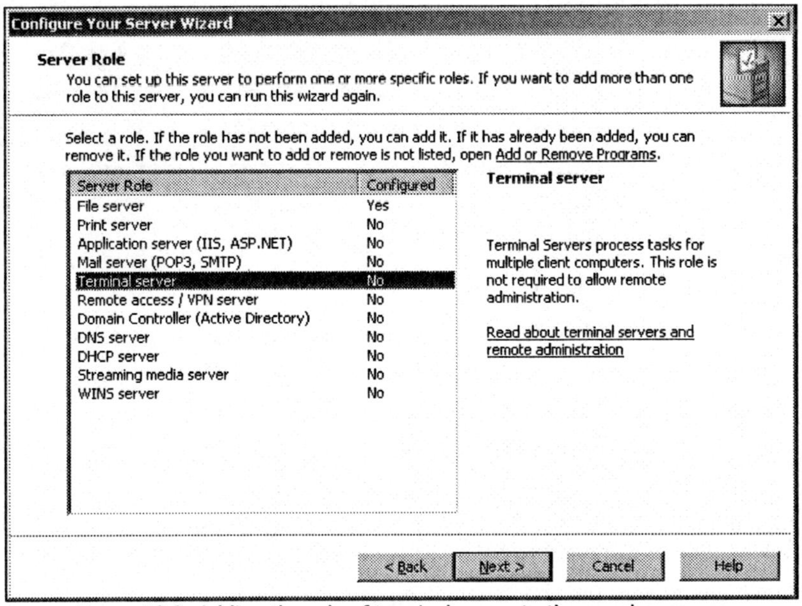

Figure 10.2: Adding the role of terminal server to the member server

3. Click on Next in the Summary of Selection window. The installation status will be displayed in the Wizard for Windows Components window. You will need the installation medium (the CD, etc.) for the installation of the terminal server. In the course of the configuration of the server as a terminal server, you will need to reboot your computer.

4. After you have rebooted your computer, you will get a message stating that this server is now a terminal server. Click on Finish. The help page for the terminal server will also be displayed.

Opening an Administrator and Computer Account and Establishing a Connection

Next, an administrator and a computer account will be opened on the SBS 2003 for the terminal server.

Carry out the following steps in order to open an administrator account:

1. Open the Users entry from Server Management and click on Add User. The wizard for adding a new user will start.

2. Select Administrator Template as the user template and do not assign any computer to the user. For further details regarding the creation of new users refer to the *User Management* section in Chapter 8.

Carry out the following steps in order to open a computer account:

1. Open the Server Computer entry in Server Management and click on Setup Server Computer. The wizard for adding a new server computer will start.

2. Follow the instructions displayed in the wizard. For further details regarding setting up server computers, refer to the *Managing Client Computers and Server Computers* section in Chapter 8.

After you have opened both the accounts, you can connect the terminal server to the network. For this, carry out the following steps:

1. Log on with the local administrator account to the terminal server.

2. Open Internet Explorer and type in the following address: `http://Name of Terminal Server/ConnectComputer`. In the subsequent page click on Establish Network Connection Now.

If this page cannot be displayed, it is probably due to a security restriction that is enabled by default. In Internet Explorer open the Tools/Internet Options menu and select the Security tab. Here, click on Trusted Sites and then on Sites.

In the Trusted Sites field add the entry http://Name of Terminal server/ConnectComputer. Disable the Require server verification (https:) for all sites in this zone checkbox.

3. A wizard for connecting the server to the network will start. Here, use the account and password that you have used while adding users.

Setting Up the Terminal Server License Server

After the terminal server is installed as such and is connected to the network, the terminal server licensing must be set up on it. For this carry out the following steps:

1. Open Start/Settings/Control Panel/Software and then click on Add/Remove Windows Components.

2. In the Components dialog box click on Terminal Server Licensing and then click on Next.

3. In the Terminal Server Licensing Setup window (see Figure 10.3) click on Next, if you would like to apply the default settings mentioned here. Specify the installation path here for the license server database and the area of validity of the license server (Domain or Workgroup). By default, the license server database will be created in the %systemroot%\System32\Lserver.

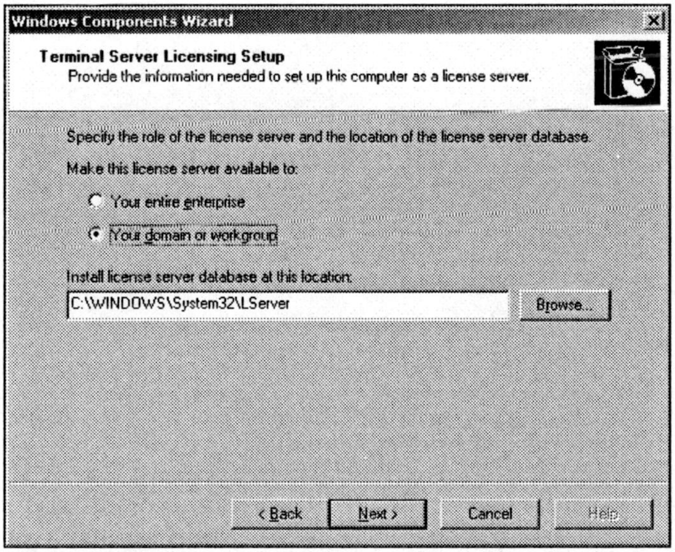

Figure 10.3: Specifying the installation path and the area of availability of the license server database

After the license server database is installed, it serves as a storing place for the terminal server client licenses. The terminal server license server is capable of issuing clients licenses that are valid for 120 days. The date of the first client login is taken as the start date. If the validity has expired, a connection to the terminal server can no longer be established; this client cannot access the terminal server license server for the issue of client licenses.

It is possible to later change the licensing wizard settings that were determined during the installation, e.g. company details or the activation method.

Take the following steps to enable the terminal server-license server:

1. Open the Terminal Server Licensing entry from Start/Settings/Control Panel/Administration.

2. In the MMC select the Enable Server entry from the context menu of the license server to be enabled. The configuration wizard will then start.

3. As the Activation Methods (see Figure 10.4), select the Automatic Connection (Recommended) option. Other activation methods possible are web browser and telephone. Then click on Next.

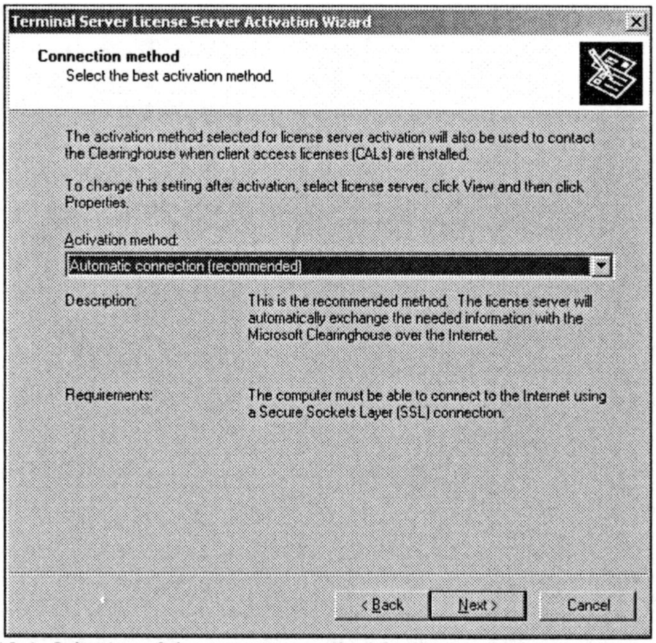

Figure 10.4: Selection of the activation method for the terminal server license server

4. An attempt is then made to establish an Internet connection with the Microsoft **Clearinghouse**. Enter the required information: your name, your company's name, and your country. In the Company Information window

enter information like e-mail, address, and city. These entries are optional. Then click on Next.

What Is Microsoft Clearinghouse?

Microsoft Clearinghouse is a database managed by Microsoft for the administration of licenses. This database can be accessed only by Microsoft customer care officials, so as to be able to provide prompt assistance in case of problems. The server configured as the terminal server-license server establishes a connection with this Microsoft database through the Internet to acquire new key packets for the client licenses, for example.

When connecting through the Internet, the following information will be transmitted to Microsoft: company name and user name, as well as the name and ID of the license server. The key packets will be sent to this server. This communication is carried out over a secure SSL connection (Secure Sockets Layer).

The key packets can also be activated via the telephone or by fax. For enabling via telephone, start the licensing wizard, select your country from the list, and call the given number. For activating via fax, generate a page with the necessary licensing information in the configuration wizard. Microsoft will reply on the fax number that you give.

5. The Finding The Microsoft Activation Server status window will appear next, followed by a message saying that the wizard was successfully completed.

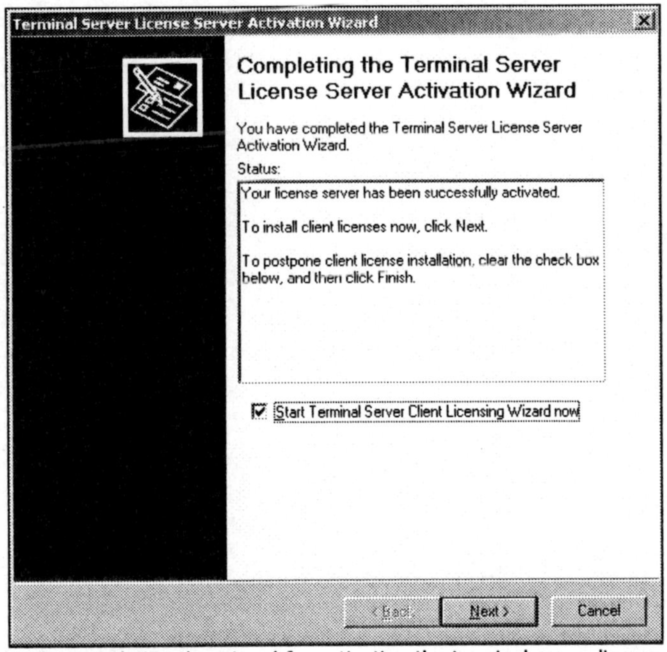

Figure 10.5: Completing the wizard for activating the terminal server license server

Make sure that in the Completing the Terminal Server License Server Activation Wizard dialog (see Figure 10.5) the Start Terminal Server Client Licensing Wizard now checkbox is enabled. Then click on Next.

The installation of client licensing is described in the following section.

Installing the License Server Database

After you have configured the terminal server license server with the help of the wizard, you can add the client licenses to the license server. For every client that has established a connection with the terminal server you will require a **Client Access License (CAL)**. These licenses are installed in the license server. By default, the Per Machine mode licensing is enabled as the access method. If you would like to change this setting to the Per User mode, open Start/Programs/Administration/Terminal Service Configuration. In the left-hand side of the console, click on Server Settings, and in the right-hand section, double-click on Licensing. In the Licensing Modes dialog box select the Per User entry and then click on OK.

The key packets for the client licenses still need to be installed. To do this, take the following steps (the first three steps are not required if the above-mentioned wizard for license server configuration has already been started):

1. Open Start/Programs/Administration/Terminal Server Licensing.
2. Verify whether the installation method for the license server is set to Automatic. To ascertain this, select the Settings entry from the context menu of the license server for which you would like to install the key packets. If required, change the appropriate entry in the Installation Methods tab.
3. Select the Install Licenses entry from the context menu of the license server and click on Next.
4. After the welcome message click on Next. In the Licensing Program window (see Figure 10.6), select the license through which you have acquired the terminal server-client access licenses from License Program, so that the key packets can be made available. Here you have eight different options, e.g. Acquire Complete Product, OPEN License, or Select License to select from. Click on Next.

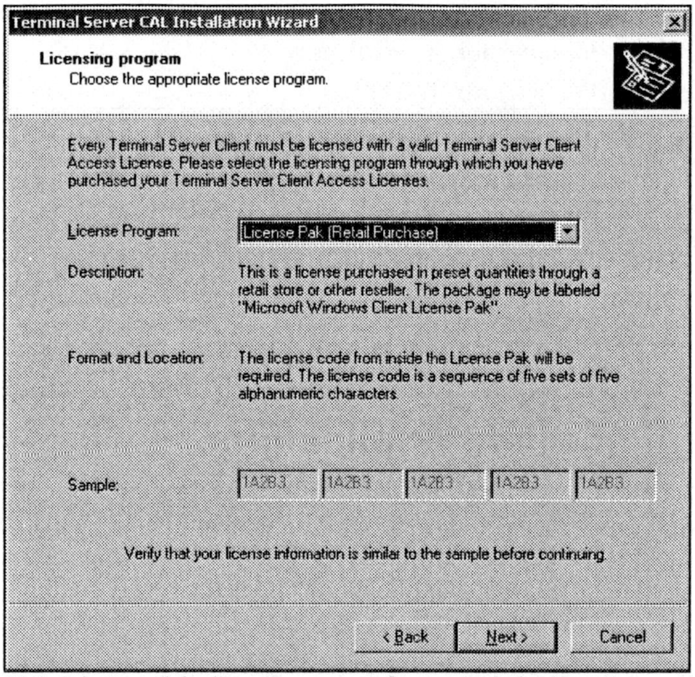

Figure 10.6: Selection of the licensing program for acquiring the Client Access Licenses

5. In the License Number window enter the license numbers of the acquired
    license packets or the agreement number of an OPEN license or similar
    information and click on Next. The encrypted client license key packet
    will be installed through Microsoft Clearinghouse on the terminal server
    license server.

6. Click on Finish. From this point, the license-server licenses can be issued to
    the clients and a connection to the terminal server can be established.

Redirecting the "My Documents" Folder

When using a terminal server, the user profile and the "My Documents" folder are stored
on the terminal server. You should, however, redirect the "My Documents" folder to the
SBS 2003. This has the advantage that you can back up the folders using the backup

program of the SBS and need not separately back up the client data in the terminal server. You can also set up disk quotas for these folders.

> The redirection of the "My Documents" folder applies to all the users of the SBS domain and cannot be set up for individual users.

In order to redirect the "My Documents" folder from the terminal server to the SBS 2003, follow the steps already described in Chapter 8 under the section *Redirecting the My Documents Folder*.

Installation of Client Applications

You can consider all those applications that can be used through the terminal server clients for installation on the terminal server. All client applications that are components of the SBS can be installed on the terminal server. In the following sections you will find tips for installing the Outlook 2003 applications, the fax services, and the Internet Explorer on the terminal server.

Installing Outlook 2003

Outlook 2003 can be installed on the terminal server from the SBS 2003.

> Before you start the installation, ascertain whether applauncher.exe has been completed. For this, open the Task Manager and verify through the Processes tab whether the applauncher.exe is still running. If required, end this process.

Take the following steps to install Outlook 2003:

1. Log in as a domain administrator on the terminal server.
2. Click on Start/Run and enter the \\Servername of the SBS.
3. Double-click on ClientApps and then on outlook2003. Double-click setup.exe and follow the instructions.
4. After the installation is complete, click on Next and Finish. The wizard that was started with the setup must definitely be closed.

As soon as a terminal server-client logs on to the SBS network for the first time, Outlook will be automatically configured during the course of the client installation.

The Exchange-Cache mode is not available to terminal server users.

Installing Fax Services

The SBS 2003 can also be installed as a fax server for the terminal server users. The installation and the configuration of the fax service on the SBS were already explained in the *Fax Services* section in Chapter 4. The clients and the terminal server must be appropriately prepared so that the terminal server users can use the fax service.

Configuring the Terminal Server

Take the following steps to configure the terminal server:

1. On the terminal server open Start/Settings/Control Panel/Software and click on Add/Remove Windows Components.
2. Select the Fax Service entry and then click on Next.
3. Click on Do not share printer and then on Next. During the course of the configuration you must have the installation medium (CD, etc.) of Windows Server 2003 handy. Click on Finish.

The configuration of the terminal server clients for the fax service is described in the *Configuring the Clients* section below.

Installing Internet Explorer

In contrast to the other two applications, Internet Explorer need not be installed on the terminal server. During the installation of the SBS clients the settings for the Internet connection and the Favorites menu are automatically configured. The Favorites menu contains a few hyperlinks that are important for some elements of the installation of ActiveX-Control Elements and ActiveX Certificates.

Configuring the Clients

The Remote Desktop Connection must be installed for every client so that they can access the terminal server. By default, the Remote Desktop Connection is automatically installed during the installation of Windows XP, Windows Server 2003, and Windows CE operating systems. For all older Windows versions and for Pocket PCs the Remote Desktop Connection has to be installed manually.

To do this, take the following steps:

1. Open Start/Run on the client and enter \\ServerName\clientapps.
2. Then click on tsclient.
3. Double-click on the Win32 folder and then on the setup.exe file in it.
4. The wizard will guide you through the installation of the Remote Desktop Connections.

After you have installed the Remote Desktop Connection, you can also configure the clients for the fax service. To do this, take the steps listed next.

As soon as a terminal server user logs on, the terminal server will ascertain the local printer of the user and install the appropriate driver for the printer on the remote system.

1. Open Start/Programs/Accessories/Communication/Remote Desktop Connection on the client.
2. Log on to the terminal server through the Remote Desktop Connection.
3. Open Start/Settings/Printers and Faxes and then click on Add Printer. The printer installation wizard will start. Then click on Next.
4. Select the Network Printer, or a Printer attached to another Computer option and click on Next.
5. Select the Browse for a Printer option and then click on Next.
6. The Search for Printer dialog box will be displayed. Here, click on the Search button. In the search results list, the printer named Fax should be available. Select this printer and click on OK. During the installation you must have the installation medium (CD, etc.) of the operating system handy.
7. Do not set the printer as the default printer (select No) and click on Finish.

The Remote Desktop Web Connection

The Remote Desktop Web Connection is an ActiveX control element that retains and further extends the functions of a conventional Remote Desktop. This makes it possible to provide the function of an application over the Web, even if the application is not installed on the client. If the ActiveX control element is embedded in a website, the user can connect with the terminal server and can display the Windows desktop within Internet Explorer through a TCP/IP or an Internet connection. The user receives the following logon form when logging on to the terminal server via the Remote Desktop Web Connection.

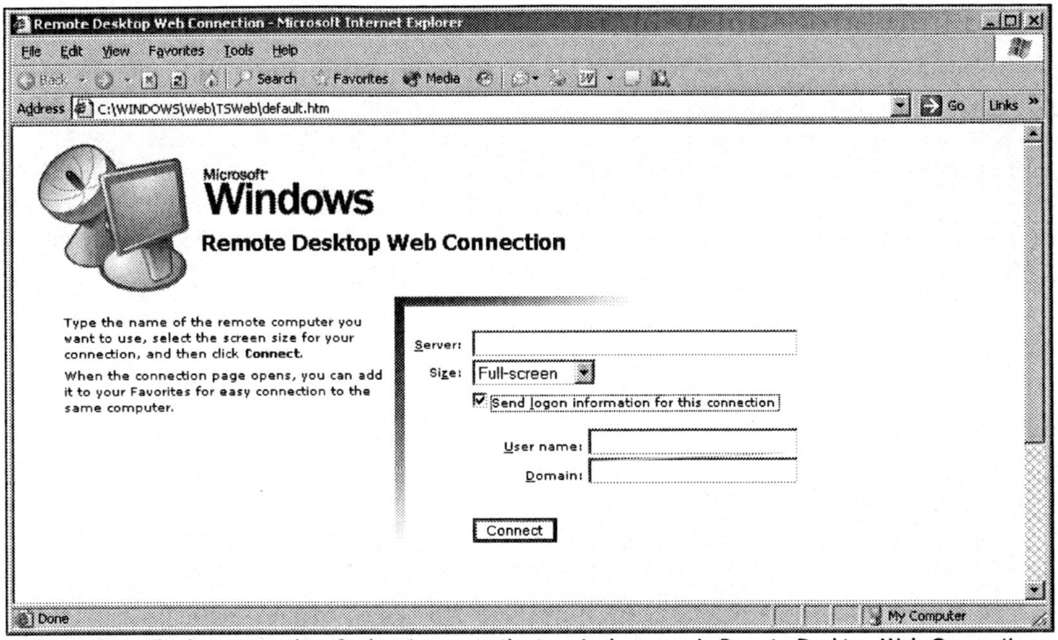

Figure 10.7: The logon template for logging on to the terminal server via Remote Desktop Web Connection

The implementation of Remote Desktop Web Connection makes sense for users without a fixed workstation (roaming users). This ensures that they can establish a secure connection to their actual client computer from any computer with Internet Explorer.

You can give your customers or partners access to your internal applications by implementing a Remote Desktop Web Connection. This way you don't have to run the application on your computer, and the danger that the internal network of your company can be accessed is eliminated.

The Remote Desktop Web Connection can only be used if the Internet Information Server and the Internet Information Service (IIS) version 4.0 or later are installed on the terminal server.

> In general, the Remote Desktop Web Connection is used for the following operating systems that have an IIS installed on them: Windows NT 4.0, Windows 2000, 2000 SP2, 2000 SP3, Windows Server 2003, Windows XP, and Windows XP Media Center Edition. If you require the components, download them from:
> `http://www.microsoft.com/downloads/details.aspx?FamilyID`
> `=e2ff8fb5-97ff-47bc-bacc-92283b52b310&displaylang=en.`

Installing and Uninstalling

While installing in a Windows Server 2003 or Windows XP environment, you must specify an installation directory for the components. For this, enter the path C:\Windows\Web\TsWeb (do *not* use the recommended path C:\Inetpub\wwwroot\TsWeb) and click on OK. If you are using IIS version 4.0 in a Windows NT environment, enter the path C:\Inetpub\wwwroot\TsWeb. You must confirm that this folder should be created if it does not exist. In order to uninstall the components, select the entry Remote Desktop Web Connection from Control Panel/Software.

Embedding ActiveX Control Elements in a Website

The ActiveX Control Element is added to the website in question via HTML. For this, the <OBJECT> HTML tag is used. The source text for the embedding can look as follows:

```
<OBJECT language="vbscript" ID="MsRdpClient">
CLASSID="CLSID:9059f30f-4eb1-4bd2-9fdc-36f43a218f4a"
CODEBASE="msrdp.cab#version=5,2,xxxx,0 WIDTH=<% resWidth =
Request.QueryString("rW") if resWidth < 200 or resWidth VIEWASTEXT >
1600 then resWidth = 800 end if Response.Write resWidth %> HEIGHT=<%
resHeight = Request.QueryString ("rH") if resHeight < 200 or
resHeight > 1200 then resHeight = 600 end if Response.Write resHeight
%>></OBJECT>
```

In this sample code, the value xxxx stands for the build number of the control element. The build number of the ActiveX element supplied with it is 3790. You will find the serial number in the source text in the CONNECT section on the default.htm page in the installation directory.

Under code base the storage location of the Msrdp.cab file is specified. This file contains the Remote Desktop Web Connection code. This file is normally located in the installation directory. You will see all the valid object parameter codes if you open the Msrdp.ocx file. This file can be found in Msrdp.cab. Open the Msrdp.ocx file with the Oleview.exe program, for example, or with the Visual Basic Object Browser.

Terminal Server on SBS 2003

On the SBS 2003 server, terminal services via Remote Desktop are only configured in administration mode. If you open the Terminal Service Configuration console in Server Management and would like to change the Licensing of the terminal server under Server Settings, you can only change the Remote Desktop for Administration entry there (see Figure 10.8).

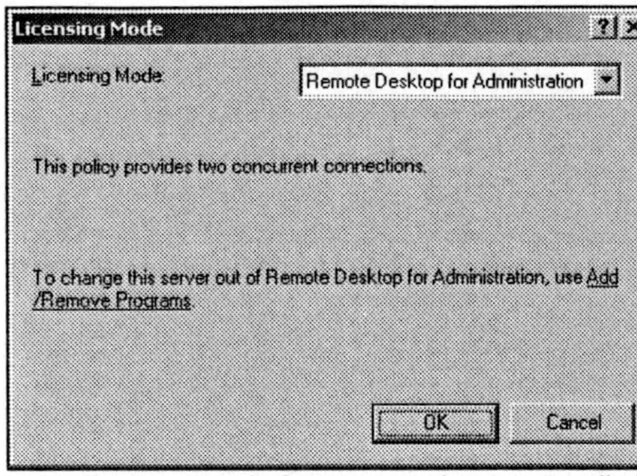

Figure 10.8: The licensing mode for a terminal server installed in SBS 2003

When you open Control Panel/Software/Add/Remove Windows Components, the terminal server will not be displayed as a Windows Component as is the case in all versions of Windows Server 2003. The reason for this is that in the SBS 2003 environment the Remote Desktop is only available in administration mode. This is a security mechanism, as SBS 2003 is basically implemented on a domain controller, and only the administration mode (not the application mode) is available on domain controllers.

To implement the terminal server in an SBS 2003 Network not just in the administration mode but also in the application mode, you must install an additional Windows Server 2003, as described earlier in this chapter, and configure it as a terminal server.

Also, you cannot update a Windows Server 2000 or SBS 2000 to SBS 2003, if the terminal server is installed on it in the application mode. If, however, you carry out the installation directly from the winnt32.exe file from the \i386 directory of SBS 2003 CD1, you will not receive any warnings regarding the terminal server application server mode. Instead, the Remote Desktop will be configured for the administration mode of the terminal server without any further notification.

11

Business Contact Manager 2003

Business Contact Manager (BCM) is an add-on for Outlook 2003; you can install it for effective customer management. The BCM features the central management of business contacts, sales information, sales records, and their respective reports in an Outlook 2003 environment. This product is specially designed for small companies having a maximum of 25 employees and is therefore ideal for the SBS 2003 domain. The BCM can also be installed as an add-on for the Outlook 2003 included with SBS 2003. The BCM can also be synchronized with other Office 2003 products and is guaranteed to work in a problem-free and flexible manner with, for example, Excel or Word 2003.

Features of BCM 2003

The advantage of integrating BCM with Outlook 2003 is that you can carry out new tasks in an environment already known to you. Thus no training period to learn how to use a completely new piece of software effectively is required.

BCM helps companies, staff members, and sales personnel to keep track of, maintain, and manage company-related contact and sales data; it also provides help for the closing of new sales possibilities. The following list discusses the features of BCM in detail:

- The data created in Office 2003 is added to the corresponding contacts in BCM so that it can be traced quickly.
- The Office data in an Outlook 2003 environment can be opened and viewed with BCM.
- Sales-related and customer-related reports can be exported to Excel or Word 2003. Data, for example the price list and the customer list, can be imported from Excel.

- It is possible to send documents to multiple recipients simultaneously from Word 2003 and Publisher 2003.

- Word 2003 and Publisher 2003 feature a multitude of templates for the dispatch of newsletters. Follow the success of these publicity measures.

- Faxes and other scanned documents can be added to customer information.

- The sorting and organizational options can be individually customized for the existing data in Outlook 2003.

- You can get statistics such as the sales status, the achievable profit, for all processes.

- Via the activity protocol you can have a quick overview of all the activities related to a specific customer, contact, or sale. This also makes the maintenance of the related information easier.

- You can create reports with extensive filter functions; for example, you can look up contacts with whom no communication was made in the last quarter or sales prospects for the following quarter. You can also select the information to be displayed to get a quick overview of the most important points.

The Integration of BCM

BCM is a component of Office Small Business Edition 2003. However, BCM can also be acquired within the framework of the Volume Licensing program. Office 2003 Home or Office 2003 Professional versions do not include BCM—contrary to all the other announcements made by Microsoft itself.

Outlook 2003, with BCM installed, can work with POP3-based, IMAP-based, or HTML-based e-mail systems. However, BCM cannot be used if Outlook 2003 is used together with an Exchange Server. However, Microsoft provides a patch that makes it possible to use Outlook 2003 together with an Exchange Server in an SBS 2003 environment.

Microsoft offers the BCM update at `http://www.microsoft.com/downloads/details.aspx?displaylang=en&FamilyID=EAB86AF5-1F5E-4EF3-9691-90F9B870B9B6`. BCM is an environment for an individual desktop. It is not possible to exchange the data processed in BCM with other users in the network. This is so because data exchange is not a priority in a small company.

To use the additional functionalities like exchanging business data, upgrade to Microsoft Customer Relationship Management (CRM). The data existing in BCM with Outlook can be imported in Microsoft CRM. In contrast to CRM, the customization possibilities for BCM are limited; hence, only customized views and reports can be created.

Installing BCM 2003

This section describes the separate installation of BCM 2003. In an Office Small Business Edition 2003 environment, BCM can be selected from the feature list during the installation and is then installed along with the other components.

During the installation of BCM, Outlook 2003 must be closed.

1. To install BCM, you require .NET Framework 1.1 on the system (see Figure 11.1). Click on OK to install it if it isn't already installed:

Figure 11.1: Verifying whether .Net-Framework version 1.1 is already installed

2. After the installation of .NET Framework, the welcome window of the installation will be displayed.

3. In the course of the installation, select only the installation directory. By default, BCM will be automatically written to the installation directory of Outlook 2003.

When you start your computer for the first time after the installation, you will be asked whether you want to apply the BCM to your current Outlook profile. After you have confirmed this, a new database will be created. Following the installation of the BCM, you will get an additional menu, Business Tools, in Outlook 2003 (see Figure 11.2). Also, the Business Contact Manager entry will be created in the All Mail Folders column.

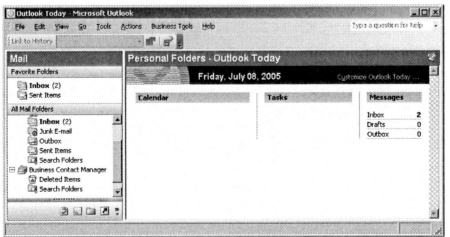

Figure 11.2: Outlook 2003 after installing the BCM

Working with BCM 2003

The basic functions of BCM 2003 are discussed in this section. As mentioned earlier, BCM is completely integrated in the Outlook 2003 interface. Thus you do not have to learn how to use a completely new piece of software.

BCM is operated through the Business Tools menu in Outlook. You will find all the available options of the program here (see Figure 11.3).

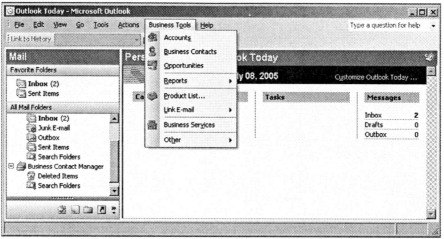

Figure 11.3: The Business Tools menu in Outlook 2003

Entering the Basic Data

To effectively work with BCM, you should first enter a series of basic data in it. This data includes company entries, business contacts, product lists, and sales opportunities.

Companies and Business Contacts

Under Companies and Business Contacts you can make new entries that are similar to the conventional contacts in Outlook. In Contacts, through the My Contacts entry, you can switch between the Contacts entries (those created in Outlook), Companies in Business Contact Manager, and Business Contacts in Business Contact Manager.

Product Master List

You can enter all the products offered by the company via the Product Master List (see Figure 11.4). In order to enter a new product in this list, click on Add. Enter the product name, a product description (optional), the unit price, and the standard quantity, and click on OK. The existing entries can also be edited or removed from the product list.

442

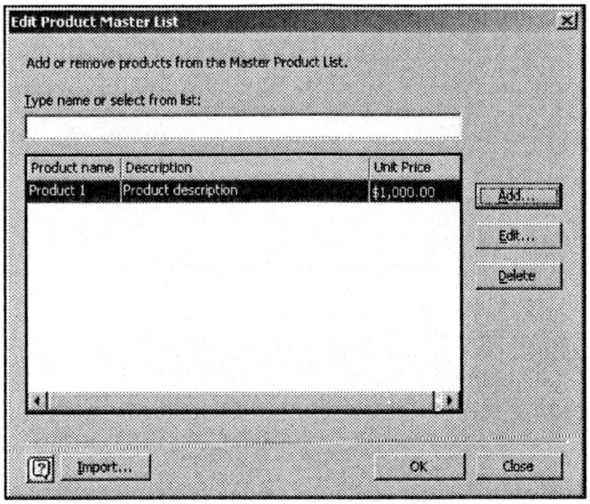

Figure 11.4: Creating a Product Master List

Sales Opportunities

Via Opportunities you can add new entries that are displayed in Tasks besides the
conventional Outlook tasks.

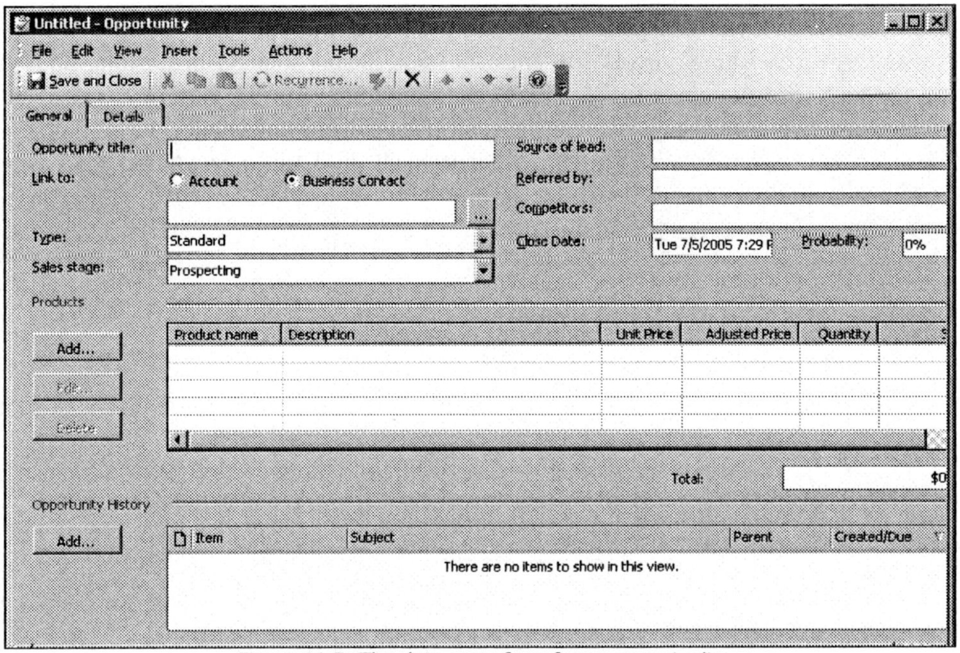

Figure 11.5: The data entry form for an opportunity

For every opportunity you can enter extensive information like the source of lead, the competitor companies, the sales stage, the expected turnover, the probability, the close date, and the possible products. Additionally, you can link an opportunity with an account or a business contact (see Figure 11.5).

Reports

Reports can be generated for the four fields Company Contacts, Companies, Sales Opportunities, and Others. Here you can generate reports according to different categories like status, assessment, category, or telephone lists. The Sales Opportunities can be listed according to the sales trend, and opportunities according to product and records. Under Others you can generate reports for lead origins and business task lists.

Other Functions

Through the Link E-mail menu item you can automatically link the incoming and outgoing e-mails to the records of the company or business contacts. To do this, select the personal folders from which BCM can create the links. Besides the automatic functions, you can manually select the folders through Link available E-mails and, additionally, specify dates. Thus all e-mails that are older than the specified date will be ignored for linking. Then click on Start in order to create the links.

The Company Services menu will take you to the BCM website. There you will find tricks and tips for working with BCM, files for Office, and other information about the product. Via Others/Business Records you can invoke the journal function. Here, BCM has created its own entry besides the default Outlook Journal in My Journals. Furthermore, you can display the trashcan of BCM through Others/Deleted Elements. The deleted elements of the BCM (not of Outlook 2003) are located here. Hence, a quick search for locating the objects is ensured.

12
A Security Strategy for SBS 2003

You will get an overview of the basic security strategies for the protection of the SBS 2003 network in this chapter. As the various points have for the most part already been discussed in the context of the individual sections, the description here takes the form of a checklist with references to the individual chapters.

- Verify your network topology and the resultant configuration of the firewall.
- Secure the routers.
- Verify the network, e-mail, firewall, and web services on the SBS 2003.
- With the help of the automatic software update make sure that the operating systems of the server and the clients are secure.
- Implement secure passwords with the help of the password policy.
- Secure the server by controlling remote access to the SBS and the SBS network.
- Verify that users are only given the minimal necessary permissions, and restrict the user rights.
- Change the account names for the predefined administrator account and take further security measures for using the account.
- Back up the server on which the SBS 2003 is installed.
- Monitor the security and system events in the SBS 2003.

Verifying the Network Topology

To secure the network effectively, a verification of the existing network structure or the network structure to be configured is essential, and it makes a difference whether your Internet connection is a dial-up connection or a broadband connection. To protect a dial-up connection, pay particular attention to the tips given in the *Verifying the Internet, E-Mail, Network, and Firewall Services on the SBS 2003* section later in the chapter.

In the case of a broadband connection there are two further possibilities: either the SBS 2003 has a network card for the LAN and a router with firewall functions for the internet traffic, or there are two network cards in the SBS 2003. In case of the latter, the server uses the internal firewall that is provided by SBS 2003.

Using a Router and Firewall for a Broadband Connection

If there is only one network card in the SBS 2003, the network topology should look as follows (Figure 12.1):

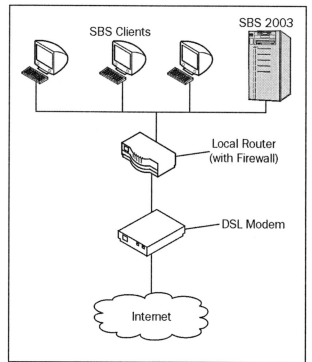

Figure 12.1: Use of a router and a firewall in the SBS 2003 Network

In this case you cannot use the integrated firewall of SBS 2003, as the SBS does not function as a gateway between the Internet and the clients. Therefore, either the router must have a firewall function, or you must install an external firewall. You need to open in the firewall the ports that are necessary for SBS 2003. A table in the *Configuring a Firewall on a Router* section gives an overview of these ports.

Using the Integrated Firewall of SBS 2003

If the SBS 2003 has two network cards, the network must be configured as follows (see Figure 12.2) to allow the integrated firewall of SBS 2003 to function correctly with a broadband connection:

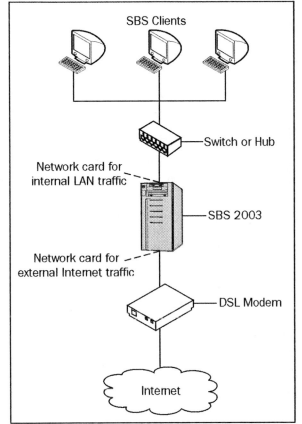

Figure 12.2: Using the integrated firewall of SBS 2003 when the SBS has two network cards

To use the integrated firewall, connect one network card of the SBS 2003 to the local network through a switch or a hub. The other network card is connected to the device used for establishing an Internet connection, for example the DSL modem. In this case it is also possible to additionally install a firewall external to the firewall integrated in the SBS 2003. This can be a router with firewall functionalities or an actual firewall. Pay attention to the tips given in the *Securing the Router* section, which follows.

In the task list of the Internet connection wizard, you must select Broadband Connection as the type of connection in this case (see the *Network Task: Setting Up an Internet Connection* section in Chapter 2). If you are using one more router with firewall functionalities, ensure that you select the Local Router Device with an IP-Address option (see the *Network Task: Setting Up an Internet Connection* section in Chapter 2).

Securing the Router

If you are using a router for the Internet connection, and it simultaneously acts as a firewall and a wireless access point, you must ensure a correct and secure configuration for this device.

Securing the Wireless Access Point (Base Station)

If the router has the wireless access point feature and if there are no wireless devices installed in your company, you should deactivate this functionality. Otherwise, there is a risk of unknown users having unauthorized access to your network. More specific details for the deactivation of this feature will be available in the manual of the router. If you use wireless devices, you must appropriately secure the access point in order to prevent or at the very least minimize the possibility of any unauthorized access.

For this you need to first assign a password for the configuration of the router. Make sure that the password is not the default password assigned by the manufacturer of the router. Next, you must enable encryption. For that you can use either the **WEP (Wired Equivalent Privacy) Encryption** or **802.lx Authentication**. The 802.lx authentication is newer and more secure than WEP. Both these procedures deal with the security protocol that encrypts the data transferred through radio waves from one device to another. In case of WEP encryption, you must manually create a security key that will then be exchanged between the access point and the wireless devices. This security key is automatically generated in 802.lx. If you have a choice between a 64-bit and a 128-bit key during WEP encryption, always use the longer key.

For making your router even more secure, enable MAC (**Media Access Control**) filtering. For this, find out the MAC addresses of the wireless cards used in the network and enter this address list in the router. This will ensure that only devices with the listed MAC addresses can access the access point.

To find out the MAC address of a network card, enter the following command at the command prompt: `ipconfig /all`. The MAC address is displayed under Physical Address (see Figure 12.3).

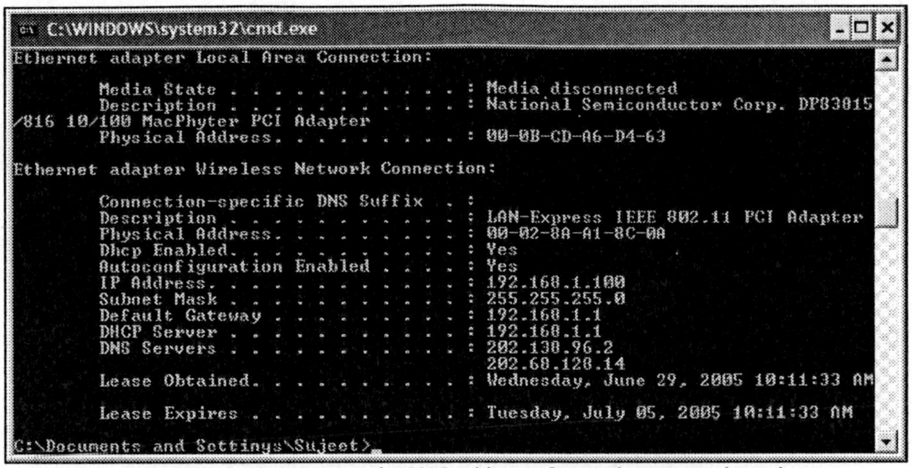

Figure 12.3: Ascertaining the MAC address of a wireless network card

If you have enabled MAC filtering, you must update the list stored in the router as soon as you add a new wireless card to or remove a wireless card from the network.

Configuring a Firewall on the Router

In this section, we discuss the configuration of a firewall for use with SBS 2003. All the ports on the SBS 2003 are automatically configured after you have completed the Establish Internet Connection wizard in the task list.

The opening of ports in a firewall is also called **port forwarding** in the relevant documentation. Here you will find an overview of all the possible ports required in the SBS 2003 network. If a port is not needed, you can block it on the firewall of the router.

If you have not purchased the SBS 2003 premium edition and consequently haven't installed the ISA Server 2000 as a firewall, a separate firewall device will likely be available in most small companies. This device can be operated along with the integrated firewall of SBS 2003 under certain circumstances. Often, the firewall is combined with the DHCP server in such cases.

If this device is **UPnP** (Universal Plug and Play) compliant, the ports required in the SBS 2003 are configured through the e-mail and Internet connection wizards. If this device is not UPnP compliant, you have to configure the firewall manually.

If the firewall also serves as a router, and the SBS is connected to the local network and to the Internet through different network cards, you can use either the SBS 2003 firewall, or the firewall functionality of the hybrid device—you can even use them both together.

The table that follows gives you an overview of the port numbers required in SBS 2003 for different services. All the services use the TCP protocol.

Port Number	Service	Description
21	FTP (File Transfer Protocol)	Before you set up the server as an FTP server, add and install the FTP service.
25	E-Mail	Sending and receiving mails through the SMTP protocol (Simple Mail Transfer Protocol).
80 (HTTP)	Web Server	Internet access, Outlook Web Access (OWA), Outlook Mobile Access (OMA), invocation of efficiency and utilization reports of the SBS, company web page (wwwroot), as well as access to Outlook through the Internet (RPC) without a VPN connection.
443 (HTTPS)	Web Server; Remote Web Workplace	HTTP requests over SSL (Secure Sockets Layer). For Remote Web Workplace, refer to the corresponding row of this table.
444	SharePoint Services –Intranet Web Page	Securing the client-server communication while accessing the intranet web page of the company and while accessing the other pages created in `http://companyweb`.
1723	VPN (Virtual Private Network)	Configuration of a secure connection from remote clients to the company network.
3389	Terminal Services	Using the terminal services of the SBS 2003 through remote clients.
4125	Remote Web Workplace	Connection to the local network through Outlook Web Access (OWA), Remote Desktop connection to the clients of the local network, access to the intranet web page of the SharePoint services, and the download of connection managers for the configuration of remote access.

If you require more ports for specific applications, you must unlock them in the firewall. For an overview of all the available ports and of ports used by specific application and services, go to `http://www.iana.org/assignments/port-numbers`.

If the router supports the logging functionality, you should enable this functionality and study the log files.

Verifying the Internet, E-Mail, Network, and Firewall Services on the SBS 2003

Non-optimally configured Internet, e-mail, network, and firewall services represent another security risk; we'll now see how to deal with these.

Verifying the Firewall Configuration

A wizard is used to configure the SBS 2003 as a firewall. In the standard version of SBS, the default firewall service is configured in the routing and RAS services. In the premium version of SBS, ISA Server is configured.

While selecting the available services, you have to remember to select only the most important services. If, for example, you are providing the users with a remote web workplace, you have to consider whether you need to provide a VPN connection at all.

If you allow the access to the company web page (wwwroot) or to the intranet site of Windows SharePoint Services over the Internet (see Figure 12.4) via the Internet connection wizard, it is possible that the login page of the Remote Web Workplace will get listed in an Internet search engine like Google.

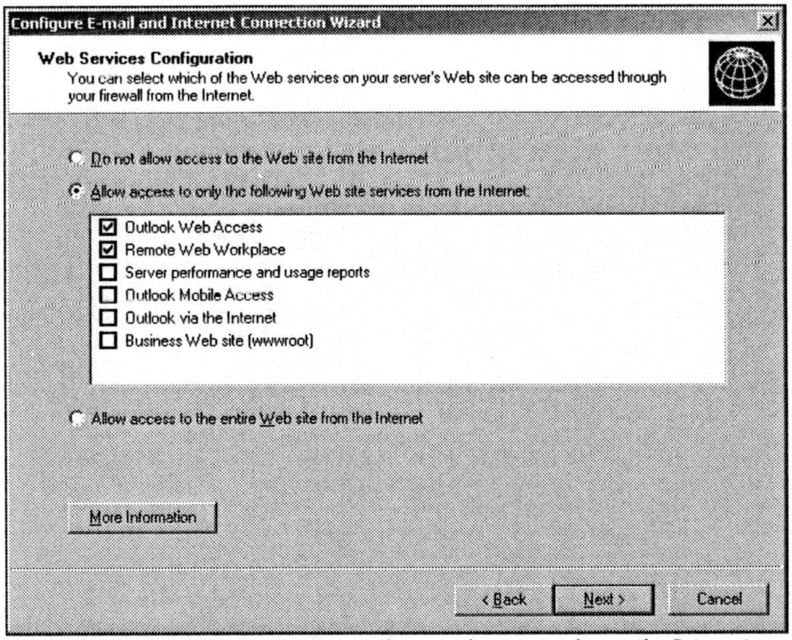

Figure 12.4: Selecting components that may be accessed over the Internet

When you allow access to the company web page over the Internet, **Web Robots** can automatically start searching for web pages and documents, in a manner similar to how you follow the hyperlinks on published pages.

In order to prevent the Web Robots from searching for and categorizing web pages (or parts of web pages), you must create a text file called robots.txt in any text editor and save it in the directory of the default website.

For the Web Robots to read the `robots.txt` file, you must publish the company website wwwroot in the Internet connection wizard.

The following listing shows the contents of `robots.txt` that will allow Web Robots to list only the contents of the company website and not the internal websites like, for example, the remote workplace.

```
User-agent:  *
Disallow:    /_vti_bin/
Disallow:    /clienthelp/
Disallow:    /exchweb/
Disallow:    /remote/
Disallow:    /tsweb/
Disallow:    /aspnet_client/
Disallow:    /images/
Disallow:    /_private/
Disallow:    /_vti_cnf/
Disallow:    /_vti_log/
Disallow:    /_vti_pvt/
Disallow:    /_vti_script/
Disallow:    /_vti_txt/
```

Managing E-Mail Attachments

Furthermore, you should use the feature of Exchange Server 2003 that makes it possible to automatically remove specific file types from e-mail attachments before the user opens an attachment and possibly compromises the security of the network.

You can install this feature by using the Internet connection wizard (see Figure 12.5):

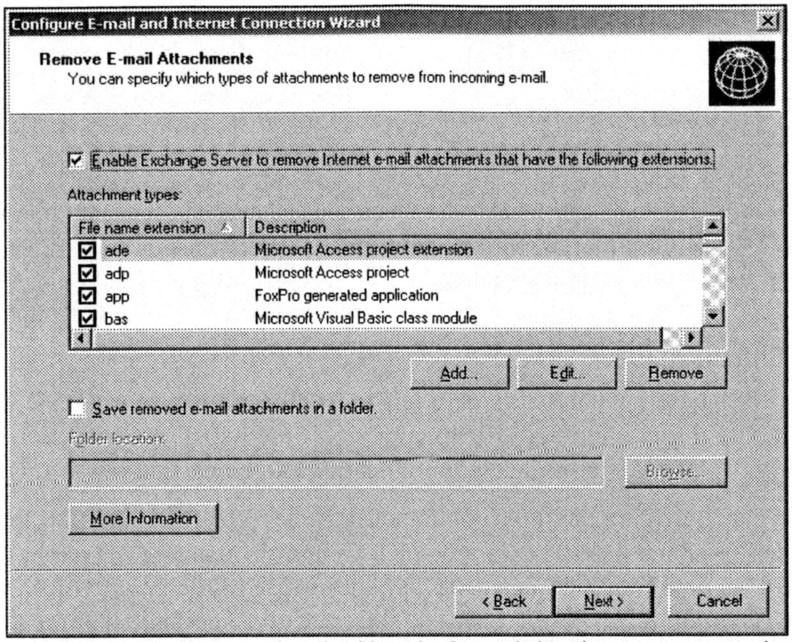

Figure 12.5: Selecting file types that should not be forwarded to the user as an attachment.

You can change the settings of the file types by restarting the wizard.

Configuring TCP/IP Filtering

TCP/IP filtering is used to control incoming access. This method is highly recommended from the security perspective as it runs in kernel mode. Other control mechanisms such as, for example, IPScc policy filter or routing server and RAS server, are operated in the user mode or in the workstation and server services. As only incoming TCP/IP access can be controlled with the help of the TCP/IP filtering, you should combine this with IPSec filtering and RAS-Packet filtering for outgoing access.

Microsoft recommends enabling the firewall function while using SBS 2003 with two network cards and to open the relevant ports in the external network card. Carry out the following steps to configure the TCP/IP filtering:

1. Open the Control Panel and select Open from the Network Connections context menu.

2. Mark the network connection that is to be configured for controlling the incoming accesses and click on Properties in its context menu.

3. In the General tab click on Internet Protocol (TCP/IP) and then on Properties in Connection Settings of [Name of the Adapter].

4. In the Internet Protocol (TCP/IP) Properties window click on Advanced and then on the Options tab.

5. Click on TCP/IP Filters and Properties.

6. Check the Enable TCP/IP Filter (all Adapters) checkbox here. Although this enables TCP/IP filtering for all adapters, the filter configuration must be separately carried out for each adapter. For the configuration you can either select the Allow All option or you can allow incoming connections only for specific IP addresses, TCP ports, and UDP ports.

Example: If for the external network card only port 80 is allowed for the incoming traffic, the port will only allow Internet traffic to come in. If the Allow All option is selected for the internal network card, unlimited communication can be carried out through this card.

7. You can configure the three columns for the TCP/IP filtering: TCP Ports, UDP Ports, and IP Protocols. For each column, you can select either the Allow All option or the Allow Only option. In case of the latter, you can restrict the TCP and the UDP traffic. To do this, click on Add and enter the port number and the protocol number in the Add Filter window. If you have only enabled the Allow Only option and have not made any entries in the list, no communication with the network card is possible. This applies equally to both the internal and the external connections.

> The following, however, cannot be blocked: TCP and UDP traffic cannot be blocked by selecting the Allow Only option for the IP protocol column and then entering the protocol numbers 6 (TCP, Transfer Control Protocol) and 17 (UDP, User Datagram Protocol). Generally, the ICMP messages (Internet Control Message Protocol) cannot be blocked, even by selecting the Allow Only option for the IP protocol column and entering the protocol number 1.

The filter options configured here refer only to the incoming traffic. In order to check the outgoing traffic, you can use the IPSec policies and the RAS packet filtering at best.

Software Updates for the Operating System

A step for further securing the network is timely updates of the operating system software through service packs, updates, and patches provided by Microsoft to close known security holes. This holds equally for the SBS 2003 and the individual client computers. For this, the best way is to install Software Update Services (refer to Chapter 9). You can also use the automatic Windows update, also described in Chapter 9.

Furthermore, regularly check for updates for applications like Microsoft Office and applications from other manufacturers, and work out a deployment strategy for them. For Microsoft Office products, the automatic deployment of updates featured in Software Update Services version 2.0 gets implemented. An automatic update is available at the following link `http://office.microsoft.com/OfficeUpdate/default.aspx`. Only the Office versions 2000, XP, and 2003 are supported for the update. To search for updates for other applications, check the relevant web pages or automatically get information about new updates, provided the manufacturer offers this service.

Upgrading the Operating Systems and Applications

You can also consider upgrading clients that still run Windows 9x, NT, or older, to Windows 2000 or XP Professional. These operating systems guarantee improved performance and security in an SBS 2003 network. Moreover, for instance, the Outlook 2003 in SBS 2003 requires Windows 2000 with service pack 3 at the very least or Windows XP, and will not run on older Windows versions.

Implementing Secure Passwords

The network can be further secured by implementing secure passwords that meet Windows complexity requirements. Besides the implementation of the appropriate policies, it is also necessary to train users to deal with passwords. There will always be enough users (including administrators) who write their passwords on a piece of paper and either put it under the keyboard or stick it to the monitor. The importance of regularly changing their passwords must be brought home to the users. Explain to the users that they have to keep their passwords as secret as, for example, the PIN number of their credit cards.

Users should take care that they do not use any such terms in their passwords that a potential attacker could easily discover, either through personal knowledge or through any other hacking methods. The following terms come under this:

- Name of their children, spouse, pet, or friends.
- Any word that can be found in the dictionary.
- A date, telephone number, or a personal number like car number or bank account number.
- A password that has already been used by the user.

You will get instructions for implementing secure passwords after you have completed the Internet connection wizard. The implementation of the requirements is already explained in detail in Chapter 2.

Remote Access to the Network

You can configure either the remote web workplace or a VPN connection to remotely access the network. The simpler solution is to configure the remote web workplace so that only authorized users connect to the network. In both the cases, teach users that they should in principle log off as soon as they stop requiring the connection. Through the remote web workplace, users can establish a connection to their computer at their workplace, receive e-mails, access the internal web page, and use the applications from outside the local network. Through the Connection Manager, users can also establish a connection to the SBS 2003 network.

To establish a connection with a computer in the local network via remote web workplace, the remote web workplace must have either the Windows XP Professional or the Windows Server 2000 operating system. If some other operating system is installed on the remote computer, you must configure a VPN connection or a dial-up connection to access the network. If the remote web workplace is not required, disable this feature.

If you do not want to (or cannot) set up the remote web workplace, you will have to use the Internet connection wizard again. With the wizard, you can install a VPN connection and/or a dial-up connection (see figure 12.6). In case of a VPN connection, the remote user first establishes an Internet connection and then connects with the company network through a tunnel. In case of the dial-up connection, the connection to the SBS 2003 is established over the telephone line with a modem.

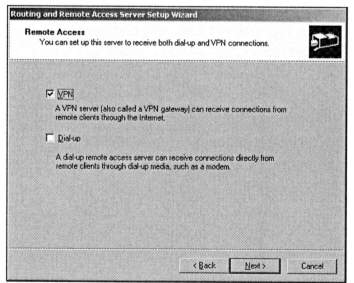

Figure 12.6: Selecting the RAS access method.

If the Enable RAS option is not available, the RAS service has not been installed on the SBS 2003. If these connection types are not required, do not install them.

Restricting User Rights

Giving the users too many rights can prove to be dangerous in two ways; On the one hand, the users themselves can unintentionally cause damage, on the other, in the event of unauthorized access to the account, an attacker will have extensive rights.

When creating a user account, ensure that the users are assigned the correct user templates. Furthermore, the user accounts for the administrator and power user templates should not be used for day-to-day work. Thus, a normal user cannot remotely access the network through the user templates. To provide this authorization, use the Mobile Users template for the concerned users. Even for network shares, issue only the truly necessary user and file rights.

Security Considerations for Administrators

From the security point of view, the administrator must log in with the administrator account (or from another account with administrator rights) only when he has to complete tasks that require administrative rights. Otherwise, he should log in from a user account that has fewer privileges. If the administrator logs in with all the administrative rights and during an Internet session contracts a virus or a Trojan, the virus will be able to perform all the functions of the current user account. With administrative rights, data can be deleted or the hard disk formatted. Therefore, it's best to log in from an account to which minimal rights are assigned.

In case it isn't foreseen that a certain task requires administrative rights so as to be executed, you can still carry out this task from the user account you are currently logged on to without logging off and then logging on as an administrator. For this, you have the Run as option in the graphical user interface and the RUNAS command-line option.

The "Run as" Option

You can start any executable file, mmc, or element of the Control Panel with the Run as option. For this, you only need to have a user name and password through which the desired program can be run. However, it is possible that this option aborts if you try to run a program on another computer through the network. This happens when the user account that you have entered in Run as is not identical to the account from which the program was originally started, even though the "Run as" account has sufficient rights. Take the following steps in order to use this option:

1. Determine whether the Run Service as option in Services is enabled. If this is not the case, start the service manually.

2. Select the program file, link, mmc, or the Control Panel element that you want to run. Press the *Enter* key and select Run as from the context menu.

3. Specify the account from which you would like to run the program. For this, the user name, password, and the domain are necessary (see figure).

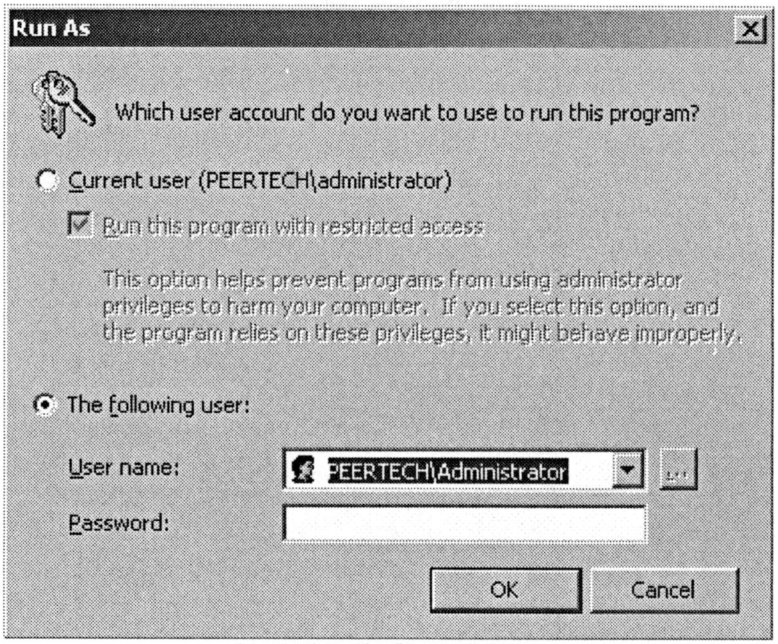

Figure 12.7: The "Run as" Option

Using RUNAS

The RUNAS program is started from the command line. It fulfills the same purpose as the Run as we just saw. First verify whether the Run Service as in Services has been started. RUNAS has the following options: runas [/profile] [/env] [/netonly] /user: Accountname Programpath:

The optional parameters have the following meaning:

• /profile: Profile path of the user account, necessary only when a profile has to be loaded.

• /env: If the network environment is to be used instead of the local environment.

- /netonly: If the user information is valid only for remote access.
- /user: In the ComputerName\Account format, or in case of 2000, Account@ComputerName.
- Program path: Path to the executable file. If there are blank spaces in the program path, the input must be given within inverted commas.

A RUNAS command line can look as follows:

```
runas /user: Administrator@hippokrates.firma.de "mmc
%windir%\system32\Konsole1.msc"
```

You can enter the password for the account after the prompt.

The following (mostly self-evident) rules should apply to the administrative account:

- In all cases, use a secure password for the account.
- Never disclose the password and do not note down the password in the vicinity of the computer.
- Do not log on with the administrative account for day-to-day tasks.
- Do not leave the computer unattended, if you have logged on with the administrator account. Lock the computer, even if you leave it for a brief period of time.

Secure the Network Shares

For all network shares that are set up during the installation of SBS 2003, the authorizations are automatically kept highly restricted so as to protect the company data against unauthorized access. You should also abide by this principle when creating additional network shares.

In order to ascertain which shares are available on the server, enter the \\Servername command at the command prompt. The following shares are automatically created during the setup of the server:

- Servername.log
- Address
- ClientApps
- Clients
- Printers and Faxes
- Faxclient
- Netlogon

- Sysvol
- Tsclient
- Tsweb
- Users

All other shares that may be listed are self-created shares whose permissions you should verify. To do this, open the Security tab via Properties and verify the permissions that are assigned to the users and the groups for the share and restrict these as needed.

Changing the Name of the Administrator Account

The administrator account can be further secured by renaming the predefined administrator account. As the administrator account cannot be locked when another account with the same permissions is being used, the only solution left is to rename the account; a potential hacker has no chance if he logs on with the administrator account and tries to guess the password, as an account with this name does not exist any more.

After you have renamed the administrator account, you must re-log on to the SBS 2003. Otherwise, you will be denied access to the administration tools or other resources as long as you are logged on with the old administrator account.

1. In order to rename the account, open the User entry in the Server Management. Select Properties from the context menu and open the General tab. In the Display Name textbox enter the new name for the account.

2. Switch to the Account tab and enter the same account name under User Login Name. This name must also be entered under User Login Name (Pre-Windows 2000). Then click on OK.

Furthermore, you can also rename the local administrator account on the clients:

3. In Windows 2000 and XP, open Control Panel/Administration/Computer Administration.

4. Open Local Users and Groups in the console and then Users. Select Rename from the context menu of Administrator and change the name.

To change the name of the administrator accounts in all client computers, use the GPMC (Group Policy Management Console).

Securing the SBS 2003

The SBS 2003 must be secured at two levels; the server itself has to be physically secured, and must also be securely configured from the software perspective.

Physically Securing the Server

For physically securing the server, the server must be located in a locked room, and no one but administrators should have the key to the room. Otherwise, there is a danger of the server hard disk being removed and read, of booting the computer with a floppy and then formatting the hard disk, or exchanging the keyboard with a specially configured keyboard that can record all the keyboard inputs, including the password. Therefore, make sure that the server room is always sealed and the key is kept in a secure location.

Additionally protect the BIOS of the server with a password. Furthermore, you should store the backup tapes of the SBS at a location other than the server room. Also, the use of a UPS system can protect the server from damage during a power outage.

Installing Software on the Server

The basic rule for a server is never to install more than the necessary applications on it. On no account should the SBS be treated as a client computer when installing software. This ensures that no hacker can access the server through possible security holes in the installed applications.

In any case, you must run a backup program on the server if you are not using the integrated Windows Backup. Furthermore, it should self-evident that anti-virus software must also be installed on the server. Here you must decide whether you want a server-based solution that will protect all the clients in the network, or want to install anti-virus software individually on each client.

Monitoring the SBS 2003

You should activate the monitoring of security-related processes in the SBS 2003. You can either read the contents of the monitoring report or have it sent to an e-mail address.

If you receive the reports as e-mail attachments, you will find a chronological overview of the system, application, and security events, as well as those of the IIS. However, keep in mind that the reports sent as e-mail attachments can be relatively large. If the size of the report is more than 5 MB, it won't be sent via e-mail. Also consider whether the mailbox of your mail provider has any size restrictions.

Moreover, enable the monitoring of failed logins and locked accounts. By default, the auditing is enabled for both these event types in the SBS 2003. If 50 invalid login attempts are made within 10 minutes, the account gets automatically locked for the next ten minutes. An entry is made in the event log of the SBS 2003 at every failed login attempt. Locked accounts due to invalid login attempts are recoded in the performance report of the SBS 2003. If you have additionally enabled the option to receive an e-mail, an e-mail will be sent to the given address every time an account gets locked.

13

Troubleshooting Small Business Server 2003

In this chapter we've discussed various error scenarios and problems that occur in SBS 2003 and have suggested comprehensive solutions for them. For a clearer overview, we have summarized the problems individually in the theme areas of group server, users, Internet, intranet, e-mail, fax, monitoring, and mobile devices.

Server Problems

This section describes problems that the administrator detects (and which can be solved) directly on the server.

Services close abruptly when shutting down and restarting SBS 2003

Problem: When shutting down or restarting the SBS 2003, services that are running can abruptly terminate before they are properly closed by the system. This can lead to loss of data.

Cause: This problem is caused by an error in the registry. This happens when the WaitToKillServiceTimeout value is set to the wrong type REG_DWORD instead of the correct type REG_SZ. The value of WaitToKillServiceTimeout is thus interpreted as a time limit of zero milliseconds, and all the running services terminate abruptly.

Solution: To solve this problem, open the registry editor by entering the regedit command in the Run dialog box.

1. Navigate to the HKEY_LOCAL_MACHINE\SYSTEM\CurrentControlSet\ Control key.
2. Select the Delete entry from the context menu of WaitToKillServiceTimeout and confirm it.

3. Select New and String from the context menu of Control. Create a new value as follows: Name, WaitToKillServiceTimeout; Value Type, REG_SZ; and Value, 120000. This sets the waiting period for closing the services at 120,000 milliseconds.

4. Close the registry editor and restart SBS 2003.

Problems with the Internet Connection Firewall (ICF)/Internet Connection Sharing (ICS) Service

Problem: After you have updated a Windows Server 2000 installation to SBS 2003, the Internet Connection Firewall (ICF)/Internet Connection Sharing (ICS) service unexpectedly starts and ends.

Cause: This problem occurs when the Internet Connection Sharing service was enabled on Windows Server 2000. Therefore, this service starts even after the system has been updated to SBS 2003, although Internet Connection Sharing is not available in SBS 2003.

Solution: This problem can be solved by disabling the service. To do this, take the following steps:

1. Open Start/Programs/Administration/Services.

2. Select the Properties entry from the context menu of the Internet Connection Firewall/Internet Connection Sharing service.

3. Select the Disabled entry from Start Type in the General tab and then click on OK.

Instead of a user e-mail address only the GUID is displayed

Problem: In the Server Management under Users, instead of the username for the E-mail address the user's GUID (Globally Unique Identifier) is displayed.

Cause: This problem occurs if the username contains Unicode characters.

Solution: This problem can be solved by changing the SMTP e-mail address for the user account. To do this, take the following steps:

1. Open the Advanced Administration entry in Server Management and then select Active Directory Users and Computers.

2. There, double-click on the name of the SBS and then open the Users or the Built-in folder, depending on where the user is stored.

3. From the context menu of the users, select Properties and switch to the E-Mail Addresses tab.

4. Under Type, select the SMTP entry and then click on Edit. Replace the displayed GUID with the correct e-mail address of the user and then click on OK.

5. Switch to the Exchange – General tab. In the Alias text box, replace the GUID with the correct e-mail alias. Click on OK.

User-Specific Problems

In the following sections, you will find a series of typical problems and error scenarios faced by users.

A user cannot change his or her password

Problem: A user who tries to change his or her password gets an error message stating that the password cannot be changed.

Cause: A password cannot be changed when a user's new password does not conform to the password policies determined by the administrator.

Solution: Inform the user about the necessary length and complexity requirements.

A user account is locked

Problem: A user cannot log in as his or her account is locked.

Cause: For security reasons, a user account will get locked when too many of the user's login attempts have failed.

Solution: In order to unlock the user's account, take the following steps:

1. Open the Users entry in Server Management and select the Properties entry from the context menu of the locked-out user.

2. Open the Account tab and disable the Account is locked checkbox. The user can now log in.

Via the settings for account locking it is specified that, by default, an account gets locked after 50 failed login attempts. The account then remains locked for ten minutes.

A new user cannot log in

Problem: A newly created user tries to log in to the domain directly after his or her account has been created. However, the login attempt fails.

Cause: A user account is not recognized by Active Directory immediately after it is created, and therefore it cannot be used. By default, it takes 15 minutes for the new account to be recognized.

Solution: Ask the user to wait for approximately 15 minutes (and in the meanwhile, maybe drink a cup of coffee).

The first login to a client takes too long

Problem: When the user logs on to the client for the first time after being added to the SBS domain, the login takes too long.

Cause: The redirection of the "My Documents" folder to the server has been enabled. At the time of the first login, the contents of the local folder must be synchronized with the server. The bigger the size of the contents, the longer it takes for the synchronization and consequently, the login. From the second login onwards, only the changes to the folder are synchronized and hence the login will not take as long.

Solution: As this is not an error, no solution is required.

The user cannot save data in the shared folders of the server

Problem: A user cannot save data in the shared folders of the server any more.

Cause: The user has exceeded the disk quota allotted to him or her for saving data.

Solution: First, you can ask the user to save data on his or her local computer. If several users face this problem, you have to consider changing the size of the disk quota. Keep in mind, however, that the quota cannot be changed for each user individually; it can only be changed for an entire hard disk partition.

Users cannot restore any previous file version

Problem: The users cannot restore the previous versions of their files as there is no Previous Versions tab in the Properties of the "My Documents" folder.

Cause: The "My Documents" folder has been redirected to a new storage location only a short while ago, as a result of which the snapshot to be taken has not yet been created. The disk space allocated to the deleted files is still active.

Solution: The tab is available when the next snapshot is created. This occurs at 7:00 a.m. and at 12:00 p.m. There is no need of any other measures.

The "My Documents" Folder is not synchronized with the server

Problem: There is no synchronization of the contents of the "My Documents" folder with the files on the server.

Cause: The user's disk quota has been exceeded, and thus no more of his or her files can be stored on the server.

Solution: You can either inform the user not to delete any more required files from the "My Documents" folder, or you can alternatively increase the disk quota. Keep in mind, however, that the quota for all the users will be increased.

Redirected folders cannot be accessed any more after the migration of the user profile

Problem: After you have imported the user profile into SBS 2003, the users cannot access the redirected folders any more.

Cause: For private user profiles, the administrative credentials of the user folders are deleted from the client computers. However, the users require these credentials to access folders that have been redirected to the server. Following the migration of the user profiles, of which the redirected folders are also a part, the users cannot possibly access the data of the server any more.

Solution: To solve this problem, you must manually restore access to the user folders on the client computer. To do this, take the following steps:

1. In the client computer open Start/Programs/Administration/ View Events. There, open the Application entry.
2. Search for an error message in the list that gives its source as Folder Redirection and double-click on this entry.
3. Note the destination and the source directory that is specified in the description of the events.
4. The next steps are carried out on the server. Navigate to the user folder noted down in step 3 using the Windows Explorer.
5. Select the Sharing and Security entry from the context menu of the folder and select the Permissions tab. Verify that the username is not available in the list of authorization entries there. If the folder is empty, delete it.
6. From here onwards, the steps are to be carried out on the client. Navigate to the user folder noted down in step 3 in Windows Explorer. Select the Sharing and Security entry from the context menu of the folder and click on Advanced in the Security tab.
7. In the Advanced Security Settings window, select the User tab. There, click on the username and enable the Replace Owners of the Objects and the subordinate Containers checkbox. Click on Apply.

8. On the Authorizations tab, the name of the user should be available in the Authorization Entries list. If this is not the case, include the user to the list via Add. Assign the Full Access authorization to this user. Then click on OK.

9. Log off from the client computer and then log on again.

After the upgrade to SBS 2003, some applications are not accessible

Problem: After the upgrade, only the applications available in SBS 2003 are present on the clients, not the applications installed before the upgrade.

Cause: Only the default applications have been installed on the client computers. Other applications have not been updated.

Solution: Install the applications on the SBS 2003 server. They are installed on the client computer after it has been upgraded. The command line for the installation of the applications on the client can be found in the registry of the SBS 2003 server under the key HKEY_LOCAL_MACHINE\SOFTWARE\Microsoft\SmallBusinessServer\clientsetup\sbs2k_archive\Client Applications\.

Open Client Computers in Server Management and then click on Add Applications to Client Computers. Enter the appropriate command lines for the installation of the application there.

A remote connection cannot be established

Problem: In Windows XP, a user cannot establish a remote connection to a computer.

Cause 1: The user account doesn't have permission to log in through the remote desktop.

Solution 1: To give the user this permission, open the User entry in Server Management. From the context menu of the concerned user select the Properties entry. On the Properties page, switch to the Terminal Service Profiles tab and enable the Allow Terminal Server Login checkbox.

Cause 2: The client computer has not been configured to use the remote desktop.

Solution 2: Take the following steps to configure the client computer:

1. Open Control Panel/System and then the Remote tab there.
2. Enable the Allow Users to establish a Remote Desktop Connection checkbox there and click on OK.

Cause 3: The client computer is configured in such a way that remote access by the user is not allowed.

Solution 3: Take the steps shown on the facing page to configure the client computer to allow remote access:

1. Open Control Panel/System and then the Remote tab there.
2. Click on Select Remote Users. The Remote Desktop Users window will then be displayed. Click on Add in this window.
3. In the Select Users or Groups window, select the desired object type (for example, Users) under Object Types. Under Locations, specify the search path for the selected object type. Under Enter the objects names to select enter the name of the user or the group objects and then click on Verify Names.
4. If the name is found, click on OK to confirm it. The name will be displayed in the list of authorized users in the Remote Desktop Users window.

Problems with the Internet

In this section you will find a few typical scenarios pertaining to problems with Internet connections and Internet-specific settings.

VPN access is not possible

Problem: A user cannot access the SBS 2003 network via VPN.

Cause: The user does not have permission to access the SBS 2003 system through the VPN or through the dial-up connection.

Solution: To give the necessary permissions to the user, add him or her to the mobile users group or apply the Mobile User template to the user through the wizard for changing user permissions.

SBS 2003 Standard doesn't allow USB devices for dialing on demand

Problem: In the standard version, a USB device cannot be used for connecting to the Internet by on-demand dialing.

Cause: The standard edition of SBS 2003 does not support connecting to the Internet by on-demand dialing using a network device connected to the USB bus like, for example, a USB modem or a USB-DSL adaptor.

Solution: When configuring e-mail and Internet connection via the wizard in the standard version, you must select a non-USB network device or use the Enterprise version of SBS 2003, to which this restriction does not apply.

There is no solution to this problem in the standard version. In this case, you cannot use a USB device.

Intranet Problems

In this section you will find a series of error scenarios that can occur in connection with the use of the intranet, particularly when SharePoint Services are used.

The installation of the intranet components or the connection with http://companyweb fails

Problem: While installing the intranet components, you receive an error message stating that an error has occurred in the installation of SharePoint Services and in creating an intranet page. You would like to access the company website after installing the SBS 2003 but you receive the message that you are not authorized to access the page.

Cause: These problems do not occur if you have installed SBS 2003 before 24 November 2003, unless you want to make major changes in the SharePoint Services such as creating a new top-level webpage. The actual problem lies in the validation of the DLLs. A few DLLs are mistakenly taken to be invalid by the installation routine.

Solution: In order to solve this problem, Microsoft provides a patch for the SharePoint services and the SOL Server 2000 MSDE. For further details you can refer to Microsoft KB articles 832880 and 833019.

The incorrect installation files of installation CD 3 have, in the meantime, been replaced. Customers that still own the older CD can receive the updated CD for free. The appropriate order form can be found by going to `https://microsoft.order-4.com/sbsrtmcd/`.

If users have already been added before installing this patch, open the User entry in Server Management and start the user permissions wizard. Give the already created users access permission to the website.

If the web site was published before installing the patches, restart the e-mail and Internet connection wizard after you have installed the patches to make the web site available on the Internet.

The user has to enter his or her login Information when accessing the company website

Problem: When the user tries to access the internal company website, he or she is prompted to enter his or her login information.

Cause: As the internal company website is based on the SharePoint Services, the user must be a member of a SharePoint services group. A user who is a member of this group does not have to enter login information.

Solution: If you create a user account on the basis of one of the user templates, users are automatically configured to access the company website without having to provide any further login information.

The search function for the internal website is not available
Problem: No search functions are available on the internal company website.

Cause: The full text search functionality is not available when MSDE is running on the SBS 2003. An instance of SQL Server is required for this.

Solution: In order to use the full text search you must upgrade the MSDE to an instance of SQL Server 2000. MSDE cannot be upgraded on an evaluation version of SBS 2003.

The documents on the company website cannot be edited
Problem: It is not possible to edit or save the documents on the internal company website.

Cause: To edit and save the documents on the internal company website, Microsoft Office XP or Microsoft Office 2003 must be installed on the client computer. The documents cannot be edited in older versions of Office.

Solution: Upgrade the appropriate Office applications on the users' computers.

The website of the SBS 2003 cannot be accessed through the FQDN
Problem: When you try to access the SBS 2003 from an internal client through its officially registered FQDN (Fully Qualified Domain Name), you receive an error message stating: DNS Error. This page cannot be displayed.

Cause: This problem occurs when the officially registered FQDN is resolved to the external page of a NAT (Network Access Translation) device that is connected to the Internet, and returns this to the internal server. At this moment, Internet Explorer tries to access the publicly registered FQDN, but the connection is blocked and an error message is displayed. The query is interpreted by the router as if it has been issued from an IP address located within the internal network. Thus the router takes the query to be false (spoofing) and does not process the packet further. However, the client, which is actually located outside the network, gets an error message instead of a reply.

Solution 1: You can first try to solve this problem by installing a current firmware update on the router.

Solution 2: If the firmware is current or if the problem cannot be solved by updating it, the clients can try to access the SBS by using the NetBIOS name when they are within the URL.

Solution 3: The third solution is to install an additional DNS Forward Lookup Zone. This zone must have the same name as the external domain name. In order to install this DNS zone, take the following steps:

1. Issue the `dnsmgmt.msc` command to open the DNS administration console.
2. Double-click on DNS Server, and in the left half of the window select the New Zone entry from the context menu of Forward Lookup Zone. Then click on Next.
3. Select the Primary Zone entry and click on Next.
4. In the Active Directory... window, click on Next.
5. On the Zone Name page specify the FQDN of the external domain. This name can be, for example, www.externalname.com. Then click on Next.
6. In the Dynamic Update window, select the Do not allow dynamic updates option and click on Next and then on Finish.
7. Now select the DNS zone just created and from its context menu select the New Host (A) entry.
8. In the New Host window, do not make an entry in the Name field. If the FQDN contains the www, you can enter it into the Name field. In the IP Address field, enter the local IP address of the SBS. Then click on Add Host.

It is also possible to create a DNS entry in the SBS that resolves the external FQDN to the internal IP address of the SBS. Here, the IP addresses that are used by the clients in the Internet to connect to the FQDN of the SBS are not applied.

In order to create an additional DNS entry, carry out the following steps:

1. Open the DNS administration console and select the New Zone entry from the context menu of the DNS server. Click on Next.
2. Select a Primary Zone as the zone type and then click on Next.
3. Select the To all Domain Controllers of the Active Directory Domain option as the Active Directory Replication area. Then click on Next.
4. Select a Forward Lookup Zone as the zone type and click on Next.
5. Under Zone Name, enter the external FQDN, e.g. www.externalname.com. Click on Next.
6. In the Dynamic Updates window, select the Do not allow Dynamic Updates option and click on Next and then on Finish.
7. Mark the zone just created in the Forward Lookup Zones entry, and from its context menu select New Host (A).

8. In the New Host window, do not enter any value in the Name field, and enter the internal IP address of the SBS in the IP Addresses field. Then click on Add Host.

9. Now, the DNS resolution cache must be deleted from the client computers (Windows 2000 and XP). To do this, enter the ipconfig /flushdns command at the command prompt.

Internal clients cannot connect to the external FQDN of the SBS

Problem: When trying to access the SBS 2003, an internal client gets the following error message: This page cannot be displayed. The possible DNS problems are given at the bottom of the page.

Cause: This problem occurs when the SBS 2003 has only one network card and is located behind a router. The user of the internal client tries in this situation to access the SBS by using its external FQDN. This problem does not apply to all these scenarios, but only to specific router models. The following router models are affected by this issue:

- 3Com OfficeConnect Cable/DSL Gateway 3C855
- D-Link Broadband VPN Router DI-804
- Microsoft Wireless Base Station MN-500
- Microsoft Base Station MN-100

Normally, the internal network users cannot access the SBS through the external FQDN. However, the users of **OMA (Outlook Mobile Access)** must access the external domain name of the SBS in order to synchronize their mobile devices with Outlook.

Solution: To work around this problem, create a DNS zone for the external FQDN of the server so that the FQDN is resolved to the internal IP address of the SBS. To do this, take the following steps:

1. Open the DNS administration console and select the Forward Lookup Zone entry and then New Zone from the context menu of the DNS server. Click on Next.

2. Select a Primary Zone as the zone type and click on Next.

3. Under Zone Name enter the external FQDN, for example, www.externalname.com. Click on Next.

4. In the Dynamic Updates window, select the Allow only secure Updates option and click on Next and then on Finish.

5. Mark the zone just created in the Forward Lookup Zone entry, and from its context menu select New Host (A).

6. In the New Host window, do not make any entries in the Name field, and in the IP Address field enter the internal IP address of the SBS.

7. Mark the Create a new PTR Entry for this Entry checkbox and click on Add Host.

8. You will then get a message that the PTR entry has been successfully added. Confirm this by clicking on OK.

E-Mail and Fax Problems

In this section you will find a listing of the typical problems faced while sending and receiving e-mails and faxes.

E-Mails cannot be sent or received anymore

Problem: After a while the problem crops up that a user can't send or receive e-mails.

Cause: This happens when the user has reached the size limit for his or her mailbox.

Solution: First, you can save the e-mails in a local folder on the client of the user. If a user faces this problem again, you have to consider increasing the size of his or her mailbox. For further details refer to Chapter 8.

Unwanted e-mails are sent to the Exchange mailboxes

Problem: The Exchange Server mailboxes receive unwanted messages (spam).

Cause: The connection filter has not been configured for the Exchange Server.

Solution: Configure the connection filter to block unwanted e-mails to the Exchange Server on the basis of the blocklists.

Several existing e-mail domains cannot be specified in the e-mail and Internet connection wizard

Problem: Only one e-mail domain can be specified in the e-mail and Internet connection wizard, even though several e-mail domains are to be used.

Cause: Only one e-mail domain is specified in the wizard as you configure the reply addresses for the domain here.

Solution: In order to use multiple e-mail domains, create a customized recipient policy for the second e-mail domain after closing the wizard in Exchange. The e-mail addresses for the users of the second e-mail domain are created via this policy. For more details refer to the *E-Mail Administration* section in Chapter 4.

Problems while downloading external POP3 e-mails through the POP3 connector

Problem: On the SBS 2003 there are a huge number of unexpected e-mails in the Exchange SMTP queue. These e-mails are exclusively for recipients outside the SBS e-mail domain. This symptom occurs after downloading e-mails from the external POP3 server; the POP3 connector wrongly sends back e-mails to recipients who are not members of the SBS 2003 e-mail domain.

Cause: This problem would not occur if the e-mails are hosted internally with the help of the Exchange Server.

Solution: This symptom is a problem with SBS 2003. For this purpose, you must install the KB835734 update, which can be found at `http://www.microsoft.com/downloads/details.aspx?FamilyID=7B1FF109-092E-4418-AA37-A53AF7B8F6FC&displaylang=en`.

A connection to the POP3 and IMAP4 services of the SBS cannot be established

Problem: Both the POP3 and IMAP4 virtual server services are stopped when the Exchange System Manager is started on the SBS 2003. When you try to restart both these services through the Exchange System Manager, you receive an error message. As both these services have been closed, no connection can be established from Microsoft Outlook and Outlook Express to SBS 2003 anymore. You receive the appropriate error messages when you try to connect to the POP3 server or the IMAP4 server.

Cause: This problem occurs because in SBS 2003 the Microsoft Exchange POP3 service and the Microsoft Exchange IMAP4 service are switched off by default.

Solution: Take the following steps in order to enable these services and to authorize the firewall for these services:

1. Open Start/Programs/Administration/Services and double-click on the Microsoft Exchange POP3 service.
2. Select Automatic from the Start Type list box. Click on Apply and click on Start in Service Status.
3. Repeat this step for the Microsoft Exchange IMAP4 service and then close the Services window.
4. Open Server Management and expand the Task List. In the right half of the window, click on Connect to the Internet.
5. Follow the instructions of the wizard till you reach the Firewall page. Here, click on Enable Firewall and then on Next.

6. Click on Add and enter Microsoft Exchange POP3 in the Service Name text box. Under Protocol enter TCP and under Port enter 110. Click on OK.

7. Click once again on Add and enter Microsoft Exchange IMAP4 for the Service Name, TCP as the Protocol, and the Port 143 in the appropriate fields and then click on OK.

8. Click on Next and close the wizard.

Error message 5120 in the event log

Problem: An error message with the event ID 5120 is found in the event log. This occurs when incoming or outgoing e-mails have attachments. However the attachments must contain MIME fields whose type is **multipart/alternative**. By default, the MIME type is **multipart/mixed**. Normally, e-mail attachments with the multipart/alternative MIME type are e-mail worms.

Cause: This error message can also be displayed when an anti-virus program scans all the folders, including the Exchange folder, at file level. During the file-level virus scan, the infected e-mail attachment can be deleted before this attachment is deleted from the SBS 2003 itself.

Solution: This event message is not an error message in the true sense. You should probably switch to another anti virus program that does not scan at file level.

Problems in sending e-mails via SMTP when a Smart Host server is used

Problem: When sending e-mail through the SMTP connector, the mails remain in the outbox queue and do not get sent. Additionally, the following three conditions must be fulfilled for this problem to occur:

- All e-mails are forwarded to a Smart Host server.
- The Smart Host server is not identical with the mail server of your Internet provider on which your e-mails are stored.
- The TURN authentication is used for retrieving the e-mails.

This configuration applies when you configure the following settings in the e-mail and Internet connection wizard:

- In the E-mail Sending Methods window, click on Forward all E-mails to the Mail Server of the ISP. In the Mail Server text box, enter the name of a Smart Host server.
- In the E-mail Sending Methods window check the Use Exchange checkbox. Click on Keep E-mails on ISP till my Server sends a Signal.

- In the E-mail Server to which the Signal should be sent field, specify the name of the server. This is the mail server of the ISP that sends a signal to your Exchange Server. This server is different from the Smart Host server. Click on Turn after Authentication.

- In the Information for TURN Authentication window, specify the username and the password of the account through which the Exchange Server authenticates itself against the mail server of the ISP.

Cause: The authentication fails in this configuration when the e-mails are sent through the SMTP connector. During the authentication of the SMTP connector on the Smart Host Server, the account settings that the server uses for the outgoing connection are the ones that you have specified for the TURN authentication. These account settings are configured for the server from which the SBS receives incoming mails, and not for the Smart Host server. Thus, as a result of the authentication problem you can only receive e-mails and not send them.

Solution: To ascertain the account settings for the outgoing SMTP connection, open the Connectors entry in the Exchange System Manager and select Properties from the context menu of Small Business SMTP Connector. In the Advanced tab click on Outgoing Security.

Faxes cannot be received

Problem: Faxes cannot be received, even though the fax modem is correctly installed and there are no error messages in the event log.

Cause: The modem must be reset.

Solution: In order to reset the modem, unplug it and then plug it in again. More details could be found in the documentation of the device.

Faxes cannot be forwarded to the document library

Problem: The option to forward faxes to the document library is available neither in the fax configuration wizard nor in the fax administration console.

Cause: The fax services have probably been uninstalled via Add/Remove Control Panel/Software/Windows Components. The option to reinstall is not available at this location in SBS 2003.

Solution: You must reinstall the fax services. Take the following steps:

1. Open Add/Remove Control Panel/Software/Windows Components and disable the Fax Services checkbox. Click on Finish.

2. In Software, switch to Currently installed Programs. Select Microsoft Windows Small Business Server 2003 and click on Change/Remove.

3. On the Select Component page select Fax Services under Action and click on Install. Click on Next and follow the instructions of the wizard.

Monitoring Problems

In this section, we discuss monitoring problems and problems with the performance and utilization reports.

No more monitoring warnings are given

Problem: No more monitoring warnings are given after the configuration of the Health Monitor has been imported.

Cause: The import of the Health Monitor configuration with the help of a wizard can cause problems with the imported actions if the actions still refer to the computer from which they have been imported—an imported SMTP server or a file path is no longer valid, and leads to problems.

Solution: To make the monitoring warnings function correctly again, you must update the imported data of the actions. For this, open Health Monitor in administration and click on Actions. Select Properties from the context menu of an action and verify the settings in all the available tabs in each case.

According to a warning notification, a user account has been hacked

Problem: A warning is displayed stating that a user account has been hacked.

Cause 1: This warning is displayed when the user has exceeded the limit of the number of login attempts that has been specified in the account lockout function.

Solution 1: Check whether the user has actually made a series of failed login attempts because of a forgotten password. In this case reset the user password and give the user the new password.

Cause 2: A user account has actually been hacked into or is still being hacked.

Solution 2: If the account has actually been hacked or is still being hacked, take the following steps:

1. Verify in the event log under Security from the monitored login events whether the local network has already been hacked.

2. Ascertain the IP address of the hacker's computer and try to get more details of this IP address through the Internet service provider.

3. Check whether the there are any unknown user accounts under Users in the Server Administration.

4. Reset the password of the hacked account and disable the account till the hack attempt has ended. Additionally, reset the administrator password.

5. Disconnect the SBS 2003 from the Internet till the hack attempt is over.

The server performance and utilization reports do not contain all the log data

Problem: The server performance and utilization reports do not contain all the selected protocol data.

Cause: Data is added as an attachment to the report only when the data to be logged has changed since the last report. Even for applications that create several log files, e.g. Internet Information Services, no new attachments are sent for the reports if there is no new data.

Solution: This is not an error, so no further steps are required.

No Information about Internet usage is found in the server utilization report

Problem: The server utilization reports do contain data, but this data does not include information about Internet usage.

Cause 1: If you are using the firewall function of the ISA server, the SBS 2003 cannot monitor the firewall statistics of the ISA server.

Solution 1: You must configure the ISA server for monitoring and report creation, and not the SBS 2003.

Cause 2: You are using a hardware router as a firewall. Even in this case the SBS cannot evaluate the relevant statistics of the device.

Solution 2: Add one more network card to the SBS 2003. Install the routing and RAS services as a firewall on the SBS 2003 via the Internet access and e-mail wizard.

The server performance and server utilization reports cannot be received in Outlook Express

Problem: It not possible to receive the server performance and server utilization reports in Outlook Express.

Cause: By default, various file attachments are blocked in Outlook Express. This done in order to minimize the risk of opening infected attachments.

Solution: To allow these attachments, in Outlook Express open the Tools menu and then Options. Switch to the Security tab and disable the Disallow Saving or Opening of Attachments that could contain a Virus checkbox.

Problems with Mobile Devices

In this section, we discuss problems that can occur while using mobile devices.

ActiveSync cannot be installed

Problem: The Active Sync application cannot be installed on the client computer.

Cause: For installing ActiveSync, the mobile device should not be connected to the client computer. If it is so connected, the installation will not be completed.

Solution: In order to reinstall the application, disconnect the mobile device from the client computer, log on again, and restart the installation.

No connection can be established between the mobile device and the client computer

Problem: It is not possible to establish a connection between the mobile device and the client computer.

Cause: Most probably, the problem lies in the USB connection of both the devices. It is also possible that the current version of ActiveSync has not been installed.

Solution: First verify whether the current version of ActiveSync has been installed on the client computer. If it is installed, remove the mobile device from its base station or disconnect its cable. Switch off the mobile device and switch it on again before you connect it to the computer.

A connected mobile device cannot surf the Internet if ISA Server 2000 is installed

Problem: If ISA Server 2000 is installed, the user cannot surf the Internet from his or her mobile device if it is connected through the base station or through a cable.

Cause: If the mobile device is connected, then its user will be treated as an anonymous user. ISA Server 2000 does not allow anonymous users to surf the Internet.

Solution: Depending on the operating system installed on the mobile device, you must try out different solutions. We'll look at these individually. At the end a few settings have to be configured in ActiveSync. These settings are the same for all and are independent of the operating system of the mobile device.

Microsoft SmartPhone 2003

1. On the mobile device open Start/Settings/Date Connections.
2. Open Menu/Edit Connections/Proxy Connections.
3. Under Menu click on Add.
4. Under Connects from select the Work option; under Connects to select the Internet option.
5. In Proxy (name: port) enter the name and the port number of the proxy server. The port number is 8080. Also enter your username and password, and click on Finish.

Microsoft Pocket PC Phone Edition 2003

1. Open Start/Settings. Under Connections click on Connections and then on Set up my proxy server.
2. Switch to the Proxy Settings tab. Enable the This Network establishes a Connection to the Internet and the This Network uses a Proxy Server checkboxes. Enter the name of the proxy server and click on Advanced.
3. In Computer Link enter the port number 8080. Confirm this procedure by clicking on OK.

Microsoft Pocket PC Phone Edition 2002

1. Open Start/Settings. In Connections click on Connections.
2. Under Work Settings click on Change and switch to the Proxy Settings tab.
3. Enable the This Network establishes a Connection to the Internet and the This Network uses a Proxy Server checkboxes and click on Advanced.
4. In Computer Link enter the port number 8080. Confirm this procedure by clicking on OK.

ActiveSync settings

These settings must be configured irrespective of the system installed:

1. Open the Tools/Options menu in ActiveSync and switch to the Rules tab.
2. Select Office under Connection.
3. When surfing the Internet for the first time, you will be prompted to enter a username and password. The user account to be entered must be a member of the Internet Users group.

The first synchronization attempt between Outlook and the mobile device fails

Problem: The first synchronization attempt between Outlook 2003 and the mobile device fails. You receive an error message stating that the profile cannot be found.

Cause: If the user has not yet run Outlook 2003, no profiles can be created. ActiveSync cannot create profiles by itself.

Solution: Start Outlook and connect the mobile device to the client computer either through its base station or through a cable. Pay attention to the following sequence while connecting the mobile device:

1. Start the ActiveSync program.
2. Connect the base station of the mobile device through the USB cable or through the COM port to the client computer. When using the COM port, ensure that the COM port used when installing ActiveSync is not used. In order to share the COM port, click on the File menu in ActiveSync and then click on Get Connected.
3. Put the mobile device in the base station or connect it with a cable. ActiveSync automatically establishes a connection with the mobile device.

The synchronization of a connected mobile device is not possible

Problem: When the mobile device is connected to the client computer through its base station or through a cable, it cannot be synchronized.

Cause: The ISA Server or Routing and RAS (RRAS) are set up on the SBS 2003. The option ActiveSync Channel is not correctly configured for this.

Solution: On the client, open the ActiveSync program. Select Options from the Tools menu and switch to the Rules tab. As the Connection option under Channel, select Internet.

Problems with Outlook Mobile Access (OMA) and SSL

Problem: On some devices with Smart Phone 2002, Pocket PC 2002, or WAP 2.0 (Wireless Application Protocol), problems occur while using Outlook Mobile Access in connection with SSL (Secure Sockets Layer).

Cause: Some devices are not supported if they do not use an SBS 2003 signed certificate.

Solution: Provide the appropriate signed certificate.

A

SBS 2003 and Firewalls without ISA Server

This appendix discusses the configuration of a firewall for use with SBS 2003. If you do not have the premium edition of SBS 2003 and consequently do not use the ISA Server as a firewall, you must have a separate firewall device available. Under certain conditions, this device can be used in conjunction with the integrated firewall of SBS 2003. One often deals with a combination of firewall and DHCP Server in such cases. If this device is UPnP (Universal Plug and Play) compatible, the various ports required by the SBS 2003 have to be configured through the e-mail and Internet connection wizards. If this device is not UPnP compatible, the firewall must be manually configured.

If the firewall additionally serves as a router and if the SBS is connected to the local network through one network card and to the Internet through another, you can either use the firewall of the SBS 2003 or the firewall functionality of the hybrid device, or use both of them together.

The following table gives an overview of the port numbers required by SBS 2003 for various services. All these services use TCP protocols. For the complete list of all the ports, go to the web address http://www.iana.org/assignments/port-numbers. This web page has a list of all ports reserved for the applications of specific manufacturers.

Port Number	Service	Description
21	FTP (File Transfer Protocol)	Before you configure the server as an FTP server, you must add and configure the FTP service.
25	E-mail	Sending and receiving e-mails via the SMTP (Simple Mail Transfer Protocol).
80 (HTTP)	Web Server	Internet access, Outlook Web Access (OWA), Outlook Mobile Access (OMA), invoking SBS performance and application reports, company web site (wwwroot), and Outlook access through the Internet (RPC) without VPN connection.

Port Number	Service	Description
443 (HTTPS)	Web Server; Remote Web Workstation	HTTP queries through SSL (Secure Sockets Layer); for web workstation, refer to the relevant row of this table.
444	Share Point Services-Intranet-Web Page	Securing the Client-Server communication while accessing the Intranet web page of the company as well as other pages available at `http://companyweb`.
1723	VPN (Virtual Private Network)	Establishing a secure connection from remote clients to the company network.
3389	Terminal Services	Use of the terminal services of the SBS 2003 by remote clients.
4125	Remote Web Workstation	Connection to the local network through Outlook Web Access (OWA), remote desktop connection to the clients of the local network, access to the intranet web page of the Share Point Services, as well as downloading the connection manager for the configuration of remote access.

B

Configuration of a DHCP Server for SBS 2003

In an SBS 2003 network, you can either use the DHCP (Dynamic Host Configuration Protocol) Server service of the SBS 2003 or that of some other DHCP server. In this case, a router with DHCP functionality or a separate DHCP server is used.

If you would like to use the DHCP service of the SBS 2003, you must only close the original DHCP service when you are prompted by the setup program to do so. Otherwise, the setup program will not be able to determine the IP address range that has been in use until now.

Configuration of an Existing DHCP Server

If you would like to operate the DHCP service from another server even after installing SBS, you must ensure that the service is correctly configured.

In the DHCP server, open the dhcp.mmc, if the DHCP server is based on Windows. For example, if you are using a Unix-based server, make the following settings in the respective configuration files:

1. Create a new DHCP range. The range option details are given in the table later in the appendix. First ensure that this field contains a sufficient number of IP addresses for all the clients and the other network devices with their own IP addresses. You must also add the IP addresses of all the planned RAS Servers and remote users.

2. Under xx exclude the DHCP server's own IP address for the local network from the list of addresses to be issued. Also, exclude the IP addresses that are used by devices with a static IP address. To be on the safe side, exclude approximately five more addresses so that, later on, you can configure network devices with a static IP address.

The following table gives the DHCP range options that are to be configured. These options are available on a Windows-based DHCP server. You should apply them to your server even if it is not Windows based.

DHCP range option	Description
Router (Standard-Gateway)	If the SBS is installed as a gateway and it contains two network cards, then enter the address of the card used for connecting to the local network.
	If the SBS 2003 has only one network card and if the Internet connection is established through a router, enter the internal IP address of the router here.
DNS Server	Enter the address of the network card used to connect to the local network.
	If the DNS service is run on a separate server, enter the IP address of the server.
DNS Domain Name	Enter the complete name (FQDN, Fully Qualified Domain Name) of the internal domain: sbs2003.local for example. This name will be automatically assigned to the clients.
WINS Server	Enter the IP address of the SBS 2003 if you have not installed another WINS server. WINS support is solely required by clients with the Windows NT 4.0 or Windows 9x operating system.
WINS Node Type	Enter the value "hybrid" or H-node (0x8) as the node type. By setting the WINS node type, unnecessary broadcast traffic is eliminated from the network.

Index

X

Printed in the United Kingdom
by Lightning Source UK Ltd.
105814UKS00002B/123-188